THE WORKING CLASS IN EUROPEAN HISTORY

Editorial Advisers:

Standish Meacham
Joan Scott
Reginald Zelnik

Books in the Series *The Working Class in European History*

The Logic of Solidarity: Artisans and Industrial Workers in Three French Towns, 1871-1914 *Michael P. Hanagan*

Ben Tillett: Portrait of a Labour Leader *Jonathan Schneer*

Sweated Industries and Sweated Labor: The London Clothing Trades, 1860-1914 *James A. Schmiechen*

South Wales and the Rising of 1839: Class Struggle as Armed Struggle *Ivor Wilks*

Divisions of Labour: Skilled Workers and Technological Change in Nineteenth-Century Britain *edited by Royden Harrison and Jonathan Zeitlin*

The Growth of Working-Class Reformism in Mid-Victorian England *Neville Kirk*

Syndicalist Legacy: Trade Unions and Politics in Two French Cities in the Era of World War I *Kathryn Amdur*

English Laundresses: A Social History, 1850-1930 *Patricia E. Malcolmson*

Workers, Society, and the Soviet State: Labor and Life in Moscow, 1918-1929 *William J. Chase*

Workers, Society, and the Soviet State

Studies of the Harriman Institute

Columbia University

The W. Averell Harriman Institute for Advanced Study of the Soviet Union, Columbia University, sponsors the *Studies of the Harriman Institute* in the belief that their publication contributes to scholarly research and public understanding. In this way the Institute, while not necessarily endorsing their conclusions, is pleased to make available the results of some of the research conducted under its auspices. A list of the *Studies* appears at the back of this book.

WILLIAM J. CHASE

Workers, Society, and the Soviet State

Labor and Life in Moscow, 1918–1929

UNIVERSITY OF ILLINOIS PRESS   Urbana and Chicago

Publication of this work was made possible in part by a grant from the Andrew W. Mellon Foundation.

This book is printed on acid-free paper.

Library of Congress Cataloging-in-Publication Data

Chase, William J., 1947–
   Workers, society, and the Soviet State.

   (The Working class in European history)
   Bibliography: p.
   Includes index.
   1. Labor and laboring classes—Russian S.F.S.R.—
Moscow History. 2. Moscow (R.S.F.S.R.)—Social
conditions. I. Title II. Series.
HD8530.M62C43 1987   305.5′62′0947312   85-28823
ISBN 0–252–01319–0

To Donna

Contents

List of Maps and Tables

Acknowledgments

Conveying my gratitude to those whose support made this book possible is a most enjoyable and yet frustrating venture. Enjoyable because without their encouragement, assistance, and support this work would not have been possible; frustrating because words are inadequate to express my thanks and appreciation.

Much of the research for this study was made possible by fellowships from the American Council of Learned Societies and the University of Pittsburgh. A Senior Fellowship from the W. Averell Harriman Institute for Advanced Study of the Soviet Union at Columbia University enabled me to write the original draft of the manuscript. I owe a special debt to Jonathan Sanders of the Harriman Institute, whose encouragment and friendship made my stay there both productive and enjoyable. The libraries and staffs of Hillman Library at the University of Pittsburgh, the Columbia University libraries, the New York Public Library, Widener Library at Harvard University, and the Hoover Institution for the Study of War, Peace and Revolution were all especially kind and helpful.

To Roberta Manning, my friend and former advisor, I extend my deepest gratitude and appreciation. From this project's inception as a dissertation until its completion, she has unselfishly offered her advice and has been my best critic and staunchest supporter. Without her encouragement and counsel, the writing of this book would have been a far more difficult experience. To Bob Supansic, I also extend my profound gratitude. Our long hours of discussion and his sharp editorial eye have benefited me and this work in untold ways. His willingness to assist me on a moment's notice is appreciated in ways he can only imagine. To Arch Getty, my friend and long-time collaborator in various ventures, a special thanks. From our first days in graduate school, his friendship, intellectual support, and sense of humor have been a touchstone for me and helped to propel me forward.

Many other colleagues and friends also contributed to this study. Robert Doherty, Sheila Fitzpatrick, Orysia Karapinka, Peter Karsten, Diane Koenker, William Rosenberg, Ronald Suny, and Reginald Zelnik all read the manuscript in one of its many forms. Their criticisms, comments, and advice were invaluable and have helped to transform and improve this study. My sincerest thanks to all of them. Of course, it goes without saying that I bear all the responsibility for the book's shortcomings. Still others contributed to this book in various ways and to them—Robert Beattie, Peter Chase, Frank Giarrantani, Hiroaki Kuromiya, Anna Melnikov, Carmine Storella, Lynn Viola, and Douglas Weiner—I extend my appreciation.

Throughout everything which went into this book—from graduate school and before to the last dotted i—one person was always there. Without her love, tireless encouragement and support, boundless patience, sense of humor, and above all her ability to bring out the best in me, none of this would ever have come to pass. It is to her, Donna Chase, that this book is dedicated.

Glossary of Terms and Abbreviations

ARA: American Relief Administration
AMO: Moscow Automobile Plant
Besprizorniki: Homeless children
Cheka: Extraordinary Commission to Combat Counter-revolution and Sabotage
Kollegial'nost': Collegial administration
Edinonachalie: One-man management
Guberniia: Province
Meshochniki: Bagmen, Civil War food traders
NOT: Scientific Organization of Labor
Oblast': Province
Ogorody: Kitchen gardens
OGPU: Unified State Political Administration; political police
Otkhodnichestvo: Seasonal migration
Otkhodniki: Seasonal migrants
Rabkrin: Workers and Peasants Inspectorate
Raion: City borough or district
RSFSR: Russian Soviet Federated Socialist Republic
Samogon: Home-brewed alcohol
Samogonshchiki: Bootleggers
Sovkhozy: State farms
Sovnarkhoz: Council of Peoples' Economy
Sovnarkom: Council of Peoples' Commissars
Spetseedstvo: Specialist-baiting
SR: Socialist Revolutionary Party
Subbotnik: Voluntary workday, usually Saturday
TNB: Norm-setting Bureau

TsIT: Central Institute of Labor
TsSU: Central Statistical Administration
VSNKh: Supreme Council of National Economy
VTsSPS: All-Union Central Council of Trade Unions
Zemliachestvo: Informal association of people from the same district
Zemliaki: Fellow villagers, people from the same district

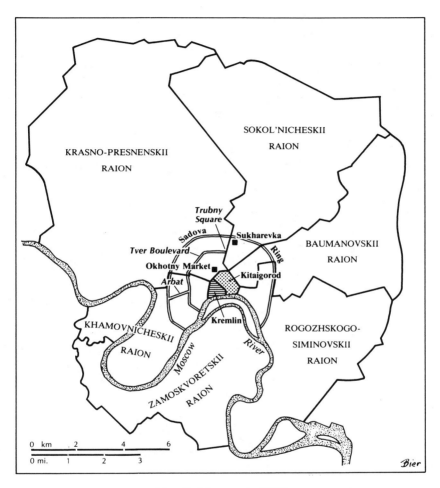

Map 1. Moscow in 1926

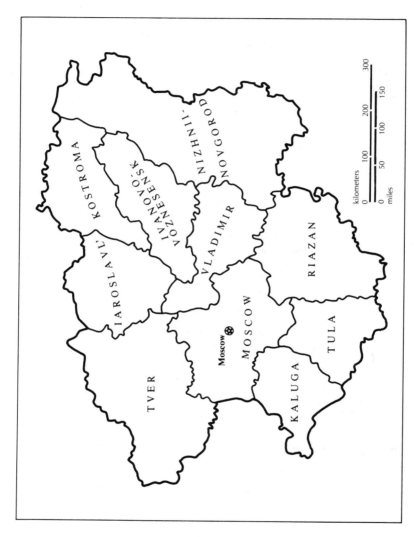

Map 2. The *Gubernii* of the Central Industrial Region, 1926

Workers, Society, and the Soviet State

Introduction

In November 1917, the Russian proletariat and Bolshevik Party united to toll the death knell for the Provisional Government and the *ancien regime* and to create the world's first socialist state. Volumes of western studies have analyzed the history of the Bolshevik Party, its leaders and institutions, and the state which it constructed. Unfortunately, western historiography on the Russian proletariat between that revolution and the transformation of Soviet society which commenced in 1928/29 devotes too little attention to that class once Bolshevik power was assured.

The published western research on Soviet labor concentrates on a narrow range of issues. The richest and liveliest literature focuses on the debates and struggles over workers' control during the immediate post-revolutionary years. Workers' control became the first major contest between the proletariat and the new state. Because it has attracted the attention of historians, sociologists and political scientists—Marxist and non-Marxist—the debates over and fate of workers' control have been relatively well documented and our understanding has been enhanced.[1] Still, questions remain and the topic demands more attention.

Aside from studies of workers' control, western historiography on the Soviet working class and issues dear to it in 1918-1929 is insufficient and uneven. Several studies of wage policy exist. However, they emphasize the formulation of wage policy and the structure of wage scales in the post-1928 period and give too little attention to the ways in which wages affected workers' daily lives.[2] Soviet labor policy has also received some attention. But save for Margaret Dewar's study, these works also focus primarily on the post-1928 years.[3] The literature most relevant to the Soviet working class of the 1920s remains trade union history.

3

Although too few in number, from these works one can catch provocative glimpses of workers' lives, hopes and frustrations prior to 1929.[4] The epic works of E. H. Carr, R. W. Davies, and Charles Bettleheim also discuss issues and problems important to Soviet workers.[5] While rich in detail on some issues and problems, they are concerned above all with interpreting the formation and early evolution of the Soviet experiment and hence focus primarily on policies, institutions, and political debates.

Recent studies of topics that intersect workers' lives and labor history have provided new windows on the Soviet working class. Kendall Bailes' and Nicholas Lampert's books on the Soviet technical intelligentsia address the strained relations between workers, their bosses, and technical specialists.[6] Several works on Soviet Taylorism and the scientific organization of labor touch briefly on workers' reactions to official attempts to rationalize the work process.[7] Finally, Sheila Fitzpatrick's pathbreaking studies of the cultural revolution from 1928 to 1931 and of education and social mobility in the 1920s and 1930s provide stimulating insights into some of the aspirations, demands, and frustrations of Soviet workers.[8]

For all their valuable contributions—and I in no way mean to minimize them—one fact clearly emerges from even a cursory survey of the existing literature. Not one western scholarly study exists that is devoted to analyzing the changing composition, and daily experiences, demands and attitudes of the Soviet proletariat, or even a part of it, in the 1918-1929 period. Considering that workers helped to bring the Soviet state to power, that they were the class on which Soviet power (truly or rhetorically) based itself, that (with the exception of the 1919-1924 period) they comprised a majority of the Communist Party in the period under investigation,[9] and that they were major participants in and beneficiaries of the dramatic policy changes which began in 1928, this glaring historiographic gap is inexcusable.

Yet it is explicable. Restricted access to source materials undoubtedly discourages and inhibits interested researchers. Students of Soviet labor do not have ready access to the abundant and rich source materials that our counterparts in British, West European, and American labor studies have at their disposal. Many available source materials, for example, newspapers and contemporary journals, have passed through official censors. Few worker memoirs from the period exist. For now, at least, historians of Soviet labor must reconcile themselves to the limits imposed by the restricted, aggregate, and often somewhat dry available evidence. It is, therefore, understandable that most existing studies of Soviet workers examine that class from the top-down, as functions in the calculus of policy formation and high-level political debate.

But this "birds-eye" view of workers is not simply a function of available evidence, because in fact that evidence is richer than most researchers assume and most existing studies suggest. The major reason for the prevalent western historiographic bias lays, I believe, in the long-held, though fortunately waning, assumption that the separation of state and society in the Soviet Union was so deep after 1920 that workers' behavior, attitudes and demands are irrelevant to understanding the Soviet system. Robert Conquest, in his book *Industrial Workers in the U.S.S.R.*, states this view most emphatically: "Henceforward [after February 1921] the Party, cut off from genuine working-class roots, rested on its ideas alone. Its justification came no longer from the politics of actuality but from the politics of prophecy."[10] Having concluded that workers no longer played a role in Soviet or party politics, Conquest is free to study industrial workers not as a political or social force, but as objects of manipulation by a party driven by the "politics of prophecy."

Regardless of one's opinion of post-1929 Soviet society, I find little evidence to support this perception in the 1918-1929 period. Although at times, particularly from 1921 to 1924, workers' relationships with the party, state, and unions were strained, workers played a significant role in the period's political developments. Their behavior and demands undeniably affected the evolution of policy and the party's political debates in the 1920s.

This book approaches the proletariat from a different vantage point. It rejects the premise that any ruling political entity can operate solely on the basis of the "politics of prophecy." The "politics of actuality" always operate in history. This work seeks to identify the "politics of actuality" of the Moscow industrial proletariat from 1918 to 1929. That class and those politics were complex.

What shapes people's lives, defines their "politics of actuality," and ultimately determines their assessment of any political order are their experiences at work, home and in the marketplace. For Moscow industrial workers during this period, the important determinative issues in their lives were: wages; the conditions and pace of work; relationships with supervisors; housing; family relations; the quality of their lives; the vagaries of the marketplace; the conflicts between old and new ways; and the rivalries, jealousies, and animosities that permeated social interaction. These issues set into motion centrifugal and centripetal forces that simultaneously worked to divide and unite the proletariat. Understanding these forces, alliances, and rivalries provides insight into workers' attitudes and behavior. To appreciate the reasons for and consequences of these centrifugal and centripetal forces and the resultant contours of working class behavior, it is essential to examine that class not from the top-down, but from the bottom-up, at least to the extent to which the evidence allows. In this way, the impact of the broad patterns of social change that workers experienced between 1918 and 1929 offers insight into their values and behavior.

Labor, economic, and political policies are important to this study (and were to workers), as they must be to any analysis of a society seeking to create a new order from revolutionary chaos. These policies became especially important during the New Economic Policy (NEP) of the 1920s. By 1921, the economy had ground to a halt, factories and transport lay idle, the exchange of goods between town and country had slowed to a trickle. Someone had to pay for economic recovery. Who would do so stood at the center of that decade's economic debates. The government demobilized the army and sought to prune the unwieldy bureaucracy, but these savings proved insufficient. The urgent demand to feed restive urban areas meant that limited resources could be extracted from the hostile peasantry. Only the industrial working class remained to bear the brunt of recovery. Policies designed to speed economic restoration and growth forced workers to labor more intensively in substandard factories, fostered rapidly rising unemployment, and deferred the reconstruction and expansion of urban housing and the municipal infrastructure. How these policies and their consequences affected industrial workers, their behavior, attitudes, and demands is this book's primary focus. Such a study required a relatively fine historical focus. For this reason, I decided to examine one city's proletariat. I chose Moscow primarily because of its economic characteristics and geographic location. Although known in pre-revolutionary times as "calico Moscow,"[11] after 1917 the city's economy was quite diverse. The textile and metal industries employed the largest number of workers, but significant numbers of printers, chemical workers, wood workers, food processing workers, construction workers and transport workers also labored there. During the 1920s, Moscow was the nation's largest city, its capital, and the major industrial and commercial center. As such, it housed large numbers of white-collar and service employees and private entrepreneurs (nepmen). For these reasons, Moscow promised to provide a representative case study of the problems which industrial workers experienced and their relations to other classes and social groups.

6

Located in the heart of the Central Industrial Region, the farm lands of which were generally infertile and overpopulated, Moscow also offered the opportunity to examine the interaction of town and country, of urbanization and industrialization, and the problems which accompanied these relations and processes. In recent years, western historians of the pre-revolutionary period have devoted considerable attention to these phenomena.[12] Although the emphasis varies, their works focus primarily on the transition from peasant to worker (or urbanite at the very least) or, as Theodore Von Laue put it, the transition from field to factory. These studies quite correctly point out that Moscow and other cities of the Russian Empire were islands in an ocean of peasants. Unlike islands, however, no sharply delineated coastline separated city and country. Most of those who swelled the cities' population migrated from the countryside and most proved reluctant to shed their rural ties, habits and attitudes. During the 1920s, as before the revolution, tens of thousands of peasants annually migrated to Moscow to establish residence; an even larger number annually inundated the city in search of seasonal employment. Hence, Moscow promised to be an excellent case study of the impact which these migrants had on workers' behavior and attitudes. That impact was often negative.

Moscow may not be typical of Russian cities of the period, but I believed it would be representative. I am more convinced of this now than when I began this research. The laws and policies that defined much of the workers' lives were common to the entire country. The conditions, problems, and concerns of industrial workers in Moscow, as well as their reactions to the impact of policy on their lives and their city, reflected those in other urban areas. The differences that existed were not fundamental, but ones of degree.

This work examines many aspects of workers' daily lives; there are other aspects that it does not examine. It is not a study of working-class culture(s). While unquestionably an area of investigation essential to understanding that class, the very magnitude of such an inquiry places it beyond the scope of this study. Nor does it examine the Moscow Communist Party organization, trade unions, or the city's soviets. This book treats some of the ways in which each of these interacted with and affected workers, but these institutions are not the subject of investigation.

Moscow industrial workers during the 1920s are this study's primary focus. But to understand their attitudes, behaviors, and the problems that they faced, it is essential to survey the 1918-1921 period. The aspirations deferred, the bitter struggles, and the enduring legacies of economic, social and demographic collapse during those harsh years defined, in large measure, the realities of the 1920s. Therefore, the first chapter surveys the disintegration of Moscow and its working class during the Civil War years, but limits itself to a discussion of those issues relevant to the later period. Finally, I have chosen not to include a chapter that describes Moscow. Several recent studies provide excellent descriptions and I refer interested readers to them.[13]

Notes

1. For brevity's sake, interested readers should consult the bibliography in Carmen Sirianni, *Workers Control and Socialist Democracy: The Soviet Experience* (London, 1982), 414-433.

2. Janet Chapman, *Real Wages in Soviet Russia* (Cambridge, Mass., 1963); A. Bergson, *The Structure of Soviet Wages* (Cambridge, Mass., 1944). S. Zagorsky, *Wages and Regulations of Conditions of Labour in the U.S.S.R.* (Geneva, 1930) provides the most complete western analysis of Soviet wages for this period.

3. Margaret Dewar, *Labour Policy in the USSR, 1917-1928* (London, 1956). For studies of Soviet labor, see: Avrid Broderson, *The Soviet Worker: Labor and Government in Soviet Society* (New York, 1966); Robert Conquest, *Industrial Workers in the U.S.S.R.* (New York, 1967); Manya Gordon, *Workers Before and After Lenin* (New York, 1941); Solomon M. Schwarz, *Labor in the Soviet Union* (New York, 1951). Among studies of workers, trade unions, or labor policy (aside from Dewar), which devote considerable attention to the period 1918-1928, the most notable is Frederick I. Kaplan, *Bolshevik Ideology and the Ethics of Soviet Labor, 1917-1920: The Formative Years* (London, 1969).

4. Jay B. Sorenson, *The Life and Death of Soviet Trade Unions* (New York, 1969); Issac Deutscher, *Soviet Trade Unions: Their Place in Soviet Labor* (London, 1950).

5. Charles Bettelheim, *Class Struggles in the USSR—First Period: 1917-1923* (translated by Brian Pearce, New York, 1976); *Class Struggles in the USSR—Second Period: 1923-1930* (translated by Brian Pearce, New York, 1978); E. H. Carr, *The Bolshevik Revolution, 1917-1923*, 3 vols. (Middlesex, 1966); *The Interregnum, 1923-1924* (New York, 1954); *Socialism in One Country, 1924-1926*, 2 vols. (London, 1973); E. H. Carr and R. W. Davies, *Foundations of a Planned Economy*, 2 vols. (New York, 1969).

6. Kendall E. Bailes, *Technology and Society under Lenin and Stalin: Origins of the Soviet Technical Intelligentsia, 1917-1941* (Princeton, 1978);

Nicholas Lampert, *The Technical Intelligentsia and the Soviet State* (New York, 1979).

7. Kendall E. Bailes, "Alexei Gastev and the Soviet Controversy over Taylorism, 1918-1924," *Soviet Studies*, 29, 3 (1977), 373-394; Zenovia A. Sochor, "Soviet Taylorism Revisited," *Soviet Studies*, 33, 2 (1981), 246-264; Samuel Lieberstein, "Technology, Work, and Sociology in the USSR: The NOT Movement," *Technology and Culture* (January 1975), 48-66; Rainer Traub, "Lenin and Taylor: The Fate of 'Scientific Management' in the (Early) Soviet Union," *Telos*, 37 (1978), 82-92.

8. Sheila Fitzpatrick, "Cultural Revolution as Class War," *Cultural Revolution in Russia, 1928-1931* (Sheila Fitzpatrick, ed., Bloomington, Indiana, 1978); *Education and Social Mobility in the Soviet Union, 1921-1934* (Cambridge, 1979).

9. Figures on the social composition of the Communist Party during this decade can be found in T. H. Rigby, *Communist Party Membership in the U.S.S.R., 1917-1967* (Princeton, 1968), 85, 116. Although workers did not comprise a majority of party members from 1919 to 1924, they were the largest single class within its ranks. See also the discussion in chapter seven below.

10. Conquest, 8.

11. For studies of pre-Soviet Moscow, see: Robert E. Johnson, *Peasant and Proletarian: The Working Class of Moscow at the End of the Nineteenth Century* (New Brunswick, N.J., 1979); Laura Engelstein, *Moscow, 1905: Working Class Organization and Political Conflict* (Stanford, 1982); Victoria E. Bonnell, *Roots of Rebellion: Workers' Politics and Organizations in St. Petersburg and Moscow, 1900-1914* (Berkeley, 1983); Diane Koenker, *Moscow Workers and the 1917 Revolution* (Princeton, 1981).

12. Barbara A. Anderson, *Internal Migration during Modernization in Late Nineteenth Century Russia* (Princeton, 1980); "Who Chose the Cities? Migrants to Moscow and St. Petersburg Cities in the Late Nineteenth Century," *Population Patterns in the Past* (Ronald D. Lee, ed., Princeton, 1977), 277-295; James H. Bater, "Some Dimensions of Urbanization and the Response of Municipal Government: Moscow and St. Petersburg," *Russian History/Histoire Russe*, 5, Part 1 (1978), 46-63; and *St. Petersburg: Industrialization and Change* (Montreal, 1976); Johnson, *Peasant and Proletarian*; "Peasant Migration and the Russian Working Class: Moscow at the End of the Nineteenth Century," *Slavic Review*, 35, 4 (1976), 652-664; Theodore Von Laue, "Russian Labor between Field and Factory, 1892-1903," *California Slavic Studies*, 3 (1964), 33-65; "Russian Peasants in the Factory," *Journal of Economic History*, 21 (1961), 61-80; Richard H. Rowland, "Urban Inmigration in Late Nineteenth Century Russia," *The City in Russian History* (Michael F. Hamm, ed., Lexington, Ky., 1976), 115-124; Roger H. Thiede, "Industry and Urbanization in New Russia," *ibid.*, 125-138; Joseph Crane Bradley, Jr., "*Muzhik* and Muscovite: Peasants in Late Nineteenth Century Urban Russia" (Ph.D. dissertation, Harvard University, 1977).

13. See the sources in note 11.

1. Political Aspiration and Political Necessity: Moscow and Its Proletariat, 1918-1921

In November 1917, Russian workers and the Bolshevik Party joined forces to make the first socialist revolution in history. The alliance between them proved durable enough to withstand onslaughts by counter-revolutionary White Armies and foreign troops. But no sooner had victory been assured when the Bolsheviks (now Communist Party) faced a new threat—mass worker unrest. Their political influence in the factories in 1917 had helped to propel the Bolsheviks to power, but by 1921, that influence had all but vanished and workers rejected the party's policy of War Communism.

How and why had this happened? A complete explanation is beyond the scope of this chapter, the purpose of which is provide essential background to our study of Moscow workers in the 1920s. But one can not begin to grasp the realities of that decade without addressing the question. The experiences and legacies of the Civil War and War Communism defined the contours of political, economic, and working-class life for many years.

The Bolsheviks and industrial working class each brought revolutionary agendas to 1917. Broadly speaking, the former sought the creation of a socialist state; the latter demanded an improvement in their daily and working lives and a transformation of political life. The Bolsheviks' revolutionary platform—peace, land, bread, all power to the soviets, and workers' control—articulated workers' demands.[1] While these slogans united the party and proletariat's revolutionary agendas, those agendas had their origins in different historical experiences. Within the party, and especially the leadership, that platform—and those that followed—was born of a profound, if not always accurate, vision of the nation's and proletariat's present and future needs and of a sophisti-

11

cated, wide-ranging analysis of the role of a socialist state in a hostile, capitalist world that lent a heroic (and sometimes paranoid) dimension to the struggle. At the highest level, a sense of mission that related to human history's totality informed and defined the party's agenda.

The party's agenda was rooted in Marxist analysis and a desire to destroy a repressive socio-economic order and to establish a socialist society. Cast in theoretical terms but molded and tempered by the realities of Russian society, that agenda focused not simply on the amelioration of the proletariat's and society's present condition but on a vision of the future. A different and historical sense of time animated the party. Its early post-revolutionary decrees were but the first steps in a long and arduous historical march. Although heated debates over what policies offered the best opportunity to achieve socialism at times divided the party, they did not diminish its shared historic vision.

The determinative realities of the working-class's revolutionary agenda were radically different. That agenda sprang from the experiences of daily life and centered on a rapid amelioration of workers' condition. Higher wages, better working conditions, more labor protection, improved housing and diets, greater respect, these were the items on the workers' early 1917 revolutionary agenda. As their conditions deteriorated in 1917, workers added the transformation of power relationships to their agenda. The mounting popular support for "workers' control" (and "all power to the soviets") stemmed from the inability or refusal of government leaders and management to reduce workers' hardships and to meet their demands.

The Bolshevik platform offered an increasingly attractive alternative to many workers who read into the slogans their own visions of the immediate and more distant future. For workers, bread was more than a slogan, it was one's next meal, the availability of which was one of their non-negotiable demands and a measure of their near-term prospects for survival. For peasants (and many workers), land promised secure access to the means of survival with as little outside interference as possible. For both, peace meant the end to the meaningless death and destruction imposed upon them by an incomprehensible logic. All power to the soviets and workers' control were the political means by which, for the first time, they would determine their lives and realize their aspirations.

In the struggle for victory, the two agendas' compatability obscured their different origins. Nor were the differences important then. But after victory, the differences surfaced and conflicts ensued. Faced with the responsibility of governing a country wracked by Civil War and economic collapse, the party increasingly viewed its role and the enactment of its agenda in broad, even historic terms. Economic collapse forced workers to defer their revolutionary agenda and struggle to survive. Conflict was inevitable, not because the party and proletariat had fundamentally different agendas—they did not—but because their historical experiences and those from 1918 to 1921 forced each to frame its agenda in profoundly different terms and to view its realization on different scales of time. Although in 1917 and later their agendas dramatically converged in impressive displays of unity, these moments obscure the two agendas' different origins, a difference that remained the source of an ongoing structural tension between the party and proletariat after 1917.

The extent to which their revolutionary agendas were compatible is underscored by the fact that alliances between groups within the party and proletariat were common after 1917. That these alliances were often fleeting indicate that differences over how best to translate the 1917 platform into reality remained. But agreement on one issue did not mean agreement of all. The most heated debates within and between the party and working class occurred over the structure of the new state, workers' control and economic policy to name but a few issues.[2] There were others. But during the Civil War, as each issue was resolved in the party leadership's favor, divergence between it and the working class widened. Periods of divergence and convergence succeeded each other dialectically in these years and the 1920s. During periods of relative unity, forces at work below the surface undermined this convergence, and vice-versa. The years immediately following 1917 afford a clear case.

Despite their differences, workers and the party shared one overriding concern—the defense of the revolution. That defense proved to be a struggle of epic proportions. Rather than ending the warfare and political and economic collapse which had helped to bring the Provisional Government to its knees, the 1918-1921 period witnessed their acceleration. To overcome the consequences of economic and social collapse, the party, working class, and individuals developed survival strategies. Dire realities dictated each strategy. By 1921, the government's strategy had engendered widespread discontent and pitted the former allies against one another.

The survival strategies developed by the party and working class reflected their revolutionary agendas. Broadly, the Bolsheviks strategy consisted of enacting central government policies that would meet the demands of workers, soldiers, and peasants and that would provide direction to grassroots initiative and energies. In this way, they hoped to gain popular support for the construction of a socialist state. The decrees on peace, land, and workers' control and the elevation of soviets to governmental status were the first bold moves. The peace decree reflected the Bolsheviks' abhorence of imperialist wars and the nation's profound warweariness and followed inexorably from the collapse of the predominantly peasant army. They had hoped that ending the war would reverse the accelerating economic collapse. But the costly Brest-Litovsk peace of March 1918 actually sped that collapse and so infuriated the anti-Bolshevik forces that they took up arms to topple the new regime. The promise of peace had given way to more war. Party leaders hoped that land redistribution would destroy the landlords' powers, win peasant support (or at least neutrality) for the revolution, and reverse the deteriorating urban food situation. But by 1921, it had achieved only the first of these. Likewise, the workers' control movement took on a dynamic of its own, one that brought it into conflict with the party's agenda. In short, the decrees on land, peace, and workers' control produced dramatically different consequences than the party had hoped.

The Bolsheviks' major strategies centered on politics and the economy. For them, every government fostered the economic and political interests of a nation's ruling class. The creation of a workers' state demanded that the new Soviet government use all the resources at its disposal to destroy the former ruling classes' power and assert that of the proletariat. In the political realm, the Bolsheviks argued that only their platform truly represented the proletariat's revolutionary demands. Hence, any party that sought to participate in the construction of the new order must endorse that platform. The party (or parties) and the political organs created by that class, the soviets, were to collaborate in governing the state. The Bolshevik-dominated central government would develop national policies that would guide the policies of and be carrried out by local soviets.

In the economic realm, many party leaders argued that the nationalization of economic resources and central direction of the economy were essential to crushing the bourgeoisie and aristocracy and the creation of a socialist economy. But save for the land, during the first eight months, nationalization proceeded in a cautious, piecemeal fashion. The nationalization of banking and finance institutions were necessary to political survival; so too were certain key industries. Otherwise, nationalization was to be considered on a case by case basis. Side by side with the nationalized enterprises, privately owned enterprises and private trade continued to operate. Lenin referred to this mixed economic system as state capitalism. What distinguished state capitalism from that found in many capitalist countries, he argued, was that political power had been transferred to the political organs of the proletariat. Under the dual restraints of centrally directed economic policy and workers' control, Lenin told his more radical comrades, state capitalism would be made to serve the workers' and state's interests. It was to be a transitional stage between capitalism and socialism.

Then in June 1918, the government abruptly abandoned state capitalism and embarked on wholesale nationalization and increasing state direction of all aspects of economic life. Three factors precipitated the adoption of this new strategy. First, the Civil War between the Red Army and the counter-revolutionary White Armies was widening and foreign troops had invaded the country in support of the Whites. Second, economic collapse accelerated daily. Finally, the government feared that Germany which, since the Brest-Litvosk peace, occupied the Ukraine would soon take over that region's economic resources. To forestall the latter and strengthen the government's ability to deal with the former two, the government nationalized all of the country's major economic resources.

Nationalization and centralization became the major economic tenets of the policy of War Communism, which dates from June 1918. Unlike state capitalism, War Communism was not a transitional stage but a bona fide survival strategy, although some Bolsheviks viewed it as the realization of the revolution. Several features characterized War Communism: the nationalization of virtually all economic enterprises and activities, the centralization of econmic policy, the requisitioning of peasant produce (*prodrazverstka*), the "abolition" of money and its replacement by natural wages and a socially organized barter system, and the increasing use of state power to raise industrial production. Each of these policies evolved in response to a series of crises and policy failures. And with each new crisis, attempts to impose centralized direction of the society and economy increased. War Communism reached its peak in late 1920, only weeks before its abandonment in March 1921.[3]

While this strategy ultimately guaranteed the the Red Army's victory and the Soviet state's survival, it also brought the state into conflict with the proletariat's revolutionary agenda and aspirations. The hardships and policies of these years shattered those dreams. The workers' revolutionary agenda centered on the amelioration of their working and daily lives and increasing their political influence. They demanded better wages and working conditions, a shorter work week, increased respect from their supervisors, influence (if not outright control) over production and the factory, and better housing and living conditions. In pursuit of these and other demands, in 1917 they organized shop and factory committees and *raion* and city soviets. These were their political organs and increasingly in 1917 they elected Bolsheviks to them.

After November, workers moved to enact their revolutionary agenda. Differences between their and the Bolshevik's agendas quickly surfaced. The most fundamental difference centered on how power was to be shared. Many workers interpreted "all power to the soviets" and workers' control as meaning that power would be decentralized and that they would define the contours of political life. Workers looked to the soviets and factory committees to enact their agenda. These organs responded eagerly in 1918. That year the assertion of local initiative and control hastened the fulfillment of many worker demands. But, it soon became apparent that local initiative, so essential to the seizure of power, offered few solutions to the crises that increasingly engulfed society. In an attempt to alleviate these crises, the party and government enacted policies that directed and restricted the activities of soviets and factory committees. Initially workers' bodies endorsed many of these policies. But as the crises continued unabated, the frustrated government extended central control and, by 1920, adopted repressive enforcement measures. As a result, soviets and factory committees were transformed into executors of unsuccessful and increasingly unpopular policies that alienated many workers from the government which they helped to bring to power. By 1921, not only were workers' lives much worse than three years earlier, but their hopes of local political control had been dashed. The inability first of local organs and then of the central government to fulfill the workers' revolutionary agenda forced workers to adopt increasingly individualistic survival strategies, strategies born of desperation. Finally, in early 1921, desperation turned to rage and workers vociferously denounced the party, government, and failed policies.

The estrangement between the state and working class developed gradually but grew ever wider. Several factors hastened the rift. The most important were the inability of state policies to halt the economic collapse (especially the food crisis) and the disintegration and transformation of the proletariat that, by 1921, bore little resemblance to that which had made the revolution. This survey of the 1918-1921 period in Moscow explores the reasons for and consequences of the collapse of the city and its proletariat. In so doing, it seeks to explain how the pursuit of revolutionary agendas created a breach that divided party and proletariat. This chapter confines itself to the issues central to our study of the

16

1920s—those of daily life, those bearing on work and factory life, and those that defined worker-party/state relations.

Economic Disintegration

Russia entered World War I ill-equipped to fight the war. Its industries and transport system proved incapable of meeting the demands of a prolonged conflict with a major industrial power. By 1917, the army lacked essential materiel and equipment, industrial centers lacked sufficient fuel to maintain production, and workers ominously complained about insufficient rations. To protest their condition, general strikes erupted in March. Several days later, the tsar abdicated and the 300-year-old Romanov dynasty ceased to exist. But after the initial revolutionary euphoria waned, Russians once again faced a dire reality—the economy continued its downward spiral. The November revolution brought no relief. In fact, the crises intensified. By 1921, Moscow's and the nation's economy had ground to a halt.

The most important reason for the disintegration of Moscow's economy was the deterioration of the nation's transport system, especially the railroad. The economy of Moscow—the hub of the national railroad network—depended on a steady flow of fuel, raw materials, manufactured goods, and food shipped there by rail. The transport system's collapse severed the city's life-line. That process began during WWI and accelerated during 1917. The excessive use of the rail system without sufficient maintenance and repair during the war years, and the strikes, work stoppages, and other revolutionary activities from 1917 to 1918 hastened that decline.[4]

Then came the Civil War. The proportion of the transport system under Bolshevik control steadily shrank until 1920, as each White Army victory put more of the railroad system under enemy control. The portion of the system that remained under Bolshevik control deteriorated. The excessive use of tracks, locomotives, and cars without the necessary maintenance, repairs, and replacement parts took its toll. In late 1918, half of all locomotives were idle; by 1921, only a small fraction of the system remained in operating order.[5]

In an effort to halt the rail system's disintegration, workers, the local soviet, and national government implemented numerous measures, but the demands placed on the railroad system, shortages of skilled railroad workers, and insufficient replacement parts frustrated all efforts. For example, in February 1918, the soviet mobilized all Muscovites ages

18 to 45, skilled workers from plants and shops that had closed, and even workers employed in unrelated industries to repair railroad lines and equipment.[6] Yet, the rail system continued to deteriorate. In April 1919, workers on the Moscow-Kazan railroad line responded to the desperate situation by initiating the first *subbotnik* (a voluntary, unpaid labor day) to repair railroad locomotives and cars. The *subbotnik* campaign quickly spread throughout the city. In 1919 and 1920, thousands of Muscovites participated in *subbotniks* organized to repair the railroads. They too failed to reverse the collapse.[7] The government militarized the railroad workers, and in 1920 Trotsky assumed control of the Commissariat of Transport and placed the entire system under military control. Only then did the crisis begin to wane.[8]

Equally as devastating to the city's economy was the fuel crisis. In 1917, Moscow received half of the fuel that it had received in 1915.[9] In 1918, the new government worked strenuously to increase the production of local peat and coal industries. Both produced more in the first half of that year than they had in the comparable period in 1913, but they could not keep pace with the demand.[10] By November, Moscow had only 12.5 percent of the coal and peat and 29 percent of the wood that it needed; this was only enough to sustain the city for two or three days. As of that date, the city had stockpiled only one-third of the wood needed for the long winter.[11] The fuel crisis reached even graver proportions the next year—the city received only 4 percent of the fuel which it had consumed in 1913. The metal industries that were vital to the war effort received less than one-quarter of the fuel they had used three years earlier.[12] The situation continued to deteriorate in 1920. The shortage of fuel affected all aspects of the city's economy—industries ceased or reduced production; railroads halted; city services were curtailed; and residents had to endure the brutal cold of three Russian winters without sufficient heat. For want of fuel, those agencies responsible for food distribution were unable to distribute hundreds of train carloads of desperately needed food which sat rotting at the railroad yards.[13]

In August 1918, the Moscow Soviet created a Central Fuel Council to oversee all aspects of the city's fuel situation and issued the first of many appeals for collectives of workers organized on a *raion* or factory basis to participate in preparing coal, peat, and wood.[14] In November 1919, as General Denikin's White Army threatened Moscow, the party Central Committee declared that "the fuel crisis threatens to disrupt all soviet work: factory workers and office employees are abandoning their jobs to escape the cold and hunger, trains carrying grain are brought to a standstill, and a veritable disaster is impending because of the fuel shortage. . . . The fuel problem has become the central problem." The Central Committee urged party organs to organize *subbotniks* and where necessary to conscript labor to gather fuel.[15] Local soviets and the unions dispatched factory-organized fuel teams to the countryside, coordinated the transport and preparation of wood, and approved the gathering of wood from demolished or uninhabited buildings. During the next eighteen months, thousands of Muscovites volunteered or were conscripted to collect and prepare fuel.[16]

Despite these efforts, fuel remained scarce. In 1921, the Moscow Soviet appealed to all workers to redouble their efforts, and set a goal of bringing no less than 400 train car loads of wood to the city.[17] The goal was not reached, and in mid-February fuel shortages forced the Moscow *Sovnarkhoz* (Council of Peoples' Economy) to close forty-eight more factories.[18]

The transport and fuel crises affected all aspects of Moscow's economy. Especially hard hit were those industries that depended on fuel and raw materials from abroad or from areas often under White Army control. For want of fuel and raw materials, many factories shut down or curtailed production. By August 1918, more than one-fifth (264 of 1,190) of the city's enterprises had already closed. By the summer of 1920, the proportion that had closed had risen to more than one-third (406).[19] The production of Moscow's census industries stood at only 15 percent of the 1913 level. Even in factories that continued to produce, many workers devoted much of their workday to producing goods such as primus stoves, candelsticks, and kerosene lamps that had no relationship to normal production but that could be exchanged for food in the villages.[20]

Spiraling inflation exacerbated the economic problems. From 1917 to 1924, rampant inflation rendered the ruble worthless and imposed severe hardships on all citizens, especially urban wage-earners. According to a price index compiled by the Central Statistical Administration, the price of a standard ration of goods rose from 1.00 unit in 1913 to 27.80 units in January 1918 to 26,900 units three years later (see appendix 1). The primary cause of the inflation was the excessive issuance of rubles by the revolutionary government to pay for the war. During these years, the printing press was the state's major source of revenue.

Shortages of fuel and raw materials and inflation were not the only reasons for industrial closings. Some enterprises closed for lack of workers. Sabotage, which took many forms, forced others to close. Anti-

Bolshevik factory owners shut down their plants so as to destabilize the revolutionary government's economic base.[21] Owners, managers, and employees took advantage of the chaotic situation and workers' ignorance of bookkeeping to embezzle huge sums of money.[22] In some cases, workers' control committees and recently created government agencies, whose personnel lacked the administrative and accounting skills necessary to industrial management, committed unwitting sabotage.[23] At the First Trade Union Congress in January 1918, Tomskii stated that the worker ignorance of accounting wreaked such havoc with factories' books that it often looked like sabotage. But, he added, "I do not think it is sabotage, only Russian illiteracy."[24] There were also many cases of "sabotage" committed by hungry workers and soldiers who stole industrial products, materials, and tools to sell or exchange for food and fuel. In whatever form, sabotage was commonplace during the Civil War. In no less than 50 percent of the cases where Sovnarkom (the Council of Peoples' Commissars) gave a specific reason for the nationalization of an industry, sabotage was the reason.[25]

The Food Crisis

The collapse of the transport system, the currency, and city's productive capability contributed to a steady deterioration of Moscow's food situation. The tsarist government had introduced food rationing in 1916; the Provisional Government continued the policy throughout 1917. But this policy did little to ensure an adequate supply of food to the city's population. On the eve of the November revolution, the food situation in Moscow showed signs of marked deterioration—the amount of food available continued to decline, prices rose steeply, and speculation in food products flourished. The Bolsheviks' promise of "bread" (that is, food) offered an increasingly attractive alternative to Moscow workers. In November, Moscow anticipated receiving more than 2,000 train carloads of grain, but only 981 arrived. In December, only 439 carloads reached the city; in February 1918, a mere 139. The average daily bread ration plummeted to 100 grams and workers consumed only an estimated 1,700 to 2,000 calories a day. (The recommended daily caloric requirement for a worker was 3,600.)[26]

The Civil War and economic collapse wrecked Bolshevik attempts to make good their promise of bread. Aside from the food grown in Moscow's immediate environs (agricultural production in the adjacent provinces was normally only enough to support the local population for part of the year), the city depended on produce transported by rail from the Central Black Earth region, Siberia, and the southern grain-producing provinces. For most of this period, however, the latter two regions were behind enemy lines and the reduced rail service frustrated the transport of food from other regions. During these years, the city received only the smallest fraction of food necessary to sustain the population.

Food became the over-riding concern of all Muscovites. Desperate citizens developed a variety of survival strategies. Thousands simply left Moscow for the countryside where food was thought to be more abundant. Many workers sent their families back to their villages while they continued to live and work in the city.[27] Some people became *meshochniki* (bagmen) trafficking in foodstuffs produced in their home village or on a family plot for sale at exorbitant prices in the city's black markets. Members of the dispossessed aristocracy and property owning classes sold their possessions—everything from furniture to ball gowns—on the black market. Many women had nothing to sell but themselves. "Prostitution is practiced by Soviet employees in order to obtain, for the sale of caresses, boots that go up to the knees; prostitution is resorted to by mothers of families, working women, peasant women, who sell their bodies to the manager of the rations division in order to obtain for their children a full bag of precious flour."[28]

Others turned to crime. Amidst the chaos of 1917, the crime rate rose rapidly—to four times that in 1900. But 1918 witnessed the steepest rise in crime. That year the murder rate was eleven times greater than in 1917; the robbery rate, 285 times greater. During the next three years, the number of recorded crimes rose by 50 percent. Theft was the most common crime. During the Civil War, theft and robbery accounted for more than 90 percent of all crimes committed in the capital. Stealing remained the only way for many to survive. Workers stole tools, equipment and materials from the factories; soldiers stole from their supply sections; and many people stole from food and exchange teams. Inevitably, many stolen goods were sold or exchanged for food on the black market.[29]

Such individual behavior was the recourse of people desperate enough to settle for short-term relief.[30] But while individual workers adopted such tactics, as a group they realized that only organized, collective efforts would improve their food situation. In search of relief, factory committees and workers demanded that their soviets provide relief and often went on strike to underscore the urgency of their demands.[31] The soviets responded eagerly. Soon after the seizure of power, the Moscow Soviet took several measures demanded by its constituents.[32] In November, it ordered its Food Committee to coordinate all food activities and all city and *raion* rations commissions to requisition grain cargoes and deliver them to city supply organs for sale at fixed prices.

Shortly thereafter, the soviet authorized the dispatching of factory organized food teams to the countryside to exchange manufactured and industrial products for grain and other foodstuffs. During early 1918, this expanded into a regular system of exchange between Moscow and Ekaterinoslav, Kherson and Tavricheskaia *gubernii*. The economic collapse frustrated this tactic. In March, the city Food Committee announced that to meet its food needs, such teams had to exchange 100 million rubles worth of goods; but as of mid-February, Moscow's industries had only produced 16 million rubles worth of "exchangable" items. From late December through February 1918, the city soviet passed a series of resolutions that organized public dining halls, fixed the prices of certain staple food items, rationed food on the basis of newly issued ration cards, and organized special teams to ferret out unknown or concealed food products.[33] These efforts also failed to ameliorate the situation. The future promised little relief.

Given the inability of locally initiated policy to reverse the increasingly desperate situation, the central government issued several decrees in May and June 1918 that concentrated all food supply and distribution policies in its hands. On June 11, the government officially decreed the "food dictatorship."[34] Under this "dictatorship," the government determined the food policy that was to be executed by local governments. The new policy had considerable support. As early as January 1918, the All-Russian Congress of Rations Councils had called for a state monopoly on food, the fixing of food prices, and a resolute struggle against speculators. Many factories demanded similar measures, and whatever other steps were necessary to ward off starvation.[35]

Despite its imposing name, the "food dictatorship" was flexible enough to allow for local initiative. To succeed, it required such initiative. Two characteristics distinguished the central government's "food dictatorship" from the earlier, unsuccessful local efforts. One was that all local initiatives had to conform to central government policies. To ensure this, the Commissariat of Food was empowered to formulate food policies and the Military Rations Bureau (*Voenprodbiuro*) of VTsSPS

(All-Russian Central Council of Trade Unions) to direct that policy's implementation.[36] *Pravda* stated that centralization of all food activities was essential because, in many cases, prior food collection work had proceeded "extremely poorly" and "time will not wait."[37]

Centralization failed to reverse the food crisis. In December 1918, a frustrated Moscow Soviet voiced its constituents' criticisms of those within the Peoples' Commissariat of Food who were responsible for supplying the city. The Commissariat had supplied it with less than half of the established rations and "a significant part" of the food that reached the capital was given to the garrison. The soviet's leaders charged that the Commissariat was riddled with bureaucratism and alienated from the working class. They demanded that worker organizations be allowed to purchase and import into the city nonrationed food products.[38] Criticisms of the Commissariat of Food and its designated agencies continued during the next two years. By late 1920, it was clear that rather than ameliorating the food crisis, the failure of governmental food policies had alienated workers from the government.

The second and most distinctive difference between the "food dictatorship" and earlier efforts was the transformation of goods-exchange teams into food requisitioning teams. The campaign to organize these teams commenced with Lenin's May 22 "Letter to the Workers of Petrograd" that called on workers to make heroic sacrifices to ensure the revolution's survival and to organize food requisitioning teams: "We need a mass 'crusade' of advanced workers to every corner of this vast country. We need ten times more *iron detachments* of the proletariat. . . . Then we shall triumph over famine and unemployment."[39] Moscow's soviet, trade union, and local party leaders responded by organizing a series of factory and *raion* meetings to explain the food policy and to recruit workers into food detachments. Soon after, the Moscow Committee issued a decree requiring each party organization to enlist no less than 5 percent of its members for food detachments. Each factory committee was to elect no less than 1 percent of the workforce to staff the teams. The city and *raion* soviets, Moscow Council of Trade Unions and the Fourth Moscow Conference of Factory Committees endorsed the decree.[40]

By November, upward of 6,000 workers staffed food detachments teams of twenty-five or more members.[41] Large factories, such as Dinamo, Danilovskii, Tsindel', and Trekhgornaia, organized their own teams; smaller enterprises often grouped their forces into *raion* teams.[42]

Although the Communist Party took the lead in organizing the teams and its members often headed them, nonparty volunteers comprised the majority of food teams' members.[43]

In theory, the food requisitioning teams had several responsibilities. Not only were they to expropriate surplus food from kulaks, but there also supposed to act as agitators, help in the formation of Committees of Poor Peasants (*Kombedy*), engage in cultural and educational work, and organize reading rooms, soviets, and party cells.[44] The real activities of the teams were often very different. Many teams, unable (or unwilling) to distinguish kulaks from other types of peasants, carried away any available food. Others abused their power and engaged in robbery.[45] Peasants often responded violently to such behavior. Bands of peasants assaulted food teams. In 1918 alone, 7,309 food team members nationwide (about 20 percent of the total) lost their lives.[46] In 1920, peasants in Tambov, western Siberia and other areas organized armed revolts against forced requisitioning.[47]

Viewed from an urban worker's perspective, food detachments were more than marauding, armed bands. Thousands of Moscow workers responded to the tocsin sounded by soviet, trade union, and party leaders.[48] To many, Lenin's warning that "the salvation of the Moscow workers from starvation is the salvation of the revolution" rang true.[49] For these workers, most of whom were not Communists, the starvation of the cities meant certain doom for them and their form of government— the soviets—and the return of the old order. Faced with the possibility of starvation, as well was the dashing of their revolutionary aspirations, the requisitioning of peasant produce seemed the lesser of two evils. But requisitioning also produced intraproletarian tensions. As the number of murdered food team members rose and as peasants—inherently less sympathetic to the policy—replaced workers in the factories, conflicts over requisitioning mounted.

Fortunately, Muscovites did not depend entirely on requisitioned foodstuffs. From late 1918, they could also legally import into the city one and a half puds of food per person for personal consumption. (One pud equals thirty-six pounds.) Many workers availed themselves of this opportunity whenever possible. But the policy had an unforeseen negative side-effect. Many factory workers devoted part of their workday to producing items such as locks, hatchets, and crowbars that they exchanged for food. Such unauthorized production reduced regular factory production.[50] Yet another source of food existed—state farms (*sovkhozy*) and kitchen gardens (*ogorody*) for use by factories, soviets, and trade unions.[51] The enterprise or agency that farmed the land dispensed with the produce as it saw fit. During these years, the amount of land devoted to food cultivation by Muscovites increased markedly and the produce from such plots proved to be a crucial supplement to rations.[52]

Still the specter of hunger daily stalked Moscow. During the first quarter of 1919, textile workers received an average daily bread ration of .55 pounds. Many received less—27 percent received from 20 to 28 percent of that ration, 16 percent received only up to 20 percent of that ration, and 3 percent received no rations. More than 900 textile workers died during this period.[53] In July 1919, when the average daily bread ration plummeted to a mere 80 grams, *Pravda* lamented that "Moscow and Petrograd are starving. . . ."[54] Workers went on strike to protest their condition and the failure of government policy, but to little avail. The size of rations increased slightly after the 1919 harvest only to decline again in mid-1920.[55] In January 1921, the government announced that the already meager official bread ration of 400 grams (in reality, few received that much) would be reduced by two-thirds. During the first ten days of February, not a single food train reached the city.[56] As we shall see, hungry workers went on strike and furiously condemned the food policy, the Commissariat of Food, and, above all, the party.

The food crisis limited both the quantity and quality of food that workers consumed. Although workers received so-called preferential rations, their diet was meager. In theory, their rations included bread, kasha, meat, fish, flour, potatoes, sugar and salt. In reality, the standard diet consisted of bread, potatoes (sometimes frozen), and kasha. Vegetables and meat were rare in Moscow, except at a very high price in the private markets. Horsemeat, pigeon, dog, and cat were eaten for as long as the supply lasted.[57] Such substandard diets guaranteed that workers would be continually undernourished and exhausted, and hence less productive and more susceptible to the diseases that plagued the city.

To ensure that the limited supply of food went to those whom the government deemed deserving of them, from mid-1918 most rations were distributed as meals in public and factory dining halls. Created in response to worker demands, the city soviet opened the first such halls in April 1918. That month from 500 to 600 people ate one daily meal there. The number of dining halls mushroomed as the food crisis deepened. By 1921, virtually all Muscovites—more than one million—ate one daily meal in the 1,734 dining halls. These facilities' conditions varied markedly. Some were adequate, but others were so overcrowded that workers had to eat in unheated corridors and shops. The quality of meals varied depending on the availability of food. During his stay in Moscow in 1920, Alexander Berkman was served a bowl of putrid fish soup; he was unable to eat it, but an engineer at his side eagerly devoured it. While the food and conditions of dining halls left much to be desired, they undoubtedly saved many from starvation. As one worker put it: "If it were not for the [factory] dining hall, I do not know how we would have held out during these years."[58]

Despite its best efforts, the government proved incapable of overcoming the food crisis. Only one alternative existed—the private market. But for ideological and political reasons, the party wanted to limit that market as much as was possible, or at least feasible. Many Bolsheviks distrusted, others abhorred, the private traders who honey-combed the country. Many hoped that the destruction of capitalist market relations would strike a death-blow to capitalism. State controlled rationing was therefore ideologically attractive to many Bolsheviks. But the failure of centralized food policies to meet workers demands forced the party to tolerate the private market. Had it not been for that market, many would not have survived. Toleration did not preclude harassment, however, and so the Cheka (the Extraordinary Commission to Combat Counter-revolution and Sabotage) periodically descended upon the markets and arrested a number of vendors. Some of those arrested were sentenced to compulsory labor, while others were merely reprimanded or fined and had their produce confiscated.[59]

During the Civil War, entrepreneurial peasants, workers, merchants, and employees all engaged in private trade. Known collectively as bagmen (meshochniki), these people provided upward of two-thirds of the country's food supply and four times more grain than did official supply organizations.[60] In Moscow, these products were sold in the few private shops and the very public black markets. The largest of these was Sukharevka, but there were others such as the Okhotny market (within a stone's throw of the Commissariat of Foreign Affairs), the Smolenskii market, and smaller ones on Tver street and around the Arbat.

The scarcity of food and consumer goods in state stores and dining facilities stood in stark contrast to the relative abundance of food and goods in these markets. One could find almost anything there. For example, at the Sukharevka market, one could buy fruit, milk, butter, fish, bread, cheeses, fresh vegetables, honey, and occasionally even meat. Sukharevka's prices were so high that most consumers could only afford to buy things at this market if they sold or bartered something themselves—usually goods or tools stolen from their place of work. Small, open air restaurants sold white rolls with butter, steaks (usually horsemeat), sausages, prepared vegetables, pastries, and tea. A glass of tea with a white roll cost 500 rubles; grains and vegetables cost 150 rubles and more. In addition to food, one could buy virtually any item imaginable: shoes, blankets, rugs, clothing, negligees, French lingerie, wigs, household items and utensils, fabrics, cigarettes, passports, ration books, even gramophones.[61] Although the quantity and selection of products in these markets declined over time, markets like Sukharevka remained oases of abundance.

Despite the high cost, the meager ration allotments forced all citizens to shop on the private market. In 1918 and 1919, Muscovites spent about three-quarters of their wages on food, half of which they purchased at private markets. But such purchases accounted for 90 percent of a worker's total food costs.[62] Given the cost of food on the private market, rationing was perhaps the only means (however unsatisfactory) available to provide the general population with even a modicum of protection from the ravages of economic collapse.

In the years after 1917, workers found themselves hungry, cold, and struggling to survive. In their factories and homes, they daily watched the economy ratcheting downward, grinding up their hopes for their and their families' future, and replacing them with the fear of tomorrow. Through it all, they watched their soviets and the party, unable to control the situation, try to implement well-intentioned but unsuccessful policies and issuing resolutions that proved to be more than "pious wishes." For many workers, it would be years before they would again cede any credence to their revolutionary state.

Housing

An improved standard of living and quality of life was fundamental to the proletariat's revolutionary agenda. The food crisis made a mockery of that hope and left workers undernourished and exhausted. Workers also experienced frustration in their quest for improved housing. But unlike food, workers, through the soviet and central government, had some control over urban housing. After the Novemeber revolution, each moved decisively to fulfill that worker demand. Direct action and official decrees quickly municipalized and redistributed housing to workers and other laboring people. By 1921, half of the city's population had moved from substandard apartments and factory barracks to dwellings formerly occupied by the city's now *declassé* wealthy and middle-class residents.

But the quality of that housing was abysmal. Shortages of fuel and building materials turned once comfortable dwellings into dilapidated hovels. Hungry and exhausted workers found little respite at home.

Before the revolution, the vast majority of workers lived in one of two types of housing: small, overcrowded apartments in one- or two-story wooden houses; or barracks located in the city's industrial districts or suburbs.[63] The barracks (*koechno-komorochnaia kvartira*) were undoubtedly one of the worst aspects of pre-revolutionary working-class life. Regardless of whether they were privately owned or factory barracks, the conditions there were horrid:

> A barrack of three to five tiny cells, hardly separated by plank partitions, contains on the average over thirteen inhabitants. Married and single, children and adults, healthy and ill, five and more persons are crowded into a single cell. The premises, frequently damp, devoid of the light of day and unventilated, strike you by their gloomy, filthy, suffocating atmosphere. The air is filled with stinking dust and reeks with (sic) human sweat and stale clothing. The inhabitants generally work the day long . . . and sleep there at night. They sleep on anything they can find: on berths, trunks, on the floor, using their clothing as bedding.[64]

Most cells had only one window which frequently opened into a hall or faced the bathrooms. Toilets and sinks either stood in unheated corridors or were far removed, often in the yard. Plumbing and running water were nonexistent. Wood and often garbage heated the barracks, many of which were situated in damp, dark basements, making them foci for the spread of disease.

Many workers lived in barracks before the revolution. In 1899, 16,140 such barracks housed 174,600 residents, about one-quarter of whom were under fourteen years of age. By 1917, more than 340,000 occupants (or 17 percent of the population) lived in an estimated 27,000 barracks.[65] Such was the *ancien regime*'s housing policy.

The revolutionary government took immediate measures to eradicate the worst aspects of the proletariat's deplorable housing conditions. In late 1917, the city soviet municipalized all houses and apartments the total monthly rents of which exceeded 750 rubles.[66] An August 1918 decree declared all urban real estate to be state or municipal property and placed it under the jurisdiction of locally elected authorities.[67] The administration of such property became the responsibility of tenant committees which in turn were responsible to the *raion* housing commissions which the city soviet empowered to redistribute housing. Although formal municipalization did not occur until August, *de facto* municipalization by zealous workers and local soviets began immediately after the revolution. The August decree simply recognized a *fait accompli.*[68]

With municipalization came the eviction of many former owners; in other cases, these people were forced to share their dwellings with working class families transferred from barracks and other squalid residences. Pasternaks's portrayal of the confiscation of the Zhivago family's house and the conditions of life there after the redistribution is probably an accurate portrayal of what occurred in the houses of many formerly well-to-do residents.[69] In 1918, more than 20,000 workers' and employees' families moved into confiscated housing. By 1921, the redistribution policy had benefitted about 500,000 people (or half the city's population).[70] For those people, the move represented a significant improvement in their living conditions. As John Hazard has stated,

> one of the most spectacular demonstrations to the working man of what the Revolution really could mean to them was the moving of people who had been living in the cellars and hovels and little shacks out in the poverty-stricken suburbs, to the palaces and mansions of the former rich. A worker had only to open his eyes in the morning and see the golden and crystal chandelier instead of the old kerosene lamp to realize that something tremendous had happened and to draw the conclusion that as the chief beneficiary he vowed allegiance to the cause.[71]

But significant problems frustrated the promise which redistribution held out. Housing construction had slowed significantly during World War I; after municipalization, construction and most routine maintenance and repairs ceased for want of funds. Consequently, between 1917 and 1920, the number of unfit apartments in the city doubled and the number of inhabitable apartments declined significantly. In early 1917, 27,872 apartment houses contained 231,597 apartments; three years later, there were 24,490 with 163,651 tenants.[72]

Shortage of home heating fuel sped the deterioration of the city's housing. During the unrelenting cold of winter months, the maximum temperature was decreed to be fifty degrees Fahrenheit. Few dwellings were that warm. To meet the home fuel crisis, the city soviet in 1918 formed a Commission for the Demolition of Houses and Country Homes for Fuel—in short, a special dismantling commission. From 1918 to 1919, the Commission authorized the razing of 903 residential buildings. But the demand for fuel was so great that freezing residents razed some 2,500 dwellings in 1919 alone.[73] People took wood from wherever they could find it. They stripped the siding, floors, doors, beams, and anything else that would burn from occupied and unoccupied buildings. They felled trees in city parks, tore down fences and removed wooden crosses from cemetery plots. By 1920, the heating systems in two-thirds of the dwellings were useless. Without heat, walls became moist, water pipes froze and burst; when they thawed, they damaged the buildings thereby making many apartments uninhabitable. The residents themselves contributed to the deterioration by knocking holes in the walls for chimney pipes, cutting wood from floors and walls for fuel, and dismantling or destroying plumbing and electrical fixtures, the use of which some did not understand. Unable to repair the damage, the soviet met residents' complaints by moving them to other dwellings.[74]

The apartment that housed the American Relief Administration (ARA) teams in the city exemplifies the housing conditions which existed during these years and for some time after. Since it was offered to foreign representatives, no doubt it was substantially better than that housing the bulk of the population.

> The condition of this building was representative of a great number of larger residences of Moscow . . . 30 Spriridonovka had contained schools; it had also housed an undetermined number of families occupying one or two rooms each. The central heating plant, since no one was responsible for it, had long since ceased to function and the occupants kept warm by setting up stoves in their rooms, making holes in the wall where necessary. The water system was also useless and a large area of the cellar was under two feet of water. The rooms were indescribably filthy, particularly the bathrooms, which had been used for every purpose but bathing. An inspection of the cellar revealed not only the wreck of the heating plant, but that some of the occupants of the house were following agricultural pursuits, either to piece out their own food supply or as a business venture. Here was an indiscriminant collection of pigs, poultry, and rabbits, whose living conditions like those of their owners left much to be desired.[75]

An unsympathetic observer surveying Moscow's housing situation in 1921 might well have concluded that the results were to be expected: the illiterate and brutish workers had descended on the city's housing like a plague of locusts and destroyed it, while the government proved unable to halt, and even tacitly encouraged, the process. In reality, the fuel shortage and economic collapse undermined what otherwise would have been one of the revolution's most important early accomplishments.

Nonetheless, by 1921, growing numbers of workers were themselves becoming unsympathetic observers.

Demographic Consequences

While Muscovites found ways to endure economic collapse, food and fuel shortages, and abysmal housing conditions, one reality defied all strategies: death. The specter of death loomed large over the city during these years. Epidemics of typhus, scarlet and relapsing fevers, cholera, diptheria and smallpox swept through Moscow and wracked the already exhausted citizens. Incidences of these diseases, which were endemic in pre-revolutionary times, rose sharply in 1918. Epidemic diseases accounted for approximately one-fifth of the deaths that year. Consequently, the city's death rate jumped from 23.7 to 29.9 (per thousand residents.) (Death rates are listed in appendix 2.) The next year epidemics of typhus (76,000 cases), cholera and smallpox, coupled with high incidences of spanish flu, scarlet fever, and diptheria ravaged the population and pushed the death rate up to 45.4. During the next two years, epidemic diseases continued to account for a significant proportion of all deaths. While they were the most dramatic killers, tuberculosis and respiratory ailments and deficiency diseases such as rickets, scurvy, and hunger edema, claimed the lives or sapped the strength of many undernourished residents.[76]

Although the most brutal, death was the least important reason for Moscow's precipitous population loss during the Civil War years. Flight and Red Army levies accounted for most of the staggering population decline. In February 1917, slightly more than two million people resided in Moscow; by late 1920, the city housed only 1,027,000—less than its 1897 population.[77]

Although many former aristocrats and bourgeois fled Moscow after the November revolution,[78] worker-peasants who returned to their villages accounted for the largest group (probably the majority) of those who left the city during these years. Members of the pre-revolutionary peasant estate (*soslovie*), they had migrated to Moscow before 1917 in search of employment. They comprised a majority of that population. Most were males. Some had lived in Moscow for many years; others were recent arrivals. After the November 1917 land decree, tens of thousands of the city's worker-peasants returned to their villages to claim their share of the recently confiscated lands. As one contemporary observer put it, "many workmen have returned to their villages and begun

31

to cultivate their own land and nothing will induce them to come back. . . ."[79] As hunger, cold, and unemployment mounted in Moscow, the number of people returning to the villages grew dramatically.[80]

Not all worker-peasants immediately left the city. Some remained and sent their relatives to the villages to claim land in the family's name and to protect them from deteriorating urban conditions. Whether because they had rejected village life or feared losing their job or chose to stay to defend the revolution, others made the same choice.[81] Despite their desire to stay in Moscow, the deteriorating economy forced many to leave. The March 1918 Congress of Labor Commissions and Directors for the Moscow Industrial Region resolved that those people who had "sufficient income or secure property" should be the first to be laid off. Some factory committees passed similar resolutions.[82] But as Moscow's woes mounted, many left voluntarily.

Red Army levies further reduced the population, especially the working class. According to the Moscow Soviet, more than 313,000 residents performed Red Army service.[83] These enlistments serve as a measure of proletarian support for the revolution, but they also contributed to the disintegration and transformation of that class. Thousands of Muscovite workers took up arms to defend the revolution. By late January 1918, more than 4,000 members of Moscow's Red Guard had enlisted to combat General Kaledin's assault on Petrograd. When Germany renewed its offensive in February, 20,000 Muscovites joined the Red Army in response to Sovnarkom's plea that "the socialist fatherland is in danger" and the urgings of local soviet officials. ("Mobilize! All to the front! Death or victory!")[84] Many who did so shared the view of the Dinamo workers that it was "better to die than to retreat from German imperialism."[85] By mid-May, more than 57,000 Muscovites, most of them workers, had enlisted.[86]

Red Army levies continually depleted the city's male population. Given the class nature of the army, Communists and workers comprised the majority of enlisted Muscovites. Beginning in July 1918, the "almost unceasing mobilization of party members to the front" commenced. Thousands of party and Komsomol members volunteered or were conscripted for service. In all, two-thirds of all Moscow Communists served in the Red Army during the Civil War. A high proportion of workers also joined the army. According to VSNKh, approximately 70 percent of Moscow workers between the ages of 20 and 24, 55 percent of those between the ages of 25 and 29, and 35 percent of those between the ages of 30 and 35 served in the Red Army.[87] In many factories, groups of workers enlisted and served together. For example, in the autumn of 1918, the Guzhon and Dinamo plants each sent a regiment of metalworkers, many of them skilled, to fight in the battle of Tsaritsyn. During the first half of 1919, the Trekhgornaia textile plant sent six detachments to the front and all of the Iakhromskii factory's male workers volunteered for service (only one-third were taken so as not to further impair productivity). Other workers enlisted in response to mobilizations such as that issued by VTsSPS in 1919 which mobilized 10 percent of the males in every union. Usually a larger percentage enlisted.[88]

In the case of Moscow, there is considerable evidence to substantiate the Soviet claim that "in the Red Army were grouped the best young forces of workers and peasants."[89] Among them were some of the revolution's most enthusiastic supporters, the Communist Party's best organizers, and the city's most physically able and skilled workers. Their presence testified to worker support for the revolution and strengthened the Red Army's fighting ability and morale, but it also entailed a considerable reduction of the city's productive population. Together with the movement of worker-peasants to the villages, these departures hastened what, in March 1918, Bukharin called the "disintegration of the proletariat."[90]

The Disintegration and Transformation of the Proletariat

The disintegration of the proletariat dramatically reduced the size and transformed the composition of that class. It also had profound political consequences. Red Army enlistments, the exodus to the villages, the closing of many shops and factories, and the rising death rate quickly depleted the working class. In 1917, Moscow's industries employed 190,000 workers. By August 1918, only about 140,000 labored there; by January 1921, a mere 81,000.[91]

During these years, virtually every factory experienced a drastic reduction in its workforce's size. For example, the Guzhon metal works (later Serp i molot) employed 3,688 workers in 1913. But by 1921, only 825 workers worked there, and fewer than half of them possessed the requisite production skills and experience. The Krasnyi proletarii plant boasted 2,394 workers in 1916, but only 700 workers three years later. Ninety percent of that factory's workers in early 1921 were "yesterday's peasants." Between 1918 and 1921, the Dinamo workforce contracted by two-thirds. The situation was even worse at the Mikhelson factory that in 1913 employed some 2,000 workers. During 1918, that factory lost 80 percent of its workers. A paltry 300 workers labored there in 1921 and only 75 of them were described as "old workers" (that is, experienced workers). The workforce in the textile and food processing industries shrank by 75 percent during the Civil War. Comparable reductions occurred in all of the city's industries save for the garment industry where in 1920 the workforce was actually 29 percent larger than in 1913, a growth due primarily to the demand for military apparel.[92]

The loss of skilled workers became particularly acute. At the Krasnyi Bogatyr' plant, where the number of male workers with ten or more years experience had contracted by 60 percent by 1919, there was an "acute shortage" of skilled workers. Such was also the case at the Third State Cast Iron Foundry. In 1914, that foundry employed 257 skilled casters (all males); by 1920, there were only 50, 38 of whom were women. The reduction in the number of mechanics was equally as steep—from 110 in 1916 to 24 in 1919. At the AMO plant in early 1921, more than half of the workers were unskilled.[93] Faced with an acute shortage of skilled workers, the Central Committee of the All-Russian Union of Metalworkers resolved in late 1919 to recruit such workers from the countryside.[94] Yet in September 1920, there were 11,105 vacancies for metalworkers in the city, many of them for skilled workers. Factories also tried to recruit former workers who had returned to the villages. The tactic failed.[95]

Two groups comprised the majority of industrial workers by 1920: peasants (some of whom were recuited or conscripted, others of whom had cut their village ties) and the spouses and offspring of workers who had left production. In 1919, 8 percent of the city's workers were seventeen years old or younger. A year later, women accounted for 45 percent of the industrial proletariat. Women dominated the work force in the textile, wool and tobacco industries, but were a distinct minority in the metals, wood and leather industries.[96] The vast majority of these new workers lacked skills and production experience. Many undoubtedly entered the factories to survive since only those who worked received rations, and, in theory at least, workers received the largest ration allotments. These new workers suffered from what Shliapnikov called an "ignorance and lack of interest in production." While their ignorance probably declined during the next three years, so too did their interest in production.[97]

As a result of these quantitative and qualitative changes, the Moscow proletariat by the end of the Civil War can be best described as a bifurcated class. In virtually every factory, there remained a small core of experienced and skilled workers, a majority of whom were males over thirty years old. Most of these remnants of a labor aristocracy were hereditary proletarians who had very few, if any, ties to the village and who "had tied their fate with the fate of the factory."[98] Despite their skills and experience, they were incapable of countering the economic collapse which paralyzed their factories. Hunger, cold, and exhaustion limited whatever desire they had to do so. But these workers comprised a minority of the rapidly disintegrating workforce, the majority of which were inexperienced and reluctant workers.

Declining Productivity and Labor Discipline

Worker productivity plummetted during the Civil War. This decline resulted from a confluence of factors—the scarcity of fuel, raw materials, and tools; the increasing disrepair of many of the city's factories; the proletariat's changing composition; the decline of labor discipline; and the undernourishment and illness that sapped the strength of workers. Although precise calculations of the decline during these years differ slightly, the general trend is unmistakable. The figures published by the Moscow Soviet show that on average the productivity of the average Moscow worker in 1917/18 fell to 46.7 percent of the 1913 level. By 1919/1920, it had declined to 25.6 percent; the following year, it rose slightly to 29 percent.[99] To stem declining productivity, party, trade union, and factory committee leaders pursued two strategies: to re-instill labor discipline among workers and to tie wages to productivity. Not until 1920 did either strategy achieve any success.

A wide variety of production traits and attitudes come under the rubric of labor discipline—punctually arriving at work; conscientiously performing one's job; respecting machinery, materials, and products; obeying the instructions of foremen and other responsible personnel; and minimizing absence from work.[100] During 1917, labor discipline broke down. Part of the problem resulted from widespread worker political activism that entailed numerous and lengthy meetings during the workday. The concomitant breakdown of worker repsect for or deference to owners, managers, technical specialists (*spetsy*), and foremen and worker rejection of work rules established by them sped the process. After Novemeber 1917, the breakdown of labor discipline intensified. Many workers interpreted the workers' control decree as a signal to sharpen class conflict in the factory and escalated their harassment of factory personnel, especially specialists (a practice referred to as *spet-seedstvo*, specialist-baiting).[101]

In early 1918, the leadership of worker institutions (factory committees, trade unions and soviets), which had fanned the flames of class conflict so as to assert working class power and hasten the old order's demise, realized that the resulting reduced productivity and labor discipline was destroying the economic base of the new state and threatened their constituents with ruin. Quickly, they issued a flurry of calls for the revival of labor dicipline. In January 1918, the First All-Russian Trade Union Congress and the Moscow City and *Guberniia* Rubber Workers Conference passed resolutions on the need to strengthen labor discipline.[102] In April, several worker organizations passed resolutions calling for better labor discipline, improving the quality of technical personnel and training qualified workers to perform technical jobs.[103] Delegates to meetings of metalworkers and the Fourth All-City Conference of Factory Committees and Trade Unions in June passed similar resolutions as did some factory committees.[104]

Although some factories apparently increased production and productivity in early 1918, the collapse of the economy and workforce and the deterioration of work conditions quickly undid these gains.[105] Trade union leader Tomskii was not exaggerating when he stated in May 1918: "The decline in labor productivity has reached catastrophic proportions. Industrial production is threatened with complete collapse."[106]

Given that inexperienced and undisciplined workers comprised an increasing proportion of the industrial labor force during these years, the absence of discipline should not be surprising. Not infrequently, these workers arrived late to work, preferred card games, revelry, and drinking to production, and consciously and unconsciously damaged machines.[107] Worker absenteeism was also common. In 1908, the average worker worked the equivalent of 320 eight-hour days;[108] in 1920, that worker reported for only 219 eight-hour workdays. Excluding vacations, the average worker missed 60 days of work, 45 of which were missed because of illness or simply because the worker failed to appear. Organizational work accounted for 15 days away from the job; idle workplaces for 8 additional days. But these figures are averages for the city's entire industrial workforce. In some industries, such as the metal industry where the average worker missed 84 days of work, the situation was far worse.[109]

While illness and the frantic search for food and fuel accounted for some of the absences, their timing provides another reason. The highest rates of absenteeism occurred in July and August and suggest that those workers with village ties extended their vacations there so as to take part in field work or simply to seek refuge from Moscow's deteriorating conditions.[110] Whatever the reasons, absenteeism frustrated all attempts to raise production and continued unabated.

Trade unions and certain factory committees simultaneously sought to raise labor productivity by re-introducing piece-rate wages. In Janaury 1918, VTsSPS called for the creation of special factory commissions to establish output norms for each shop and category of worker and for the introduction of production registers.[111] The Labor Code of December 1918 also recommended the use of piece-rate wages. But worker resistance slowed the shift from time-based wages until 1920. Prior to the revolution, most workers received piece-rate wages. Many resented this method of payment and during 1917 demanded the adoption of time-based wages. After November 1917, the shift to hourly or daily wages accelerated. By August 1918, only one-third of the nation's workers received piece-rate wages.[112] The establishment of output norms also proceeded slowly. In its appeal for the setting of such norms, VTsSPS recommended that all unions and factories create norm-setting bureaus (*tarifno-normirovochnye biuro*—TNB). However, the failure of many factories and some unions to establish TNBs, worker resistance to them, poor work conditions, and economic collapse frustrated attempts to carry out the VTsSPS directive.[113]

Although efforts to use monetary incentives to increase productivity intensified from 1918, the rate of inflation reduced the value of such incentives. As inflation obliterated the ruble and prices soared, calls for natural wages (that is, the payment of wages in food, clothing, shoes, and so forth instead of money) increased. After hearing a report that food costs exceeded the average worker's wage by 300 percent, the Second Congress of Commissars of Labor in May 1918 urged the introduction of natural wages for workers. During the next several months, worker convocations, including All-Russian Conference of Metalworkers, passed similar resolutions.[114] From late 1918, natural wages were gradually introduced. At that time, 48 percent of the average wage consisted of allowances in kind; two years later, the proportion had risen to 93 percent.[115]

Resolutions, wage policies, and natural wages all failed to halt declining productivity in 1918 and 1919. Nor could they have been expected to do so. The forces of deterioration and chaos that swept the land were more powerful than any policy. The food crisis remained the major obstacle to improved productivity. Hungry and undernourished workers are never productive. But the wage policies themselves also hampered attempts to raise productivity. The increasing use of natural wages was in essence a policy of social maintenance. Regardless of how productive one was, one received wages in kind. This was even true for workers receiving piece-rate wages because they were assured of a minimum wage. Since rations were determined by occupation rather than productivity and bonuses were paid in inflated rubles, no material incentive for increasing productivity existed. In short, the social maintenance policy undermined those designed to raise productivity. Not until 1920 were the two policies brought into harmony.

Workers' Control and the Nationalization of Factories

The November 16, 1917 decree on workers' control (*rabochii kontrol*) formally initiated that short-lived experiment in industrial management. It was also a recognition of what was occurring on a *de facto* basis. As early as August 21, 1917, the Moscow Soviet passed a resolution in support of workers' control. A week before the November 16 decree the soviet responded to an owner's attempt to close his factory by confiscating the plant and empowering the factory committee to operate it. Soon after, workers at the Dinamo plant responded to a similar attempt in the same way. While meeting the demands of workers, the November 16 decree further intensified worker-management conflicts and hastened the closing of many enterprises, which in turn increased the number of plants taken over by workers.[116] By January 1918, workers' control commissions had been established in more than half of the city's industrial plants; by March, the proportion rose to three-quarters.[117]

Bolsheviks and workers alike enthusiastically supported workers' control. But the nature and limits of workers' control proved to be a deeply divisive issue that pitted workers against Bolsheviks, and workers and Bolsheviks against themselves. Two interpretations of workers' control—productivist and radical—quickly emerged.[118] What distinguished the two positions was their perception of the relative roles of collegial administration (*kollegial'nost'*) and one-man management (*edinonachalie*). Collegial administration meant that workers' control commissions elected by factory committees would administer a factory or enterprise. One-man management meant that an individual had that responsibility. The two also differed on the role of factory committees. The productivists envisioned them as the base of a nationally integrated, industrial trade union hierarchy. They were to execute, not formulate,

38

union and state labor policies. The radicals saw them as the base of a national economic hierarchy.

The conflict between the productivists and radicals occurred over that issue where the party's and proletariat's revolutionary agendas met most directly. The radicals' position reflected the direct experience of the working class, which had seen firsthand the effects of the shortsightedness of capitalist factory owners and the often incomprehensible actions of their hired managers. The workers believed that they could do better. A natural human desire to gain control of their lives also motivated them. But the radical position, starting as it did from the proletariat's direct experience and interests, could not transcend the limits of that experience, limits that shaped the working-class's revolutionary agenda.

While the party had consciously created the political opening into which the working class could press its demands for workers' control, the party acted under the restraints imposed on it as guardian of the state and revolution. Effective worker output had to be increased if the nation was to be able to defend itself, if the proletariat's material demands were to be met, and if the progress achieved by the revolution was to inspire the workers of the world. *Les raisons d'etat* underlay the productivist position.

Because the link between the control of production and the level of effective output (or production efficiency) is manifold and objectively verifiable, the party could not simply surrender to the radicals' interpretation of workers' control. While for the radicals and workers, workers' control was an end itself, the party's productivist leaders viewed it as a means to an end. Thus, it was on this issue that the very different origins of the two revolutionary agendas became most clear and the structural tension between the party and proletariat was sharpest. In the immediate post-revolutionary years (and in the 1920s), control of production remained the issue over which the party and working class and productivists and radicals would struggle to implement their respective revolutionary agendas.

Lenin and his party supporters as well as some trade union and factory committee leaders advocated the productivist position. For them, the purpose of workers' control was not to have the factories run by workers (*pod upravlenie rabochikh*), but to have workers' control commissions (composed of union and factory committee representatives) take stock of equipment, goods, materials and fuel, oversee and organize production, and check on administrative and hiring and firing practices.[119] One-man management was to remain in operation so as to ensure the maintenance of production. In short, workers' control commissions were to oversee and advise, but not interfere with management. The two were to collaborate in developing policies which would meet workers' demands and yet still raise production without exploiting workers. For productivists, one-man management and collegial administration were not contradictory, but rather complemented each other—workers participated in collegial administration alongside management without destroying the organizational hierarchy that productivists believed essential to efficient production.

Such an interpretation of workers' control reflected two of the productivists' major concerns. One was that, as Lenin often argued, left to their own devices most workers were incapable of achieving anything more than trade union consciousness, that is, they lacked the ability to grasp and assimilate the political implications of a given situation or set of policies and hence contented themselves with achieving merely their economic demands. The productivists feared that factories exclusively controlled by workers would move first to satisfy their long-repressed and justifiable economic grievances at the expense of factory productivity and the country's economic well-being, both of which were essential if workers demands were to be met. Second, the productivists argued that too few workers possessed the knowledge, skills, and abilities to competently manage factories on their own. Factory supply and distribution networks, sources of capital, accounting procedures, and other technical requirements remained a mystery to many workers. Hence managerial and technical personnel had to be retained and utilized if workers' control was to succeed. By exploiting the knowledge and skills of these personnel, workers' control commissions could better ensure the realization of their economic demands. In the process, they became practical schools of administration in which workers learned that knowledge required to one day manage the factories.

The radicals viewed workers' control differently and in the broadest of terms. The radicals drew their support from factory committees, the Regional Councils of Factory Committees, the left wing of the party and unions, and above all workers. They endorsed factory take-overs by workers' control commissions that were freely elected by workers. The commissions were to oversee their factory's entire operations and to formulate production policies and priorities. Worker-controlled factories were to be the base of a national economic policy apparatus. Individual factories were to elect representatives to regional Peoples' Economic Councils that would coordinate regional economic activities. In turn, the regional councils would elect representatives to a national economic council that would formulate and coordinate national economic policies and development.

Factory committees and workers heartily endorsed the radicals' call for factory take-overs. And with the decree on workers' control, there commenced the massive transfer of Moscow's factories from private ownership to workers' control commissions in a flurry of "wild-cat nationalization." Factory committees viewed workers' control and nationalization as synonomous means to vital ends—keeping the factory open and thereby assuring workers of a livelihood, and furthering the socialization of the economy by hastening the demise of bourgeois power.

Because workers usually petitioned local political bodies when they wanted their factory nationalized, prior to late June 1918, the term nationalization is somewhat misleading. Less than a quarter of the city's industries that were "nationalized" (and in which workers' control was established) were in fact nationalized. Virtually half (46 percent) of the "nationalized" enterprises were actually "provincialized" by the Moscow *oblast* SNKh; one-third (31 percent) were municipalized by local agencies, normally the city soviet.[120] Without minimizing the importance of nationalization as an organizational aspect of socialist construction by party leaders, until June 1918 the vast majority of factory nationalizations clearly occured in response to worker demands and initiative. The trade union official Lozovskii dubbed this rapid proliferation of workers' control and "wildcat nationalization" as attempts to achieve "socialism in one factory."[121]

Unfortunately for the radicals, localism, accelerating economic collapse, declining worker productivity, the disintegration of the proletariat, and, until March 1918, the lack of a systematic platform undermined their position at a time when the productivists, who dominated the government leadership, were asserting their power. The disintegration of the proletariat caused particular problems. The working class that aided in the seizure of power consisted of a diverse group of workers. The most prominent were the experienced, skilled, male workers. During 1917, these workers assumed command of the factory committees. Their election to the committees reflected their co-workers' recognition that they possessed essential leadership skills and abilities. They understood how the factories operated, knowledge essential to challenging management's assertions and demands. After the establishment of workers' control, the factory's very survival often rested on this knowledge. Skilled, male workers were more literate, and negotiations with management, factory committee functions, and the factories' successful operation demanded literacy. They also possessed considerable political experience. Some had participated in the 1905 revolution, the prewar trade union movement, and strike organizations. All these qualities made them natural political leaders during 1917.[122]

What gave the 1917 factory committee movement its power was the coalesence of these workers with the younger, inexperienced, and often unskilled workers, many of whom had only recently joined the workforce. During World War I, military service claimed upward of 28 percent of Moscow's working class, and wartime orders created many new jobs. Inexperienced and unskilled juveniles, women, and males unfit for military service, many of whom were peasants, filled the vacated and new positions.[123] What they lacked in skills, literacy, and political and work experience, they often more than made up for with their militance and rejection of authority.

This combination of workers proved to be a very volatile and powerful. But it also created considerable centrifugal intraclass strains. To establish their vision of workers' control, factory committee leaders had to prove that they could successfully manage the factories and halt the decline in production. To do so required that workers increase their labor discipline and productivity. Toward this end, many regional councils of factory committees passed resolutions designed to do just that. Here the radical factory committee leadership often came into conflict with their new co-workers somewhat different revolutionary agenda. The latter tended to view the seizure of power and assertion of workers' control as a signal that their economic demands would soon be met. Many still lacked the poltical consciousness of their experienced co-workers. They insisted upon an immediate amelioration of their economic condition, but often resisted the demands that their leaders believed the fulfillment of their economic demands required.

No sooner had workers taken over their factories than they had to contend with severe problems. Fuel and raw materials shortages curtailed production. Worker ignorance of bookkeeping, supply, and distribution proceedures created significant interruptions. To meet workers' wage demands, some factories began to sell essential tools and raw materials. Absenteeism mounted and labor discipline declined. Although some factories managed to increase productivity in early 1918, the general trend was clear.

These bitter realities severely weakened the radicals. For their vision of workers' control to be realized a measure of economic stability was required. Such stability would provide workers with the time necessary to overcome their mistakes, to master managerial techniques, and to quell the chaos that engulfed the factories. But in early 1918, economic stability and time were scarce commodities. In a collapsing economy, mistakes were magnified.

At this point, the disintegration of the proletariat became of crucial importance. That process witnessed not only the exodus of workers to the villages but also the removal from production of many of the factories' political leaders and experienced workers. Many left to staff the state, party or union bureaucracies or to join the Red Army. Their departure could not have come at a worse time. With sound leadership and a willingness to raise productivity, the radicals' view of workers' control might have been realized. But departures and economic collapse undermined these dreams.

From March 1918, a series of central government and trade union policies enacted the productivist program. That month VSNKh (the Supreme Council of National Economy) ordered all nationalized plants to establish managerial troikas. Composed of a factory manager, technical director, and government commissar, the troika had unrestricted authority over the factory. Worker, employee, and union representatives sat on an advisory committee that discussed policy, but they had no power over the troika.[124] The policy institutionalized the productivist platform. But amidst the chaos of 1918-1919, the issuance and enactment of decrees often remained separate activities.[125] Until early 1920, collegial administration in which workers participated existed in many factories. The quality and abilities of factory committees and management more than central dictates determined the configuration of industrial management. Not until 1920 did the state finally succeed in transforming power relations in the factories.

War Communism in the Factory

On June 28, 1918, Sovnarkom decreed the nationalization of all large-scale industrial enterprises. The decree, which formally initiated the policy of War Communism, came in response to the deteriorating economic and military situations and was precipitated by the government's fear that Germany would lay claim to vital Ukrainian industries. But the Bolsheviks' ideological predisposition toward and political preference for a centrally organized economy added to the decree's attractiveness.

Nationalization not only introduced a measure of order into a patchwork system of municipalized, provincialized, and nationalized enterprises, it also provided an administrative hierarchy necessary to centralization. By late 1918, more than 600 industrial enterprises in Moscow had been nationalized (or municipalized). Nationalization continued in 1919 and 1920, and not infrequently it occurred because workers demanded it to keep their factories open. Like the policy of War Communism, nationalization did not reach its peak until late 1920.[126]

In late 1919, the fledgling Soviet state's fortunes reached their lowest ebb. The economic collapse continued to accelerate, food shortages threatened Moscow with starvation, and White Army victories and foreign occupation reduced the country to the size of late sixteenth-century Muscovy. During that autumn, General Denikin's White Army marched to within 200 miles of Moscow. More so than ever before, the revolution was endangered. Faced with the threat of defeat, party leaders concluded that centralization and increased control should be extended to the factory level. Beginning in November 1919, they introduced punitive measures to combat labor indiscipline, militarized the labor force, tied rations to productivity, and replaced collegial administration with one-man management, all in an attempt to reverse the economic collapse.

Under the new system of factory administration, the powers of managers were dramatically increased and those of the factory committees severely restricted. Factory committees had to relinquish all administrative responsibilities and to concentrate their energies on cultural work, seeking to improve issues of daily life (*byt*) (such as food, fuel and clothing), and strengthening labor discipline. Factory managers had the right to enforce unilaterally all labor policies as they interpreted them and by whatever means they deemed appropriate, including firing the offender and withholding wages and, most importantly, rations. The latter became a common means of enforcing labor discipline. For example, at the Trekhgornaia textile plant, workers who were absent for nine days were denied rations from the factory's thirty-hectare farm; those absent for six days received only half of their share of the produce.[127] The use of food to enforce policy portended a significant change in policy.

The re-imposition of one-man management also enhanced the power and privileges of technical specialists. To reverse the exodus of harassed but valuable specialists, party leaders favored using all possible means to attract specialists back to work. They granted specialists very high salaries and preferential rations and increased their control over factory affairs.[128] This "pandering to the specialists" enraged many workers and

Communists who continued their harassment and abuse of these personnel. Even after the policy change, the Democratic Centralists and Workers Opposition—two prominent party opposition groups—vociferously condemned such preferential treatment and labeled party policy "everything for the specialists."[129]

Most workers did not share the opinion that enhancing managers' and specialists' power and hamstringing the factory committees was a necessary policy. Workers' resentment of their "demotion" was widespread. Workers at the AMO plant rejected the need for a new system of administration and managerial prerogatives and responded with energetic protests and strikes. Workers at Serp i molot bitterly complained: "The working class was boss (*khoziain*) only in '18-'19."[130] Denied the opportunity to influence factory life, worker hostility mounted in 1920.

To re-instill labor discipline and thereby raise productivity, in November 1919 the government ordered the creation of Workers' Disciplinary Courts (also known as Comradely Courts) in the factories. These courts were empowered to punish violators of wage agreements, labor decrees, factory regulations, and labor discipline. Local trade union organizations oversaw the courts, the judges of which consisted of one delegate each from the factory administration, the trade union, and the factory committee. The courts held public hearings and could impose sentences ranging from a mere reprimand to hard labor.[131]

Incomplete data from workers' disciplinary courts in Moscow *guberniia* in 1920 indicate the types of problems that plagued industry. Of 5,182 cases which appeared before these courts, metalworkers committed 42 percent of the offenses (2,218); garment workers, 18 percent of them (962). No other occupational group accounted for more than 5 percent of the cases. In these two industries, a large proportion of the workforce was new workers. Absence and tardiness accounted for the majority of the offenses (55 percent); theft for 15 percent. Other offenses included: negligence, violations of labor discipline, and sabotage (9 percent); violations of rules (7.6 percent); and disobedience of orders (4.7 percent). Males were more likely be absent from or tardy to work (61 percent vs. 50 percent) and more likely to be charged with negligence and violations of discipline and rules (18.4 percent vs. 15.1 percent). But women committed more serious offenses such as theft (20.7 percent vs. 9.1 percent) and abuse of administrators (20 cases vs. 5 cases). In industries such as textiles, weaving, and food processing where women dominated the labor force, theft and refusal of orders accounted for a high proportion of offenses.[132]

But disciplinary courts and coercion could not remedy the shortage of labor. The government addressed this problem by pursuing two different, but in the long run complementary, policies—the militarization of labor and the increasing use of *subbotniks* (voluntary, unpaid workdays, usually on a Saturday).

Throughout 1919 and 1920, the Council of Labor and Defense and other agencies turned to the conscription of labor in order to alleviate the labor shortage. Introduced on an industry by industry basis in response to specific crises or needs, labor conscription became common practice by late 1919.[133] Still labor shortages continued. The party Central Committee responded to the crisis in January 1920 by adopting theses on compulsory labor proposed by Trotsky. The theses noted that it was essential to draw skilled and experienced workers back into industry by gradually recalling them from the army, food detachments, state institutions, and the ranks of the peasantry and speculators. To accomplish this, universal compulsory labor was deemed essential. The theses also called for the militarization of labor and the economy. Such a policy, it was hoped, would reduce labor desertion and improve labor discipline. On January 29, 1920, Sovnarkom enacted a law based on the theses. Felix Dzerzhinskii, the head of the Cheka, was appointed chairman of the newly created Central Committee on Compulsory Labor.[134]

This policy was not without its critics. Debate over the issue among party leaders was heated. Prior to and during the Ninth Party Congress, the Democratic Centralists opposed the policy because it turned workers into soldiers. Many trade union leaders and Mensheviks also criticized the policy.[135] Despite such opposition the policy not only came into being but was steadily extended. In the course of 1920, state decrees militarized a wide range of workers. These decrees were usually issued on an industry by industry basis, for example the militarization of metalworkers or of garment workers.[136] Stiff penalties for people who were repeatedly absent from work augmented the militarization of labor. An April 1920 Sovnarkom decree prescribed the following penalties for absentees: for one days absence, a 15 percent deduction in the monthly bonus; for two days absence, a 25 percent deduction; and for three days absence, a 60 percent deduction. Lost time had to be made up by compulsory labor. Absences in excess of three days were considered sabotage, and such cases were referred to factory disciplinary courts.[137]

Given the draconian nature of labor militarization, one wonders about the extent to which it was successful. The desertion rate among militarized workers suggests the policy's limited effectiveness. Of 38,514 workers mobilized for work in thirty-five armament plants during the first nine months of 1920, 34,939 deserted—a net addition of only 3,575 to the workforce.[138] Although this sample represents only a portion of those workers militarized, it suggests that forces of chaos and disorder outstripped the state's ability to enforce its labor legislation.

To reverse the labor shortage, the party also sought to coopt its supporters' voluntary labor. The *subbotnik* movement began in April 1919.[139] During the next twenty months, the number of participants (*subbotniki*) grew dramatically and the nature of movement changed. Originally, *subbotniks* consisted of Communists and communist sympathizers who voluntarily devoted several hours or a day's labor to problems, such as railroad repairs and fuel preparation, which needed attention. Until September 1919, *subbotniks* retained the character of locally initiated, voluntary labor. That month the Moscow City party committee ordered its members to participate in two *subbotniks* a month.[140] By January 1920, Red Army soldiers garrisoned in the city regularly participated in *subbotniks*. Yet the number of nonparty, civilian participants continued to increase. The movement reached its peak on May 1, 1920 when more than 450,000 people, including Lenin and other party leaders, participated in the famed May Day *subbotnik*. Throughout 1920, no fewer than 72,000 people a month, more than 75 percent of whom were noncommunists, engaged in *subbotnik* activities.

What accounts for this widespread participation at a time of deepening immiseration and discontent? Given the increasing militarization of labor, one might be tempted to interpret *subbotniks* as conscript labor. If they were, the party was doing a poor job of imposing such service. Party members accounted for no more than one-third of *subbotniki* in 1920; Red Army soldiers, an estimated 35 percent. This means that only 5 to 15 percent of the city's nonparty civilians participated in *subbotniks*. Why did these people do so? Some undoubtedly saw *subbotniks* as a means of overcoming the economic crisis. Self-interest motivated others, such as those who worked on fuel *subbotniks*. The wood collected by these volunteers was commonly divided between the factory and participants, and was often sufficient to heat one's dwelling for two to three months. Many *subbotniks* were devoted to aiding the Red Army and thus attracted many soldiers' relatives. Likewise, many probably saw such work in support of the Red Army as an act of revolutionary consciousness or patriotism. It is interesting to note that in those months in 1919 and early 1920 when Denikin's Army threatened Moscow, the number of *subbotniki* grew markedly. In September and October 1920, when *subbotniks* reached their post-May 1920 peak, the Red Army was engaged in a new conflict—the Russo-Polish War. Managerial and peer pressure motivated others. Last but not least, participants received extra rations. In short, while the *subbotnik* movement helped somewhat to relieve the labor shortage, it remained distinct from the militarization of labor.

Labor militarization and the *subbotnik* movement achieved limited success in overcoming the labor shortage. Of equal concern to the government was declining worker productivity. Piece-rate wages, monetary bonuses for those who exceeded their production norms, and disciplinary courts all failed to raise productivity. Not until June 1920 did an effective solution arise. That month Sovnarkom issued a decree authorizing the payment of "natural bonuses" (that is, food, clothing, and so forth) for those piece-rate workers who exceeded their output norm. Prior to that decree, workers had resisted attempts to abandon hourly or daily wages, but beginning in June there began a "massive transfer of enterprises to piece-rate wages."[141] In January 1920, 52 percent of all Moscow workers received time-based wages and 41 percent received piece-rate wages. By December, the figures were 16 percent and 69 percent respectively.[142] For the first time in five years, industrial productivity rose.

The new wage policy succeeded, but it also had negative side-effects. Until mid-1920, the government pursued two policies. On the one hand, its wage policy sought unsuccessfully to tie wages to productivity. Paralleling that wage policy was one of social maintenance, that is, the payment of wages not in rubles but in kind. Given that monetary bonuses offered little incentive and that natural wages, which were paid regardless of one's level of productivity, offered a measure of support, one should not be surprised that workers ignored pleas to be more productive. By blending the heretofore parellel policies, the government discovered a means to spur productivity. But, by forcing workers to intensify their labor in order to survive, the policy actually gave rise to discontent. A showdown between workers and the government was becoming inevitable.

"Arise Ye Prisoners of Starvation"

In late 1920 and early 1921, widespread worker unrest engulfed Moscow and other industrial centers. The wave of unrest erupted at a time when the policies of War Communism reached their peak, but when the justification for such policies—the Civil War—was virtually over. According to the Central Statistical Administration, strikes occured at 77 percent of the medium and large enterprises in the country. Approximately 90 percent of all strikes were in nationalized industries and most strikes were over food.[143] Factory meetings and conferences passed Menshevik, and Socialist Revolutionary (SR) sponsored resolutions and Bolshevik spokesmen were shouted down. Street demonstrations occurred in Moscow and other cities. In some cases, the unrest had to be quelled by troops. Workers from Moscow's Goznak, Kauchuk, Krasnyi Bogatyr', AMO, Krasnyi proletarii, and Mars factories among others went on strike. Mensheviks and SRs had considerable influence in these and other factories.[144]

The primary concern was food. The workers deeply resented their pitiful rations and the policy of requisitioning that in 1920 also gave rise to peasant unrest. Worker dissatisfaction with requisitioning resulted from two factors: its failure to ensure adequate food and the resentment that it engendered among workers' relatives in the villages. Some workers retained close ties to the villages and were well aware of mounting dissatisfaction there. Worker criticism of the Commissariat of Food became particularly virulent in 1920/21, and forced the dismissal of Sviderskii, a collegium member and one of the most vocal supporters of the requisitioning policy.[145]

The heated exchanges at the February 1921 metalworkers conference in Moscow revealed the workers' grievances and the depths of their bitterness. The conference convened at a time when food and fuel shortages were particularly acute. In January, the meager official ration was cut by two-thirds; during early February, not a single food shipment reached the city.[146] The nonparty members who dominated the conference of some 1,000 delegates condemned the policy of War Communism and listened closely "only to those who attacked the insufficiencies of our system. . . . Hardly anyone spoke in its defense. . . ." Delegates shouted down Kamenev and other party leaders. According to A. Vyshinskii, the Commissar of Food who attended the conference, food was the participants' primary concern, although debates over production rates, the role of trade unions and worker-peasant relations also occurred. Those in attendance were defiant of anyone who defended the government's food policy: "The semi-peasant masses of Moscow workers seemed to be more concerned with this issue than any other."[147] Menshevik and SR delegates who attacked the food policy were well received; speakers who denounced the food privileges enjoyed by Communists and specialists received stormy applause.

Among the resolutions passed, one demanded that workers' rations not be lowered, that "privileged rations" and the issuing of "products of production" in lieu of wages be abolished, and that the quality of food in factory and public dining halls be improved. Another called for the abolition of requisitioning. Many delegates drew the clear distinction between "we" (*my*) and "you" (*vy*) when speaking of officials. Vyshinskii stated: "By their words, one could sense a complete breach between the masses and the party, between the masses and the unions."[148] Delegates to the Garment Workers Congress that same month also condemned the food policy and production rate-setting efforts.[149]

Other sources of dissatisfaction existed. Many workers deeply resented managers and specialists whose influence in the factory and over workers' lives had grown dramatically since 1919. In the factories, these people restored production norms, punished underproductive workers, and implemented the state's increasingly harsh labor policies. Their increasing power stood as a symbol of a broader process that many workers condemned: the supplanting of worker initiative by ineffective bureaucratic processes. To many workers, "you" (the bureaucrats) had repeatedly co-opted the various initiatives that "we" began. Yet the assertion of centralized control rarely improved the situation. Not surprisingly, then, workers and even some party members, especially the Workers' Opposition, openly expressed their antibureaucratic sentiment.[150]

The "complete breach between the masses and the party" was not simply political, it was also physical. In March 1918, the Moscow party organization claimed 20,000 members; three years later, it boasted 40,000 members and candidate members, more than half of whom were workers by social origin. But in 1921, only 6,000 members worked in the city's factories, and more than half of them performed administrative work.[151] Most factory party cells consisted of only a handful of Communists. For example, the Dinamo party cell counted thirty-two people, only eight of whom worked in production; at Russkabel, the figures were twenty-seven and nine respectively.[152] The party that had risen to power in 1917 in large measure because of their influence in the factories and shops had lost its grassroots organization and influence. Significantly, most of the party's members in factories were managers and administrators. Whereas in 1917, Communists actively participated in the assault on such personnel, by 1921 they were often the enforcers of unpopular policies not dissimilar from those enacted by their "bourgeois" predecessors.

The unions' isolation from the workers was equally serious. A resolution passed by the Third Moscow *Guberniia* Trade Union Congress in 1921 stated clearly: "The fundamental weakness of union building is the weak connection of union organs to the masses, the insufficient concentration of work with factory committees." Strengthening those ties was an issue that all speakers addressed.[153] Undoubtedly, one major reason for this "weakness" was the production-oriented policies adopted by the Bolshevik-dominated union leadership. Unions had participated with government and management to implement piece-rate wages and bonuses, penalties for absentee and underproductive workers, and workers disciplinary courts. Rather than protecting workers against violations of labor agreements and the Labor Code, the unions had participated in the drive to increase worker productivity. This participation became particularly galling after the linking of productivity and food in 1920.[154] Nor had unions been able to ameliorate the food shortages. Given the extent of economic collapse, this was beyond their abilities. But their failure to perform their basic functions severely undermined their credibility among many workers.

Given the party's and unions' loss of influence, the criticisms that workers stridently voiced are hardly surprising. But why had that unrest not erupted earlier? Work conditions and food shortages in 1919 had been deplorable, far worse than those before and during 1917. Yet strikes and work stoppages protesting those conditions had been comparatively few in number and unrest had been an amorphous, factory-centered phenomenon.[155] The answer lies not in the conditions against which workers struggled daily, but in the changed military situation. In 1919, the existence of the revolution remained in doubt as Red and White Armies engaged in pitched battle. But by late 1920, the Civil War was virtually over. The revolution, maimed and deformed by the trials between 1918 and 1920, had survived. So long as the battles raged, an explanation for the hardships existed. So long as the deprivations appeared to be due to circumstances beyond the government's control, most workers were begrudgingly resigned to endure them. However much they objected to the existing policies, while the revolution itself was in danger workers withheld their discontent. Only when the policies of War Communism continued after victory seemed assured did wide-spread labor unrest break out. Only then did workers demand the fruits of victory that they justly deserved and that had been promised them.

The Tenth Party Congress and the End of War Communism

Widespread worker unrest, armed peasant rebellions, and the revolt at the Kronstadt naval base formed the backdrop against which the Communist Party held its Tenth Congress in March 1921. Two policy changes of direct bearing on this study emerged from that congress—a final definition of the role of trade unions and the replacement of War Communism with the New Economic Policy (NEP).

The role and functions of trade unions in a workers' state had been an ongoing debate since the seizure of power. The Tenth Congress delegates sought to resolve that debate. They had to choose between three platforms.[156] The first was that of the Workers' Opposition which argued that trade unions should manage major sectors of the economy. Their platform was similar to that of the radicals in early 1918. It proposed that an All-Russian Producers Council should manage the economy and take over the functions performed by VSNKh and the Commissariat of Labor. The policies enacted by this council would be implemented by subordinate unions and state agencies. Such a proposal, its authors argued, would reduce bureaucratism and hasten the realization of a workers' state. Toward this end, the opposition called for: the reinstatement of collective management; the democratization of the unions, soviets, and party; a purge of bourgeois and petty bourgeois from the state bureaucracy and the party; and the transformation of the party into a purely workers party.

At the other extreme stood Trotsky's proposal that urged the unions' complete subjugation to party and state authority. Consistent with his desire for the total militarization of labor, he argued that the role of the unions should be limited to the management of compulsory labor programs, the enforcement of labor discipline, and the improvement of labor productivity. In a workers' state, he argued, the exploitation of workers ceased to exist, and therefore the unions' role should center on the implementation and enforcement of policy and the education of its members.

Between the two extremes stood the platform of the Group of Ten led by Lenin. Their proposal, which represented a refinement of the earlier productivist platform, offered a compromise between those of the "militarizers" and the Workers' Opposition. Because the country was a workers' state, Lenin argued, unions must implement and enforce party and state policies and actively strive to increase labor productivity, to improve labor discipline and to raise the cultural and political level of their members. But in the transition to the full realization of a workers' state, the vestiges of the old order would remain. To guard against the possible exploitation of the proletariat, unions must also defend the rights of workers. To do this they must have certain rights such as those to negotiate collective agreements, to appeal violations of those agreements, and, as a last resort, to strike to defend workers' rights. Unions (and factory committees) must also retain their right to advise management when appropriate. Unions, then, were to be agents of production and protection as well as schools of communism.

Lenin's resolution carried the congress. But, the compromise placed the unions in an awkward role. As the executors of policy, they had to urge workers on to greater productivity and to struggle against poor discipline and work habits. At the same time, they were to represent and protect their constitutents against managements' excesses and to cultivate the initiative of their class conscious members. The underlying assumption of Lenin's proposal was that the workers' state would not exploit workers—all problems would result from improper policy implementation. But what if workers believed that a given policy was exploitative, or at least objectionable? With whom would the unions side? To whom did they owe their primary allegiance? As we shall see, the delicate balancing act required by the unions' newly defined dual role was more than they were capable of performing.

The Tenth Congress also addressed the issue of economic policy. War Communism had failed. Its food policy had proved especially disastrous. To alleviate the food crisis, Lenin proposed (and the Congress approved) that a food tax (*prodnalog*, the payment of taxes with produce) replace food requisitioning. (In 1924, after the stabilization of the currency, a money tax replaced the food tax.) After their tax payments, peasants were free to dispose of their produce in whatever way they saw fit. The food tax became effective immediately. The New Economic Policy had begun.[157]

Since the policy's purpose was to increase the flow of food to areas where it was desperately needed, and since it was unrealistic to expect peasants to transport their produce over long distances, private trade was legalized soon after. The number of private traders rose dramatically. So too did their role in the economy. Known as nepmen (a term contemporaries used to describe all private entrepreneurs), private traders by

1923 controlled upward of two-thirds of all goods circulated in Moscow.[158]

The food tax and legalization of private trade quickly replenished the city's markets. This had been their goal, but other policy changes followed in their wake. While the state retained control of what Lenin called the economy's "commanding heights"—banking, foreign trade, most industrial enterprises, mechanized transport, and the country's natural resources—private enterprise was legally resuscitated. In May 1921, the state revoked those decrees which had nationalized most small-scale industries, and announced in July that every citizen could legally engage in handicraft production and could operate small-scale industrial enterprises (not to exceed twenty workers). A property-owning class was thus given a new lease on life. Subsequently, the state leased certain industrial enterprises to private individuals, Soviet citizens as well as foreigners.[159]

Private producers responded eagerly to the new policies. Small private industries and artisan shops quickly opened for business. They produced such desperately needed goods as clothes, shoes, domestic wares, and a variety of wooden and metal craft items essential to the maintenance of a farm or domestic household. Because they required little capital and the producers often sold their wares directly to consumers, private enterprises gained an early competitive edge on larger, state-owned enterprises. But the legal restrictions placed on them and the shortage of capital limited their share of the market. In 1922/23, privately owned industries in Moscow city and *guberniia* accounted for only 3.4 percent of all the industrial goods produced there.[160]

A major goal of the NEP was industrial restoration. To stimulate industrial production, the state ordered sweeping industrial reorganization. In 1921 and 1922, a series of measures consolidated a large number of industrial enterprises into trusts in an effort to ensure maximum efficiency in the distribution of fuel, raw materials and other supplies. By late 1922, thirty-three tusts employed 163,000 workers in Moscow.[161] Despite the efficiencies thus gained, production costs and the prices of industrial goods remained quite high. The next year witnessed the implementation of a policy of industrial concentration, the purpose of which was to eliminate weak, unproductive enterprises and to transfer the appropriate equipment and personnel to larger, more productive plants. Although the transfer did permit a more rational allocation of labor and resources, much of the city's productive capacity remained underutilized at the end of 1923 and many people lost their jobs.[162]

The government enacted other policies designed to force industries and commercial establishments to lower costs. One was the policy of cost accounting (*khozrachet*) that required state-owned enterprises to pay for all purchases and wages from sales receipts and to balance their books. Coupled with this was the reduction and eventual elimination of state subsidies to industries. Universal during the Civil War, state subsidies had guaranteed the survival of and continued production by many nationalized plants, but had done little to promote efficiency. The withdrawal of subsidies and the implementation of *khozrachet* severely undermined the financial solvency of some enterprises. The results of these policies were double-edged: plant closings allowed for a more rational allocation of scarce capital and skilled workers, but they also contributed to a rise in unemployment.[163]

The government also sought to stabilize the currency. Until March 1924, rampant inflation robbed the ruble of all value. A standard ration of goods which cost one unit in 1913 cost 5,400,000,000 units by 1924 (see appendix 1). E. Preobrazhenskii's claim that the value of the ruble fluctuated "not only in the course of days, but in the course of hours" was no exaggeration.[164] From 1921 to 1924, as in the Civil War, excessive currency issuance fueled hyper-inflation. But the re-establishment of market relations, *khozrachet*, and the elimination of state subsidies necessitated a sound currency. In 1922, the government issued a new currency, the *Sovznak* (or Soviet goods ruble), in an attempt to stabilize the situation. Its excessive issuance spelled its demise. In late 1922 and 1923, the government issued yet another currency, the *chervonetsi* (ten ruble bank notes legally equal to the gold content of the prewar ruble coin). The gold-based *chervonetsi* (later renamed the ruble) inspired market confidence and provided the basis for the return of monetary stability in 1924. From then on, the currency remained reasonably stable thereby hastening economic recovery.[165]

The commercial, industrial, and monetary policies enacted during the early NEP marked a decisive break with those of War Communism. Such was not the case with labor policy. During 1921, the militarization of labor ended and the shift from natural to monetary wages commenced. But the over-riding goal of labor policy remained increasing worker productivity. Toward this end, the government merely expanded upon the the labor and wage policies in force in 1921. Piece-rate wages were extended and production norms raised repeatedly during the decade. The pace of work intensified and the number of machines which workers had to operate increased steadily. Improving the quality of work conditions remained secondary to increasing the quantity of goods produced.

One-man management remained the operative principle of industrial administration, although from the mid-1920s the party enlisted workers in campaigns to improve the quality of management. In only one major area did NEP labor policies differ from those of high War Communism: they sanctioned and contributed to high unemployment.

The NEP proved remarkably successful in restoring the city's and nation's economy. By 1921, hundreds of industrial plants had ceased operations; the remainder had shut down part of their operations. Machinery and equipment were in severe disrepair; tools were in short supply. Fuel remained scarce and rationed until late 1923. Shortages of raw materials affected many industries, particularly the metal and textile industries. Inflation limited the operations and capital accumulation of industry until 1924. But as each problem was overcome, the pace of recovery quickened. The production of Moscow's census industries in late 1926 exceeded their prewar level by 4 percent.[166] The speed with which the economy recovered, especially in 1924/25, surpassed many party leaders' expectations and emboldened them to embark on the socialist reconstruction of the economy. The Fourteenth Party Congress in 1925 signaled the beginning of this reconstruction as well as Soviet industrialization.

The NEP's success was not achieved without cost. Industrial workers bore the brunt of that cost. The drives for productivity and large-scale unemployment fell disproportionately upon the working class. Throughout the 1920s, party leaders debated how best to distribute the burden of recovery. While they debated, worker discontent festered. As we shall see, from 1926 worker dissatisfaction played an important role in the transformation of factory life.

The legacies of the 1918-1921 period remained for many years. Until 1924/25, bureaucratic methods held sway and curtailed worker initiative. The primacy of the party remained unchallenged. The famine of 1921-1922 delayed any marked improvement of the food situation until late 1922. Home fuel shortages also continued into 1922. Not until 1926 did industry attain prewar levels of production. The repair of the city's housing stock proceeded slowly and the amount of available housing space contracted sharply with the repopulation of the city. Add to this list, the enduring effects of disease, crime, severe shortages of goods, and rampant inflation (until 1924), and it is clear that the legacies of the Civil War years loomed large over the city during the 1920s. Some Soviet historians have described the Civil War as the "heroic period of the Russian revolution."[167] There was indeed considerable heroism during these years. It was born not only of a belief in the righteousness of the cause but also of the necessity of sacrifice in the face of seemingly overwhelming odds. The period was also one of severe deprivation, frustration, and agony. While some may laud the glorious achievements of an era, the heroes remember too vividly the fear and desperation that called forth such valor.

The proletariat and party each brought its own agenda to the November revolution. The bitter realities of the 1918-1921 period crushed and deformed those agendas. Circumstances had deferred and driven underground the workers' agenda. The party's fared only slightly better: it had been partially realized in form, but its content had been tranformed. During the 1920s, both workers and the party would seek to revive and enact their respective agendas. The revival of the workers' agenda would proceed slowly. It would be years before they would cede to the party the credibility and confidence that had enabled them together to make the revolution. For its part, the party would ponder their dissatisfaction and move cautiously as it struggled with the massive mission of socialist construction. For both, the scars of the 1918-1921 period were slow to heal.

Notes

1. For discussions of worker support for the Bolshevik platform, see: Koenker, *Moscow Workers;* Alexander Rabinowitch, *The Bolsheviks Come to Power: The Revolution of 1917 in Petrograd* (New York, 1976).

2. Robert Vincent Daniels, *The Conscience of the Revolution: Communist Opposition in Soviet Russia* (New York, 1960), chapters 2-5; Carr, *Bolshevik Revolution,* I, chapters 5-10; II, chapters 16-17; Sirianni, Part One.

3. On early economic policies, state capitalism and War Communism, see: Maurice Dobb, *Russian Economic Development Since the Revolution* (New York, 1928), chapters 1-4.; Alec Nove, *An Economic History of the U.S.S.R.* (Middlesex, 1982), chapters 2-3.

4. On 1918 strikes, see: *Moskovskii sovet rabochikh, krest'ianskikh i krasnoarmeiskikh deputatov, 1917-1927* (Moscow, 1927), 256 (hereafter abbreviated as *Moskovskii sovet, 1917-1927);* William Henry Chamberlin, *The Russian Revolution,* 2 vols. (New York, 1965), II, 48-49.

5. N. M. Aleshchenko, *Moskovskii sovet v 1917-1941gg.* (Moscow, 1966), 140.

6. N. M. Aleshchenko, "Moskovskii sovet v 1918-1920gg.," *Istoricheskie zapiski,* 91 (1973), 105.

7. See the discussion of *subbotniks* below and note 139.

8. For a discussion, see: Daniels, *Conscience,* 129-132; and Issac

Deutscher, *The Prophet Armed, Trotsky: 1897-1921* (New York, 1965), 501-503.

9. Based on a survey of 383 Moscow industrial enterprises conducted at the time of the 1918 census. Tsentral'noe statisticheskoe upravlenie, (TsSU) *Vserossiiskaia promyshlennaia i professional'naia perepis' 1918g.* (Moscow, 1926), 268-269 (hereafter abbreviated as *Perepis' 1918g.).*

10. *Istoriia Moskvy,* 6 vols. (Moscow, 1957), tom. VI, kn. 1, 139-140; *Ocherki istorii Moskovskoi organizatsii KPSS: 1883-1965* (Moscow, 1966), 311.

11. *Pravda,* November 15, 1918. The article laid the blame for this predicament on the lack of transport and the failure of the fuel departments of VSNKh and the Commissariats of War and Means of Communications.

12. *Moskva za 50 let sovetskoi vlasti* (Moscow, 1968), 56-57; *Ocherki Moskovskoi KPSS,* 350; Iu. Larin and L. and Kritsman, *Ocherk khoziaistvennoi zhizni i organizatsii narodnogo khoziaistve Sovetskoi Rossii, 1 noiabria 1917-1 iiulia 1920g.* (Moscow, 1920), 29.

13. *Pravda,* October 30, 1918. Meshcheriakov, the article's author, claimed that 400 to 500 train carloads of food sat in the railroad yards, but for lack of fuel, they could not be distributed. The vehicles existed, but the fuel did not. Nor was there any draft power: "On the streets of Moscow horses drop from hunger. There is no feed for them."

14. The Central Fuel Council replaced the Central Council to Supply the City with Fuel that was created in June 1918. In September, the Central Fuel Council announced that it could only guarantee fuel for essential state-owned industries. Aleshchenko, *Moskovskii sovet,* 162-164. The lack of fuel contributed significantly to the sharp rise in unemployment in 1918. For two examples of the impact of this shortage on unemployment, see: *Pravda,* February, 17, 1918; *Istoriia zavoda "Dinamo."* 3 vols. (Moscow, 1964), II, 25.

15. *Pravda,* November 13, 1919.

16. Iu. A. Poliakov, *Moskovskie trudiashchiesia v oborone sovetskoi stolitsy v 1919 godu* (Moscow, 1965), 11; *Moskovskii sovet, 1917-1927,* 88. See also: *"Dinamo,"* II, 39; *Pravda,* July 11, November 19, 1919. By early 1921, there were eighteen different organizations in the city concerned with fuel affairs; they often issued contradictory orders. In an effort to introduce some order and to organize fuel affairs on a systematic basis, STO (the Council of Labor and Defense) created an Extraordinary Fuel Commission in January 1921. V. A. Avanesov chaired the commission that VSNkh disbanded at the end of March 1921 when all responsibilities were shifted to VSNKh itself. E. D. Safronov and V. A. Tikhonov, "Iz istorii resheniia toplivnoi problemy v vosstanovitel'nyi period (1921-1925gg.)," *Istoriia SSSR,* 4 (1973), 113.

17. *Pravda,* February 1, 1921.

18. A. A. Matiugin, *Moskva v period vosstanovleniia narodnogo khoziaistva (1921-1925)* (Moscow, 1947), 12-13.

19. *Perepis' 1918g.,* chast' I, tab. I, 2-3; *Moskva za 50 let,* 75.

20. *Istoriia Moskvy: kratkii ocherk* (Moscow, 1974), 245; N. Shikheev, "Iz istoriia zavoda AMO," *Bor'ba klassov,* 3-4 (1931), 60; *Ocherki Moskov-*

skoi KPSS, 394. Census industries are those industrial enterprises that employ fifteen or more workers and use mechanical power and those that employ thirty or more workers but do not use such power.

21. One example of such a closure was the book publishing house of L. A. Stoliar. He closed down his business in late 1917 and moved to the south of Russia where he joined a "White band" and fought against the Soviets. *Rabochaia Moskva*, December 12, 1922.

22. At the Krasnyi Bogatyr' (former Bromlei) rubber works, workers discovered in early 1918 that thirty-seven administrative personnel had embezzled 3.3 million rubles. Even after the discovery, some employees continued to embezzle funds. A. M. Panfilova, *Istoriia zavoda Krasnyi bogatyr' 1887-1925* (Moscow, 1958), 58-59. For a similar situation at another factory, see V. Bogdanovskii, *Imeni Vladimira Il'icha* (Moscow, 1962), 110-112. See also, *Ocherki Moskovskoi KPSS*, 312-313.

23. In early 1918, workers at the Treugol'nik rubber works complained that the newly created Central Rubber Trust *(Tsentrorezin)* was sabotaging the plant. Panfilova, *Istoriia*, 64.

24. As quoted in Roger Pethybridge, *The Social Prelude to Stalinism* (New York, 1974), 171.

25. Dobb, *Russian Economic Development*, 34-36.

26. G. S. Ignat'ev, *Moskva v pervyi god proletarskoi diktatury* (Moscow, 1975), 243, 247; *Istoriia Moskvy*, VI, 1, 145.

27. Such was the case with metalworker B. at the Guzhon (later Serp i molot) plant, who sent his family to live with his parents in their native village in Vladimir. E. O. Kabo, *Ocherki rabochego byta* (Moscow, 1928), 103-107.

28. Louise Bryant, *Mirrors of Moscow* (New York, 1923), 126. See also: the discussions in Emma Goldman, *My Disillusionment in Moscow* (New York, 1970), 11; and Marguerite E. Harrison, *Marooned in Moscow: The Story of an American Woman Imprisoned in Moscow* (New York, 1921), 93.

29. A. G., "Moskovskaia obshcheugolovnaia prestupnost' v period voennogo kommunizma," *Prestupnik i prestupnost'* (Moscow, 1927), sbornik II, 355-384. According to this source, economic crimes—robbery, theft, appropriations, and swindling—accounted for 90 percent of the city's reported crime. Whereas in 1918 and 1919, fines were the most common punishment for such crimes (48 percent and 44 percent respectively), by 1920 deprivation of freedom and forced labor were the most common punishments (57 percent and 29 percent respectively). Moscow had the second highest crime rate in the country; only Petrograd, where the struggle for survival was even more intense, had a higher rate. See also *Statisticheskii ezhegodnik 1918-1920* (Moscow, 1921), chast' XIX, tab. XII, 95. A comparison of the data on crime in these two sources suggests that more than half of the city's crimes were committed by children under the age of seventeen. Whether the statisitics in the two sources are comparable is open to question.

30. That many citizens had reached desperate straits was evident in a number of ways, the most brutal of which was the "ferocious lynching of thieves by mobs, which were often half-crazed by hunger." According to

Chamberlin, II, 61, this incident was reported "in a newspaper" but unfortunately no citation was given.

31. Ignat'ev, *Moskva*, 247; D. A. Baevskii, *Rabochii klass v pervye gody sovetskoi vlasti (1917-1921 gg.)* (Moscow, 1974), 132.

32. N. Dobrotvor, "Moskovskie rabochie v prodotriadakh," *Bor'ba klassov*, 7-8 (1934), 182-188.

33. On goods-exchange teams, see: *Pravda*, January 24, January 25, February 1, February 8, February 18, March 10, 1918; Ignat'ev, *Moskva*, 235-236; Aleshchenko, *Moskovskii sovet*, 61-65; *Moskovskii sovet 1917-1927*, 71-77. The ferreting out of concealed grain stores yielded only short-term relief during the first months of 1918. The goods-exchange teams also produced some minor short-term relief. Three rations categories existed: (1) those engaged in physically demanding labor; (2) those engaged in light physical labor as well as the sick and young children; (3) those engaged in mental work and adolescents. The nonworking population (e.g., speculators) received no rations. *Rabochii klass sovetskoi Rossii v pervyi god diktatury proletariata: sbornik dokumentov i materialov* (Moscow, 1964), dok. 184, 32-33; *Pravda*, September 17, 1918; *Krasnaia Moskva, 1917-1920gg.* (Moscow, 1920), 90-131.

34. For the decrees that preceded the establishment of the "food dictatorship," see: *Dekrety sovetskoi vlasti*, 10 vols. (Moscow, 1957-1959), II, dok. 8, 23-24; II, dok. 153, 262-264; II, dok. 178, 307-312. The June 11, 1918 decree can be found in *Sobranie uzakoneni i rasporiazheni rabochego i krestian'skogo pravitel'stva, 1917-1924* (Moscow, 1917-1924), 1918, 43, 524. (Hereafter abbreviated as *SU*).

35. *Krasnyi arkhiv*, 106 vols. (Moscow, 1922-1941), tom. 97, 13-14; *Pravda*, June 11, June 12, 1918; Dobrotvor, 182.

36. *Krasnyi arkhiv*, tom. 4-5, 105; *Pravda*, August 14, August 23, 1918; February 7, 1919. The trade unions were chosen to direct food teams because they reputedly had the best apparatus to oversee the work and the closest ties to the mass of workers.

37. *Pravda*, August 25, 1918.

38. *Moskovskii sovet 1917-1927*, 84.

39. *Pravda*, May 24, 1918. See also V. I. Lenin, *Polnoe sobranie sochinenii*, 55 vols. (Moscow, 1958-1965), tom. 36, 357-364.

40. *Krasnyi arkhiv*, tom. 89-90, 104-110; *Rabochii klass: sbornik*, dok. 177, 180; K. I. Antonova, "Bor'ba rabochikh tsentral'nogo promyshlennogo raiona za khleb v 1918 gody," *Iz istorii bor'by trudiashchikhsia sovetskoi vlasti i sotsialisticheskoe stroitel'stvo: sbornik trudov* (Moscow, 1977), 28; *Ocherki Moskovskoi KPSS*, 317; Aleshchenko, *Moskovskii sovet*, 183; Dobrotvor, 183.

41. According to *Pravda*, October 30, 1918, there were 6,000 volunteers from Moscow as of that date. Yet according to a report of the Central Military Rations Bureau of VTsSPS, during the 1918 to 1919 period, there were 5,000 volunteers from Moscow city and *guberniia*. *Krasnyi arkhiv*, tom. 89-90, 112-113.

42. *Ibid.*

43. For example, detachment no. 43 from Sokol'nicheskii *raion* had twenty-three members, twelve of whom were nonparty workers; detachment no. 1258 from *raion* had twenty-eight members, only five of whom were communists. Detachment no. 1989, comprised of workers from the Danilovskii, Tsindel', and Bromlei factories, consisted of thirty-one members, a minority of whom were communists. Twenty members of no. 1989 team were under twenty years of age, four were ages twenty-one to thirty, three were ages thirty-one to forty, and four were over forty years old. Among their ranks were seven metalworkers, two switchmen, nine unskilled workers, and one employee. For these and other examples of factory organized teams, see: S. Lapitskaia, *Byt rabochikh Trekhgornoi manufaktury* (Moscow, 1935), 123; V. M. Kurakhantov, *Pervaia sittsenabivnaia* (Moscow, 1960), 79. Pervaia sittsenabivnaia is the former Tsindel' factory. See also: *Rabochii klass: sbornik*, dok. 180, 189-190; *Krasnyi arkhiv*, tom. 89-90, 127-130; Dobrotvor, 184; *Pravda*, October 30, 1918.

44. Such was the charge given to the forty-five man Dinamo food team, which in August 1918, established a base of operations near Elets in Orlov province. *"Dinamo,"* II, 33-35. In May 1918, the Moscow Committee passed a resolution calling for the equipping and arming of food team personnel. Antonova, 27.

45. Lenin admitted that some food team members were "unstable, weak-willed workers whom kulaks have bribed with home-distilled vodka." Lenin, *Polnoe sobranie*, tom. 36, 424-425. See also: Dobrotvor, 188; Lapitskaia, *Byt*, 122.

46. Ignat'ev, *Moskva*, 252-253.

47. Oliver H. Radkey. *The Unknown Civil War in Soviet Russia: A Study of the Green Movement in the Tambov Region, 1920-1921* (Stanford, 1976).

48. The precise number of Muscovites in food detachments is difficult to ascertain. *Ocherki Moskovskoi KPSS*, 351, puts the total number of members of such teams from 1918 to 1920 at 22,000, 15,000 of whom were from Moscow city and *guberniia*. According to Poliakov, *Moskovskie trudiashchie-sia*, 14, in 1919 alone there were 31,534 people in food detachments, 12,479 of whom were from Moscow city. The chaos of the period and the continuing practice of factories sending out factory-organized teams may account in part for the discrepancy in estimates.

49. See Lenin's letter to the Tula *Guberniia* party committee in *Krasnyi arkhiv*, tom. 78, 248.

50. *"Dinamo,"* II, 49; Matiugin, *Moskva*, 8.

51. A February 1919 Sovnarkom decree authorized the creation of these farms and gardens. *SU*, 1919, 9, 87.

52. For a discussion, see *Pravda*, May 8, May 29, July 2, 1919. Virtually all of these "factory farms" remained operational until after the famine of 1921/22. For examples, see *Rabochaia Moskva*, March 4, April 22, May 4, August 4, 1922; N. Shikheev, "Iz istoriia zavoda AMO," *Bor'ba klassov*, 3-4 (1931), 62.

53. *Pravda*, June 17, 1919; E. G. Gimpel'son, "Zarabotnaia plata i material'noe obeshchenie rabochikh v 1918-1920gg.," *Istoricheskie zapiski*, 87 (1971), 75.

54. *Pravda*, July 12, 1919. See also: *Ekonomicheskaia zhizn'*, October 16, 1919; Poliakov, *Oborone 1919*, 12, 54; *Moskovskii sovet, 1917-1927*, 86.

55. For estimates of caloric intake, see: *Statisticheskii ezhegodnik 1918-1920*, vyp. 8, 115; *Statisticheskii ezhegodnik 1924-1925* (Moscow, 1926), vyp. 1, chast' VIII, tab. 1, 304; E. O. Kabo, *Pitanie russkogo rabochego do i posle voiny: po statisticheskim materialiam 1908-24gg.* (Moscow, 1926), 40; TsSU, *Sostoianie pitaniia gorodskogo naseleniia SSSR, 1914-1924* (Moscow, 1926), 5-147 passim.

56. *Pravda*, January 22, 1921; N. Rodionova, *Gody napriazhennogo truda iz istorii Moskovskoi partiinoi organizatsii 1921-1925gg.* (Moscow, 1963), 6; Iu. A. Poliakov, *Perekhod k NEPu i sovetskoe krest'ianstvo* (Moscow, 1967), 232.

57. H. H. Fischer, *The Famine in Soviet Russia, 1919-1923: The Operations of the American Relief Administration* (New York, 1927), 82-85. See also Harrison, 126.

58. As quoted in Lapitskaia, *Byt*, 121; *Istoriia moskovskogo avtozavoda imeni I. A. Likacheva* (Moscow, 1966), 80-81 (hereafter abbreviated as *Istoriia . . . Likacheva*); Alexander Berkman, *The Bolshevik Myth (Diary, 1920-1922)* (London, 1925), 57; Arthur Ransome, *Russia in 1919* (New York, 1919), 30. In December 1918, a local doctor described the work of the city Commission on Public Nutrition, which was responsible for the maintenance of dining halls, as "catastrophic." *Pravda*, December 4, 1918.

59. For a discussion of such a raid, see: Harrison, 151-157; Ignat'ev, *Moskva*, 240-242.

60. S. G. Strumilin, *Na planovom fronte* (Moscow, 1958), 243; I. Ia. Trifonov, *Klassy i klassovaia bor'ba v SSSR v nachale NEPa (1921-1925gg.)* (Leningrad, 1969), 45. See also *Izmeneniia sotsial'noi struktury sovetskogo obshchevtsa: oktiabr' 1917-1920* (Moscow, 1976), 254-255.

61. For a description of Sukharevka and other markets and restaurants, see: Berkman, 56-60; Goldman, 23; Harrison, 150-157; Poliakov, *Moskovskie trudiashchiesia*, 13. A sense of the outrageous prices at private markets can be gotten from the experience of Marguerite Harrison. In 1920, she followed the prescribed procedures to buy a saucepan. She spent three days going to the proper authorities and waiting in lines. Finally, she purchased the pan for three rubles. A similar saucepan at Sukharevka cost 2,500 rubles. Harrison, 93.

62. Strumilin, *Na planovom fronte*, 243; Trifonov, *Klassy i klassovaia bor'ba*, 45. According to a NKT investigation, food accounted for 72.5 percent of an average Moscow worker's budget in November 1918. The vast majority of the food purchased was bought on the black market, Larin and Kritsman, *Ocherk khoziaistvennoi zhizni*, 53.

63. Joseph Crane Bradley, Jr., "*Muzhik* and Muscovite: Peasants in Late Nineteenth Century Urban Russia" (unpublished Ph.D. dissertation, Harvard

University, 1977), 119-140, has a good description and discussion of pre-revolutionary housing conditions.

64. As quoted in T. Kholodny, *Moscow: Old and New* (Moscow, 1933), 16. See also I. Verner, "Zhilishcha bedneishevo naseleniia Moskvy," *Izvestiia Moskovskoi Gorodskoi Dumy*, October 1902, as quoted in Timothy Sosnovy, *The Housing Problem in the Soviet Union* (New York, 1954), 7.

65. *Moskovskii sovet 1917-1927*, 355; *Stroitel'stvo Moskvy*, 10 (1927), 2. See also: Aleshchenko, *Moskovskii sovet*, 314; Poliakov, *Moskovskie trudiashchiesia*, 19; Sosnovy, 5-8.

66. This decree resulted in the municipalization of 4,000 of the city's 28,000 apartment houses. *Moskovskii sovet 1917-1927*, 74. An October 30 (November 12) 1917 decree declared a moratorium on the payment of rent for the duration of the war plus three months for workers earning less than 400 rubles a month and for families of mobilized men whose families' income was less than the above figure per person. This figure was the average wage of a skilled worker. See John N. Hazard, *Soviet Housing Law* (New Haven, 1939), 5. In April 1918, the presidium of the city soviet called for the limiting of housing space per family—the maximum allowable space was one room per adult. The purpose of this was to ensure a better and more equitable distribution of the housing fund. *Moskovskii sovet 1917-1927*, 78. At that time, a report in *Pravda*, April 20, 1918, placed the number of uninhabitable dwellings in the city at about 15 percent of the general housing fund. Considering the onset of the construction season and demobilization of the army, this shortage provoked considerable anxiety.

67. *Dekrety Sovetskoi vlasti*, I, 132-137. In September 1918, a city soviet resolution created *raion* housing commissions comprised of representatives of *raion* soviets, factory committees, trade unions, *raion* party committees, and *raion* Cheka organizations. These commissions were responsible for the redistribution of municipalized housing space. The soviet divided the population into four categories: workers, responsible Soviet employees, the remaining working population, and "nonworking parasitic elements." The first two categories were given preference in the allocation of housing. *Moskovskii sovet 1917-1927*, 83-84.

68. *Stroitel'stvo Moskvy*, 10 (1927), 3; Hazard, 4; Alexander Block, "Soviet Housing—The Historical Aspect: Problems of Amount, Cost, and Quality in Urban Housing—I," *Soviet Studies*, III, 1 (January 1951), 9-11.

69. For a discussion of the activities following the confiscation of an eight-story apartment building, see *Pravda*, April 11, 1919. See also S. Lapitskaia, "Zhilishchnoe stroitel'stvo novoi Moskvy posle oktiabr'skoi revoliutsii," *Bor'ba klassov*, 7-8 (1934), 216-217. For a discussion of the city soviet resolution on the confiscation and redistribution of furniture, see *Moskovskii sovet 1917-1927*, 84.

70. For a discussion of the redistribution see: Lapitskaia, "Zhilishchnoe stroitel'stvo," *Bor'ba klassov*, 7-8 (1934), 217; Aleshchenko, *Moskovskii sovet*, 193-195; Ignat'ev, *Moskva*, 283; *Istoriia Moskvy*, VI, 1, 142-143; Sos-

novy, 12. For a discussion of the redistribution of housing at Trekhgornaia, see Lapitskaia, *Byt*, 125.

71. Hazard, 3.

72. *Rabochaia Moskva*, February 19, 1922.

73. For a discussion, see: *Ibid.*; *Pravda*, February 15, 1921; Block, "Soviet Housing—I," 13; Alfred John DiMaio, *Soviet Urban Housing: Problems and Policies* (New York, 1974), 9; *Moskovskii sovet 1917-1927*, 433. In 1919, the city soviet investigated 1,552 worker dwellings and closed 267 for unhealthy conditons; in 1920, 452 were closed for the same reason. The displaced persons were moved to other dwellings. *Moskovskii sovet 1917-1927*, 433.

74. For a discussion, see: *Gorodoe zvanie—il'ichevtsy po zalam muzeia zavoda imeni Vladaimir Il'icha* (Moscow, 1970), 47; Lapitskaia, *Byt*, 126-127 (the Trekhgornaia workers organized *subbotniks* to strip wood from dilapidated housing); *"Dinamo," II, 50; Pravda*, January 16, 1919, February 7, 1921; Block, "Soviet Housing—I," 12; Alexander Block, "Soviet Housing—The Historical Aspect: Some Notes on Policy—II," *Soviet Studies*, III, 3 (January 1952), 230; Walter Duranty, *I Write as I Please* (New York, 1935), 111; *Moskva za 50 let*, 67; Sosnovy, 39; H. H. Fischer, *Famine*, 87. See also *Rabochaia Moskva*, March 23, May 13, 1922.

75. H. H. Fischer, *Famine*, 75.

76. E. Z. Volkov, *Dinamika naseleniia SSSR za vosem'desiat let* (Moscow, 1930), 272. Despite the high death rates in the period, Frank Lorimer has suggested that Soviet statisticians "unwittingly" underestimated the force of mortality in the period. Frank Lorimer, *The Population of the Soviet Union: History and Prospects* (Geneva, 1946), 119. For death rates by age groups in 1919, see *Krasnaia Moskva*, 74. The highest death rates were for those ages 1-4 (98), 40-49 (36), 50-59 (69), and 60 and older (178). For infant mortality and birth rates, see appendices 3 and 4. For a discussion of epidemics from 1913 to 1924, see *Stroitel'stvo Moskvy*, 7 (1925), 15-16. For a discussion of the soviet's attempts to deal with epidemics, see: *Moskovskii sovet 1917-1927*, 91; Aleshchenko, *Moskovskii sovet*, 199, 315-316.

77. *Statisticheskii spravochnik g. Moskvy i Moskovskoi gub., 1927g.* (Moscow, 1928), 12-13; TsSU, *Itogi vserossiskoi gorodskoi perepisi 1923g.* 4 vols. (Moscow, 1924-1927), chast' I, tab. I, 13 and chast' II, tab. 1, 20; TsSU, *Vsesoiuznaia perepis' naseleniia 1926g.* 56 vols. (Moscow, 1928-1933), tom. 2, tab. V, 110; M. Ia. Vydro, *Naselenie Moskva* (Moscow, 1976), 11-13; A. Ia. Grunt, "Moskovskii proletariat v 1917g (k voprosu o chislennosti, sostave i territorial'nom razmeshchenii)," *Istoricheskie zapiski*, 85 (1970), 77.

78. Precise estimates of the number of aristocrats and bourgeois who fled Moscow do not exist, but nationally the figure is estimated to have been between 1.5 and 2 million. I. Ia. Trifonov, *Ocherki istorii klassovoi bor'by v SSSR v gody NEPa (1921-1937)* (Moscow, 1960), 7.

79. *Krasnaia gazeta*, 240, 1920 as quoted in K. Leites, *Recent Economic Developments in Russia* (Oxford, 1922), 197. For a discussion of rural migrants to Moscow before the revolution, see Johnson, *Peasant and Proletarian*.

80. Given the pre-revolutionary migration patterns to Moscow, the most likely destinations of out-migrants were: Moscow, Riazan, Kaluga, Smolensk, Tver, Vladimir, Tambov, Iaroslavl', and Orel *gubernii*. Migration patterns will be discussed in chapter 2.

81. O. I. Shkaratan, *Problemy sotsial'noi struktury rabochego klassa SSSR* (Moscow, 1970), 250. For a contemporary discussion of worker ties to the land, see *Pravda*, June 30, 1918. See also Kabo, *Ocherki*, 103-107.

82. Shkaratan, 238.

83. According to the Moscow Soviet, 313,853 Muscovites enlisted in the Red Army between 1918 and the end of 1920. The annual figures were: 1918—133,254; 1919—111,267; 1920—69,332. *Krasnaia Moskva*, 648.

84. The Sovnarkom plea can be found in *Pravda*, February 22, 1918. For the battlecry "death or victory," see *Istoriia . . . Likacheva*, 66. See also: *Pravda*, February 9, 1918; *Krasnyi arkhiv*, tom. 86, 62-84; *Ocherki Moskov-skoi KPSS*, 104-106.

85. *"Dinamo,"* II, 37-38.

86. Aleshchenko, *Moskovskii sovet*, 104-106; *Rabochii klass: sbornik*, dok. 40, 42.

87. G. Kostomarov, "Moskovskii Sovet i oborone strany (1918-1920)," *Istoriia proletariata SSSR*, 3 (19), (1934), 142-145; *Pravda*, August 20, 1918; *Ocherkii Moskovskoi KPSS*, 331-338; *Rabochii klass: sbornik*, dok. 40, 42; L. Bychkov, "Moskovskii Komsomol v grazhdanskoi voine," *Bor'ba klassov*, 7-8 (1934), 179-180; Poliakov, *Moskovskie trudiashchiesia*, 119; *Moskovskie bol'sheviki v bor'be s pravym i "levym" opportunizmom 1921-1928gg.* (Moscow, 1969), 16, puts the proportion of Moscow Communists in the Red Army at 70 percent. The VSNKh figures can be found in Larin and Kritsman, 43.

88. *"Dinamo,"* II, 42-43; *Ocherki Moskovskoi KPSS*, 331, 337. See also: *Pravda*, October 22, October 23, October 24, October 25, 1919; Bychkov, 179; Poliakov, *Moskovskie trudiashchiesia*, 78-79. In response to the 1919 VTsSPS mobilization, 250 of the 1,765 male members of the Moscow Garment Workers Union enlisted. *Izmeneniia sotsial'noi struktury . . . 1917-1920*, 164. See also *Krasnyi arkhiv*, tom. 83, 14-15.

89. Kostomarov, 154.

90. *Sed'moi s"ezd Rossiiskoi Kommunisticheskoi Partii* (Moscow, 1924), 33, 45. See also: *Izmeneniia sotsial'noi struktury . . . 1917-1920*, 123-126; and Grunt, "Moskovskii proletariat," 109. In December 1925, the Fourteenth Party Congress noted that the cohesion of the urban proletariat had increased and underlined the fact that the process of the "declassing of the proletariat" was a thing of the past. *XIV S"ezd Vsesoiuznoi Kommunisticheskoi Partii (B): Stenograficheskii otchet* (Moscow, 1926), 973.

91. Estimates on the declining number of industrial workers can be found in: Grunt, "Moskovskii proletariat," 101; *Statisticheskii ezhegodnik g. Moskvy i Moskovskoi gubernii, 1914-1925* (Moscow, 1927), vyp. 2, 171; *Perepis' 1918*, tab. 1, 3; *Statistika truda v promyshlennykh zavedeniiakh* (Moscow, 1922), 14; TsSU, *Vserossiiskaia perepis' promyshlennykh zavedenii 1920g.* 4 vols. (Moscow, 1922), tom. III, 52, 106; *Materialy po tekushchei*

promyshlennoi statistike za 1919 i 1920 (Moscow, 1920), 20; Matiugin, *Moskva*, 7; Aleshchenko, *Moskovskii sovet*, 190; F. D. Markuzon, "Polozhenie truda v g. Moskve v 1921 godu," *Voprosy truda* 2 (1922), 138.

92. *Rabochii klass: sbornik*, dok. 59, 62; *"Dinamo,"* II, 57; Bogdanovskii, 114; Matiugin, *Moskva*, 7-8; *Istoriia Moskvy*, VI, 1, 206; Aleshchenko, *Moskovskii sovet*, 222; Poliakov, *Moskovskie trudiashchiesia*, 10.

93. *Krasnyi arkhiv*, tom. 96, 106-108; Panfilova, *Istoriia*, 38, 75; *Istoriia . . . Likacheva*, 80, 95; Shikheev, 62.

94. *Izmeneniia sotsial'noi struktury . . . 1917-1920.* In April 1919, a plenary meeting of the city soviet, after noting a significant change in the composition of the workforce, passed a resolution "to enlist members of the middle section, that is people who are less experienced than the advanced workers and peasants, to replace the weary, advanced section." That same meeting also called for more workers to enter the army and to assume more responsible positions in the food and transport sections of the *apparat* and in the State Control Commission, a plea that could only hasten the disintegration of the working class. *Pravda*, April 4, 1919.

95. *Ekonomicheskaia zhizn'*, November 4, 1920; Dewar, 184. Although the predominant trend was for people to migrate from town to country, the reverse process also occurred. During the Civil War years, more than 160,000 people took up residence in Moscow and remained residents there in 1926. In the latter year, some 30,000 of these people were workers. *Perepis' . . . 1926g.*, tom. 36, tab. IV, 142; dop. I k tab. III-IV, 174-183; dop. III k tab. III-IV, 190-201.

96. *Perepis' promyshlennykh zavedenii 1920g.*, Svodnyi vyp., tab. XIV, 56.

97. As quoted in James Bunyan, *The Origins of Forced Labor in the Soviet State, 1917-1921: Documents and Materials* (Baltimore, 1967), 20-21. See also: *Rabochii klass: sbornik*, dok. 267, 298; *Izmeneniia sotsial'noi struktury . . . 1917-1920*, 145-146.

98. As quoted in F. Babun, "Komsomol zavoda 'Serp i molot'," *Iunost' nasha Komsomol'skaia: dokumental'nye materialy, ocherki i vospominaniia iz istorii Komsomola Kalinskogo raion goroda Moskvy, 1917-1970* (Moscow, 1970), 65.

99. *Moskovskii sovet 1917-1927*, 219. Estimates of the decline in worker productivity nationally from 1913 to 1920 can be found in S. Strumilin, "Dinamika produktivnosti truda v Rossii," *Vestnik truda*, 5-6 (1924), 144-146.

100. *Pravda*, July 23, 1918. See also *Ocherki Moskovskii KPSS*, 308-311.

101. For example, see *Pravda*, January 1, 1918. See also: Bailes, *Technology and Society*, 52-66; Lampert, 12-22.

102. Panfilova, *Istoriia*, 62. For other examples of early 1918 calls for productivity and discipline, see: *Pravda*, February 12, 1918; *Rabochii klass: sbornik*, dok. 136, 147.

103. *Krasnyi arkhiv*, tom. 96, 74; *Rabochii klass: sbornik*, dok. 138, 148-150, dok. 145, 155-156. For a discussion, see Dewar, 28-44.

104. *Rabochii klass: sbornik*, dok. 138, 148-150, dok. 145, 155-156; *Uprochenie sovetskoi vlasti v Moskve i Moskovskoi gubernii: dokumenty i materialy* (Moscow, 1958), dok. 199, 241-242, dok. 203, 251-252, dok. 205, 253, dok. 208, 255; *Pravda*, July 4, 1918; *Ocherki Moskovskoi KPSS* 309.

105. Complaints about deteriorating conditions in the city's factories proliferated in the press. For examples, see: *Pravda*, December 5, 1918; January 5, January 30, February 21, March 2, 1919.

106. As quoted in Bunyan, 21.

107. *Pravda*, July 23, 1918.

108. In reality, the average worker in 1908 worked 270 nine and one-half hour days, but the figure has been converted to allow for comparison. Markuzon, 144.

109. *Statisticheskii ezhegodnik 1918-1920*, chast' XXXV, tab. IV, 174-175. See also: *Pravda*, January 6, February 3, 1921; Markuzon, 145-146; Lapitskaia, *Byt*, 123.

110. *Statistika truda v promyshlennykh zavedeniiakh*, 13.

111. See note 103.

112. *Perepis' 1918*, vyp. 2, 186-187; P. Petrochenko and K. Kuznetsova, *Organizatsiia i normirovanie truda v promyshlennosti SSSR* (Moscow, 1971), 25. The VTsSPS resolution can be found in *Profsoiuzy SSSR: dokumenty i materialy*, 4 vols. (Moscow, 1963), II, 129-131 (hereafter referred to as *Profsoiuzy SSSR*).

113. Petrochenko and Kuznetsova, 27-28; E. G. Gimpel'son, "Zarabotnaia plata i material'noe obespechenie rabochikh v 1918-1920gg.," *Istoricheskie zapiski*, 87 (1971), 70; E. G. Gimpel'son, "Rabochii klass v upravlenii promyshlennost'iu v pervye gody sovetskoi vlasti (noiabr' 1917-1920)," *Istoriia SSSR*, 2 (1977), 7. Although TNB originally was the acronym for *tarifno-normirovochnye biuro*, beginning in 1925 it came to refer to *tekhniko-normirovochnye biuro*. The change, which occurred on an *ad hoc* basis reflected the drive to establish scientific or technically based output norms.

114. Gimpel'son, "Zarabotnaia plata," 60-62; Larin and Kritsman, 48-50; Dewar, 38.

115. S. G. Strumilin, *Zarabotnaia plata i proizvoditel'nost' truda v russkoi promyshlennosti v 1913-1922gg.* (Moscow, 1923), 28; Gimpel'son, "Zarabotnaia plata," 62-63; *Pravda*, October 15, 1919; *Ekonomicheskaia zhizn'*, May 15, September 11, 1919; Dewar, 183-202 passim.; Matiugin, *Moskva*, 8-9. The futility of raising money wages to relieve the desperate economic condition of workers was recognized by the Third All-Russian Congress of Trade Unions in April 1920. *Profsoiuzy SSSR*, II, 234-237. By the end of 1920, the average Moscow worker earned about 400 times more in wages than in 1913, but the cost of food and consumer goods had risen by 20,000 times. Gimpel'son, "Zarabotnaia plata," 60. For a debate on the reasons for and ideas behind the naturalization of the economy, see: *ibid.*; V. I. Billik, "V. I. Lenin o sushchnosti i periodizatsii sovetskoi ekonomicheskoi politiki 1917-1921gg. i o povorote k nepu," *Istoricheskie zapiski*, 80 (1967), 126-169. See also L. Kritsman, *Geroicheskii period russkoi revoliutsii* (Moscow-Leningrad, 1925).

116. Aleshchenko, *Moskovskii sovet*, 41-43; *"Dinamo,"* II, 22-23; Dewar, 22-23. In December 1917, the All-Russian Congress of Manufacturers' Association resolved to close any enterprise in which workers' control assumed active interference in the enterprise's administration. Many of the city's factory owners made good this threat.

117. Aleshchenko, *Moskovskii sovet*, 45; *Ocherkii Moskovskoi KPSS*, 300-301.

118. The following discussion of productivist and radical interpretations of workers' control is based on: Sirianni, chapters 1-7; Carr, *Bolshevik Revolution*, II, 64-194; Kaplan, *Bolshevik Ideology*; Chris Goodey, "Factory Committees and the Dictatorship of the Proletariat (1918)," *Critique*, 3 (1974), 24-47; and "Factory Committees and the Dictatorship of the Proletariat: Additional Notes," *ibid.*, 5 (1975), 85-89; William G. Rosenberg, "Workers' Control on the Railroads and Some Suggestions Concerning Social Aspects of Labor Politics in the Russian Revolution," *Journal of Modern History*, 49, 2 (1977), D1181-D1219; Maurice Brinton, *The Bolsheviks and Workers Control* (London, 1970); and "Factory Committees and the Dictatorship of the Proletariat," *Critique*, 4 (1975), 78-86; S. A. Smith, *Red Petrograd: Revolution in the Factories, 1917-1918* (Cambridge, 1983).

119. Such guidelines were laid down by the Presidium of the Moscow Soviet, Aleshchenko, *Moskovskii sovet*, 45. The workers' control commissionat Trekhgornaia assumed these responsibilities and also organized teams of workers to procure supplies of fuel and raw materials and to combat sabotage. Lapitskaia, *Byt*, 118.

120. Ia. Rezvushkin, "Proletariat na pervom etape sotsialisticheskogo stroitel'stva (ot oktiabria do 'voennogo kommunizma')," *Istoriia proletariata SSSR*, 11 (1932), 80-86. For examples of appeals by factories to local organs, see *Pravda*, March 15, March 18, 1918; *"Dinamo,"* II, 36; *Uprochenie sovetskoi vlasti*, dok. 202, 250-251. When workers sought the 'nationalization' of their factories, they often submitted their request to the city soviet. For examples, see Bogdanovskii, 11; Shikheev, 59. One reason that workers chose to appeal to local bodies for the "nationalization" of their factories was that most such requests were quickly honored. Such was not the case when a factory appealed to a national body. For example, as early as February 1918, workers at the Krasnyi Bogatyr' factory called for the nationalization of the plant. VSNKh gave responsibility for administering the plant to the Central Rubber Trust (*Tsentrorezin*) whose performance was apparently disastrous. Not until the June 28, 1918 decree was the plant nationalized. Panfilova, *Istoriia*, 64-67.

The role of local soviets in the nationalization process is not generally appreciated by western historians. The Moscow Soviet was very active in this area. However, local officials often created problems for themselves when it came to administering the newly confiscated plants. From January to April 1918, the city soviet municipalized fifty-eight plants. But the Moscow Region Economic Committee (MREK) was also active in the nationalization process, nationalizing twenty-one enterprises during the same period. To minimize administrative confusion, the city soviet supplanted MREK with the Moscow *Oblast'* SNKh (MOSNKh). But new problems of jurisdiction and authority arose and in September 1918 the city soviet replaced MOSNKh with a new city SNKh (MGSNKh). During 1918 and 1919, both MOSNKh and MGSNKh municipalized or sequestered more than 150 enterprises, while VSNKh nationalized more than 300 local enterprises. Aleshchenko, "Moskovskii sovet," 82-96; *Pravda*, March 18, 1918.

121. As quoted in Rosenberg, D1198.

122. See Sirianni, Part One; Goodey, "Factory Committees: 1918"; and "Factory Committees (Additional Notes)"; Koenker, *Moscow Workers*, 25-28, 150-170.

123. According to L. S. Rogachevskaia, *Likvidatsiia bezrabotitsy v SSSR, 1917-1930gg.* (Moscow, 1973), 54, 20-28 percent of all Moscow workers were mobilized for military service during World War I. Shkaratan, 211-213, claims that nationally no more than 20 percent of all workers were mobilized. He provides no overall figures for Moscow, but puts the proportion of mobilized Muscovite metalworkers at 27 percent and of printers at 38.7 percent.

124. Sirianni, chapter 4.

125. For example, after the nationalization of the List factory, the former owners, who had cooperated with the factory committee prior to June 1918, were hired as engineers and sat on the factory administrative board with three workers. Aleshchenko, *Moskovskii sovet*, 152.

126. For the June 28, 1918 decree, see *Direktivy KPSS i sovetskogo pravitel'stva*, I, 79-84. Immediately after this decree, 175 factories in the city were nationalized. In the ensuing months, the pace of nationalization and municpalization increased. The city SNKh was particularly active in this regard. During 1919, it asserted its jurisdiction over several hundred plants. *Raion* soviets played an active role in the fulfiflment of the nationalization decree. Aleshchenko, "Moskovskii sovet," 82-96.

127. On the shift to one-man management, see: Carr, *Bolshevik Revolution*, II, 190-194; Kaplan, *Bolshevik Ideology*, 320-331. By the end of 1920, one-man management existed in 85 percent of the country's enterprises. Dobb, 106. See also Lapitskaia, *Byt*, 123.

128. Bailes, *Technology and Society*, 52-66; Lampert, 12-22.

129. Bailes, *Technology and Society*, 52-66; Bunyan, 86; Dewar, 178-180. On the Workers Opposition, see A. Kolantay (sic), *The Workers Opposition in Russia* (Chicago, 1921).

130. See the discussion in *Istoriia . . . Likacheva*, 78-79; *Partiinoe stroitel'stvo*, 2 (1930), 57.

131. *SU*, 1919, 56, 537. For early 1918 examples that factory disciplinary courts be established see: *Pravda*, February 12, July 4, 1918; Panfilova, *Istoriia*, 62.

132. *Statisticheskii ezhegodnik 1918-1920*, vyp. II, 99-101. Data on sentences imposed are lacking. An April 1921 Sovnarkom decree extended the range of jurisdiction of disciplinary courts to include such offenses as the

nonfulfillment of output norms and neglecting safety precautions. *SU*, 1921, 23/24, 142.

133. Labor service for those who lived on unearned income was introduced in December 1918. The Labor Code of 1918, published in December, stipulated that labor service was required of all able-bodied people between the ages of sixteen and fifty. But labor service, that is, the requirement that people work and the militarization of labor were different phenomena. The concept of labor service reflected both an ideological belief that people should work and a policy of necessity born of the increasing shortage of labor. For the Labor Code, see *SU*, 1918, 87/88, 905. See also: Dewar, 42-52; Sorenson, 130-132, 151-152.

134. *SU*, 1920, 8, 49. See the discussion in Bunyan, 95-114; and Dewar, 52-60.

135. Dewar, 121-136.

136. For examples, see *ibid.*, 187-204 passim.

137. *SU*, 1920, 36, 172.

138. A. Anikst, *Organizatsiia rabochei sily v 1920 gody* (Moscow, 1930), 50-51.

139. The following discussion of *subbotniks* in Moscow is based upon: *Dokumenty trudovoi slavy moskvichei, 1919-1965—iz istorii bor'by za razvitie kommunisticheskikh form truda: sbornik dokumentov i materialov* (Moscow, 1967); Iu. Kukushkin and D. Shelestov, *Pervyi Kommunisticheskie subbotniki* (Moscow, 1959); G. D. Kostomarov, ed., *Kommunisticheskie subbotniki v Moskve i Moskovskoi gubernii v 1919-1920gg.* (Moscow, 1950); *Pravda*, May 17, May 23, June 7, September 24, September 26, 1919.

140. In September, the Moscow party committee created a Bureau of *Subbotniks* (later the Department of Subbotniks) to coordinate and direct *subbotnik* activities. The original troika that headed the bureau consisted of V. M. Zagorskii (chairman) and comrades Kvash and Ivanov. During a meeting of the bureau on September 25, 1919, a bomb exploded killing twelve people including Zagorskii and Kvash and injuring fifty-five others. Kukushkin and Shelestov, 34.

141. Petrochenko and Kuznetsova, 28-29; *Direktivy KPSS i sovetskogo pravitel'stva*, I, 176-178. See also Gimpel'son, "Zarabotnaia plata," 78-81.

142. *Statistika truda v promyshlennykh zavedeniia*, 28.

143. Leites, 195-197.

144. *Ibid.*; Aleshchenko, *Moskovskii sovet*, 224; Matiugin, *Moskva*, 16-17; Sorenson, 60. For factory examples, see: Lapitskaia, *Byt*, 124; N. Marmerstein, ed., *Slavnye traditsii: k 100-letiiu zavoda 'Krasnyi proletarii' imeni A. I. Efremova* (Moscow, 1957), 106; Rodionova, 73-76; *Istoriia . . . Likacheva*, 84, 100. See also Paul Avrich, *Kronstadt 1921* (New York, 1974), 64, 67, 75, 78, 164.

145. *Leninskii sbornik*, 39 vols. (Moscow, 1924-1980), XXXIX, 260-262. On Menshevik pressure at the Eighth Congress of Soviets to end food requisitioning, see David Dallin, "Between the World War and NEP," *The Mensheviks from the Revolution of 1917 to the Second World War* (Leopold H. Haimson, ed., Chicago, 1974), 234-239.

146. *Pravda*, January 22, 1921; Rodionova, 6; Poliakov, *Perekhod*, 232.

147. *Pravda*, February 8, 1921.

148. *Ibid.*, See also Lenin, *Polnoe sobranie*, tom. 42, 486n; *Dva mesiatsa rabotei V. I. Lenina; ianvar'-fevral' 1921* (Moscow, 1934), 54n. The resolution calling for an end to requisitioning was based on the report of V. V. Kuraev who, in March 1921, began work in NKZ RSFSR. My thanks to Bert Patenaude for bringing this to my attention. According to a report in *The New York Times*, March 6, 1921, Lenin appeared at this meeting and asked delegates if they preferred the return of the Whites. One delegate allegedly responded: "Let come who may—whites, blacks, or the devils themselves—just you clear out." According to *Dva mesiatsa*, 54n., Lenin's speech "was heard with intense attention" and after it "the conference changed for the better."

149. The Fourth All-Russian Congress of Garment Workers in February was especially critical of rate-setting efforts. Lenin, *Polnoe sobranie*, tom. 42, 486n.

150. Kolantay (sic).

151. Party membership figures can be found in *Moskovskaia gorodskaia i Moskovskaia oblastnaia organizatsiia KPSS v tsifrakh* (Moscow, 1972), 27-29. Data on the growth of the city's party organization can be found in: *ibid.*, 22, 35; *Pravda*, October 18, October 24, December 15, 1919; *Rabochii klass: sbornik*, dok. 78, 76, dok. 101, 96-99; *Ocherki Moskovskoi KPSS*, 361-373; Rodionova, 17.

152. *Ocherkii Moskovskoi KPSS*, 382; Rodionova, 29.

153. *Moskovskaia gubernskaia konferentsiia professional'nykh soiuzov* (14-15 sentiabr' 1921), (Moscow, 1921), 3-33.

154. During late 1920, the party press devoted increasing attention to the issues of production including rate-setting. For examples, see *Pravda*, November 15, November 26, November 27, December 3, December 7, 1920.

155. Data on 1918-1920 unrest are very incomplete; for a representative treatment, see: *Moskovskii sovet 1917-1927*, 256; Panfilova, *Istoriia*, 76.

156. For treatments of the trade union debates, see: Carr, *Bolshevik Revolution*, II, 200-229; Daniels, *Conscience*, 119-136. On the Workers Opposition, see Kolantay (sic).

157. For a discussion of the NEP, see: Dobb, chapters 5-7; Nove, chapter 4.

158. Trifonov, *Klassy*, 19, 32; *Istoriia Moskvy*, VI, 1, 238-250; Carr, *The Interregnum*, 111; Nove, 103; *Report of the American Trade Union Delegation to the Soviet Union* (New York, 1927), 54.

159. For resolutions which sanctioned the re-appearance of private enterprise, see *Direktivy KPSS i sovetskogo pravitel'stva*, I, 237-241, 254-259. For a discussion of the change of policy, see: Matiugin, *Moskva*, 31; Dobb, chapter 5.

160. *Istoriia Moskvy*, VI, 1, 238-250.

161. *Ibid.*, 240.

162. As a result of this policy, one-quarter of the textile, metal and chemical plants in Moscow city and *guberniia* were shut down and the average

number of workers per factory grew from 581 to 666. In 1923, Moscow factories suffered from a host of problems; many experienced considerable interruptions. The textile industry operated at only 60 percent of capacity, the metal industry at only 25 percent and the chemical industry at only 63 percent. Rodionova, 136-138; Shkaratan, *Problemy*, 240. See also *KPSS v rezoliutsiiakh*, I, 687-705.

163. For a discussion of these policies see Carr, *Socialism*, I, 354. See also *KPSS v Rezoliutsiiakh*, I, 687-705.

164. As quoted in Carr, *Bolshevik Revolution*, II, 343. Because of the rate of inflation, newspapers such as *Rabochaia Moskva* carried weekly columns entitled "*Valuta*" that gave the changing values of the currencies in circulation. The cost of a copy of this newspaper provides a graphic example of the inflation rate. On February 17, 1922, a single issue cost 3,000 rubles; by May 3, 1922, it cost 30,000 rubles.

165. For a discussion of inflation and currencies, see S. S. Katzenellenbaum, *Russian Currency and Banking, 1914-1924* (London, 1925), 74-137.

166. Matiugin, *Moskva*, 71-74.

167. Kritsman.

2. The Demographic Recovery and Composition of Moscow

By early 1921, Moscow's exhausted population was only half the size it had been in 1917, approximately the same size it had been a quarter century earlier. Industrial production had ground to a virtual halt. Residents complained about hunger, cold, economic deprivations and the policies that failed to alleviate them. The future seemed uncertain, if not bleak, and the task of rebuilding Moscow seemed formidable. In five years, however, the city's population doubled and, in the process, exceeded the two million mark (2,026,000).[1] Although still plagued by problems, the city's economy had surpassed most prewar indices. Muscovites still complained about economic woes, but hunger and cold were not among them. The recovery seemed miraculous.

The rapid demographic recovery of the city, which by 1926 was the country's largest, resulted from a significant natural population increase—due to declining infant mortality and death rates and a high birth rate—and mass in-migration. Moscow's hearty natural population growth during the 1920s represented a dramatic improvement over with the city's prewar tradition when the population often struggled to replenish itself. For the first time in decades, life rapidly outdistanced its gruesome rival. In-migration, on the other hand, represented the continuation of a long-standing tradition. During the half century before 1917, tens of thousands of people annually had moved to Moscow from the surrounding rural hinterlands. Rural-born residents comprised a majority of the city's population.

During the 1920s, Moscow experienced record high annual growth rates—11 percent per annum from 1920 to 1923, 7 percent from 1923 to 1926, and 6.2 percent from 1927 to 1928. The previous record had been set during World War I when average annual population growth reached 5.6 percent.[2] Even after reaching its prewar population in 1926, the annual rate of population growth continued to exceed that of the war years.

With this growth came a host of inter-related problems. The city's housing in the early 1920s was smaller and more dilapidated than it was in 1917. Migrants had a difficult time finding places to live, and by 1922, a housing shortage existed. To meet the rising demand, factory and temporary barracks, which the soviet had closed just a few years earlier, had to be re-opened. Still, demand exceeded supply, and, throughout the decade, thousands of residents were forced to live on the streets. Likewise, many returning veterans and migrants who flocked to the city hoping to secure work found that there were too few jobs. The city's demographic recovery outstripped its economic recovery. Even after the prewar economic indices were surpassed, fewer jobs existed than did in 1913. Unemployment rose steeply, steadily forcing native Muscovites and other established residents to compete with rural migrants for the few full-time and temporary jobs. In short, the city's rapid population growth gave rise to severe problems and mounting dissatisfaction.

The social, economic, and political impact of this growth will be discussed in ensuing chapters. This chapter's purpose is to analyze the dimensions of and reasons for that growth and to provide a profile of the city's population. Such background is essential to appreciate the proletariat's composition and behavior and the problems that afflicted Moscow during the NEP.

Moscow's Demographic Profile

Nowhere was the impact of seven years of warfare and social and economic collapse more noticeable than in northern industrial cities such as Moscow. The most striking difference between pre- and post-revolutionary Moscow was its changed sexual composition. For the first time in its history, from 1917 females comprised a majority of Muscovites. As Table 2-1 indicates, prior to World War I males significantly outnumbered females though the gap continually diminished. In 1902, there were 767 females for every thousand male residents. This severe imbalance reflected the preponderance of males among the migrant population. Many of those males were unmarried; others had left their wives and families in the villages. By 1917, the exodus of males to the front and the influx of women to fill their jobs evened the sexual ratio. During the next three years, Red Army levies, the flight of many males to their villages, and higher male death rates continued to skew the city's sexual composition. Beginning in 1921, the demobilization of the army and return of males from the villages somewhat redressed the sexual ratio. But females remained a majority of the population throughout the decade. Moscow, like most major Soviet cities, was to remain a predominantly female city, hardly surprising in view of the enormous carnage of World War I and the Civil War.[3]

Both before and after the revolution, Moscow's population was quite young (see table 2-2). About 60 percent of the residents in both eras were less than thirty years old. But the two periods differed in one striking way: during the 1920s, there was a higher proportion of children under the age of ten. Whereas in 1912 only 15 percent of the residents were younger than ten, by 1926 that proportion had risen to one-fifth.[4] Given the high death rates among children and infants and the low birth rates during the Civil War years, the increase is quite significant.

Three factors account for the presence of more children. The first was the postwar baby boom (see appendix 3). From 1914 to 1920, the city's birth rate stayed well below its prewar counterpart. But with the increased number of marriages after 1917 and the demobilization of the army beginning in 1921, the birth rate rose sharply and remained high until 1926. The next year it began a steady, long-term decline. Precisely

TABLE 2-1
Sexual Composition of Moscow, 1897-1926

Year	Number of females per 1,000 males
1897	755
1902	767
1907	803
1912	843
1915	891
1917 (March)	983
1917 (November)	1,016
1920	1,063-1,235[a]
1923	1,006-1,067[a]
1926	1,047

SOURCES: *Itogi . . . perepisi 1923g.*, tom I, otd. I, tab. I, 13; *Perepis' . . . 1926g.*, tom. 2, tab. IX, 198-199; Vydro, *Naselenie*, 16-21.

a. These figures represent the estimated ratios for these years. They serve as a reminder that the chaos and mobility of the period made the fixing of precise ratios a difficult task.

TABLE 2-2
Age Structure of Moscow by Sex, 1926

Age group	Males	Females	Number	Percent
up to 1 year	24,794	24,082	48,876	2.4%
1-4 years	113,049	109,422	222,473	11.0%
5-9	59,345	59,596	118,942	5.9%
10-14	65,885	70,704	136,589	6.7%
15-19	89,765	102,809	192,574	9.5%
20-24	129,976	130,436	260,412	12.9%
25-29	128,398	141,878	270,276	13.3%
30-34	104,847	100,859	205,706	10.2%
35-39	86,453	81,816	168,269	8.3%
40-44	69,105	56,852	125,957	6.2%
45-49	52,801	48,140	100,841	5.0%
50-54	38,111	39,686	77,800	3.8%
55-59	24,009	32,483	56,492	2.8%
60-64	14,073	25,259	39,232	1.9%
65-69	7,822	18,178	26,000	1.3%
70 and older	5,922	17,792	23,744	1.2%
Totals	989,592	1,036,355	2,025,947	100.0%

SOURCE: *Perepis' . . . 1926g.*, tom. 2, tab. IX, 198-199.

why it did so remains unclear. The higher incidence of abortions (to be discussed in chapter 5) undoubtedly was a major factor.

The second reason was the dramatic decline in the city's infant mortality rate, undoubtedly one of the young Soviet state's most important early accomplishments. In the decade after the revolution, that rate declined from 355 deaths per thousand births to 133 (see appendix 2). The low infant mortality rate during the 1920s stood in stark contrast to that of pre-revolutionary times when Russia had the highest infant mortality rate in Europe, a rate more than twice that of the other European countries.[5] Under the *ancien regime*, urban conditions were so unhealthy and available health-care so limited and expensive that many expectant mothers returned to their native villages to have their children.[6] The Soviet government significantly expanded the number of facilities and services available to expectant and recent mothers. These facilities provided free medical care for the mother and child as well as instruction on prenatal and postnatal care.[7] That such care contributed to the declining urban infant mortality rate can be assumed given the higher rate in rural areas where the new government lacked the capacity to develop comparable services.

Not only did fewer of the city's infants die after the revolution, but the average new-born Muscovite could be assured of living a longer life than his ancestors. The average life-expectancy of a Russian child born in 1896-1897 was thirty-two years, whereas that of a child born thirty years later was forty-four years.[8]

The third reason for the greater proportion of children was the presence of more families in the city. In 1902, only 568 males and 422 females per thousand residents (over the age of fifteen) were married, and many of the males' spouses and families resided in the villages. In 1926, the figures were 642 and 509 respectively. The greater number of marriages after 1917 accounts for part of the increase; three times as many marriages occured in 1923 than in 1905.[9] No doubt the excess of females between the ages of twenty and twenty-nine and war widows spurred the nuptiality rate; in pre-revolutionary days, young, marriageable women were a distinct minority. But equally as siginificant is that more families—as opposed to married or unmarried individuals—migrated to Moscow after 1920. Half of those migrants were females, and by 1926 half of the city's residents were classified as economically inactive (most of them were dependent family members) compared to only one-third fourteen years earlier.[10] Precisely who those families were and from where they came remains unclear. Some were undoubtedly the families of state and party officials and employees who had moved to the capital from diverse geographic locations. Others were peasants who had migrated from the surrounding countryside.

The migration of entire families to Moscow indicates a marked change from pre-revolutionary times when most married males who moved to the city left their families in the villages. Moscow, for decades a town composed predominantly of male migrants, was becoming a family town. Equally as important was that a growing proportion of Muscovites were severing their ties to the land and establishing permanent residence there.

Moscow in the 1920s differed from its pre-revolutionary counterpart in yet another significant way—a decreasing proportion of people died (see appendix 2). As we have already seen, death was no stranger to Moscow from 1918 to 1921. The diseases, cold and malnutrition of those years joined with the effects of epidemics and the 1921-1922 famine to keep the death rate inordinately high in 1922 (29.0 deaths per thousand residents). Only in the next year did that rate drop below the pre-1917 level, and then precipitously so to 14.4. Throughout the 1920s, the death rate declined; by 1929, it stood at 12.9, slighty more than half the average between 1912 and 1916. This dramatic lowering of the mortality rate resulted from the interaction of several factors: the elimination of epidemics, a steady improvement in the population's diet and health, ample food and fuel supplies, the gradual expansion and upgrading of the free health-care system, better municipal sanitation, and the restoration and expansion of the city's water and sewer systems. Thanks to the declining death and infant mortality rates, Moscow experienced something rare in its history— a dramatic natural population increase.[11]

The declining mortality rate should not be construed to imply that Muscovites were healthy. Such was not the case. A study of some 20,000 Muscovite industrial workers and employees conducted in the mid-1920s revealed that 80 percent of them suffered from some sort of chronic illness or pathological condition. The study concluded that most of the problems resulted from the prolonged hardships and deprivations of the war years (1914-1921).[12] Physical examinations of juveniles revealed that they too suffered from a host of chronic medical problems. In one study, upward of 85 percent were anemic and had tubercular tendencies; many others were underdeveloped and had deformed spines.[13] Despite the efforts of soviets and trade unions to develop sanatoriums and rest homes for workers, the need continued to exceed the supply. The slow pace of improvements in housing and work conditions, especially up to 1925, often exacerbated the frail physical condition of many Muscovites. In that year, tuberculosis, pneumonia, and other respiratory diseases accounted for more than one-quarter of the city's deaths.[14] These grim statistics testify to the human cost of substandard conditions that characterized the lives of citizens for too many years.

While the demographic profile of post-1922 Moscow contrasted sharply with that of pre-revolutionary times, there remained one significant similarity—the continued preponderance of women over the age of fifty. The reasons for the imbalance remain unclear. Surely, longer female life expectancy was a factor. But the ratios are such that, even given the greater susceptibility of males to infectious diseases and death in battle, one suspects additional factors at work. In his study of late nineteenth-century Moscow, Robert Johnson found that the low proportion of peasant males among the older age groups was due to an absolute decrease in their number. After accounting for various factors affecting mortality rates, Johnson was "left with the impression" that a significant proportion of male worker-peasants simply left the city after age forty. He suggested that many of them returned to their family lands in the villages.[15]

Data on the city's age and sex structure during the 1920s are insufficiently precise to test Johnson's hypothesis. However, there was a substantial absolute decrease in the number of males over fifty years of age. A comparison of the data found in table 2-2 with a model life table reveals that there were significantly fewer males in this age group than there should have been (see appendix 4).[16] Even after accounting for males' shorter life expectancy and higher death rates during the period, it appears that the decline in males over fifty resulted from the actions of one or more independent variables. Their returning to the villages remains a plausible hypothesis and one in accord with the rural habits and ties of Muscovites discussed below.

In-Migration

Natural population growth, while significant relative to pre-revolutionary times, accounted for only 15 percent of Moscow's burgeoning population.[17] As had been the case for decades, migration remained the primary reason for the city's demographic growth. In 1926, native Muscovites accounted for only one-third (33.7 percent) of the city's population. Rural-born residents of Moscow comprised slightly less than one-half (48 percent) of the population; the remaining 18 percent had been born in other urban settlements.[18]

Most migrants to Moscow during the 1920s came from the provinces of the Central Industrial Region (CIR), a pattern that had existed before 1917. There were two major reasons for this migration: rural economic hardships and the city's promise of jobs and independence. However, one important difference distinguished the two periods: the annual rate of migration was greater during the NEP.[19] Of course, many who migrated to Moscow during the 1920s were actually returning there from Red Army service or from the villages to which they had fled after 1917. Unfortunately, the available evidence makes no distinction between new and returning migrants.

The largest number of migrants to the city came from Moscow *guberniia* and bordering provinces. A 1926 examination of the birthplace of 1,178,977 migrants living in Moscow reveals that almost two-thirds (64.2 percent) of them had moved from the CIR (or within 200 miles of Moscow). Approximately one-fifth (18.8 percent) came from the Central Black Earth and Western regions, Leningrad-Karelia and Belorussia. The remainder had moved there from all over the USSR, although, as a rule, the farther one lived from Moscow, the less chance there was that he or she would migrate there.[20] Table 2-3 lists those *gubernii* from which

10,000 or more people migrated to Moscow by 1926. Unlike pre-revolutionary times, when males dominated the ranks of in-migrants, equal proportions of males and females migrated to Moscow.

The *gubernii* listed in table 2-3, and those of the CIR in particular, traditionally had been the source of the pre-revolutionary city's growing population. At the turn of the century, three-quarters of the migrants to Moscow were peasants, primarily from the provinces of Moscow, Tver, Iaroslavl', Vladimir, Riazan, Kaluga, Tula, and Smolensk.[21] Approximately 75 percent of these migrants came from within a radius of 100 miles. In the 1920s, a similar pattern existed.

Two factors help determine whether or not people will leave their native province: local population density and local economic opportunites. In the case of the CIR, the largest number of migrants to Moscow

TABLE 2-3
Guberniia of Origin of Migrants to Moscow, 1926

Guberniia	Number of people	Percent of all migrants to Moscow	Of migrants to Moscow, percent of males
Moscow	228,616	19.4%	48.6%
Riazan	169,739	14.4%	49.3%
Tula	123,357	10.5%	45.3%
Kaluga	76,434	6.5%	52.4%
Smolensk	54,348	4.6%	50.3%
Tver	50,710	4.3%	48.0%
Vladimir	48,086	3.5%	54.8%
Leningrad-Karelia	32,269	2.7%	42.3%
Tambov	28,067	2.4%	51.7%
Iaroslavl'	23,948	2.0%	52.7%
Orel	22,491	1.9%	48.1%
Nizhnii-Novgorod	19,452	1.6%	61.2%
Kostroma	12,750	1.1%	58.1%
Briansk	12,245	1.0%	54.8%
Penza	12,071	1.0%	53.2%
Saratov	11,022	.9%	49.4%
Ivanovo-Voznesensk	10,170	.8%	53.5%
Totals	928,775	75.9%	49.5%[a]

SOURCE: *Perepis'* . . . *1926g.*, tom. 36, tab. V, 216-221.
a. Average.
NB. The Central Industrial Region consists of the following *gubernii*: Moscow, Riazan, Tula, Kaluga, Tver, Vladimir, Iaroslavl', Nizhnii-Novgorod, Kostroma, and Ivanovo-Voznesensk.

came from the region's most densely populated and least industrialized provinces—Riazan and Tula. Together they accounted for more than 290,000 people, or one-quarter of the city's migrant population.[22] Nizhnii-Novgorod, Kostroma, and Ivanovo-Voznesensk, the CIR *gubernii* that sent the fewest number of people, were less densely populated and had numerous industries that provided jobs for local residents. Studies have shown that the higher the percentage of urban workers in a province, the less likely were the chances that people would migrate beyond its borders.[23] This is hardly surprising considering that most migrants were peasants who usually preferred to remain as close to home as possible.

When did migrants move to Moscow? In late 1926, slightly less than half (46.8 percent) of the city's migrant population (excluding temporary residents) had moved there after 1920. Many others were long-time residents—one-fifth had lived there for twenty years or more; 10 percent since 1897. In all, 626,082 migrants had maintained continuous residence for six or more years.[24] Unfortunately, because the census data listed in table 2-4 reflect only continuous residence, it is impossible to determine what proportion of the post-1920 migrants formerly had resided there. Given the city's rapid population growth from 1921 to 1923, one suspects that many who moved there during these years were former residents returning from the Red Army and villages.

Nonetheless, many others were first-time visitors, who were inexperienced in the ways of the city and brought with them rural values and perceptions which often had a noticeable impact on urban life. As the decade wore on, the number of first-time migrants mounted. The slight decline in per annum growth after 1924 reflects several factors: those who were returning to the city had already done so, the rising unemployment rate and the scarcity of available housing discouraged many, and local employment opportunities gradually increased.

Only one-fifth (19.1 percent) of the city's workers in 1926 were native residents. Of those workers born elsewhere, 40 percent had moved or returned there only within the last six years, and 44 percent had maintained continous residence there for more than ten years. (Almost one-quarter had been there for twenty years or more.)[25] The demographic composition of the Moscow proletariat can be likened to a spectrum. At one extreme stood urban-born, hereditary workers; at the other, their inexperienced, often unskilled "country cousins" undergoing their first exposure to urban industrial life.

Between them one could find workers such as K. and C., rural-born,

TABLE 2-4
Duration of Residence of Migrant Moscow Population, 1926

Occupation	Tem-porary	1926 Up to 1 yr.	1925 1 year	1924 2 years	1921-1923 3-5 years	1917-1920 6-9 years	1914-1916 10-12 years	1907-1913 13-19 years	1897-1906 20-29 years	Prior to 1897 30+ years	Total[a]
All residents	58,470	93,333	91,057	106,056	312,707	161,007	93,010	117,408	128,936	125,721	1,287,705
Percent	4.5%	7.2%	7.1%	8.2%	24.3%	12.5%	7.2%	9.1%	10.0%	9.8%	
Active population	38,082	52,349	54,166	61,860	192,125	105,467	60,759	79,515	93,291	87,962	825,576
Percent	4.6%	6.3%	6.6%	7.5%	23.3%	12.8%	7.4%	9.6%	11.3%	10.7%	
Workers	6,299	12,068	15,010	17,667	49,682	30,348	18,663	27,842	32,268	23,832	233,619
Percent	2.7%	5.2%	6.4%	7.6%	21.3%	13.0%	8.0%	11.9%	13.8%	10.2%	
Employees	7,729	18,361	20,535	23,169	79,988	44,122	23,670	28,872	33,387	26,528	306,361
Percent	2.5%	6.0%	6.7%	7.6%	26.1%	14.4%	7.7%	9.4%	10.9%	8.7%	
Free professionals	127	152	178	226	1,475	739	398	517	652	625	5,089
Percent	2.5%	3.0%	3.5%	4.4%	29.0%	14.5%	7.8%	10.1%	12.8%	12.3%	
Proprietors and self-employed	9,229	5,018	4,873	5,812	17,839	8,201	5,125	6,473	9,735	12,581	83,886
Percent	11.0%	6.0%	5.8%	6.9%	20.0%	9.8%	6.1%	7.7%	11.6	15.0%	

SOURCE: *Perepis'* . . . *1926g*, tom. 36, tab. IV, 142; dop. I k tab. IV, 174-183; dop. III-IV, 174-183; dop. III k tab. III-IV, 190-201.
[a]Total excludes those who did not know their duration of residence in Moscow.

long-time residents who had turned their backs to their villages and had "tied their fate with the fate of the factory."[26] In 1924, K. was a thirty-eight-year-old caster at the Serp i molot (former Guzhon) metal works. His wife, one year his junior, had been a factory worker in Moscow from 1915 to 1922. Like many women who entered the workforce during those years, she had lost her job upon the return of veterans and males from the villages. Born to a peasant family in Smolensk province, K. had migrated to Moscow at the age of thirteen and went to work at the Guzhon plant. His wife, also born in Smolensk to peasant parents, moved there when she married K. some time after 1905.[27] C. was a thirty-eight-year-old metal lathe operator in 1924. Born in a semi-industrialized village in Moscow *guberniia*, his father was a factory worker, his mother tilled the small family plot. He attended school until age seventeen, at which time (1898) he moved to Moscow and secured a factory job. His wife, who had lived in Moscow for several years during her childhood, returned there in 1911 after marrying C.[28] Both couples had remained in Moscow during the trying Civil War years. Although rural-born, both had cut their rural ties.

The move from village to city could often be difficult. Fortunately, informal associational networks eased the transition. For decades, an elaborate urban-rural network had existed by which *zemliaki* (fellow villagers, or people from neighboring villages) transmitted news about urban employment opportunities and conditions as well as stories about urban life. These networks helped people to overcome their hesitancy to migrate and helped determine where they would migrate. Upon their arrival in Moscow, migrants usually sought out *zemliaki* who helped them to secure jobs and housing and "taught them the ropes" of factory and urban life.[29] Not infrequently, factory foremen preferred to hire *zemliaki*, and on occasion even sent word back "home" when they were hiring. Although such preferential treatment aided migrants, during the 1920s as the city's unemployment rate climbed, many urban workers came to resent this practice. Conflict between jobless residents and their migrant competitors mounted.

Why did peasants migrate to Moscow? In analyzing the causes of rural-urban migration, it is essential to distinguish between the conditions or situations *from* which migrants fled, and those *to* which they moved. Often a combination of these "push" and "pull" factors convinced a person to migrate. Peasants of the Central Industrial Region were "pushed" from their villages by a host of factors: overcrowded land; the declining economic viability of many peasant holdings; reduced rural economic opportunities; shortages of cash, consumer items and agricultural tools; and the cultural backwardness of village life. Yet other factors drew or "pulled" people to Moscow: the prospect of employment, relatively high wages, the promise of independence from parental authority and village tradition, and the excitement of city life with its 'bright lights' and new experiences. As in pre-revolutionary times, "push-pull" factors were deeply intertwined and resulted in a steady stream of migrants to Moscow.[30]

Economic hardships forced many villagers to migrate to urban areas. The land redistribution which lasted from 1917 to 1922 resulted in a significant rise in the number of rural households and a levelling of the size of peasant holdings. The latter was accomplished by reducing the proportion of landless households by two-thirds and that of large holdings (four or more *desiatini*) by one-third. Unquestionably, the redistribution resulted in a more egalitarian pattern of land ownership, but just as significant was the fact that most households had too little land to engage in anything more than subsistence farming. Prior to the revolution, about 40 percent of the rural households in the CIR tilled less than two *desiatini*; by 1922, more than half of the households did so.[31] Consequently, during the 1920s, much of the rural population was economically superfluous. Although estimates vary with the region studied, it appears that about 30 percent of the rural labor force was underutilized. This was an annual average. During the summer months when work demands and employment opportunities increased, the proportion of idle hands decreased; during the winter months, it was rose sharply.[32]

Cultivation methods employed in the CIR further undermined the economic viability of many households. About 90 percent of its rural households tilled strips of land as opposed to enclosed farms.[33] In accordance with time-honored custom, village communes allotted to each household strips of land consisting of a prescribed mix of good, medium and poor soil. Considerable distances often separated a household's strips. Hours, even days, of valuable labor were lost in travel back and forth, and much land remained uncultivated so as to allow for foot paths. Many strips were quite narrow, discouraging the scientific application of fertilizer and use of machinery, though the latter was scarce in the Russian countryside. In Riazan *guberniia*, a delegate to the Fifteenth Party Congress in 1927 reported: "there are places with up to 50 strips [per household] at a distance of 15-20 or even 25 *versts* 16-22, or even 28 kilometers."[34] Such practices rendered agricultural production inefficient and underproductive.

In normal times, most of the peasants in the overcrowded country-side could eke out a subsistence. But the post-Civil War years were far from normal times. Between 1914 and 1921, the amount of cultivated land in the CIR decreased by about one-third.[35] When households sought to restore their farms, they faced unusually high expenses. During the Civil War, agricultural tools and equipment had fallen into disrepair and many draft animals had perished. And during the 1920s, they experienced a consistent trade disadvantage. The prices of agricultural products remained low relative to those of equipment, tools, and consumer goods, a disparity at the root of the "scissors crises" which occurred periodically during the NEP. (The "scissors crisis" resulted from the increasing price differential between agricultural and industrial goods, the latter being much more expensive than the former. As the price gap increased, the "scissors" opened wider.) Not only were agricultural prices relatively low, but the demand for industrial crops had declined. In 1925, the production of flax and hemp, the main cash crops for the less fertile, northern provinces, stood at only 75 percent of the 1916 level. Consequently, many of the region's households experienced considerable economic hardships.[36] For the typical peasant, farming proved to be a losing financial proposition. Throughout the NEP, the number of liquidated households grew steadily, and many of their members emigrated to urban areas.[37]

Supplementing their farm income became imperative for many peasant families. Some engaged in trade and artisan production. But whereas in 1917, 40 percent of the Moscow industrial region's rural households had engaged in crafts and trade, in 1922 only 22 percent did so.[38] Others became agricultural day-laborers, but the excess rural population, the elimination of large estates, and limitations on the hiring of labor until 1925 reduced the demand for such work. Many rural industries that had once provided jobs for local peasants either did not re-open after 1921 or were slow to recover. Those that did offered fewer employment opportunities than before 1917. Debt and fewer local jobs forced many peasant families to send members to urban areas in search of permanent or seasonal work or to market foodstuffs and other items produced by rural households. While the significantly higher wages earned by urban workers made migrating to cities like Moscow economically attractive, economic hardships often made it imperative.[39]

The backwardness of the countryside induced many peasants to migrate to Moscow. Although the provinces of the CIR were more culturally modern than most *gubernii* in the country, they were still backward by urban standards.[40] The weight of village tradition, the conservatism of peasant society, and the boredom of rural life weighed heavily on some villagers. Those exposed to urban life through previous employment, military service or simply the stories of friends who had lived in a city were eager to depart. Often the first to leave were the young, better educated, and those who embraced the revolution's new ideas and aspirations in defiance of the backwardness and unceasing routine of rural life. For many, cities stood as symbols of the revolution. Urban industry, educational opportunities, and political activism offered them the possibility of realizing their personal and political dreams, finding the means with which to "attack backward agriculture," and thereby hastening the fulfillments of socialism's promises.[41] For them, as for the economically disadvantaged, Moscow was a magnet.

During the 1920s, both "push" and "pull" factors drew migrants to Moscow. Which were the more powerful can not be definitely ascertained, but the circumstantial evidence suggests that the critical economic conditions in the countryside provided the primary stimulant to migration. The subsistence nature of most rural households and the need for cash to restore the farm forced many peasants to urban areas in search of wages. Yet most urban industries recovered slowly, and even after they had recovered most enterprises employed a smaller work force than they had before the revolution. Likewise, substantially fewer domestic servants worked in Moscow in the 1920s than had before 1917. The transfer of the capital to Moscow in 1918 provided thousands of new job opportunities, but most were beyond the reach of the illiterate or semi-literate migrant.

Seasonal Migration (*Otkhodnichestvo*)

Although unemployment rose steeply in Moscow during the decade, upwards of 100,000 migrants annually flocked there to compete for increasingly scarce jobs and housing. But twice that many annually sought seasonal work in Moscow, compounding the problems. While some seasonal workers (*otkhodniki*) ultimately established permanent residence there, most returned to their villages at the season's end. Although fewer *otkhodniki* made the seasonal trek to Moscow than in pre-revolutionary times, each year during the NEP their ranks increased. In 1926, more than 200,000 *otkhodniki* descended on the city.[42]

Seasonal migration had a long tradition and seasonal workers engaged in a wide variety of nonagricultural pursuits, the most notable being construction, transport, and industrial work. In construction work—the largest single seasonal occupation—certain provinces specialized in specific skills. *Otkhodniki* from Riazan, Moscow, Ivanovo-Voznesensk, Kostroma, and Tver were renown for their carpentry skills and dominated that trade. Those from Vladimir, Kaluga, Nizhnii-Novgorod, and Tver comprised the vast majority of the city's seasonal masons. *Otkhodniki* from Moscow and Ivanovo-Voznesensk *gubernii* specialized in industrial work, especially textile production. Often whole villages engaged in seasonal textile work. For example, the village of Tereninskaia (Orekho-Zuevo uezd', Moscow *guberniia*) annually sent more than 100 seasonal textile workers to area factories. Other villages specialized in leather working; in Ivanovo-Voznesensk *guberniia*, three villages annually had a "massive *otkhod* of leather workers."[43]

The migration itself was also fairly well organized internally. Most seasonal workers continued the pre-revolutionary practice of forming *arteli* (work groups). *Artel* members came from one village or possibly neighboring villages, and chose one from their ranks to be the leader (*starosta*). This person possessed considerable seasonal work experience and the trust of his co-workers. His responsibilities included securing employment and housing, overseeing the group's work and behavior, and often holding that portion of their pay which the workers wanted to take back to their family.

Unlike permanent migrants, seasonal migrants remained firmly rooted in the countryside. But in many other respects, their social profile was similar to that of those who had moved to Moscow. The vast majority came from the villages of the Central Industrial Region; some came from the Western, Central Black Earth, and Mid-Volga regions. The largest number of *otkhodniki* came from the poor soil, northeastern provinces and the overpopulated, sparsely industrialized, southeastern provinces. The fewest came from those provinces, such as Moscow and Ivanovo-Voznesensk that housed local industries. Most seasonal workers were poor (*bedniak*) and middle (*seredniak*) peasants who possessed insufficient land to sustain their households.[44] For them, seasonal labor was an important, often essential, source of livelihood, contributing an average of between 20 and 25 percent of their family's total income. Although other urban areas in the region offered economic opportunities, Moscow's relatively high wages made it a favorite destination for seasonal workers.[45] In only one respect did the composition of *otkhodniki* differ from that of peasant migrants—the vast majority (80 percent) were males.[46]

The skill levels of *otkhodniki* varied widely. Aside from experienced construction workers and those with some industrial skills, most *otkhodniki* possessed few marketable skills and were thereby restricted to securing work as carters, haulers, domestics, food workers, and unskilled factory workers.

People of all ages comprised the *otkhodniki*'s ranks. A 1928 study of some ten thousand seasonal construction workers in Moscow revealed that their ranks spanned two generations. An equal proportion (46 percent) were younger than thirty and between thirty and thirty-five years old; 8 percent were older than fifty. Half of the workers had three or less years experience; about a quarter had ten or more years. Some 40 percent had performed seasonal construction work before 1914. Experienced builders often imparted their knowledge to the younger workers, especially if they were fellow *artel* members.[47]

The *otkhod* season began in March and usually lasted for five months, although some people stayed for seven months or more. During March, April, and May, thousands of seasonal workers left their villages. Many in this first wave of migrants were construction workers seeking to secure employment at the very beginning of the building season, or transport workers arriving at the river docks as soon as the ice had melted. Among those who departed later, many descended on the factory gates in hopes of replacing workers who, ironically, used their annual vacation to return to their villages and work the family lands. By June, the job market was saturated and the number of *otkhodniki* entering Moscow declined markedly. The competition for the limited number of jobs was so intense that temporary unemployment was a regular feaure of seasonal labor, especially for construction workers. As many as one-third of the city's construction workers were out of work in July, the height of the building season. During August and September, the ranks of the seasonal labor force swelled slightly, and then diminished slowly until December. In that month, the number of seasonal migrants reached its annual nadir: not only were there few job opportunities, but the holiday season began. After the holidays, the number of migrants grew steadily until March when, once again, the season commenced.[48]

Urban-Rural Ties

The annual influx into Moscow of more than a quarter of a million migrants—permanent or seasonal—underscores the close economic and social relationships between town and country. Symbiotic relations between the two characterize all industrializing societies. In Russia, they permeated virtually all aspects of life.

Many Muscovites retained strong rural ties, not the least of which was ownership of village land. The phenomenon of landowning urban dwellers had long existed in Russia. In the 1880s, the majority of workers in the Moscow region possessed land allotments. With the growth of an hereditary, urban proletariat, the proportion of landowning urban workers slowly declined. By 1912, almost one-quarter of the city's workers owned land, three-quarters of whom sent part of their wages to their families in the countryside. By 1917, only about one-fifth of all Moscow workers owned land.[49] The proportion of landowning Muscovites continued to diminish after the revolution, but as late as 1926 one of every six Moscow workers still owned land.[50] Such urban-rural ties in central Russia continued into the 1950s.[51] Nonetheless, while land ownership remained common, more and more Muscovites were severing their village ties.

As table 2-5 indicates, with the exception of professionals and employees, all occupational groups in Moscow included a significant proportion of landowners. Given that professionals and employees were usually either native urbanites or migrants from distant regions, their weak ties to the land are to be expected. Among workers and proprietors, however, land ownership and agricultural labor were quite common. Proprietors who operated their enterprises with the aid of family or *artel* members were the occupational group with the highest proportion of landowning members; in many cases, the land and village ties were essential to their trade.[52] But the largest number of families owning land were those headed by workers. More than 20,000 working-class families (consisting of approximately 75,000 family members) possessed rural land holdings. This represented 13.4 percent of all proletarian families in the capital. An even larger proportion (almost 40 percent) of individual workers fell into this group.

Factory workers and workers employed in small and handicraft (*kustar*) industries had the most extensive ties to the land. Among factory workers, land ownership was most frequent in industries, such as metal processing and machine construction, where males comprised the majority of workers. Weavers, printers, textile workers, and chemical workers had the fewest ties to the land. Women dominated the labor force in all of these industries except printing. However, the characteristics of workers who owned land was remarkably similar regardless of the industry in which they were employed. The vast majority were males. About half of

TABLE 2-5
Urban Ties to the Land, Moscow, 1926

Occupation	1[a]	2[b]	3[c]	4[d]	5[e]	6[f]
Workers						
All categories	13.4%	7.7%	3.7%	39.9%	21.0%	21.5%
Factory workers	12.5%	7.2%	3.4%	33.3%	17.5%	18.3%
Workers in small and *kustar* industries	14.2%	9.0%	4.4%	40.7%	24.1%	24.7%
Railroad workers	10.7%	6.2%	2.8%	44.0%	22.7%	10.0%
Employees						
All categories	6.4%	3.6%	1.8%	18.5%	8.7%	10.2%
Free Professionals						
All categories	1.4%	—	.05%	.2%	.05%	1.4%
Proprietors with wage labor						
All categories	9.7%	6.6%	3.3%	19.0%	11.4%	10.9%
Proprietors with family or *artel* members' labor						
All categories	23.4%	18.3%	9.9%	51.8%	17.9%	30.6%
Self-employed						
All categories	13.7%	9.7%	5.3%	41.3%	32.1%	23.6%
Unemployed						
All categories	6.9%	3.3%	1.7%	19.9%	9.5%	12.8%
Totals	9.6%	5.7%	2.9%	25.1%	13.8%	15.1%

SOURCE: *Perepis'* . . . *1926g.*, tom. 55, tab. II, 128-129.
a. Column 1: Families owning land in the countryside.
b. Column 2: Families, members of which do agricultural work in the countryside
c. Column 3: Family members who do agricultural work in the countryside.
d. Column 4: Individuals owning land in the countryside.
e. Column 5: Of those individuals, those who do agricultural work in the countryside.
f. Column 6: Families and individuals owning land as a proportion of all families and individuals.

them had more than ten years of production experience (*stazh*), and many were skilled. Their ownership of land notwithstanding, many propertied workers were the children of workers.[53] A majority (57.6 percent) of these families also had family members who worked that land. In some cases, family members lived in the village; in others, one or more members worked the land seasonally. Thus, even among the most experienced and skilled workers, the ties which bound the working class to the land ran deep.

Land ownership by urban residents was more than a short-term phenomenon. The practice continued for a number of reasons. Some rural-born workers viewed urban industrial work as temporary and either planned to return to the land in a few years or, at the very least, to retire to their holdings. Second, and deriving from the first, the income earned by such urban workers and the produce from the family's holding were often viewed as part of a single family income, an attitude reinforced by the hardships of the Civil War.[54]

An example of a working-class family that owned land in Vladimir *guberniia* clearly illustrates the depth of rural-urban ties. B., a trade union member since 1917 who joined the Communist Party in 1924, was a skilled metalworker. Born in 1884 to peasant parents in Vladimir *guberniia*, he moved to Moscow at the age of thirteen and, with the help of a *zemliak*, secured employment at the Guzhon factory where he still worked in 1924. Prior to the revolution, he married an illiterate peasant woman and they had three sons and a daughter. His parents and sister continued to live on the family farm in Vladimir, consisting of three *desiatini* (8.1 acres). In 1920, B. sent his family back to Vladimir to escape the hardships which gripped Moscow. During the next four years, the family experienced some dramatic changes in living arrangements. By 1924, two of B.'s sons (ages nineteen and twelve) and his sister lived in Vladimir and tended the family plot. B. resided in Moscow with his fourteen-year-old son and sixty-three-year-old father; B.'s wife and five-year-old daughter divided their time between Vladimir and Moscow. Throughout his life, B. sent money to his family in the country; in 1924, he sent them almost one-fifth (18.8 percent) of his income.[55] There were many such families in Moscow.

Significant migration also took place in the opposite direction—from city to country—and often had an adverse impact on industrial productivity and efficiency. During the summer months, thousands of Muscovites returned to their villages for their annual vacation. Throughout the 1920s, newspaper articles referring to this annual exodus of urban residents announced that "the time has come for the annual leave."[56] Although some residents departed in May to help sow crops, most who returned to the land did so in July so as to participate in haymowing. As one contemporary observer noted: "The issue of the July holiday is above all an issue of the connections of the factory workers with the land." While these two months witnessed the largest exodus, the movement from town to country was continuous from May through September. Only in October did the permanent workforce return to its normal size. While this draining of the industrial workforce during the summer months obviously affected overall factory production, one study of the textile industry revealed that average worker productivity was highest during May, June, and July.[57] The impact that large numbers of worker-peasants had on factory life and productivity will be discussed later. Suffice to say for now that their presence in (and temporary absence from) the factories affected industrial life in many ways.

Seasonal urban-rural migration was largely a function of two factors: the degree of mechanization in a given enterprise and skill. The largest number of workers who annually returned to the villages were employed in unmechanized enterprises that were often forced to cease production temporarily.[58] Mechanized factories, however, could not afford shutdowns that entailed significant costs and loss of revenue, undermined production schedules, and wreaked havoc with the flow and storage of raw materials and supplies. Rather than disrupt production, some factories hired seasonal workers to replace vacationing personnel. Unskilled and semiskilled workers were more apt to return to their holdings during vacation. This was not a new phenomenon. Before the revolution, such workers behaved the same way. But skilled workers rarely left their jobs for the village. Most skilled workers who owned land preferred to follow the example of worker B. above and sent their family members to work their land.

While industrial skill helped to determine who returned to the land, the duration of urban residence did not. Such was the case in both pre- and post-revolutionary times.[59] Consider the case of metalworker B. and his family. In 1924, B. was a thirty-six-year-old grinder (presumably semiskilled) at a small metal foundry in Moscow. He lived with his wife, a semiskilled textile worker at the Trekhgornaia factory, and their four children. The son of a peasant-artisan from Moscow *guberniia* and a mother who worked in a factory, B. moved to Moscow to work at the age of thirteen and had worked there ever since. His wife, the daughter of peasant parents from the same province, also moved to the city at the age of thirteen. Although both B. and his wife had lived in the city for twenty-three years, they both returned to their families' holdings for thirty or forty days a year to work the land. In this family at least, the pattern of urban-rural seasonal migration had remained unchanged since the turn of the century.[60]

While many Muscovites placed great value on the ownership of land, party and state officials took a dimmer view of it. One commentator called the ties of the Moscow population to the land "one of the major problems of our city."[61] Although officials disliked the annual departure of workers, they sought to make the best of the situation. Beginning in May and throughout the summer months, newspapers ran numerous articles on "Work among the Vacationeers" and "Preparing for the Vacation." After a brief introduction noting the depth of worker ties to the villages, the typical article urged vacationeers to bring newspapers, books, and pamphlets with them so as to engage in propaganda activities among their rural brethren. The party counseled its members to do the same and, in particular, to explain the ideas found in Lenin's *On Cooperation.*[62]

Unions also sought to use the vacationers to their advantage. The Moscow Construction Workers Union is a case in point. To strengthen union support in the village and add seasonal builders to the union rolls, the union contacted those construction workers who vacationed in the villages and urged them to recruit seasonal builders to join the union. It considered these "semipeasant" (*polukrest'ian*) seasonal builders susceptible to union influence. Factories and unions also employed vacationing workers to aid in the extension of factory *shefstvo* (patronage) work, the purpose of which was to speed the realization of the *smychka* (town-country alliance) by conducting educational, cultural, and political work in the villages.[63]

The transition from village to city, from field to factory, was a protracted historical process spanning decades. To speak of migration to Moscow as a process distinct from migration away from the city or to speak of either as a singular experience is impossible. Moscow's rapid growth in the 1920s was due primarily to the fact that more migrants remained there than left there. Many Muscovites retained not only their land but many rural perspectives and habits as well and the continuing in-migration ensured the survival of rural culture and values in the city.

The maintenance of peasant traits and habits manifested itself in subtle ways and in such intimate areas of life as marriage. During the 1920s, many Muscovites continued to marry in accordance with the agricultural and liturgical calendar. An examination of monthly marital patterns in the capital from 1924 to 1928 reveals that marriages decreased significantly during the Lenten season and remained low throughout the summer, when the demands of agriculture were great and when many residents were back in their villages. After the September harvest, the number of marriages increased and remained high until Lent. The only exceptions during this latter flurry of marital activity were the months of December and, to a lesser extent, January, the Advent and Christmas seasons. Toward the end of the decade, however, the seasonal oscillation became somewhat muted. Whether this was a temporary fluctuation or an early sign of an increasingly urban, secularized outlook is impossible to determine.[64]

The pattern of Muscovite births also reflected the demands of agriculture. From 1924 to 1928, the number of births per month rose from September to January and then, with the exception of March, declined. During the summer months, there was a relative lull in the birth rate. Thus, the fewest number of conceptions occurred between July and October when the agricultural workday was longest and most exhausting, and when many Muscovite couples were separated—one mate remaining in Moscow, the other returning to the village to work the land. From January to March, the number of conceptions increased significantly. Viewed with the agricultural calendar in mind, these suggest a behavior well-suited to the needs of a peasant economy. During the summer months when all available labor was needed, women, even those in the late stages of pregnancy, were capable of performing their expected tasks. During the winter months when females' work was centered in or near the house, women reared their new children.[65]

Given that workers and owners of small enterprises in Moscow had the most extensive ties to the land, one suspects that these groups would be more likely to perpetuate such behavior. A study of birth rates in Moscow from 1925 to 1927 confirms this suspicion. B. Iagolin, the study's author, examined the birth rates in each of the city's militia districts (otdelenie). In 1927, the citywide birth rate was 25.6 with the range running from 15.3 in the first Arbatskii district in the center of the city to 43.7 in the outlying Siminosvkii district. Based on birth rates, Iagolin divided the city into two sectors: center and periphery. Employees and professionals (the groups with the fewest ties to the land) comprised a majority of the population of the center; workers and owners accounted for less than one-quarter. The social composition was the reverse in the periphery. The birth rate in the predominately worker periphery stood at 39.37 in 1925 and 33.74 in 1927; in the center, the figures were 25.31 and 18.22 respectively. Thus, Moscow's working class, with its extensive ties to the country, was the heaviest contributor to the city's overall birth rate, one characterized by strong rural, seasonal patterns. This suggests that working class birth rates reflected these patterns more strongly than those for the city as a whole.

Not only did proletarian districts have considerably higher birth rates, but their rates declined more slowly than in the center. When one considers that females of child-bearing age were heavily concentrated in the central districts, the importance of these reproductive patterns becomes even more dramatic.[66] Clearly, many rural-born Muscovites viewed families with a perspective less reflective of urban than rural life, where large families provided the labor with which to increase the family's income.

The implications of such worker behavior are of more than demographic interest. It was the proletariat to which the party looked for political support, and which it enlisted for various campaigns to increase labor discipline and productivity and to destroy the vestiges of the old order. Yet a significant portion of this class continued to live in accordance with rural and religious customs and practices and retained close ties to the village, the symbol of Russian backwardness to many in the party.

Workers seemed to find little contradiction between their behavior and support for the revolution or party. After all, what was wrong with proletarians in a workers' and peasants' state owning land, especially when such land was used simply to enhance their material well-being? In the abstract, of course, no contradiction existed. But what many party members disliked about the village was its conservatism and backwardness, which they believed slowed the march to socialism, and its potential stranglehold on urban food supplies and the urban standard of living. During the Civil War, many worker-peasants chose the village over the city. In another crisis, with whom would such workers side? Many feared the worst and endorsed the NEP as a way to hasten the town-country alliance and avoid any possibility of a showdown. Simultaneously, they worked to disseminate urban values in the village and to increase worker support for the party.

Others in the party no doubt took a less compromising stance; and they were not without their case. While the NEP sought to hasten the *smychka*, it also created new dilemmas, dilemmas which contributed to mounting worker resentment. The NEP policies sought to accomplish two goals: to restore agricultural production and revive rural-urban trade, and to restore and then raise industrial production. To achieve the former, peasants required capital for the purchase of seed, equipment, draft animals, and the like. But capital was scarce during the 1920s, and the state and peasantry competed for it. The state devised two methods to accumulate capital. The first we have briefly discussed—reducing the cost of industrial production by "belt-tightening" policies and by intensifying industrial labor. These policies resulted in fewer employment opportunites in the 1920s, even after recovery, than before the revolution. The other method was to make the peasantry "pay" for recovery by having the state purchase agricultural produce at relatively low prices and by charging relatively high prices for manufactured goods.[67]

The latter policy had two negative side-effects. The first was the "scissors crisis" that occurred several times during the decade. During each crisis, those peasants who could afford to do so (and usually they were only the rich peasants, or kulaks) withheld their produce and thereby threatened the urban standard of living. Given that most rural households engaged in subsistence agriculture, they could not afford to withhold, even temporarily, what little marketable produce they had, and were forced to seek urban work so as to maintain their households.

But fewer jobs existed. Herein lay the vicious cycle of the NEP. Mass rural-urban migration required the government to provide jobs or to face the social and political consequences of high unemployment. To provide jobs required capital, capital raised by policies which simultaneously induced rural-urban migration and limited the size of the workforce. The result was a steep rise in urban unemployment. Competition for jobs intensified. To compound the problem, the scarcity of capital limited the restoration and expansion of urban housing. As population growth outstripped that of housing, a housing crisis arose. During the 1920s, the unemployment and housing crises, which weighed most heavily on the city's proletariat, gave rise to mounting dissatisfaction and tension.

The spontaneous demographic processes of the 1920s threatened to drive a wedge between the party and the working class, amplifying the qualitative differences in their revolutionary agendas. Considerations of high policy led to a gradual recognition within the party that an industrial transformation of the nation could not proceed without a similar transformation of the countryside. As the decade drew to a close, a growing segment of the party came to believe that this transformation could not be accomplished by gradualist methods.

Considerations of high policy meant little to the machinists, weavers, seamstresses, and masons who made up Moscow's working class. Nonetheless, as a group the working class was of two minds concerning the countryside as much as was the party. The seasonal migrants and urban landowners within the working class had found a way to marginally improve their situation within the existing order. But the traditional bias of the urban dweller against the countryside as well as the latent repudiation of rural society often implicit in the departure of many migrants meant that many within the city's working class harbored critical attitudes toward rural society and culture. Likewise, the strains created by the continuing high rates of in-migration created tensions within the working class. The deep, subterranean ties that linked Moscow's proletariat to the countryside proved to be in political terms a double-edged sword.

Notes

1. *Statisticheskii spravochnik . . . 1927g.*, 12-13; *Perepis' . . . 1926g.*, tom. 2, tab. V, 110. While the sources agree on the 1920 and 1926 population figures, there exist two different figures for that of 1923. The 1923 census puts it at 1,511,025. *Perepisi 1923g.*, chast' I, tab. I, 13; chast' II, tab. I, 20. However, another TsSU source puts the figure 1,542,874. *Statisticheski ezhegodnik 1922-1923* (Moscow, 1924), vyp. 1, chast' I, tab. 1, 1-2. Regardless of the figure used, the rate of growth from 1920 to 1923 was about 45 percent.

2. *Vsia Moskva, adresnaia i spravochnaia kniga na 1929g.* (Moscow, 1929), otd. 1, 19; Aleshchenko, *Moskovskii sovet*, 400. Between 1923 and 1926, the rate of population growth in Moscow was the tenth highest of all urban areas in the USSR. However, save for Leningrad, none of the nine fastest growing urban centers had a population in excess of one million. In 1926, Leningrad with a population of 1,592,158 was the second largest city. The ten fastest growing urban centers during these years were: Novosibirsk (+62 percent), Ivanovo-Voznesensk (+55 percent), Leningrad (+49 percent), Dnepropetrovsk (+48 percent), Samarkand (+42 percent), Sverdlovsk (+40 percent), Stalingrad (+38 percent), Kharkov (+33 percent), Baku and its suburbs (+33 percent), and Moscow (+31 percent). NKVD, *Goroda soiuza SSR* (Moscow, 1927), 17. The reason for the discrepancy in the growth rate of Moscow in 1923-1926 between this source and *Vsia Moskva, 1929* is unclear.

3. Of the major urban areas in the USSR, females accounted for a majority of the populations in all but Baku and Tashkent. NKVD, *Goroda soiuza*, 18.

4. *Statisticheskii spravochnik . . . 1927*, 30-31; *Perepis' . . . 1926g.*, tom. 2, tab. IX, 198-199.

5. Boris Urlanis, "Some Demographic Trends," *Town, Country and People* (ed. G. V. Osipov, London, 1969), 42. In 1919, the infant mortality rates

in European countries ranged from a high of 156.4 in Austria to a low of 61.8 in Norway. U. S. Public Health Service, National Office of Vital Statistics, *Summary of International Vital Statistics* (Washington, 1947). During the 1920s, European infant mortality rates ranged from a high of 128 in Germany (1924-1925) to a low of 52 in Norway (1921-1925). *Le Mouvement Natural de la Population dans le Monde de 1906 a 1936* (Paris, 1954), 65.

6. Bradley, " 'Muzhik' and Muscovite, " 161-163.

7. See the discussion in Susan M. Kingsbury and Mildred Fairchild, *Factory, Family and Woman in the Soviet Union* (New York, 1935), 151-157.

8.

AVERAGE LIFE EXPECTANCY IN RUSSIA AND THE SOVIET UNION

AGE GROUP	1895-1897	1926-1927
UP TO 1 YEAR	32 YEARS	44 YEARS
1-5	50	57
6-10	49	54
11-20	34	38
21-40	27	30
41-50	20	23
51-60	14	16
61-70	10	10
71-80	7	6

SOURCE: V. N. Starovskii, "The Analysis of Population Growth," *Town, Country and People*, 37.

9. Moscow's nuptiality rate for selected years was: 1905 - 4.8; 1910 - 5.7; 1916 - 3.9; 1917 - 5.4; 1918 - 7.5; 1919 - 17.4; 1920 - 19.1; 1921 - 16.9; 1922 - 15.3; 1923 - 15.6; 1924 - 14.2. Private owners had the highest and workers the second highest nuptiality rates in 1926. I. Iu. Pisarev, *Narodonaselenie SSSR: sotsial'no-ekonomicheskii ocherk* (Moscow, 1967), 180; *Moskovskii sovet 1917-1927*, 182-183.

10. *Trud v Moskovskoi gubernii v 1923-1925gg.: sbornik statisticheskh materialov* (Moscow, 1925), 2-3.

11. For data on the cause of death, see: *Ezhemesiachyi statisticheskii bulleten' po gorodu Moskve i Moskovskii gubernii* (Moscow, 1924-1928), Jan. 1924-Dec. 1928, otd. III, tab. 1, 5; *Moskva i Moskovskaia guberniia: statistiko-ekonomicheskii spravochnik, 1923/24-1927/28* (Moscow, 1929), tab. 13, 12-13. During the cholera epidemic of 1922, the press gave considerable coverage to the incidence of diseases—typhus as well as cholera—and gave advice on how to prevent contracting the diseases. For examples, see: *Rabochaia Moskva*, March 21, May 27, June 8, July 15, 1922; *Stroitel'stvo Moskvy*, 3 (1924), 34-35; 7 (1925), 15-16. On the natural population increase, see *Statisticheskii spravochnik . . . 1927g.*, 12-13.

12. S. Bogoslovskii, "Sostoianie zdorov'ia promyshlennykh rabochikh i sluzashchikh," *Statisticheskoe obozrenie*, 12 (1927), 91-98.

13. A 1924 study of juveniles revealed that 43 percent had medical problems—43 percent were anemic, 15 percent had tuberculosis, and 30 percent were underdeveloped or had other illnesses. *Professional'nye soiuzy SSSR, 1924-1926gg.: otchet V.Ts.S.P.S. k VII s"ezdu professional'nykh soiuzov*

(Moscow, 1926), 128-129. A 1928 study of pupils in Khamovnicheskii *raion*, a working-class district in Moscow, revealed that 85 percent were anemic, 75 percent had tuberculosis, and 40 percent suffered from deformation of the spine. *Komsomol'skaia Pravda*, January 18, 1929.

14. *Ezhemesiachyi statisticheskii bulleten'*, January 1925-December 1928, otd. III, tab. 1, 5; *Moskva i Moskovskaia guberniia*, tab. 13, 12-13. For a discussion of the relationship between housing and working conditions and tuberculosis, see *Rabochaia Moskva*, November 21, 1922. See also *Moskovskii sovet, 1917-1927*, 414-418.

15. Robert E. Johnson, "Peasant Migration and the Russian Working Class: Moscow at the End of the Nineteenth Century," *Slavic Review*, 35, 4, (1976), 656; Johnson, *Peasant and Proletarian*, 42-50.

16. The model life table can be found in United Nations, *Methods of Population Projection by Sex and Age* (New York, 1956), tab. 3. *Perepis'...1926g.*, tom. 2, tab. IX, 198-199.

17. The natural increase of the city's population from 1921 to 1927 inclusive was 141,976. That figure includes a natural population decrease of 4,670 in 1922 as a result of epidemics and the famine of 1921-1922. *Statisticheskii spravochnik...1927*, 12-13. The average annual rate of natural growth from 1923 to 1927 was 15.5 per thousand residents per annum; the comparable figure for the period 1910-1914 was 8.2.

18. *Perepis' . . . 1926g.*, tom. 36, tab. IV, 142.

19. Teodor Shanin, *The Awkward Class: Political Sociology of Peasantry in a Developing Society, Russia, 1910-1925* (Oxford, 1972), 92-93.

20. *Perepis' . . . 1926g.*, tom. 36, tab. V, 216-221. The CIR included the following *gubernii* in 1926: Moscow, Kaluga, Tula, Riazan, Tver, Iaroslavl', Kostroma, Ivanovo-Voznesensk, Vladimir, and Nizhnii-Novgorod. The TsSU considered only certain *volosti* in Tambov as part of the CIR. Unfortunately, it is impossible to distinguish *volosti* in the 1926 census and, for this reason, I have considered all of Tambov as part of the Central Black Earth Region. The CIR in 1926 differed slightly from its namesake in the pre-revolutionary period. For a discussion of the changes in its composition, see Lorimer, 68, 245.

21. Johnson, *Peasant and Proletarian*, 31-35. Bradley, "*Muzhik* and Muscovite," 29-35.

22. Data on the population density of the provinces of the CIR can be found in M. Vol'f and G. A. Mebus, *Tsentral'no-promyshlennaia oblast'* (Moscow, 1926), 3.

23. Thomas Fedor, *Patterns of Urban Growth in the Russian Empire* (Chicago, 1975), 120; J. William Leasure and Robert A. Lewis, "Internal Migration in the USSR: 1897-1926," *Demography*, 4, 2 (1967), 479-496.

24. *Perepis' . . . 1926g.*, tom. 36, dop. I k tab. III-IV, 174-183. See Johnson, "Peasant Migration," 658, for a discussion of duration of residence patterns of peasants residing in Moscow in 1882-1902.

25. *Perepis' . . . 1926g.*, tom. 36, tab. IV, 142.

26. As quoted in Babun, 65.

27. Kabo, *Ocherki*, 34-39.

28. *Ibid.*, 69-72.

29. On *zemliachestvo*, see Johnson, *Peasant and Proletarian*, 68-77. Comparable networks performed the same functions in nineteenth century England. Michael Anderson, *Family Structure in Nineteenth Century Lancashire* (Cambridge, 1971). For an example of a Russian worker who had had prior contact with the city before moving there permanently and obtained work with the help of *zemliaki*, see Kabo, *Ocherki*, 55.

30. Bradley, "*Muzhik* and Muscovite," 29-32, discusses some of the "push-pull" factors which caused peasants in pre-revolutionary time to migrate. See also Johnson, *Peasant and Proletarian*, 28-42.

31. Vol'f and Mebus, 24-28; I. Stepanov, *25 biudzhetov krest'ianskikh khoziastv Moskovskoi gubernii* (Moscow, 1925), 11-12; A. M. Bol'shakov, *Sovetskaia derevnia* (Leningrad, 1924), 13-23. For a discussion of the methods of redistribution, see: Shanin; D. J. Male, *Russian Peasant Organization before Collectivization: A Study of Commune and Gathering, 1925-1930* (London, 1971); Moshe Lewin, *Russian Peasants and Soviet Power: A Study of Collectivization* (Evanston, Ill., 1968).

32. The various estimates of the size of the excess rural population are discussed in V. P. Danilov, "Krest'ianskii otkhod na promyshly v 1920-kh godakh," *Istoricheskie zapiski*, 94 (1974), 62-67. See also Bol'shakov, 5-16.

33. Vol'f and Mebus, 26.

34. As quoted in Male, 37.

35. For a discussion of the economic situation in the CIR, see: Vol'f and Mebus, 4-7, 24-36; George H. Pavolvsky, *Agricultural Russia on the Eve of the Revolution* (London, 1930), 39-45, 323-325.

36. Bol'shakov, 5-6; Vol'f and Mebus, 45; Lewin, *Russian Peasants*, 184-185; Stepanov, *25 biudzhetov*, 147-151. See also Louis Fischer, *Men and Politics: Europe Between the Two World Wars* (New York, 1965), 82. According to Lewin, *Russian Peasants*, 36, not until 1925/26 did the peasantry begin to live above the poverty line for the first time since the revolution.

37. Shanin, 70-128.

38. *Sbornik statisticheskikh svedenii po SSSR* (Moscow, 1924), 108-111. According to Anita Baker, "Deterioration or Development: The Peasant Economy of Moscow Province Prior to 1914," *Russian History/Histoire Russe*, 5, Part 1 (1978), 14, in 1911 94 percent of the families in the province were both laborers and farmers. The most common types of activities were spinning, weaving, wood and metalworking, and food processing; many were performed on a putting-out basis.

39. On wages in rural and urban areas and the role of the latter in luring migrants, see: Danilov, "Krest'ianskii otkhod," 73; L. D. Mints, *Agrarnoe perenaselenie i rynok trud SSSR* (Moscow, 1929), 338-339. Wages are discussed at length in chapter 5.

40. For a discussion of cultural modernity, see Barbara Anderson, *Internal Migration*, 5-6, 85-120.

41. As quoted in Petro G. Grigorenko, *Memoirs* (Thomas P. Whitney, trans., New York, 1982), 22. See also Pearl S. Buck, *Talk about Russia with Masha Scott* (New York, 1945). Evidence of this spectrum of opinion regard-

ing cities can be found in literature as well. For examples, see: F. V. Gladkov, *Cement* (A. S. Arthur and C. Ashleigh, trans., New York, 1971); Mikhail Sholokhov, *And Quiet Flows the Don* (Stephen Garry, trans., New York, 1966)

42. Danilov, "Krest'ianskii otkhod," 71-72; Mints, *Agrarnoe perenaselenie*, 408-415. For discussions of *otkhodnichestvo* within the CIR, see: *ibid.*, 289-299, 350-354; L. E. Mints, ed., *Voprosy truda v tsifrakh: statisticheskii spravochnik za 1927-1930gg. k XVI s"ezdu VKP(b)* (Moscow, 1930), tab. 16, 34-35; Vol'f and Mebus, 15; *Voprosy truda*, 8-9 (1927), 316; *ibid.*, 10 (1927), 206-207; Danilov, "Krest'ianskii otkhod," 71-80.

43. Danilov, "Krest'ianskii otkhod," 74-94; Mints, *Agrarnoe perenaselenie*, 326-391 passim; E. Zakgeim, "Stroiteli-otkhodniki," *Statisticheskoe obozrenie*, 10 (1929), 66-72.

44. *Statisticheskii ezhegodnik g. Moskvy i Moskovskoi gubernii za 1926g.* (Moscow, 1928), 350-354, 408-415; A. I. Khriashcheva, *Gruppy i klassy v krest'ianstve* (Moscow, 1926), 35 as noted in Suvorov, *Istoricheskii opyt*, 73; Danilov, "Krest'ianskii otkhod," 97-100.

45. *Voprosy truda*, 10 (1927), 316. *Otkhodniki*-builders could earn in four months the income produced by the average peasant household in a year. Mints, *Voprosy*, 39. See also: Danilov: "Krest'ianskii otkhod," 73; *Statisticheskii ezhegodnik . . . 1926g.*, 160-178.

46. *Statisticheskii ezhegodnik . . . 1926g.*, 81; *Voprosy truda*, 8-9 (1927), 316; Mints *Agrarnoe perenaselenie*, 350-354.

47. Zakgeim, "Stroiteli-otkhodniki," 66-72

48. Mints, *Agrarnoe perenaselenie*, 312-315; Zakgeim, "Stroiteli-otkhodniki," 66-72. For data on seasonal oscillations of *otkhodnichestvo* by *guberniia* within the CIR, see *Voprosy truda*, 6 (1927), 171.

49. Grunt, "Moskovskii proletariat," 101; *Moskva za desiat' let*, 9-10.

50. *Perepis' . . . 1926g.*, tom. 55, tab. II, 128-129. See also M. Krasil'-nikov, "Sviaz naseleniia g. Moskvy s nadel'noi zemlei," *Statisticheskoe obozrenie*, 6 (1928), 103-107.

51. Sula Benet, trans. and ed., *The Village of Viriatino* (New York, 1970), 203; Stephen F. Dunn and Ethel Dunn, *The Peasants of Central Russia* (New York, 1967), 81-85.

52. Krasil'nikov, 104-105.

53. A. G. Rashin, *Sostav fabrichno-zavodskogo proletariata SSSR. Predvaritel'nye itogi perepisi metalistov, gornorabochikh i tekstil'shchikov v 1929g.* (Moscow, 1930), 16-46; Shkaratan, 264.

54. A worker told Emma Goldman that he and his family would have perished during the Civil War had it not been for his relatives in the countryside and the sale of their produce on the black market. Goldman, 53.

55. Kabo, *Ocherki*, 103-107.

56. *Rabochaia Moskva*, July 7, 1922.

57. S. V. Antronov, "Sviaz tekstil'nykh rabochikh s zemleiu i iiul'skie otpuska," *Izvestiia tekstil'noi promyshlennosti i torgovli*, 23-24 (1927), 4-7. Within the CIR and Moscow *guberniia*, about one-quarter of the textile workers had a *nadel* in the countryside. See also *Moskovskii proletarii*, June 22, June 29, 1924.

58. For the announcement that the Staro-Gorkinskaia manufactory would close during the sowing season, see *Rabochaia Moskva*, February 2, 1922.

59. Johnson, *Peasant and Proletarian*, 28-50. According to Schwartz, *Labor*, 3, the percentage of workers (by industry) who returned to their villages to help work the land was: food and beverage, 65.4 percent; animal products, 46.1 percent; minerals, 35.4 percent; lumber, 30.3 percent; textiles, 16.5 percent; metals, 11.1 percent.

60. Kabo, *Ocherki*, 47-51.

61. Krasil'nikov, 103.

62. For examples, see: *Moskovskii proletarii*, June 22, June 29, 1924; *Rabochaia Moskva*, July 7, 1922.

63. A. Aluf, "Profsoiuzy i krest'ianstvo," *Vestnik truda*, 1 (1925), 47-54.

64. *Ezhemesiachyi statisticheskii bulleten'*, Jan. 1924-Mar. 1928, otd. II, tab. 1, 4; Apr.-Aug. 1928, otd. I, tab. 1, 4; Sep.-Dec. 1928, otd. II, tab. 1, 5. Comparable seasonal oscillations occurred in marital patterns in the village of Selo Bol'she in Riazan guberniia during 1906-1925. L. K. Khotsianov, *Opyt izucheniia demografichskikh sdvigov v sel'skom naselenii Moskovskoi i Riazanskoi oblastei, 1851-1960* (Moscow, 1963), 97. The marital patterns in Moscow during the 1920s also resembled those in rural France in the 1860s and in the years before World War I. However, they bore no resemblance to the marital patterns of the Parisian population. See Henri Leridon, *Natalite, Saisons et Conjuncture Economique* (Paris, 1975), 65.

65. *Ezhemesiachyi statisticheskii bulleten'*, Jan. 1924-Mar. 1928, otd. II, tab. 1, 4; Apr.-Aug. 1928, otd. I, tab. 1, 4; Sep.-Dec. 1928, otd. II, tab. 1, 5. A similar pattern of births prevailed in Moscow at the end of the nineteenth century. P. I. Kurikin, *Statistika dvizheniia naseleniia v Moskovskoi gubernii, 1883-1897* (Moscow, 1902), as discussed in Bradley, "*Muzhik* and Muscovite," 308.

66. B. Iagolin, "Rozhdaemost po g. Moskve v sviazi s sotsial'nym sostavom naseleniia," *Statisticheskoe obozrenie*, 10 (1928), 85-88.

67. The extent to which the rural sector should "pay" was at the heart of the industrialization debates of the 1920s. See Alexander Ehrlich, *The Soviet Industrialization Debate, 1924-1928* (Cambridge, Mass., 1960).

3. The Moscow Labor Force, 1921-1929

By 1921, the working class's disintegration halted and its restoration began. Skilled and experienced workers left the army and villages and re-entered the factories. But that restoration was never completed because too few former workers returned to the factories. By 1923 or 1924 at the latest, those former workers who planned to return to the bench had done so. However, they were not the only ones to enter the industrial labor force. Peasant migrants joined them. During the very early 1920s, migrants unfamilar with production were a minority. The demands of industrial restoration and the official policies designed to spur it favored experienced workers. To hire them, factory managers fired the women, juveniles, and "yesterdays peasants" who staffed the factories during the Civil War. But from 1923, the restoration of the proletariat began to give way to its dilution as increasing numbers of inexperienced and unskilled rural migrants secured factory employment.

During the NEP, Moscow's proletariat was quite heterogeneous in terms of social origins, skill levels, work experience, and attitudes, and consciousness. It was a class in which centrifugal and centripetal forces were at work. Its changing composition, the period's labor policies and work conditions, and its relations with other social groups combined both to unite and divide the working class. But the fracture lines were not always clean. Groups within that class, such as hereditary, urban workers and new workers fresh from the villages, came into conflict over such issues as labor discipline. Other issues, such as attitudes toward management, simultaneously worked to unify that class. The remainder of this study will examine in detail these centrifugal and centripetal forces and their consequences. To do so, however, requires that we first analyze the composition of and general lines of division within the pro-letariat. Because workers did not live in social isolation, we will also briefly examine the other major occupational groups with which they interacted.

Let us begin by examining the general characteristics of the city's workforce. Throughout the decade, the working population accounted for 54 percent of all residents.[1] But as table 3-1 indicates, this stability did not reflect the restoration of the pre-revolutionary pattern. On the contrary, the relatively low proportion of working residents stood in sharp contrast to the situation in 1912, when two-thirds of the population worked.

Given that by 1926, the city's economy had reached its prewar indices, what explains this significant shift? Two important reasons have already been discussed—rising natural population growth, and the increased number of families and dependents, especially young children. Of greater importance was the changed composition of the city's labor force. A comparison of the occupational structure in 1912 and 1926 graphically illustrates the change (see appendix 5). In the former year, workers were the largest occupational group and comprised 40 percent of the working population; in the latter year, they accounted for about one-quarter of that population and their numbers had shrunken by 113,000. Employees, whose ranks had grown by one-third during the period, replaced workers as the largest occupational group in the capital of the workers' state. The presence of the national and RSFSR governments there accounts for most of the growth. Domestics, free professionals, and proprietors all shared the proletariat's experience; each had fewer members in 1926 than in 1912. Only one other group witnessed an expansion of their ranks: the unemployed, whose ranks quadrupled. Excluding the unemployed, the city's working population in 1926 counted 54,000 fewer people than in 1912.[2]

TABLE 3-1
Working and Nonworking Residents of Moscow, 1912-1926

Year	Working	Nonworking	Per 100 people Working	Nonworking
1912	1,051,000	565,000	65	35
1918	917,000	781,000	54	46
1920	564,000	388,000	60	40
1923	794,000	687,000	54	46
1926	1,101,667	924,280	54	46

SOURCE: *Trud v Moskovskoi gubernii*, 2; *Perepis' . . . 1926g.*, tom. 19, tab. I, 118.

As before the revolution, males dominated the workforce. By 1926, they outnumbered females by almost two to one (63.2 percent vs. 36.8 percent). That gap, which widened as the decade progressed, was particularly evident in industry where males comprised three-quarters of the workforce. Industrial employers preferred to hire males, a perference based on higher average male productivity and patriarchal attitudes. The only occupational groups in which the ratio of males to females narrowed during the 1920s were employees, domestics, family members helping proprietors, and "others," that is, jobs that defy precise categorization and were dull and low paying. The higher proportion of female employees was due almost entirely to their increased numbers among secretaries, clerical personnel, and minor service personnel such as launderers, cleaners, and wetnurses. Women accounted for 99 percent of the city's domestics.[3] The decreasing proportion of working women marked a sharp reversal from the war years (1914-1921) when their ranks swelled steadily. Although they were a majority of the city's residents and males' legal equal, women often found the quest to assert their rights to be a difficult one. Old attitudes died hard.

Working Class

The Moscow proletariat in 1917 numbered between 410,000 and 420,000 members, 45 percent of whom worked in factories.[4] By late 1920, that class's ranks were halved and only 81,000 were industrial workers. With economic restoration went that of the proletariat. By mid-1923, the industrial working class had grown by 58 percent; during the next three years, it expanded by another 34 percent (see appendix 6). Nonetheless in 1926, the city's proletariat was 46 percent smaller than it had been in 1912—it numbered only 293,000, almost 60 percent of whom were industrial workers. During the NEP, there were fewer workers in virtually occupation.[5] This reduction resulted from fundamental structural changes in the city's economy.

The state had become the major employer of industrial labor. As such, its systematic application of the policies of industrial concentration and *khozrachet* restricted the working-class's growth and dramatically changed its size and structure. These policies together with those designed to rationalize and intensify labor sharply reduced the demand for labor. The inflation of the early 1920s, continual shortages of capital, and legal restrictions imposed on private enterprise served to retard the restoration of small industries and thereby further limit employment opportunities. As table 3-2 demonstrates, the policy of industrial concentration resulted in a slight expansion in the number of large and very large industries and a 30 percent decline in that of small industries.[6] The demands of *khozrachet*, in turn, meant that state enterprises had to hire fewer people if they were to remain profitable. The table clearly indicates these policies' success and consequences. While they forced a more rational allocation of labor, machinery, and capital, Moscow had fewer productive enterprises and workers in the 1920s than in 1917. In light of this, the rapid economic recovery during the NEP is all the more impressive.

Seven years of warfare also significantly changed the occupational structure of the city's proletariat. In pre-revolutionary times, the city was known as "calico Moscow," the country's textile production center. Cut off from domestic and imported materials during the Civil War, the textile industry virtually collapsed. During the NEP, the partial eco-

TABLE 3-2
Concentration of Industry and the Working Class, Moscow, 1917, 1924/25

Size of industrial plant	1917		1924/25	
Small (1-100 workers)				
No. of establishments	738	69.4%	520	63.9%
No. of workers	29,663	15.9%	19,993	12.9%
Medium (101-500 workers)				
No. of establishments	253	23.8%	218	26.8%
No. of workers	54,550	29.1%	50,835	32.8%
Large (501-1,000 workers)				
No. of establishments	45	4.2%	47	5.8%
No. of workers	32,026	17.1%	31,958	20.6%
Very large (1,001 or more workers)				
No. of establishments	28	2.6%	29	3.6%
No. of workers	70,909	37.9%	52,071	33.6%
Totals				
No. of establishments	1,064	100%	814	100.1%[a]
No. of workers	187,148	100%	158,857	99.9%[a]

SOURCE: Grunt, "Moskovskii proletariat," 94-97; *Fabrichno-zavodskaia promyshlennost' gor. Moskvy i Moskovskoi gubernii, 1917-1927gg.* (Moscow, 1928), tab. 21, 102-109.
a. Due to rounding.

nomic blockade slowed the restoration of the city's once premier industry and rationalization and mechanization reduced the demand for labor. By 1923, it employed fewer than half the workers it had in 1917. The rapid economic recovery during the next two years permitted the industry to replenish its ranks somewhat, but in 1926, it employed 20 percent fewer workers than in 1917. Only after the introduction of the seven-hour day in 1928 (to be discussed in chapter six) did the textile industry witness its workforce's restoration. While the size of that industry's workforce differed markedly from pre-revolutionary times, its composition did not. Women continued to account for a majority (71 percent in 1926) of textile workers. Upward of half (47.5 percent) of them were skilled; most of them were weavers.[7]

During the 1920s, metalworkers were the largest group of industrial laborers. The demand for military wares during World War I spurred the growth of the metal industry and, by 1917, its workforce rivalled that of textile workers.[8] Although it too experienced a dramatic reduction during the Civil War, military orders and deferments for skilled workers somewhat muted the metal industry's collapse. Because its products were essential to industrial restoration and economic recovery, the ranks of metalworkers expanded sharply during the early 1920s, but then leveled off after 1924. One-third of the industry's laborers in 1926 were classified as metalworkers (*slesari*), the most general occupational category and one which could be filled by a less-than-skilled worker. An equal proportion of the newly hired metalworkers were unskilled peasants. Males dominated that industry; only 8.5 percent of all metalworkers were females. Skilled workers were in the minority. In this industry, the polarization between new and experienced workers was greater than in most others.

Metal and textile workers were far and away the city's two largest industrial occupations; together they accounted for 42.5 percent of its 1926 factory workforce. In both industries, most workers labored in large, mechanized enterprises in which the drive to lower production costs by means of rationalization, intensification, and mechanization was most intense. They were also the industries in which one found the highest proportion of Communist Party members and large numbers of new and inexperienced workers. As such, they were volatile microcosms of the proletariat at large and will receive the brunt of our attention.

In absolute terms, the city's printers trailed a distant third behind these two occupations; yet their ranks expanded rapidly during the decade. Their growth reflected the mounting demand for their products by the party and state, but it also acts as a crude barometer of the city's and country's rising literacy rate. For the same reasons, the number of paper industry workers rose. The number of railroad and power plant workers also increased in the 1920s. The former's growth represented the continuation of an historic process. As the railroad transport sector expanded, so too did the size of its hubs' workforce. The growth of the power plant workers' ranks reflected the government's determined policy to extend electrification to the entire country. The metal, printing, paper, and railroad industries were unique during the NEP—their workforces were larger than before the revolution, and they grew steadily. In the others, particularly the garment, leather, food, and tobacco industries, the state's labor policies and the shortage of capital with which to open private enterprises meant that their labor forces either declined or stagnated throughout the 1920s. Consequently, many experienced and skilled workers in these industries had to change occupations or suffered prolonged unemployment.

As this brief survey of the city's occupational structure indicates, the restoration of its proletariat was anything but a linear process. The failure of many former enterprises, especially small and medium size ones, to reopen and the consolidation of others limited employment opportunities at a time of rapid population growth. The return of experienced and skilled workers from the army and villages meant that many women and juveniles lost their jobs. The supply of labor outstripped demand for it throughout the decade. The flip-side of economic recovery was widespread unemployment. While economic restoration brought renewed hope to most Muscovites, for others it was a frustrating and traumatic time.

Nonetheless, during the 1920s, increasing numbers of peasants secured industrial employment and thereby strengthened the proletariat's ties to the land. By 1926, one of every six Moscow workers owned land, and a majority of them worked that land. The proportion of landowning workers varied from occupation to occupation, but it was highest in male-dominated industries. For example, among metalworkers about one-quarter owned land and the steady influx of peasants into this industry—35 percent of all new workers—ensured that rural ties remained strong. Among textile workers, however, rural bonds appear to have been loosening. Half as many textile workers as metalworkers owned land, a reflection of the industry's sexual composition and the fact that with each passing year the proportion of new textile workers who were of peasant origin declined.[9] Land ownership remained common in those occupations, especially construction and transport work (e.g. carters, cabmen, stevedores, and so forth), which traditionally attracted migrants. Most workers in these occupations usually worked for only a year or so and then returned to their villages, but some used their union membership to secure better paying, industrial jobs. Forced to keep labor costs low, many factories hired these and other inexperienced rural migrants to fill new positions or those vacated by departing skilled workers. In this way, the restoration of the proletariat gave way to the dilution of that class during the second half of the decade.[10]

As significant as the influx of peasants into the factories was, a different but equally important process was also taking place—the growth of an urban hereditary proletariat. Although hereditary workers remained a minority during the NEP, their ranks grew steadily. A survey of the social background of newly hired metal and cotton workers revealed that about half in the former industry and upward of 60 percent in the latter industry were the offspring of workers.[11] Within the proletariat at large, this process was even more pronounced. In families headed by workers, two-thirds of the family members were also workers; where the family head was an industrial worker, the proportion was still greater—90 percent.[12]

Although historically significant, the difficulty that many workers' children had getting jobs slowed the hereditary proletariat's growth. According to the 1922 Labor Code, a fixed quota (7 percent) of an enterprise's workforce had to be juveniles (*podrostki*, ages sixteen to eighteen). Juvenile workers worked only six hours a day, but earned a full day's wages. While on the job, they received training; after work, they attended factory schools. Because of the policy's high costs, many factory directors refused to meet the hiring quota. In 1928, the quotas were revised downward, but many still ignored them. Throughout the decade, juveniles comprised less than 5 percent of the workforce.[13]

Some employers also resisted establishing apprenticeship programs for *podrostki*. Many such programs were periodically dismantled and revived. In many cases, factory directors organized such training programs only under intense pressure from their workers who wanted their children to learn a skill. But upon "graduation," very few jobs awaited these young and often qualified applicants. The inability of many workers' children to find employment and receive training angered their parents and many union, party, and especially Komsomol officials.[14] The rising juvenile unemployment rate became a major concern.

Employers also discriminated against women. By 1921, females comprised half of the city's work force and 40 percent of its proletariat. With the demobilization of the Red Army and the return of former workers from the villages, males replaced many women. The proportion of female workers declined steadily during the NEP—from 35.7 percent in 1923 to 25.6 percent in 1926.[15] There were numerous reasons for this trend, not the least of which was an official policy to hire demobilized soldiers even if it meant dismissing women workers. Employers did not have to be pressured to execute this policy. They preferred to hire males who were, on average, more literate, skilled, experienced, productive and, above all, men.[16]

Women had to struggle not only against employers' patriarchal attitudes but also those of workers. The struggle was an arduous one. Their harassment often proved so intolerable that many women were forced to quit their jobs. This mistreatment usually consisted of verbal taunts and a steady stream of petty annoyances. On occasion, however, male workers forcibly removed unwanted females from the factory.[17] Despite the party's call for a "more resolute involvement of a wide strata of the female proletariat" in the workforce, discrimination against women remained a reality of factory life.[18] Females accounted for a majority of only five of the city's industries in 1926: tobacco (90.4 percent), garment (73.5 percent), textiles (71.1 percent), paper production (62.9 percent), and chemicals (56.8 percent).[19] Many jobs in these industries required no skill, and consequently women had few opportunities to improve their qualifications. Males dominated the skilled jobs that did exist. The relatively low female literacy rate also hindered their chances for promotion.

The problem of worker illiteracy was not confined to females. The revolutionary government set the elimination of illiteracy as one of its primary goals. Correctly, it viewed literacy as an avenue to personal advancement, increased skill acquisition and hence productivity, and the integration of workers into the government and higher echelons of the economy. Toward this end, the party, soviets, and trade unions opened schools and literacy classes in workplaces, factory clubs and neighborhoods. The quality of these classes varied markedly. But even taking the insufficiencies into account, the struggle against illiteracy remained one of the Soviet government's great early accomplishments. Whereas in 1902, three-quarters of the city's males and slightly less than half of its females were literate, by 1926 the literacy rate had risen to 91.5 percent for males and 77.6 percent for females. Yet, more than 51,000 workers (most of whom were recent migrants) remained illiterate. Literacy rates varied with occupation, skill levels, and age group. In general, young workers and skilled workers had the highest rates and the most amount of formal education; semiskilled and unskilled workers who owned land were more likely to be illiterate.[20]

While worker illiteracy remained an obstacle to greater worker productivity, its importance paled in comparison with the shortage of skilled workers. As we have seen, that shortage reached crisis proportions from 1918 to 1920. In the early 1920s, the ranks of these valued workers expanded somewhat. But in February 1926, Gosplan reported that "the supplies of skilled labor on the labor market have been exhausted."[21] Speaking of the textile industry in that same year, one author claimed that "all the reasons for our backwardness [relative to the west—W. C.] can be found in the low quality of our workforce."[22] Throughout the decade, press articles repeatedly stated that the lack of skilled workers frustrated raising worker productivity. As time passed, the number of lamentations increased.[23] A study of selected Moscow workers in 1929 revealed that only one-quarter of the metal and machine construction workers were skilled or highly skilled. One-third of all new workers hired in these industries were unskilled rural migrants. The situation was slightly better in the cotton industry where about 40 percent of the workers were skilled or highly skilled. Despite the differences between industries, one undeniable fact remained—most workers were unskilled or semiskilled and too few were technically literate.[24]

Skill is often a function of age and duration of work experience. The vast majority of Moscow's highly skilled and skilled metal and cotton workers in 1929 were in their late thirties or older and had more than fifteen years of production experience.[25] During the 1920s, half of the proletariat was younger than thirty, and that proportion crept upward annually as young migrants entered the workforce. It is easy to understand the urgency that party and union officials attached to the development of technical training. But the creation of training institutions required considerable capital, a commodity in short supply during the decade. Even in those schools that were created, the dearth of skilled workers meant that the faculty was not of the highest quality. Worker training proceeded at too slow a pace and the quality of some graduates left much to be desired.[26]

High worker turnover compounded the shortage of skilled workers. On average, highly skilled and skilled metal and cotton workers in Moscow in 1929 possessed eighteen to twenty years of production experience (*stazh*). But the average duration of employment in those industries was about eight and one-half years. Most of those industries' workers had only a few years of continuous experience in any given factory. Unskilled and semiskilled workers frequently changed jobs in hopes of securing better wages, work conditions, and housing. Such mobility frustrated attempts to impart skills to workers.[27]

Clearly the Moscow industrial proletariat in the 1920s was a heterogeneous and changing social class. Within its ranks, one could find workers who were skilled and unskilled, experienced and inexperienced, literate and illiterate, hereditary urban proletarians and uninitiated peasants. At times, these differences created significant intraclass tensions, tensions exacerbated by the demands of labor policies and practices. Examining these tensions provides the focus for the rest of this study. But to appreciate the manner in which they gave rise to intraclass divisions and alliances, it is important to first identify the fracture lines that divided the class.

Three reasonably distinct groups existed within the proletariat; two of the three possessed a distinct *oblik* (cast of mind, mentalité, or political and social outlook). The three groups occupy points on a spectrum. At one extreme stood the urban and urbanized workers; at the other, new workers. Between them was the semiproletariat. Within the latter group, there existed a myriad of gradations; it was a transitional group—some of its members possessed the characteristics of urban workers, while others had only recently emerged from the ranks of new workers. The model is a dynamic one; it allows for workers' evolution from one point on the spectrum to another.[28]

What distinguished the urban worker was an urban-industrial worldview. Most were urban-born, hereditary proletarians. During the 1920s, such workers were the exception; only one-fifth of the city's proletariat were locally born. Within their ranks could be found people of all age groups, none of whom had direct village ties. Another group supplemented the urban proletarians—urbanized workers who had spent the majority of their lives immersed in an urban, industrial environment, andwho had wholeheartedly assimilated and embraced that world's values. While urbanized workers will be included under the rubric of urban worker, it must be understood that it was not simply the passage of time, but the manifestation of the values attributed to the urban worker which permit their inclusion.

To urban workers, the world was by and large rational. They could subject their economic and occupational environment to analysis and, by so doing, understand and, within limits, master it. The products of reason and science permeated and defined their lives: they labored in factories that, like the urban setting in which they lived, testified to the power of science and technology; they used tools and machinery to process and transform the products of nature. Their labors' results were part of the larger industrial process, and their role in its creation and growth was intelligible. They believed that industrial progress held the key to their and society's future.

Literacy and education, the tools that permit one to understand and, to a certain extent, direct their environment were virtually universal among urban workers. Skilled workers over thirty had very high literacy rates; so too did workers in their early twenties. What distinguished the two was that many of the latter had studied in Soviet schools, the most popular of which were apprentice and technical schools.[29] These institutions inculated and reinforced urban-industrial values. Of course, there were some uneducated and illiterate urban workers. Most were over forty and possessed extensive industrial experience. But even among this group, some people availed themselves of the many post-revolutionary educational opportunities.

Positive attitudes toward their work also characterized the urban workers. They displayed discipline and initiative on the job and took pride in their performance. They possessed self-discipline, time-discipline, and labor-discipline. These types of discipline extended to all aspects of their job performance: they arrived at work punctually, worked a full day, coordinated the pace of their work to the machine's movement, took breaks only at the prescribed time, and abstained from drinking and horseplay on the job. They believed that discipline produced its own rewards which rebounded to the individual's and society's favor.

Urban workers were more likely than other workers to concern themselves not simply with their own narrow responsibilities, but also with the improvement of overall factory operations. Many actively participated in factory meetings and production meetings, where they expressed their criticisms, opinions, and ideas to improve production. What motivated this participation was their desire to improve their and the factory's well-being, and "the great idea that the industries are theirs (sic) and that some day they would come in for the fruits of their own labor."[30]

Among urban workers, literacy, skill, interest in socio-political issues, and social activism went hand-in-hand. As one observor of the proletariat aptly stated: "The greater the skill [and level of education— W. C.], the more frequent the attendance at lectures, circles, especially

113

political ones, and the greater the number of newspapers read."[31] This was undoubtedly true of urban workers. Skilled workers and younger, educated, hereditary workers read newspapers more often than did their fellow workers.[32] They also exhibited the highest degree of political activism and class consciousness. According to the 1929 trade union census, about one-quarter of the skilled metal and cotton workers belonged to the Communist Party and Komsomol; membership among younger, semiskilled workers was almost as high. Urban workers also had the highest participation rates in soviet, trade union, and factory-centered activities such as factory committees, circles, clubs, and production meetings. Although participation rates did not vary markedly with age, urban workers from twenty-three to twenty-nine years of age had the highest percentage of Communists and the highest rate of political activism. Most of them were well educated and skilled.[33]

Urban worker involvement in the political and social organs of the Soviet state heightened their identity with the new regime. Given the party's domination of all political organizations after 1917, worker political participation entailed an increasing identification with the party. Although worker-party relations were strained from 1920 to 1924, beginning in the latter year, as we shall see, they began to improve. The question is not whether the party embodied the will of the working class, but what alternatives to political participation existed outside of the party's influence, and how successfully did party policies address the workers' agenda? To engage in political activities meant coming to some accommodation with the limitations of political life. To not participate meant foregoing any prospects of workers realizing their dreams. The party offered the most direct access to power and the possibility of influencing policies that bore directly on workers' lives. For this reason many urban workers joined the party after 1923. Each sought to use the other to legitimize and enact their respective agendas.

The party's control of the printed word and use of this media to transmit its values and ideals hastened the identification process. It was from the press that one "understood" and interpreted the world, and that the youth learned history. Without alternative analyses, the assimilation of some party values, perspectives, or goals was inevitable. This proved particularly true among those who became literate or began to read the daily press after the revolution. Literacy brought intellectual liberation, and what they read promised political and economic liberation.

Political organizations provided the forums in which urban workers expressed and honed their class consciousness, while simultaneously

114

asserting their power. Among urban workers, different historical experiences forged somewhat different perceptions of power and consciousness. The evolution and development of consciousness was by no means linear. For those old enough to have experienced or participated in them, the Civil War, revolution, pre-1914 labor unrest, and, for some, even the 1905 revolution provided the forges in which their consciousness was molded, steeled, and tempered. They understood their class's power and limits, assets and liabilities, successes and failures; and they had opinions on each of these. But among its youngest members, consciousness had different roots. What nurtured it was the rhetoric, legends, and slogans of the epic historical battles in which they were too young to participate. They totally imbibed the revolution's values, but they lacked an historical frame of reference. Their youthful enthusiasm and inexperience often meant that their zeal was unrestrained by the subtlety, caution and appreciation of change that experience brings. These differences notwithstanding, during the 1920s worker consciousness, first "of itself" as a class and then "for itself," came to the fore once again. Urban workers led their co-workers in defining and articulating this growing class consciousness.

Given the party's monopoly of the press and many other aspects of Soviet life, it is difficult to ascertain the extent to which these urban workers' values sprang from their work experience, from the transmission of values by family members, friends, workmates, and schoolmates, from the assimilation of the party values and attitudes toward work, or from adaptation to work rules and practices. Undoubtedly, each source contributed to and reinforced the adoption of these values. What is most important for our purposes is not the source of these values but their manifestations. To endow this social profile with life, consider the following worker biographies, which come as close to personifying it as the available evidence permits.

Metalworker P. was born in Moscow in 1884. His father worked as a carpenter on a railroad line; his mother was a domestic servant. At the age of fifteen, after three years of schooling, he secured a job at the Guzhon metal factory. Save for two tours of military service (1905-1908 and 1914-1918), he worked there all of his life. Upon his return to Guzhon in 1918, he became politically active. He joined the metalworkers union, and in 1920 was elected to his *raion* soviet (presumably Basmannyi *raion*). During the early 1920s, he regularly attended and participated in union and factory committee meetings and activities. P.'s political activism stimulated his curiousity about the world around him.

He became keenly interested in politics, particularly international and party affairs. After the revolution, P. avidly read the newspaper; in 1924, he read either *Izvestiia* or *Rabochaia Moskva* daily. He particularly enjoyed reading books and articles about science and electrificiation. P. also broadened his cultural horizons. He and his wife frequently attended the theater, museums, galleries (the Tretiakov was his favorite), and public lectures.[34]

Metalworker D. provides an example of an urbanized worker who had turned his back to the village and fervently embraced the revolution. The son of a rural cobbler who also tended a small landholding, D. moved to Moscow in 1899 at the age of fifteen and found a job in a silk factory. A few years later he went to work in a metal plant, and by 1905 was a semiskilled worker. That year he joined the Russian Social Democratic Workers Party (RSDRP) and actively participated in the revolutionary movement. Arrested in 1907, he served six years at hard labor in the Amur River region and then was exiled to the Caucasus. He escaped in early 1917 and returned to Moscow where he once again became a metalworker. In 1920, he was elected to the Rogozhsko-Simonovskii *raion* soviet; he did not rejoin the party until early 1924. D.'s life centered around work and politics. He spent all of his free time attending factory and union meetings, visiting co-workers and party members to discuss the day's issues, and reading books and newspapers. For entertainment, he went to the factory club.[35]

That village ties did not preclude the adoption of an urban worldview is clear from metalworker B.'s biography. We have already met B.; he was the worker discussed in chapter 2 whose family divided its time between its native village in Vladimir and Moscow. But B. himself never left the city after moving there in 1897. From then on, he worked at the Guzhon plant, first as an apprentice and later as a semiskilled lathe operator. He actively participated in the 1905 revolution. During 1917, he joined the union and became very involved in union affairs and other revolutionary activities. But not until early 1925 did he join the party. Like worker D. above, B. remained on the job during the Civil War and, by the early 1920s, he was a highly skilled instrument maker and an instructor at the factory school. Factory affairs and devising ways to improve productivity occupied much of his time. He read *Izvestiia* and *Rabochaia Moskva* daily and also enjoyed reading trade journals and books. He became an ardent advocate of education. All of his children attended school and B. frequently helped them with their studies. Much of his social life centered around the factory and union club.[36]

Born in 1874 to peasant parents in Tula province, worker A. attended school on and off for ten years. He left his village at age seventeen for Moscow and got a job as a repariman on the Moscow-Kursk railroad line. He served in the army from 1896 to 1901. After being discharged, A. returned to Moscow where he got a job in a metal factory. Drafted again in 1915, he fought at the front until 1917, when he returned to Moscow to work in an electrical power station. That year, he became politically active. He joined the union and regularly attended political meetings. His union activities and interest in working conditions brought him to the attention of union officials who sent him to Vitebsk in 1920 as a factory inspector. Nineteen-twenty-four proved to be a major turning point in A.'s life. He joined the Communist Party (over the objections of his wife) and was elected to his factory committee. His reading habits also changed. Before 1924, A. read the newspaper only occasionally. But that year, he began to read *Izvestiia* daily and *Pravda* and *Ekonomicheskaia zhizn'* frequently. He paid particular attention to articles on occupational issues. He also began reading books on politics, history, and Lenin's life. His party and factory committee responsibilities added yet another dimension to A.'s life—regular meetings at which he met a wider circle of people who shared his interests and political perspective. A. also began to frequent the factory club.[37]

New workers were, in many respects, the antithesis of urban workers. Rural-born and bred, these recent migrants carried a host of peasant values and behaviors to the city and factory. In the villages, they had lived and worked in accordance with the seasons, weather, and position of the sun. The time-discipline and labor-discipline that industrial labor demanded were alien and oppressive concepts and traits that many found difficult to assimilate. On the farm, regular breaks to rest, smoke a cigarette, or talk were accepted modes of behavior. In the factories, they incurred the wrath of foremen and sometimes of other workers. New workers resented the demands, routine, and orders that defined industrial work. They also resisted attempts to increase worker productivity. They had been their own boss in the village, but in the factory, they seemed like cogs in an incomprehensible machine. Their ignorance of the production process and lack of interest in their work reinforced this perception and intensified their alienation. They frequently missed work. To quiet their frustrations and relieve their alienation, they regularly resorted to drink, sometimes even before and during work. For entertainment, some of them engaged in organized fist fights. The vast majority of new workers were unskilled and less educated and literate than their fellow workers.[38]

Superstition also hedged their understanding of reality. On occasion, those new workers who did not comprehend how the machinery, which surrounded them, operated invoked the power of saints to repair a broken machine.[39] New workers tended to be politically illiterate and passive. Few belonged to the party, and they had the lowest participation rates in party, soviet, union, and factory committee activities.[40] New workers displayed little evidence of any form of consciousness. If they identified with any class, it was most often the peasantry. But this identification usually reflected a mixture of tradition, village loyalties, nostalgia, and proprietorial interests rather than class consciousness.[41] For all these reasons, many new workers sought to escape the urban, industrial world either permanently or during their vacations; if that was impossible, they withdrew from it whenever they could.

Between these two cultural extremes stood the broad mass of the workforce—the semiproletariat. A wide variety of people populated its ranks: some were rural-born people with considerable industrial experience; some were relatively new workers who quickly adapted to urban, industrial life; others were urban-born former employees, artisans, shopkeepers, and members of the dispossessed classes. There is no quintessential semiproletarian. Within this group, one could find people who were akin to new workers and others who possessed some of the urban workers' characteristics. Predominantly semiskilled, this group's work attitudes and habits, ties to the land, literacy, education, and political activism varied markedly. Precisely because they lacked unique group characteristics, identifying a distinct semiproletarian behavior is quite difficult. When they did become roused over issues, they seem to have sided with either new or urban workers. For this reason, their behavior often escapes the historian's analysis. They were, nontheless, a large and significant group within the working class.

Proletarianized former artisans embodied some of the divergent characteristics of one element of this group. Though often skilled, concepts such as labor-discipline and time-discipline had a different meaning for them. Unlike industrial workers for whom the clock and the machine defined the workday and pace of work, artisans were accustomed to working at their own pace and in accordance with customary and unmechanized production techniques. Having once been their own bosses, they often resented others defining their work tasks. For them, progress and modernization implied the end of the world that they knew.

118

The factory was not to be admired and mastered, but rather feared or even despised. The city, on the other hand, was not necessarily an alien world; for some, it was the only environment they knew. Former artisans were but one group within the semiproletariat. The following worker biographies convey the attitudes and behavior of some members of the semiproletariat. The differences between these two workers and the urban and urbanized workers discussed above help to convey the diversity found within the city's working class.

Worker O. was an illiterate and unskilled textile worker who was born was in 1882 to peasant parents in Kaluga province. She moved to Moscow in 1900 and got a job at the Trekhgornaia textile factory. Although she worked there for twenty-four years, she remained unskilled. Her husband was a semiskilled factory worker. He was semi-literate and occasionally read the newspaper, but he was incapable of reading much else. Their son attended the Trekhgornaia factory school; the daughter attended a day-care center. O. had no interest in politics and consistently refused to participate in her trade union's activities. Nor did she participate in social and cultural activities. She was a religious woman, and in 1924 spent more money on religion than on social and cultural activities or personal hygiene. Her husband claimed that he was interested in union affairs, yet he was not active in the union. He went to the cinema occasionally and once attended the Bolshoi Theater, but otherwise he too led a very limited social life. In 1924, the couple spent only 1 percent (7 rubles 48 kopecks) of their combined income on cultural, social and political activities. But they spent 6.7 percent (52 rubles) on alcohol and tobaccco. Their priorities were obvious. When reading about this family, one is left with the image of a bored, middle-aged couple who passed their evenings, tired from a hard day's work, in their one-room apartment with little else but their family and alcohol to break the monotony.[42]

Another example of a semiproletarian is worker K. He was born to peasant parents in Smolensk *guberniia* in 1885, and attended school for four years. In 1897, he moved to Moscow and got a job in the Guzhon factory where he worked until he joined the army in 1915. He returned there in 1918 and worked as a caster. Although literate, K. read very little. He occasionally read *Izvestiia*, but apparently only at the instigation of his eldest son, a technical school student and Komsomol member. Neither K. nor his wife led active social and cultural lives; in fact, K. had only been to the movies twice, and that was twice as often as his wife had been. Aside from her domestic responsibilities, the one activity that

119

Mrs. K. pursued with regularity was attending church. Three large icons adorned their apartment. K. had not been to church since 1914 and apparently that was a rare appearance. In 1924, the family spent 3.9 percent (65 rubles) of their income on cultural, social and political activities. But the children actually spent much of this. They spent 2.9 percent (50 rubles) on alcohol and tobacco. Two activities occupied most of their free time: raising their children and caring for their animals. Mrs. K. daily devoted three hours to the latter activity. The practice of Muscovites maintaining animals was not uncommon. Where the K. family kept them and precisely what animals they owned is not clear.[43]

In discussions of the transition from peasant to proletarian, or from the field to the factory, two distinct views have emerged. That put forward by Marxist historians, Soviet and non-Soviet alike, emphasizes the process' liberating aspects: the elimination of customary relations; the acquisition of new and progressive values, education and culture; the growth of political consciousness. The other view tends to emphasize that changes' diruptive effects, the confusion and alienation experienced by the peasant-turned-worker, and, by implication, the crushing of the person's spirit. Obviously, the above workers' biographies stand as examples of the two arguments. Workers P., D., B., and A. are evidence of the positive and constructive changes which can be made in an urban, industrial setting. Workers O. and K. stand as examples of people who were alienated, and possibly even overwhelmed, by the experience. For the O.s, alcohol, not newspapers and books, was the way out of their dilemma. That their children grew up and attended school in Soviet Moscow, and in one case belonged to the Komsomol, suggests that their lives would differ from their parents'. Precisely because the urban, industrial world can be both literating and disruptive, the model discussed above is a dynamic one. Like members of any class, workers are capable of change. As the above biographies suggest, some did change and others did not.

The differences between urban workers, semiproletarians, and new workers created significant centrifugal tensions that divided the proletariat. Urban workers, especially those who were skilled and experienced, frequently resented and complained about the lack of labor discipline, the sloppy and often dangerous work habits, and the disrespectful behavior of new workers. Many ridiculed these "country bumpkins" (derevenshchiny). As the competition for scarce jobs intensified, so too did urban worker hostility toward new workers who secured employment that might have gone to the former's family members or friends. But divisions between new and urban workers were not the only ones that divided the class. In some cases, those policies designed to rationalize and intensify labor created breaches between generations as older, skilled workers (especially the highly skilled) resented young workers who adopted those techniques which threatened the former's skills and status. Likewise, party and union activists frequently looked down on and expressed frustration with new workers' and semiproletarians' lack of interest and involvement in factory affairs.

There were many fractures within the city's working class. Equally as important, however, were those centripetal forces that drew workers together. Chief among them were their complaints about work conditions and processes, and, above all, managerial personnel. But the motives behind these criticisms differed. New workers tended to resent the authority that foremen, technical specialists, and managers embodied. These personnel enforced rules that symbolized all that many new workers disliked about industrial life. Their taunting and abuse of their bosses represented a revolt, real and symbolic, against undesired authority and conformity. Urban workers, especially the skilled and experienced labor aristocrats, had other reasons for criticizing management. Many saw them as incompetents who hindered production and worker initiative. They resented the condescending manner of managerial personnel who belittled worker knowledge and experience. For yet other workers, managerial and technical personnel were "bourgeois" and their natural class enemies. Their substandard housing and relatively low standard of living also fostered worker solidarity. But until the late 1920s, workers lacked a credible and legitimate forum in which to air their grievances. So long as that remained the case, these centrifugal and centripetal forces tended to neutralize each other, and worker discontent remained amorphous and unfocused, but no less volatile.

Employees and Professionals

Workers are this study's subject. But their behavior and attitudes cannot be fully understood without reference to the city's other major social groups. Employees, professionals, and nepmen all interacted with workers on a daily basis in factories, government offices, apartment houses, or marketplaces. This interaction often gave rise to class tensions and resentment. When the party began its public campaigns against bureaucratism and nepmen in the mid-1920s, its appeals for worker participation often elicited an enthusiastic response. To begin to understand why, it is important to examine briefly the composition of these social groups. Later chapters will focus on these groups' relations with workers.

From 1920 on, employees were Moscow's largest occupational group—one-third of the workforce (see appendix 5). In Soviet parlance, an employee (*sluzhashchii*) is a person who earns a salary or wage, but is not directly involved in the production process. Included in their ranks are a wide variety of personnel who defy the western stereotype of employee as a white collar worker. Their upper echelons consisted of administrative and managerial personnel in industry, commerce and government. With the transfer of the capital to Moscow, the number of such personnel increased sharply. The largest single concentration of employees (more than 150,000 or 43.5 percent) worked for state or party institutions at the local, provincial, republic, or national level. Moscow was becoming a town of bureaucrats.

Growth also occured within the ranks of technical personnel (such as engineers, technicians, team leaders, and foremen) and industrial administrators. Although a relatively small proportion of the total pool of employees (9.3 percent), their heightened presence in industry was undeniable. For every factory employee in 1902, there were 14.4 workers; by 1926, the ratio was 1:4.7.[44] Throughout the NEP, officials and workers alike complained about the quality and excessive numbers of factory administrative personnel. Policies designed to lower costs and reduce bureaucratism at these people's expense punctuated the period, but to little avail until 1928. What changed then was not only the group's size but also its composition.[45]

It was not simply the bloated numbers of bureaucrats and technical personnel which made officials and workers anxious. They also worried about that group's social composition and political reliability. There was reason for concern. A 1920 study revealed that the vast majority of the country's bureaucratic officials had been deeply enmeshed—professionally, economically, and politically—in the old regime's bureaucracy and social elite. Among those surveyed, approximately 60 percent were former "working *intelligenty*" and another 20 percent were former landowners, priests, military officers, tsarist officials, and managers. Only 17 percent were former workers.[46] Although the number and proportion of former workers employed in the state bureaucracy increased steadily during the 1920s, the pre-revolutionary activities of many bureaucrats provided ample reason for party members' and workers' distrust. Politically hostile or at least politically suspect (from the party's viewpoint) personnel also held prominent positions in industry. For example, the

AMO factory's technical department consisted of thirty engineers, model builders, and draftsmen, a majority of whom were allegedly former "White guards," tsarist army officers, Mensheviks, and SRs.[47] Given the shortage of competent technical specialists and administrators who were loyal supporters of the regime, hiring such personnel was essential to restoring production. But many workers and party members did not appreciate their presence.

The remainder of the employee category consisted of a rather heterogeneous collection of people who belonged to five categories: economic and clerical personnel (agents, inspectors, accountants, statisticians, clerical workers), minor service personnel (laundresses, doormen, cooks, watchmen), security personnel (police and firemen), medical personnel, and cultural and educational personnel (academics, editors, *literati*, artists, musicians). Employees were obviously a diverse lot.

Although many employees were professionals (e.g., engineers, doctors), they did not account for all of the city's professionals. There also existed independent professionals (*litsa "svobodnykh professii"*), the ranks of which included technical, medical, cultural, and educational personnel, and priests. What delineated these professionals from those classified as employees was that they were not employed by a state enterprise or agency. During the 1920s, the ranks of independent professionals group thinned significantly—between 1923 and 1926, their numbers shrank by one-third to 6,752. In 1923, there were 45,512 professionals (employees and independents); three years later the figure was 46,532. The number of engineers and architects (the sources make no finer distinction) increased by only 2,632 to 7,974, a paltry sum considering the demand in the 1920s.[48]

The shortage and social composition of technical personnel help to illuminate the party's desire to create a new Soviet technical intelligentsia. There were political as well as practical considerations behind that desire. The party may have wielded power in the proletariat's name, but the execution of policy (especially in the factories) was the responsibility of managers and "bourgeois" technical specialists whose fealty to the regime remained questionable. Workers and officials felt the need to keep a watchful eye on these essential personnel. There was little else that could be done until workers could be trained to replace them; that process did not begin until the end of the decade.

If one excludes from the ranks of the employees security and minor service personnel, who more properly belong in the category of minor service personnel, then the social and cultural characteristics of employees stand in sharp contrast to the city's other occupational groups. They came from diverse geographic areas and had few ties to the land. Literacy was universal and some had considerable formal education.[49] But within the employee category existed two distinct cultural groups—those who had worked as professionals and employees before 1917, and the proletarian and communist *vydvizhentsy* who entered the bureaucracy and industrial administration after the revolution.[50] When workers and officials expressed their anxiety about bureaucrats and specialists, especially after 1925, they often had the former group in mind.

Workers were particularly suspicious of those "bourgeois" managers and *spetsy* who wielded power in the factories and who differed from their subordinates in virtually every respect—bearing, demeanor, patterns of speech, preferences, and social values. Their continued presence in responsible and influential positions stood as a vivid daily reminder to workers of the revolution's incompleteness. Political power emanated from the party and organs of the Soviet state to which workers from 1924 had preferential access, but these "bourgeois elements," wherever they worked, had a more subtle form of power—expertise. The political revolution had been won; the social revolution remained unfinished. For this reason, some of the strife and tension which characterized life at the workplace in pre-revolutionary times remained alive. Comparable tensions permeated daily life outside of the workplace.

Nepmen

During the 1920s, workers regularly interacted with private entrepreneurs (nepmen). That entrepreneurial class's composition and economic activities differed dramatically from its pre-revolutionary counterpart. Most nepmen either had been small-scale producers or shopkeepers before the revolution or traced their origins to the Civil War years when they were bagmen, speculators and black marketeers.[51] Some were peasants who peddled village wares. With the legalization of private ownership and trade, their ranks grew rapidly. In 1923, there were more than 75,000 nepmen in Moscow; by 1926, their ranks exceeded 100,000[52] (see appendix 5). Throughout the decade, citizens and officials alike looked to them to provide scarce and much needed goods. But from 1926 on, their activities became increasingly restricted and their ranks dwindled.

The decisive turning point in the nepmen's short existence came at the Fourteenth Party Congress in 1925, where antinepmen sentiment abounded and delegates passed resolutions which called for a systematic limitation of private entrepreneurs. That congress's approval of the policy of socialist industrialization made the nepmen's eventual elimination a virtual political necessity. This congress initiated what Soviet historians call the two-stage antinepmen campaign. During the first stage (1926-1927), the party and state intensified the development of socialist industry and commerce while simultaneously enacting a series of policies, laws, and taxes designed to restrict private economic activity. The decision of the Fifteenth Party Congress in 1927 to proceed with "more systematic and insistent restrictions on the kulak and private property owner (*chastnik*)" extended those policies and hastened the elimination of nepmen.[53]

The state employed another method to curb the nepmen's activities—arrest and exile. The police kept a close eye on and used various means at their disposal to harass them. Throughout the decade, nepmen were arrested on charges of violating labor laws, engaging in tax resistance and fraud, and transgressing other limitations. Although arrests and their publication served a political purpose, some were justified. Legal harassment was particularly intense in 1921-1922 and after 1925. Under the pressure of this two-pronged offensive, nepmen who engaged in legal economic activities virtually disappeared by 1930.

Soviet sources divide nepmen into three groups based on their relationship to labor: owners with wage labor, owners with family or *artel* labor, and self-employed. By far the smallest, the first group accounted for only 6 percent of all nepmen; the self-employed comprised the majority.[54] Among owners who hired wage labor could be found the closest thing to a real bourgeoisie—factory owners. In 1926, however, there were only 145 such owners, a decrease of eleven compared to 1923. The vast majority of privately owned factories employed fewer than twenty workers, although some employed more than one hundred people. The proportion of the proletariat employed in private factories declined steadily during the decade.[55] Despite this, press reports of the low wages, poor work conditions and violations of labor laws in private factories remained common fare. Although few in number, private factory owners had a high social profile.

Most nepmen engaged in some type of artisanal or handicraft activity; bootmakers, saddlemakers, cobblers, weavers, stockingmakers, tinsmiths, blacksmiths, coopersmiths, hatters, tailors, bakers, and confectioners were the most common occupations. The next largest group of nepmen engaged in commercial activities either as wholesalers (*optoviki*), wholesalers/retailers (*poluoptoviki*), shopkeepers (*magazinsh-chiki*), kiosk owners or peddlers and hawkers (*raznoschiki*). In 1926, the latter three comprised 82 percent of all Moscow traders. Many were peasants who traveled to the city to sell their wares or produce; others were the unemployed who tried to eke out an existence. Although the number of wholesalers was small, they controlled a considerable propor-tion of the city's private trade and commercial capital.[56] Some of them dealt extensively with state enterprises, but most preferred to operate in "exclusive circles" (*zamknutye krugi*), thereby avoiding potentially entangling contracts with the state. For this reason, the dealings of this important group of nepmen remain a mystery. Among their ranks were the speculators, those savvy entrepreneurs who took advantage of any opportunity to make a financial killing. They too experienced the press's constant scrutiny.[57]

Shopkeepers had the most frequent contacts with the public. After the legalization of private trade, many entrepreneurs hurriedly opened stores and shops. During the first four months of 1922 alone, the number of shops (*magazini*) in Moscow mushroomed from 2,900 to 5,300. Shop-keepers dragged out old stock which they had hidden during the Civil War. Their shelves often abounded with a wide variety of food stuffs (fresh eggs and fruit, dairy products, candies, and pastries), clothing, shoes, other consumer goods, and even luxury items, such as diamonds, fur coats, and silk.[58] Alongside the retail shops, bakeries and restaurants opened. Although these stores provided many goods that were in great demand, the high prices often excluded workers and made them primar-ily the haunts of the better-off residents, a fact that angered many work-ers.[59]

The vast majority of nepmen were self-employed. In 1926, there were 36,000 self-employed artisans or handicraftsmen. These people owned their tools or the necessary means of production but little else. They were transitional characters: "Today they may be taking orders, tomorrow they may be working in a factory."[60] Many of the self-employed were peddlers and hawkers who sold any item on which they could lay their hands—pots and pans one day, tools or tobacco the next day. Some peddled junk and old clothes that, in years when new clothes and other goods were scarce, were in considerable demand. The appela-tion "rag and bone" traders aptly applies to most of these people. Many self-employed had strong ties to their villages and engaged in their urban enterprise on a short-term or even seasonal basis, selling their wares and services and then returning to the village. The more enterprising of these people accumulated enough money to retire in comfort.[61]

Although they were relatively few in number, private entrepreneurs played an important economic role during the early 1920s. This was especially true of private traders, who in 1923 controlled upward of two-thirds of the goods circulated in Moscow. But as restrictions on them mounted and the state and cooperative commercial network grew, the ranks of the commercial nepmen and the amount of trade which they controlled diminished. At the end of 1926, state agencies and cooperatives controlled 89 percent of the city's trade; by 1930, they controlled virtually all trade, though illegal private trade continued.[62]

The nepmen's social composition also distinguished them from the city's other occupational groups. More than three quarters of them were males; an equal portion were over thirty years of age. Save for domestics, they had the lowest literacy rate of any occupational group in the city. Only 17 percent of them were native Muscovites; three-quarters of the migrants were born in the Central Industrial Region (CIR).[63] A quarter of them owned land. Many nepmen utilized their rural connections in their business. Not only did they serve as an outlet for peasant wares and food products, but many tapped their *zemliaki* to provide cheap labor. Workers and officials frequently complained that these entrepreneurs often by-passed the Labor Exchange and hired (illegally before 1925) *zemliaki* and peasant migrants "off the street."[64] As unemployment mounted and the number of new workers who secured jobs increased, worker hostility to such behavior intensified. Conservative, closely tied to the land, steeped in rural habits, patriarchal, and leery if not outright hostile to any infringement on their freedom, such were the traits of many nepmen. Despite their tenacity in the face of overwhelming political and legal pressure, their livelihood was a doomed one.

Domestics

One other occupational group remains to be introduced—domestics. Their importance to this study is indirect. During the 1920s, most domestics worked for nepmen, professionals, academics and other well-to-do residents. Even some party members (e.g., Lenin and Trotsky) and workers hired domestics. When the latter did so it was usually because both adults worked and hiring a domestic was preferable to leaving children unattended or giving up one income so as to tend to daily chores. Whatever the reason, having a domestic remained a symbol of wealth, social status, and class distinction. The housewife who did not work and had a domestic was "looked upon with contempt as a 'parasite' and a 'bourgeois.' "[65] Because many domestics were workers' spouses, family members, girlfriends, *zemliaki*, or neighbors, and because the press frequently ran articles on their exploitation by nepmen and other prosperous residents, their experiences and stories served to reinforce worker prejudice against the city's well-to-do.

Despite the sweeping social changes brought about by the revolution, the demand for household domestics, after dropping sharply during the Civil War, increased steadily during the 1920s. In 1912, there were 99,000 domestics in the city; by 1923, their numbers had dwindled to only 14,335. But during the next three years, their ranks trebled, a consequence of both increased supply and demand (see appendix 5). Virtually all (99 percent) were females. Three quarters were young peasant girls who migrated from within the CIR; more than half came from Moscow, Riazan and Tula *gubernii*. Most were unskilled, and they had the lowest literacy rate in the city.[66] Being unskilled females, domestic service was often the only work available to them. In fact, most domestics apparently only took the job until they could find something better.[67]

Domestics' working conditions varied considerably depending on their employer. For some, the jobs were burdensome. One fourteen-year-old orphan girl, who lived with her employer, worked from 8:00 a.m. until the late evening; another young girl worked upward of seventeen hours a day. Both were employed by nepmen and earned very low wages. Because many feared losing their jobs and had no union protection, such exploitation was common.[68] Fortunately, not every domestic was forced to endure such treatment.[69]

Continuity and Change

While Moscow's social composition during the 1920s differed in some significant ways from that in pre-revolutionary times, several features underscored the continuity between the old and new city. One of the most important proved to be social tensions. Although they were the class on which Soviet power was based, workers had only to peruse their environment to realize how great the continuities between the two eras were. Successful private entrepreneurs and "bourgeois" factory administrators and specialists continued to influence, and in some cases determine, the course of their lives. That these people earned significantly higher wages, enjoyed better living conditions, and sometimes flaunted their wealth evoked workers' jealousy, envy, frustration, and animosity.

Judging from letters to the editors and other newspaper columns, many workers, especially those in the party, viewed Soviet society as a Manichean world. Within it co-existed, however precariously, workers and their allies and those deemed antiworker either by virtue of their class background or current economic activities. Workers distrusted and resented these social remnants of the *ancien regime* and those who prospered at workers' expense. They complained about the material privileges that these alleged class enemies enjoyed. Newspaper articles and cartoons reinforced this social analysis. That "bourgeois" managers and *spetsy* treated workers rudely and frequented the same nightspots as nepmen, speculators, and *declassé* elements of the old elite only reinforced their dualistic view of society. The "we" versus "you" viewpoint expressed by workers in 1921 endured. In 1928 as in 1921, the latter had privilege.[70]

Whatever differences existed within the proletariat, widespread worker resentment (frequently fueled by the press) of "bourgeois" elements' privileges and power drew that class together. Until the late 1920s, however, there were few organized means available to settle their social grudges. Until then, those emotions simmered.

Notes

1. The working population actually includes people other than those earning a wage or salary. Working people, the unemployed with previous work experience, pensioners or those receiving public assistance and who formerly had a job, and military personnel comprised the working population's ranks. The nonworking population consisted of all other residents; children under fifteen accounted for the bulk of this group. For a discussion of the active and inactive classification, see L. I. Vas'kina, "Rabochii klass SSSR po materialam vsesoiuznoi perepisi naseleniia 1926g.," *Istoricheskie zapiski*, 92 (1973), 16, 55.

2. For a discussion, see *Trud v Moskovskoi gubernii*, 2.

3. A detailed breakdown of the labor force by sex in 1926 can be found in *Perepis'* . . . *1926g.*, tom. 19, tab. IV, 276-409. This table is reproduced in William J. Chase, "Moscow and its Working Class, 1918-1928: A Social Analysis" (unpublished Ph.D. dissertation, Boston College, 1979), 390-413. In some sources, minor service personnel comprise a separate occupational group, but such is not always the case. The 1926 census does not consistently make the distinction. For the sake of consistency and for more accurate calculations, I have treated them as employees.

4. There is considerable dispute over the size of the city's proletariat in 1917. For a discussion, see Grunt, "Moskovskii proletariat," 67-86.

5. *Trud v Moskovskoi gubernii*, 1-35.

6. As a result of this policy, one quarter of the textile, metal and chemical plants in Moscow city and *guberniia* were shut down and the average number of workers per factory rose from 581 to 666. Rodionova, 135-138; Shkaratan, 240.

7. For a breakdown of the number of workers in specific jobs in this and all of the city's industries in 1926, see *Perepis'* . . . *1926g.*, tom. 19, tab. IV, 376-409.

8. Precisely which group of workers—metalworkers or textile workers—was the largest is the subject of debate. That debate can be found in A. Ia. Grunt, *Pobeda oktiabr'skoi revoliutsii v Moskve* (Moscow, 1961); and "Moskovskii proletariat"; F. L. Kurlat, "Nekotorye voprosy istorii oktiabr'skoi revoliutsii v Moskve," *Vestnik Moskovskogo gosudarstvennogo universiteta*, 6 (1963), 31-43. Grunt argues that textile workers were the single largest industrial occupation; Kurlat claims that metalworkers had that honor. Given Grunt's carefully documented argument, I find it more convincing. *Istoriia Moskva*, VI, 1, 19, also claims that metalworkers were the largest single group of industrial workers.

9. Rashin, *Sostav*, 19-21, 150-151; Shkaratan, 258.

10. As many as 40 percent of the transport workers were considered temporary residents. *Trud*, September 28, 1928. On the dilution of the proletariat by the peasantry, see *ibid.*, September 27, 1929. Nationally in 1929, one-fifth of the workforce had three or fewer years of experience. Of those, 45 percent were from peasant families and 46.3 percent were from worker families. *Trud v SSSR, 1926-1930: Spravochnik* (Moscow, 1930), 28-29. See also *Statistika truda*, 2-3 (1929), 18. The infiltration of these workers into production will be discussed in chapter 5.

11. Rashin, *Sostav*, 19-21. See also note 10.

12. *Perepis'* . . . *1926g.*, tom. 55, tab. III, 136-154.

13. *SZ*, 1928, 49, 437; *Perepis'* . . . *1926g.*, tom. 19, tab. IV, 376-409; Matiugin, *Moskva*, 35; Rashin, *Sostav*, 48. This issue will be discussed in chapter 5.

14. K. I. Suvorov, *Istoricheskii opyt KPSS po likvidatsii bezrabotitsy (1917-1930)* (Moscow, 1968), 190. See the discussion in chapter 5.

15. *Trud v Moskovskoi gubernii*, 29; *Statisticheskii spravochnik* . . . *1927*, 42-43.

16. Sexual discrimination by unions will be discussed in chapter 5. See also Jessica Smith, *Woman in Soviet Russia* (New York, 1928), 15-16.

17. For examples, see *Trud*, January 10, January 29, 1928.

18. G. N. Serebrennikov, *Zhenskii trud v SSSR* (Moscow-Leningrad, 1934), 8.

19. *Perepis'* . . . *1926g.*, tom. 19, tab. IV, 376-409. Even in some of these industries, the proportion of females declined during the decade. Serebrennikov, 50-52.

20. *Perepis'* . . . *1926g.*, tom. 19, tab. II, 144-155. The literacy rate

reflects the percentage of the population over ten years of age who could read. For literacy rates of the working population by sex and occupation, see *Statis-ticheskii spravochnik . . . 1927*, tab. 19, 42-43. See also: Aleshchenko, *Mos-kovskii sovet*, 424; Rashin, *Sostav*, 97-122, 160-161. Although the literacy rate rose in the decade before World War I, precise statistics are lacking. For a discussion of the growth of schools, see Robert W. Thurston, "Developing Education in Late Imperial Russia: Concerns of State, 'Society', and People in Moscow, 1906-1914," *Russian History/Histoire Russe*, 11, 1 (1984), 59-82.

21. As quoted in Carr, *Socialism*, I, 390.

22. S. V. Antronov, "K voprosu o kachestve rabochei sily," *Izvestiia tek-stil'noi promyshlennosti i torgovli*, 33-34 (September 15, 1926), 1-3.

23. For examples, see: *Rabochaia Moskva*, March 25, 1922; *Pravda*, January 30, April 10, October 4, October 27, November 28, 1925; *Trud*, August 24, 1927.

24. Rashin, *Sostav*, 75-81; Mints, *Voprosy*, 30; *Perepis' . . . 1926g.*, tom. 19, tab. III, 287-290; Aleshchenko, *Moskovskii sovet*, 381; Sorenson, 205-207.

25. Rashin, *Sostav*, 76-81; Mints, *Voprosy*, 30.

26. Sheila Fitzpatrick, *Education and Social Mobility in the Soviet Union, 1921-1934* (Cambridge, 1979), 18-63.

27. Rashin, *Sostav*, 76-81; Antronov, "K voprosu," 1-3; Mints, *Voprosy*, 30. The issue of labor turnover will be discussed in chapter 6.

28. In recent years, western scholars who study the Russian working class have offered a number of models of workers and working-class behavior. This model is offered as a contribution to the on-going effort to delineate impor-tant worker typologies. For examples of this effort, see: Bonnell, *Roots of Rebellion*; Koenker, *Moscow Workers*; David Mandel, *The Petrograd Work-ers and the Fall of the Old Regime: From the February Revolution to the July Days, 1917* (New York, 1983); and *The Petrograd Workers and the Soviet Seizure of Power* (New York, 1984); Smith, *Red Petrograd*; Reginald E. Zel-nik, "Russian Bebels: An Introduction to the Memoirs of Semen Kanatchikov and Matvei Fischer," *Russian Review*, (part I) 35, 3 (July 1976), 249-289; (part II) 35, 4 (October 1976), 417-448.

The sources from which this model is derived are too numerous to list in a single footnote, but they can be found throughout the text. The only sources cited in the presentation of this model represent those from which particular supporting examples are drawn.

29. Rashin, *Sostav*, 107-122. Other schools popular with workers and their offspring were the *Rabfak*, and higher technical schools. But the gradu-ates of these institutions often left production. Fitzpatrick, *Education and Social Mobility*, 51-63.

30. See the report of Charles Butterworth, *American Engineers in Russia)* (unpublished collection at the Hoover Institution, Stanford University), box 2. To western observors, two types of workers consistently displayed these characteristics: certain skilled workers, and young, urban workers who were relatively new to the factories. Among the latter group, party and Komsomol members were especially prominent. For examples, see the reports of T. R.

Holcombe, Walter N. Poliakov, Joseph L. Thomson, Albert W. Hahn, E. H. Collester, *ibid.*, boxes 2 and 3.

31. Kabo, *Ocherki*, 195.

32. Rashin, *Sostav*, 154-155.

33. *Ibid.*, 135-151. These activities will be discussed in chapter7.

34. Kabo, *Ocherki*, 75-80.

35. *Ibid.*, 63-64.

36. *Ibid.*, 103-107.

37. *Ibid.*, 80-83.

38. One-third of the city's cotton workers and about 15 percent of its metalworkers were illiterate and lacked formal education. Rashin, *Sostav*, 117-127, 141-151. On fist-fighting, see *Pravda*, December 25, 1928; Daniel Brower, "Labor Violence in Russia in the Late Nineteenth Century," *Slavic Review*, 41, 3 (1982), 417-431.

39. Consider the incident related by V. N. Ipatieff, the renown chemical technologist: "When a blast furnace broke down and workers had troubles getting it back into production, they would sometimes appeal to saints for help, lowering a religious picture or icon into the furnace, not unlike the way peasants arranged religious processions with icons, praying for rain during a drought." As quoted in Bailes, *Technology and Society*, 38.

40. According to Rashin, *Sostav*, 141-151, only 2 percent of those new workers surveyed belonged to the party and their rate of participation in factory and Soviet activities was half that of urban workers.

41. For a discussion of these values, see G. Iastrebo, *Partiinoe stroitel'stvo*, 3-4 (5-6) (February 1930).

42. Kabo, *Ocherki*, 29-34.

43. *Ibid.*, 35-39.

44. *Perepis'* . . . *1926g.*, tom. 19, tab. IV, 379-409 (my calculations); Bradley, "*Muzhik* and Muscovite," 453. Bradley's computations are based on the 1902 census. The 1:4.7 ratio reflects the ratio of employees designated as leading, technical, economic, and registration and control personnel in factories to factory workers. Clerical, communications, security, and minor service personnel have been excluded from this computation; their inclusion changes the ratio to 1:3.3. The ratio of factory employees to workers is a citywide ratio. In some factories, the ratio was quite different. For example, at Serp i molot in November 1924, there were 3598 workers and 294 employees; in 1913-1914, the respective figures were 3658 and 334. *Stroitel'stvo Moskvy*, 4 (November 1924), 21.

45. This will be discussed in chapter seven. See also, Fizpatrick, *Education and Social Mobility*.

46. L. M. Spirin, *Klassy i partii v grazhdanskoi voine v Rossii 1917-1920* (Moscow, 1968), 386-387. For a discussion of the increasing number of former workers in the state bureaucracy, see Don Karl Rowney, "Proletarianization, Political Control and the Soviet State Administration in the 1920s: Their Impact on Upward Social Mobility," unpublished paper presented at the Third Annual Conference of the National Seminar on Russian Social History, Philadelphia, January 29-30, 1983.

47. *Istoriia . . . Likacheva*, 108.

48. For a discussion of technical professionals, see Bailes, *Technology and Society*, 44-264 passim. See also, Sheila Fitzpatrick, *Education and Social Mobility*, 48-51. The ranks of the city's doctors, veterinarians and teachers actually decreased during these years. One reason for the decrease in the number of teachers was the very low wages that they received. See Moshe Lewin, "Society, State, and Ideology during the First Five-Year Plan," *Cultural Revolution in Russia, 1928-1931* (Sheila Fitzpatrick, ed., Bloomington, Ind., 1978), 41.

49. The literacy rate for all Moscow employees by sex was: males—98.4 percent, females—85.4 percent. Although femalescomprised 41 percent of this occupational group, they were disproportionately concentrated in clerical and minor service personnel positions. Literacy rates for the population can be found in *Perepis' . . . 1926g.*, tom. 19, tab. II, 144-155. Nationally in 1927 fewer than 3 percent of all administrative and technical personnel were women. A. G. Rashin, *Fabrichno-zavodskie sluzhashchie v SSSR (chislennost', sostav, zarabotnaia plata)* (Moscow, 1929), 24.

50. According to the 1927 party census, 21.3 percent of all factory employees were Communist Party members, whereas only 10.5 percent of the workers were members. Rashin, *Fabrichno-zavodskie*, 26-27.

51. Trifonov, *Klassy*, 31-32, 71-74.

52. For a breakdown of private owners by economic activity and sector of the economy, see *Statisticheskii spravochnik . . . 1927*, tab. 17, 36-37.

53. L. F. Morozov, *Rezhaiushchii etap bor'by s NEPmanskoi burzhuaziei (1926-1929gg.)* (Moscow, 1960), 27; *KPSS v resoliutsiiakh*, II, 450-454, especially 454. During the 1920s, taxes on nepmen rose steadily. In 1923/24, more than one third of the average private entrepreneur's income went to pay taxes. A 1926 law raised these taxes which reached their peak in 1928/29. Trifonov, *Klassy*, 186-187; I. Ia. Trifonov, *Likvidatsiia ekspluatatorskikh klassov v SSSR* (Moscow, 1975), 234. Morozov, *Rezhaiushchii etap*, 44-45. The state also restricted nepmen's access to credit. A law to this effect was enacted in 1924, but until at least 1927 some continued to receive credit from state banks. Trifonov, *Klassy*, 55-63, 71-74, 161. For other limitations on nepmen, see: Morozov, *Rezhaiushchii etap*, 39, 79-80; Trifonov, *Likvidatsiia*, 223.

54. Data on the type of labor which nepmen employed and the nature of their activities in 1926 can be found in *Statisticheskii spravochnik . . . 1927*, tab. 17, 36-37. According to this source, owners with wage labor accounted for only 6 percent of all private entrepreneurs in the city, those who employed family or *artel* labor for 20 percent, and the self-employed for 74 percent.

55. At the end of 1924, there were only twenty private factories in Moscow that, under special leasing arrangements, employed one hundred or more workers. Among these was the Maikonar tobacco factory (240 workers and employees). Trifonov, *Klassy*, 52. In 1923/24, 6.5 percent of the city's proletariat worked in private factories; only 1.3 percent did so in 1927/28. *Moskva i Moskovskaia gubernii*, tab. 215, 318-319.

56. In 1925, four private commercial firms reportedly had capital assets valued at between 100,000 and 200,000 rubles each, considerable sums of

money considering the tight money market. *Pravda*, January 9, 1925. See also, I. Ia. Trifonov, *Ocherkii istorii klassovoi bor'by v SSSR v gody NEPa, 1921-1937* (Moscow, 1960), 131-135. *Trud*, February 17, 1928, stated that in 1927/28 private trade in Moscow declined by 62 percent.

57. Some speculators illegally sold goods purchased from state enterprises and trusts. The directors of the Maslo-muka factory were arrested in late 1922 because they sold goods destined for cooperative and state outlets to private retailers. *Rabochaia Moskva*, October 28, 1922. In March 1928, workers at a private iron works complained that the owner received suspiciously preferential treatment and advances on goods from certain state agencies. *Trud*, March 25, 1928. For an example of the arrest of a speculator in state manufactured goods, see *Trud*, December 24, 1927.

58. L. Fischer, *Men*, 51; Goldman, 23-24; Allan Monkhouse, *Moscow, 1911-33: Being the Memoirs of Allan Monkhouse*, (London, 1933), 142-143.

59. For an example, see *Rabochaia Moskva*, December 13, 1922.

60. Vas'kina, "Rabochii klass," 10-11.

61. Walter Duranty tells of a Finn in Moscow who, in October 1921, sold ARA food packets from a sidewalk table of "two boards across trestles." Within a week, his "table" doubled in size and he was selling eggs and vegetables. A month later he was able to rent a small store and sell produce. In May 1922, he had four salesmen and during that summer he opened a dry goods and hardware section. He left Moscow after one year with enough money to live independently for the rest of his life. Duranty, 149.

62. In November 1922, there were more than 24,000 private traders in Moscow; four years later, there were about 22,000. *Perepis' . . . 1926g.*, tom. 19, tab. IV, 376-409; *Statisticheskii spravochnik . . . 1927*, 218-219. In 1922, nepmen controlled 14 percent of the wholesale trade, 50 percent of the mixed wholesale and retail trade, and 83 percent of the retail trade. Nationally private trade constituted 78 percent of all retail trade in 1922/23, 57 percent in 1923/24, 42.5 percent in 1924/25, 42.3 percent in 1925/26, and 36.9 percent in 1926/27. Carr, *Interregnum*, 111; Nove, 103; *Russia After Ten Years*, 54. See *Trud*, February 17, 1926; December 4, 1927 for reports on the declining number of nepmen in the commercial sector. See also Trifonov, *Likidatsiia*, 228; Morozov, *Rezhaiushchii etap*, 46-48.

63. *Perepis' . . . 1926g.*, tom. 19, tab. I, 118; tab. II, 144-155; tab. IV, 376-409.

64. Trifonov, *Klassy*, 52.

65. Theodore Dreiser, *Dreiser Looks at Russia* (New York, 1928), 168.

66. Migrants from the three provinces listed in the text accounted for 57 percent of the city's domestics. *Perepis' . . . 1926g.*, tom. 19, tab. II, 144-155.

67. Anderson, "Female Labor."

68. *Rabochaia Moskva*, May 10, 1923. See *ibid.*, February 15, 1923, for a discussion of attempts by domestics to organize a union. All present at the meeting had migrated from either Moscow, Riazan, Orel, or Tula *gubernii*.

69. For a discussion of the Fischer family's domestic and their relationship, see Markoosha Fischer, *My Lives in Russia* (New York, 1944), 46.

70. On "we" versus "you," see *Pravda*, February 8, 1921, and chapter

one. The tensions between workers, and *spetsy*, managers and speculators will be discussed in chapters four, six and seven. For examples of this attitude as expressed in the press, see the letter from workers complaining that "specialists and speculators" controlled the factory organs and deprived workers of their just desserts. *Rabochaia Moskva*, April 6, 1922. See *ibid.*, September 7, 1922, for a cartoon of a nepman dressed in a fancy suit with two-tone shoes, a yachting cap, and a cane. The accompanying article states that his kind can be found everywhere—in factories, trusts, and Soviet institutions—and that all must struggle against his ideology. According to Dreiser, 73: "your true Communist considers the NEP-man a snake who is trying to undermine the success of Communism. Also he fancies him—(whether truly or not I do not know)—rich, whereas your Communist is poor."

4. The Unemployment Crisis

In the decade after the revolution, the employment situation in Soviet Russia was extremely fluid. The demobilization of the tsarist army and economic collapse in late 1917 and early 1918 spurred a sharp rise in unemployment. This proved to be a temporary phenomenon that quickly gave way to a labor shortage. So scarce was labor during 1919-1920 that the state resorted to militarization and other draconian labor policies to maintain the workforce necessary for the war effort. The job market changed course again in 1921. During the NEP, unemployment grew steadily and rapidly. Although unemployment was a national phenomenon, in Moscow the problem became particularly acute. From January 1923 to October 1928, the ranks of the unemployed nationwide more than doubled—from 640,000 to 1,364,000, a jobless rate of approximately 12 percent.[1] But in the capital, their ranks more than tripled between February 1923 and April 1929 (from 60,000 to 200,000). The city's unemployment rate in late 1927 exceeded 20 percent and hovered at that level for two years.[2] Such a high unemployment rate is intolerable in any society, but two facts made it particularly embarassing to the leaders of the world's first socialist workers' state: workers had the highest unemployment rate; and in 1912, when the tsar and capitalism reigned, that rate stood at only 3.8 percent (29,400).[3]

The NEP's economic and labor policies and mass migration to Moscow were the primary reasons for the city's growing unemployment. Those policies designed to lower production costs and raise productivity proved remarkably successful in restoring the economy to its 1913 levels by 1926 and in providing the basis for continued economic expansion. But those very same policies demanded that recovery be achieved with a smaller workforce that existed in 1913. While official policy sought to

136

limit the labor force's size, the city's population grew by about 100,000 a year, a growth that annually exceeded the number of available jobs. Consequently, although the numberof working Muscovites increased steadily, the ranks of unemployed Muscovites rose more rapidly.

The mounting unemployment crisis contributed to and exacerbated social tensions in the city. Economic security had been one of the proletariat's major revolutionary demands. The economic collapse of 1918-1921 forestalled its realization. Economic recovery rekindled that dream, but recovery had its costs. For most Muscovites, the 1920s was a decade of rising expectations; for others, whose ranks swelled annually, it proved to be a period of insecurity, setbacks, and deferred hopes. Their misfortune affected all workers. Many working-class families experienced the pain and hardships of unemployment. Others lived in fear of it. As the competition for jobs intensified, so too did those centrifugal tendencies that divided the proletariat. Men and women, the youth and their elders, urban workers and new workers, urban workers and seasonal migrants, unemployment pitted each against the other.

Centripetal forces were also at work. Divided though they often were, resident workers deeply resented those from the villages with whom they competed for jobs. Some unemployed workers blamed the state for implementing policies that forced them out of work and for not assisting them in their darkest hour. That nepmen and former "bourgeois," whose skills and knowledge were in great demand, enjoyed virtually full employment deepened worker resentment and envy of them. But relative to the intraclass divisions that unemployment fanned, these centripetal forces proved to be relatively minor. Only when they joined with other tensions that divided the city's classes would their full dimension be realized.

The Problem of Data and the Labor Exchange

Before beginning this examination of unemployment in Moscow, a word of caution is in order. There is considerable disagreement in the sources over the precise number of jobless Muscovites at any given time. The trade unions and the Labor Exchange (*Birzha truda*, which served as both employment and unemployment office) both compiled unemployment figures. The former's figures consisted only of union members and, therefore, tend to underestimate the problem's dimensions. The latter's figures included all those registered on their rolls, union and nonunion members alike. However, the Labor Exchange suffered from a series of defects, and, at times, their figures often included a large number of fake registrants. Rather than choose one organization's figures over the other's in the absence of evidence necessary to make a reasoned judgment, table 4-1 often presents two figures—the highest and lowest "official" figures.

For example, in April 1922 there were between 16,714 and 20,500 unemployed Muscovites. The former figure comes from Grigorii Mel'nichanskii, a VTsSPS presidium member; the latter figure, from the city's Labor Exchange.[4] That there often exists a third figure further complicates the problem. In this case, *Trud*, the national trade union newspaper, claimed that 18,193 Muscovites were jobless in April 1922.[5] That such varying "official" figures exist suggests some of the difficulties which one encounters in attempting to ascertain a precise figure.

The task of determining precise unemployment figures is made all the more difficult by the fact that, after 1925, the unemployed were not required to register at the exchanges. During the years of War Communism when everyone was employed, the exchanges were charged with mobilizing and directing labor. With the ending of compulsory labor and the reappearance of unemployment in 1921, they resumed the normal function of registering those out of work and helping them to find jobs. Until January 1925, all hiring had to be conducted through them. The primary reason for this practice was to enable the agency to control the flow of labor within the city. At this the exchange was rather unsuccessful.

One reason for the exchanges' failure was the behavior of and pressure put on them by employers who wanted a free labor market so that they could hire whomever they wished. These critics argued that the exchanges were incapable of rationally and efficiently regulating the workforce and that their poor performance hindered employers' ability to meet the demands placed on them by official policies. Rather than deal with them, many employers in the early 1920s took advantage of the city's available surplus labor and hired their workers illegally, that is, without going through the exchange. Private employers frequently engaged in this practice.[6] Unions staunchly defended the exchanges' rights and monopoly power which, they believed, protected unemployed and unionized urban workers from competition with rural in-migrants who were willing to work for less. Until late 1924, union pressure ensured that the exchanges gave urban workers first priority when it came to hiring.[7] However, a November 1924 decree granted rural migrants equal rights at the exchanges, a decree which the unions rightfully perceived as a blow to urban union protectionism.[8]

TABLE 4-1
Unemployment in Moscow,
April 1921-April 1929

Date	Registered unemployed
Apr. 1921	1,845
Jan. 1922	15,024-17,217
Apr. 1922	16,714-20,500
Jul. 1922	32,671
Sep. 1922	39,153
Feb. 1923[a]	59,673
Apr. 1923	84,830
Jul. 1923	113,136
Oct. 1923	105,121
Jan. 1924	106,974-111,740
Apr. 1924	114,399-128,292
Jul. 1924[a]	114,639-117,804
Oct. 1924	64,024
Jan. 1925	79,225
Apr. 1925	104,504
Jul. 1925	86,908-113,898
Oct. 1925	104,961-112,930
Jan. 1926	114,846
Apr. 1926	129,396-131,401
Jul. 1926	143,897-157,000
Oct. 1926	160,525-166,993
Jan. 1927	180,065-192,934
Apr. 1927[a]	175,614-204,080
Jul. 1927	159,480-180,000
Oct. 1927	178,194-185,413
Jan. 1928	141,072-197,342
Apr. 1928	197,035-255,762
Jul. 1928	166,869-223,549
Oct. 1928	192,617
Jan. 1929	189,551
Apr. 1929	200,271

SOURCE: *Ezhemesiachyi statisticheskii bulleten'*, Jan.
1925-Oct. 1928, otd. V, tab. 4, 14; ILO, "Russian
Supplement," 1, No. 1 (Jan. 6, 1922) and 5, No. 4,
(Feb. 16, 1923); *Perepisi 1923g.*, tom. 19, tab. I, 118;
Rabochaia Moskva, May 16, 1922; July 21, 1922;
Trud, November 5, 1922, July 14, 1927; *Moskva i
Moskovskaia guberniia*, 148; *Voprosy truda*, 9
(1928), 158-159; 12 (1928), 158-159; 2 (1929), 154-
156; 5 (1929), 142-143; 8 (1929), 140-142.
a. Denotes a *chistka* (purge) of Labor Exchange rolls.

In 1923, employers won the right to hire certain people (e.g. specialists, managers, bookkeepers) without going through the exchanges. Encouraged by the victory, they continued to attack that agency's monopoly on labor, arguing that it could not satisfy the demands of industry for certain workers. By 1925, employers' pressure and arguments that the exchanges' shortcomings hindered the pace of economic recovery broke their monopoly on labor. The obligatory hiring of workers through the exchange was abolished and a free labor market was established.[9] Employers now had the power to hire and fire workers as they saw fit. Despite the change, the exchanges did not lose all of their importance. To qualify for unemployment compensation, the jobless had to register there. In March 1927, two Sovnarkom resolutions (to be discussed below) partially restored the exchanges' right to allocate labor.

That the Labor Exchange's registers often carried a number of unqualified people further frustrates the quest for precise unemployment figures. In its defense, it should be noted that any agency charged with registering all of the unemployed in a city with a rapidly rising population, high labor turnover, and mass seasonal migrations no doubt would have difficulties in keeping impeccable and up-to-date lists. This was surely the case in Moscow. As early as December 1922, newspaper articles claimed that many people registered at the Moscow Exchange were employed or in some way falsely registered.[10] A review of its rolls bore out the charge—one of every six people was unqualified for one reason or another.[11] The problem of false registrants quickly reappeared. In July 1924, another major purge *chistka* reduced the unemployment rolls by about half, though many legal registrants were probably eliminated.[12]

No sooner were the lists purged than the number of registrants began to rise sharply. By April 1925, the number of registered unemployed approached its July 1924 level. How many of those registered in 1925 had been removed from the lists in 1924 is difficult to ascertain. In mid-1927, the exchanges once again came under fire. *Trud* reported that thirty percent of those who received unemployment compensation did so illegally. Of the 70,421 aid recipients, 20,785 were unqualified and of that group, 14,443 had jobs.[13] Such disclosures coupled with the difficulties many people had in locating full-time employment gave rise to numerous complaints and charges that bureaucratism riddled the exchange.[14]

In May 1928, *Trud* reported that a Rabkrin investigation of the city's Labor Exchange confirmed the accusations levelled against it. Entitled "Bribe-takers in the Labor Exchange," the front page article revealed that, in order to get a full time or public works job, many people had been forced to bribe officials. The article went on to charge that patronage, favoritism, and bribery undermined the agency's functions and that the responsible officials neither within the exchange nor in the city soviet had properly investigated the numerous allegations. As a result of the investigation, an unspecified number of exchange officials were arrested. Quite understandably, *Trud* demanded another purge of the exchange.[15]

Finally, the fact that seasonal migrants often registered at the exchange in hopes of securing not only temporary but also permanent work further frustrates the quest for precise unemployment figures. Given these problems, the numbers presented in Table 4-1 must be treated with caution. Whereas before January 1925, those figures may overestimate unemployment, after the abolition of the exchanges' monopoly they probably underestimate unemployment, although by how much is difficult to determine. In October 1925, *Pravda* claimed that unemployment figures at the exchanges nationwide underestimated the real level of unemployment by as much as 20 percent.[16] That the number of registered unemployed continued to rise even after the exchange lost its monopoly on labor underscores the fact that the problem of joblessness in Moscow was an increasingly severe one. During that period, the city's unemployment rate rose from 16.4 percent in late 1925 to more than 20 percent by 1928.[17]

The Reasons for Unemployment

During the 1920s, there were two major enduring causes of unemployment: the economic and labor policies of the NEP, and the massive influx of migrants into the city. To these must be added a significant short-term factor—the demobilization of the Red Army at a time of industrial dislocation. In January 1921, there were more than 4.1 million Red Army soldiers. More than two and a half million left the service during the next year; by January 1924, another million had re-entered civilian life. Although most veterans were peasants, many of them went not to their villages but to urban areas in search of work. The problems of urban unemployment began to become serious. Many veterans lacked not only jobs but also food, winter clothes, and housing, all of which were in short supply. Faced with such dire realities, some veterans turned to robbery, others organized demonstrations at which they demanded jobs and voiced their dissatisfaction. One unemployed veteran's letter to *Pravda* succinctly conveyed their demands. He complained that the veterans had endured many hardships to defend the country and now there were no jobs: "The Soviet power should pay attention to our needs and help us."[18]

Rather than incur the wrath of the Civil War's heroes, party and state officials moved to defuse the situation. A February 1922 Commissariat of Labor decree announced that veterans should receive preferential treatment when seeking work. The Moscow party organization, which supported the decree, reportedly used it and other methods to pressure the exchange into finding work for the returning soldiers.[19] Many employers needed little inducement to hire veterans, and in many cases, they fired female and juvenile workers to make room for veterans who had skills and production experience.

While demobilization spurred unemployment in the early 1920s, it proved to be a secondary, short-term factor. Far more important and enduring were the NEP's economic and labor policies. Without denying that they succeeded in restoring the economy, the policies' human costs were steep. To hasten the recovery, during the NEP's first two years, the party enacted a series of classical economic policies that reflected the values of the party's productivist wing and that were the direct descendants of the productivist policies enacted from mid-1918. The policy of *khozrachet*, which demanded that enterprises balance their books, and the phasing out of government subsidies to industry forced the dismissal of many workers and employees. Industrial concentration and the creation of industrial trusts so as to permit a more efficient utilization of factories, machinery, tools, fuel, and personnel further contributed to rising unemployment. Such was the case in the Moscow Machine-building Trust that consisted of eleven factories. Just prior to the trust's creation, these factories employed some 12,000 people. After a series of reorganizations mandated by trust officials, the workforce declined by 50 percent.[20]

The campaign to cut costs and increase worker productivity gained momentum in 1924. That year a resolution on wage policy sought to raise productivity by tying wages to output, raising production norms, and rationalizing labor and production. Rationalization became the word of the day. The rationalization campaign that began in 1924 sought to lower production costs by mechanizing operations, increasing the division and intensification of labor, and reducing superfluous workers and staff. While these policies increased productivity and lowered costs, they did so by firing workers and limiting new employment opportunities. In short, rationalization stimulated unemployment.[21]

Workers were not the only people to lose jobs as a result of official policy. The perennial struggle to reduce the bureaucracy's size also contributed to an expansion of the unemployed's ranks. The campaign began in Moscow in October 1921. Three months later, the Eleventh Party Conference passed a resolution demanding that the size of the state bureaucracy be reduced. During 1921/22, the local bureaucracy shrank by 40 percent. More calls for pruning the bureaucracy's size accompanied the rationalization campaign and its 1926 successor, the regime of economy. An August 1927 Sovnarkom resolution pushed the campaign even further by urging a 20 percent reduction in administrative costs. Significant numbers of employees lost their job as a result of these policies.[22]

As table 4-2 clearly indicates, these policies were a major cause of unemployment in Moscow. The table's data represent the results of a study, conducted by the Moscow City Statistical Bureau, of people who were unemployed and registered at the Labor Exchange between January and June 1925. The "Industrial Group" includes all workers directly involved in industrial production (e.g., metalworkers, textile workers, chemical workers); the "Nonindustrial Group" includes those occupations described as employees, minor service personnel and domestics. The "Unskilled" category includes the remaining job groups (e.g., carters, haulers).

According to this data, policy mandated personnel reductions were the single most important cause of unemployment. Slightly less than one-third of the total sample and almost half of the workers and employees

TABLE 4-2
The Causes of Unemployment in Moscow, January-June 1925[a]

Reasons	Industrial groups	Nonindustrial groups	Unskilled	Total
Closing of enterprise	18.0%	18.7%	3.0%	11.7%
Reduction of staff	48.4%	47.1%	25.2%	32.5%
Illness	1.6%	2.0%	.8%	1.1%
Demobilization	2.3%	4.6%	1.0%	1.7%
Other (e.g., marriage, family)	23.9%	23.2%	23.8%	25.4%
No previous work experience	5.7%	4.0%	46.2%	27.4%
Total	99.9%	99.6%	100.0%	99.8%

SOURCE: *Trud v Moskovskoi gubernii*, 87.
a. The figures are listed as they were reported.

143

lost their jobs for this reason. If the closing of enterprises also resulted from official policy, the proportions increase significantly. If this was the impact of policy in 1925, surely the effect of the regime of economy must have been comparable, if not greater, especially in light of the August 1927 Sovnarkom resolution. Among the unskilled, official policies were secondary causes of unemployment. The most formidable obstacle to employment for them was simply their lack of skills and previous work experience. Large numbers of rural migrants and urban born youth populated their ranks. One-quarter of those who were unemployed apparently left work voluntarily; most were probably women who quit either to marry or to have children. Unfortunately, it was often difficult for these people to re-enter the workforce.

Massive in-migration was the other major reason for the period's spiralling unemployment.[23] As noted earlier, Moscow's population doubled between 1921 and 1926 and grew by more than 10 percent a year in 1927 and 1928. The expanding city economy was simply unable to provide jobs for all of the new residents. Although urban residents bore the burden and costs of unemployment, the problem's dimensions reflected fundamental structural problems in the agrarian sector. While the lure of urban life with its new opportunities attracted some migrants to the city, economic necessity forced most of them to migrate to Moscow and other urban areas.

Although precise estimates of the dimensions of rural overpopulation differ somewhat, all contemporary observers agreed that the number was substantial—between 10 and 19 million.[24] Researchers noted a direct correlation between the size of peasant holdings and the proportion of underutilized rural labor—the smaller the plot, the higher the proportion of superfluous labor. It was from the ranks of the poor *(bedniak)* and middle *(seredniak)* peasantry that the vast majority of migrants came.[25] To peasants such studies merely proved the obvious. As a peasant delegate to the Fifteenth Moscow *Guberniia* Party Conference stated: "the peasant population goes to the city for wages with which to support his household."[26]

Contemporary agrarian analysts repeatedly stressed the interrelationship between urban unemployment and agrarian overpopulation. One analyst stated: "The issue of urban unemployment is closely tied to the issue of labor utilization in the rural economy and to the issue of the standard of living of the town and country."[27] Defenders and critics of party policy both agreed that what fueled unemployment was the fact that the country "is once more throwing on to the town a 'reserve army

144

of labor' and at the present time our industry is not in a position to digest all of the labor offered."[28] A Central Committee plenum in April 1925 and the Fifteenth Party Congress passed resolutions which shared this analysis.[29] The Left Opposition also linked the problem of urban unemployment and rural overpopulation and warned that the unemployment crisis had grave political consequences: "The discontent of the unemployed links the discontent of the countryside to the discontent of the town."[30]

Union officials also attributed the growing unemployment problem to rural migration. The Communist faction *(Komfraktsiia)* of VTsSPS noted that "the rise in unemployment among union members" resulted from the influx into unions of migrants "who have settled in cities in droves."[31] Unions displayed little sympathy for unemployed migrants whom they viewed as stealing jobs from their urban, proletarian constituents. To concern themselves with the fate of jobless migrants was not "their business" and would mean that unions would "lose their class character and deny their essence—the defense of their members interests."[32]

The elimination of the exchanges' preferential treatment of urban workers and labor monopoly only intensified the unions' opposition to the free labor market and emboldened their defense of urban workers' rights. After the abolition of this monopoly, unions urged their members to register at the exchanges so as to qualify for assistance and to increase their chances of getting a job. But by 1926, it became clear that the establishment of the free labor market enhanced the job prospects of rural migrants. According to one calculation, seasonal migrants had a 15 to 20 percent advantage over their urban counterparts in securing employment and many who did so remained on the job after the season had ended.[33] The major reason for this advantage was that these people were willing to work for lower wages and "under any conditions at all." These migrants often bypassed the Labor Exchange and got jobs at the expense of unemployed, unionized workers. At times, they "even occasioned the expulsion of the latter from their jobs."[34] Commissar of Labor Shmidt reported incidences on which factory managers dismissed large numbers of workers, in one case up to 2000, and replaced them the next week with peasant recruits.[35]

Seasonal migrants entered industrial employment in stages. First, they would procure a seasonal job (e.g., construction work) and join the union. Then, taking advantage of their union membership, they would "infiltrate into production"—often at the expense of urban workers—

and stay on as full-time workers. So common did this infiltration become that, after 1925, seasonal workers accounted for more than three-quarters of all newly hired workers.[36]

The "stealing" of urban workers' jobs by migrants angered workers and union officials alike, and heightened urban worker resentment of rural migrants. But they were also concerned about the competition between the two groups for seasonal work. For the urban unemployed, seasonal employment offered the opportunity to earn much needed income. Historically, *otkhodniki* had dominated the workforce in seasonal occupations such as construction and transport. But as the ranks of the urban unemployed expanded, the competition for such jobs, as well as the tensions between the two groups, intensified.

The tension was especially noticeable in the construction industry. In 1925, the Communist faction *(komfraktsiia)* within the Central Committee of the Construction Workers Union noted that urban workers viewed seasonal workers as "dangerous competitors" who took their jobs and income. These workers insisted that they receive preferential treatment in hiring and that when lay-offs were necessary, *otkhodniki* should be dismissed first.[37] Their demands went unmet and the struggle for seasonal work deepened. Two years later—and in obvious response to the growing antagonism between the urban unemployed and seasonal workers— Commissar of Labor Shmidt suggested that the urban unemployed should replace seasonal workers in the construction industry. Shmidt was not the only person to call for preferential hiring of unemployed workers.[38] No such action was taken.

Suggestions alone offered little solace to the urban unemployed in the face of mounting *otkhodnichestvo*. Between 1923/24 and 1926/27, the number of seasonal migrants nationwide practically doubled from 1,872,000 to 3,500,000. Commissariat of Labor officials estimated that 1927/28 would see a 17 percent increase.[39] For most of the decade, more than 200,000 seasonal migrants annually migrated to Moscow. Although the number of seasonal migrants was less than in pre-revolutionary times, the city's high unemployment rate and the inability of its economy to absorb this mass made the situation critical. One Commissariat of Labor official stated in 1927: "The necessity of regulating this enormous, spontaneous movement of masses of seasonal workers is as clear as day."[40]

The unions and Sovnarkom agreed. The Seventh Trade Union Congress in December 1926 passed a resolution calling for the re-establishment of the Labor Exchanges' exclusive control of labor allocation and the strengthening of these offices. In spring 1927, Sovnarkom issued several resolutions designed to control the flow of *otkhodniki* and the conditions under which they could be employed, but stopped short of re-investing the exchanges' pre-1925 powers. The first resolution, issued on March 1, 1927, stated that no enterprise or institution could hire such workers without concluding prior agreements with the Commissariat of Labor. A March 4, 1927 decree extended the former resolution's restrictions to all occupations. Specifically, it forbade the hiring of nonresident workers without Commissariat of Labor approval.[41] Nonetheless, the practice continued.

The pressure exerted by unions for greater protection of urban workers and by planners, who viewed the restoration of theexchanges' powers as a means to control and direct labor in accordance with the anticipated demands of a planned economy, proved to be the significant factor in the issuance of these decrees. In fact, when it came to dealing with unemployment, urban workers, unions, and planners were often allies.[42]

In an effort to control *otkhodnichestvo*, the Commissariat of Labor established a network of correspondent points *(korpunkty)* in rural locales. The organization of *korpunkty* began in mid-1926, and, with the passage of the above laws, they took on a new importance. Their functions were to direct seasonal workers to areas where there were jobs and to contract for seasonal labor on behalf of urban Labor Exchanges. In 1927, 741 *korpunkty* existed in the RSFSR, but the vast majority suffered from great difficulties, not the least of which were the lack of trained recruiters and poor coordination. That many peasants simply bypassed these offices further undermined their effectiveness. Nor did the situation improve in 1928 and 1929. With the onset of collectivization, the problem of rural-urban migration intensified, and the ability of the *korpunkty* to direct this movement declined commensurately.[43]

Despite the establishment of *korpunkty* and decrees regulating the labor market, seasonal workers continued to flock to Moscow in 1927 and 1928 in search of construction work. In the spring of 1928, so many seasonal workers descended on Moscow that those who wished to return home were offered the fare to do so.[44] Every morning during the construction season thousands of unemployed residents and *otkhodniki* lined up at *Krasnaia vorota* (known also as *chernaia vorota*—black gate)[45] to vie for the available jobs. The overwhelming peasant composition of this crowd is clear from the following description:

147

For the entire width of the sidewalk, on the pavement, along the walls, in the doorways of nearby houses in a dense human agglomeration, people crowd around. They are dressed almost identically—in *valenki* (felt boots), worn-out *sapogi* (boots), some in *lapti* (bast shoes) with cord wrapped around *onucha* (a sock worn with bast shoes), in thick coats or *polushuby* (sheepskin coats), *shapkiushanki* (caps with earflaps), *kartuzy* (peaked caps), many with a set of tools, a saw, axes, planes. Here the construction section of the Moscow *Birzha truda* is congregating.[46]

So great was the demand for jobs that people began to queue up at *Krasnaia vorota* before dawn. In some cases, the contending builders had to prove their skills to the hiring officials by taking tests such as stacking a row of bricks. Some workers had to "compete" for jobs by the "hand-over-hand on a stick" method. Many *otkhodniki* at *Krasnaia vorota* were hired as *arteli* of ten, fifteen or even thirty people.[47] The members of an *artel* brought their own tools and selected an elder *starosta* from among their skilled members to represent them. As noted earlier, *artels* often specialized in a given skill such as masonry or carpentry.

The massive influx of *otkhodniki* put a severe strain on many aspects of city life. The increased competition for jobs pitted unemployed urban workers (and their unions) against new workers and *otkhodniki*. While urbanites' hostility toward their "dangerous competitors" was greatest among the unemployed, as we shall see, this attitude also permeated the factories where new workers secured jobs.

The competition for the city's very limited housing space was particularly acute. Throughout the 1920s, Moscow's rapid population growth outstripped the supply of available housing. So severe did the city's housing shortage become that, by 1926, there were some 100,000 homeless Muscovites. Many of them were unemployed. Because of the shortage, the housing opportunities available to seasonal workers were limited to dosshouses or overnight barracks *(nochlezhyi dom, or nochlezhnyi barak)*. The demand for such quarters far exceeded the supply—in 1925, there were only 20,000 beds for ten times that many *otkhodniki*. Nightly, homeless residents and seasonal workers engaged in an anguishing competition for a place to sleep. The losers spent the night sleeping in the streets, public parks, or uninhabited buildings. Although the pace of housing and barracks construction increased significantly from 1925, the demand continually exceeded the supply.[48]

The Left Opposition may have been correct when it asserted that "the discontent of the unemployed links the discontent of the countryside to that of the town," but it appears unlikely. What the unemployment crisis did was to fuel urban worker hostility toward rural migrants—permanent and seasonal—with whom their comrades competed for jobs and housing. In this way, it widened rather than narrowed the division between town and country.

Who Bore the Brunt of Unemployment?

Depending on the criteria used, there are several answers to this question. For example, if we seek the occupational group with the highest unemployment rate, we find it was the working class. However, if we ask on which social groups did unemployment weigh most heavily, the answer is women and youths, especially juveniles. The point is not to expose the potential of statistical manipulation, but rather to underscore the fact that certain groups within the proletariat carried a disproportionate burden of unemployment. The result was that unemployment served not to unify the proletariat, but to divide it along sexual and generational lines.

Throughout the NEP, women accounted for a disproportionately large number of the city's jobless. This was the case from the very beginning of the NEP. Replacing female with male workers was an accepted practice among employers who, in 1921-1922, dimissed many women to make room for skilled and experienced workers returning from the army and the countryside.[49] The call by officials for preferential hiring of veterans has already been discussed. However, at the same time that the Commissariat of Labor urged this preferential hiring, it also issued a decree stating that, in the event of lay-offs, employers should consider men and women on an equal basis.[50] But this plea for equal treatment was often ignored. In some industries, especially male-dominated ones such as metals and printing, there was a conscious policy by employers and unions to discriminate against females.[51] But even in female-dominated industries, such as textiles, employers dismissed women to make room for men. The consequences were both immediate and dramatic. Among those occupational groups with high unemployment rates in July 1922, women accounted for the vast majority. For example, of 1,485 jobless textile workers, 1,354 (91 percent) were females; of 12,131 unemployed unskilled laborers, 10,707 (88 percent) were females.[52]

From early 1921, the female unemployment rate exceeded that of males, and the absolute number of jobless females rose annually.[53] From 1923 to 1928, females accounted for 48 to 50 percent of the city's registered unemployed. Yet in 1926, they accounted for only 37 percent of the city's working population.[54] The disproportionately high female unemployment rate was especially notable among workers and employees. In 1926, women accounted for one-quarter of the employed workers, but more than one-third of the unemployed workers. Among employees, the respective figures were 42 percent and 58 percent (see table 4-3). By 1925, the shortage of skilled workers forced factories to hire unskilled workers. Unfortunately, this situation did not rebound to the advantage of unemployed women. When given the choice, most industrial employers preferred to hire male migrants before women. Clearly, employers' patriarchal attitudes and women's low skill level combined to force women to carry an inordinate burden of the city's unemployment problem.[55] For women, who were the first to be fired and the last to be hired and who earned lower wages than males, there was little new in the New Economic Policy.

The problem of juvenile *(podrostki)* unemployment also became increasingly severe during the NEP. In the labor scarce Civil War years, juveniles had little difficulty in securing employment. But with the return of workers from the Red Army and villages, juveniles, like females, were among the first to be fired. Nationally, 120,000 juveniles worked in industrial enterprises in 1921; two years later their ranks had plummeted to 5,000.[56] In the hopes of reversing this trend, a 1922 decree established a quota *(bronia)* for these young people—7 percent of an industry's workforce were supposed to be juveniles. The sustained growth of the economy ensured that the ranks of employed youth rose, but few industries met the established quota. Throughout the 1920s, the proportion of juveniles in the workforce actually declined and the number of those unemployed grew dramatically.[57] In mid-1926, more than two-thirds of the country's juveniles were jobless and their ranks continued to expand; they accounted for almost one-fifth of the city's unemployed by October 1928.[58] Despite the spiralling juvenile unemployment rate, an August 1928 decree actually lowered the quota to 4.5 percent—the proportion of juveniles working as of January 1928. But even this quota proved to be "unattainable."[59] Youth unemployment was not confined to juveniles. In 1928, 44 percent of the nation's registered unemployed were between the ages of eighteen and twenty-four; another 31 percent were between the ages of twenty-four and twenty-nine. One factor that limited youth employment opportunities was the influx of rural migrants into the labor force. This became especially important after 1925. From 1922 to 1925, workers' children comprised more than half of those entering the work-

TABLE 4-3
Unemployment by Previous Occupation and Sex, December, 1926[a]

Occupation	Number unemployed	Males	Females	Unemployment rate
Workers (total)	48,820	65.6%	34.4%	14.3%
Rural economy	825	38.5%	61.5%	35.1%
Factory industry	23,665	55.6%	44.4%	12.1%
Artisan industry	4,769	55.6%	44.4%	25.7%
Construction	4,395	97.9%	2.1%	25.4%
Railroad	2,077	78.0%	22.0%	6.4%
Other transport	1,838	86.5%	13.5%	8.3%
Trade and credit	2,389	74.5%	25.5%	18.2%
Institutional	3,858	77.1%	22.9%	22.8%
Other branches	5,004	72.3%	27.7%	21.7%
Employees	59,117	42.3%	57.7%	13.0%
Free professionals	242	27.7%	72.3%	3.5%
Proprietors with wage labor	54	81.5%	18.5%	.9%
Proprietors with family or *artel* members' labor	393	85.0%	15.0%	1.9%
Self-employed	1,573	52.1%	47.9%	2.1%
Family members helping proprietors	282	62.0%	38.0%	2.0%
Others	3,953	51.4%	48.6%	—
Total	114,434	52.9%	47.1%	—

SOURCE: *Perepis'* . . . *1926g.*, tom. 19, tab. VI, 577.
a. Excludes those seeking work for the first time even if they were registered at the Labor Exchange; also excludes temporary residents.

force. But after 1925, that is after the introduction of the free labor market, the proportion dropped to less than one-quarter.[60]

Their lack of skills or work experience also served to keep the juvenile unemployment rate high. Denied the opportunity to learn skills on the job, the only avenue open to jobless juveniles was to enroll in technical schools. But the demand for admission far exceeded the number of spaces available. In 1926, more than 15,000 juveniles studied in technical schools, factory schools (FZU), Central Institute of Labor (TsIT) courses and production homes for homeless adolescents. That

151

year, the number of unemployed juveniles exceeded one million. Party, Komsomol, and union officials justifiably complained that the shortage of schools restricted the youths' opportunities, yet little was done to improve the situation.[61] But technical training and the acquisition of a skill did not guarantee that a juvenile would get a job. A letter from some technical school graduates succinctly expressed the disappointment and anxiety experienced by many youths: "When we finished our studies we expected to be able to work at once but our hopes have proven vain . . . we want to be active and useful children. Give us work and help us."[62]

Unskilled and inexperienced, most juveniles were particularly unattractive hiring prospects. Given official policies which stressed productivity and efficiency, juvenile hiring quotas, VTsSPS frankly admitted, did "not meet the requirements of the rationalizing of industry."[63] Inexperienced youth were also expensive workers. By law, employed juveniles could only work for six hours a day; the remainder of their day was devoted to study. If an employer had a choice between an inexperienced and unskilled juvenile and a comparable new worker from the village, financial considerations made the former a poor investment.

Given the shortage of skilled workers, why, one might ask, did young technical school graduates have such a hard time finding work? For many older workers and union representatives, it was these youths' training— not the lack thereof—that often made them unattractive co-workers. At technical schools and especially in Central Institute of Labor courses, students learned more efficient and intensive work patterns, and, on the job, they were often eager to adopt more intensive forms of labor. Their willingness to raise production norms fueled tensions between young workers and older, more skilled workers who saw them as threatening rivals. Generational tensions influenced youth unemployment in another, yet similar way. Rather than train their "replacements" many older, skilled workers apparently refused to take them on as apprentices or to teach young workers the "secrets" of production.[64] It may well be that those workers who refused to train apprentices did so in hopes of saving scarce apprenticeships for their own children. The unions' practice of placing only their constituents' children in apprenticeship programs underscores their members' concern not only for their children but also for controlling the pace of work.[65]

Many working-class parents found themselves in a difficult position. They may have shared their co-workers' suspicion and fear of "rival" juveniles, but often it was their children who could not find a job. During the late 1920s, about 60 percent of the unemployed juveniles were of proletarian ancestory.[66] Their idleness proved to be a financial and emotional drain on some families. Many working-class parents of retirement age complained that their children's inability to secure employment forced them to continue working. They also worried because many unemployed juveniles fell "under the influence of the street" where they associated with criminal types and engaged in begging, hooliganism, and prostitution, and freely used drugs and alcohol.[67]

The enforced idleness of many of the country's most physically able members brought sharp criticisms of economic and labor policies from the Left Opposition and the Komsomol. High-ranking party officials were sensitive to and defensive about the problem. As Commissar of Labor Shmidt put it, "a generation of young workers is growing up which does not have the opportunity to find employment in factories and plants in the near future."[68] But recognition and sympathy did little to ameliorate the plight of jobless juveniles or soothe the anger of Komsomol members who, throughout the decade, criticized union leaders for their failure to respond to the youth unemployment crisis. What especially infuriated the Komsomol was the August 1928 lowering of juvenile hiring quotas. This proved to be the proverbial "last straw" and forged an alliance between the Komosomol and those party leaders who spearheaded the 1928-1929 successful attack on Tomskii and the trade union leadership.[69] Komsomol fury did not confine itself to the unions. During the 1928-1931 cultural revolution, that organization played an active role in the iconoclastic assault on alleged class enemies and "rightists" whom they viewed as enemies of the revolution and the young.[70]

Let us now turn our attention from social to occupational groups. During the 1920s, the working class had the highest unemployment rate (see table 4-3). At the end of 1926, the jobless rate among the city's proletariat was between 14 percent and 20 percent depending on figures used. It rose steadily during the next two years. Former industrial workers accounted for about half of the unemployed proletarians, but former artisanal and construction workers had the highest rates. The high jobless rate (25 percent) among artisanal workers can be attributed to that mode of production's precarious position within the economy. Many independent artisans operated with little capital and the ever rising taxation rates levied on them after 1925 forced many to dismiss workers and/or shut down. The increasing mechanization of industry also undermined the demand for skilled artisan's wares. Considering the seasonal nature of the building trades, the high unemployment rate (25 percent) for construction workers in December 1926 must be seen as a temporary rate.

High unemployment rates plagued all branches of industry, but some were more affected than others. During the early 1920s, the metals, textiles, food processing, leather working and printing industries were particularly hard hit.[71] Three factors accounted for their high unemployment rates—the dismissing of female and juvenile workers, the end of war-time orders and the concentration and rationalization of industry. But even after the initial wave of lay-offs in these and other industries, the influx of new workers, the extension of policies aimed at rationalizing and intensifying labor, and increased mechanization served to keep the jobless rate quite high. In 1925, for every hundred unemployed workers of the same occupation, there were only forty openings for garment workers, forty-nine for metal workers, and eighty-two for textile workers.[72] These industries, which were the major ones in the city, continued to have high and rising unemployment rates until the onset of the First Five-Year Plan.[73]

Surprising as it may seem in light of official lamentations over the shortage of skilled workers, many skilled workers were unemployed. In 1925, skilled workers accounted for 18.5 percent of the city's jobless residents.[74] One explanation for this ironic situation lies in the policies of rationalization and industrial concentration. Some skilled workers lost their jobs because of factory closings or cutbacks; others did so because mechanization and new divisions of labor rendered their skills obsolete or unnecesary. Undoubtedly, some unemployed skilled workers were former artisans whose skills were not readily adaptable to industry. Fortunately for some skilled workers, retraining programs and the opening of new factories offered them new opportunities and, from mid-1927, their unemployment rate reportedly declined.[75]

A large number of experienced workers also endured unemployment during the NEP. In 1925, half of the registered unemployed industrial workers had ten or more years of production experience *(stazh)*; another 25 percent had five to ten years experience (see table 4-4). Compared to all jobless workers and all unemployed, these figures were extremely high. Once again, the policies of industrial concentration and rationalization were the primary reasons for this phenomenon. Data from the city's Labor Exchange indicate that, after 1925, the proportion of the unemployed with five or more years of experience declined slightly—from 50 percent in 1925 to 45 percent in 1927. But the nature of the data makes it impossible to discern whether this trend resulted from more rural migrants registering at the exchange or from the rehiring of experienced personnel.[76] That raw peasant recruits and seasonal migrants were securing jobs (and from 1925 had an advantage in doing so) while many skilled and experienced workers sat idle fueled urban worker resentment of their village rivals. But given the pressures exerted by official policy to raise production and lower costs, this anomaly also raises significant questions about how industrial managers were applying these policies. As we shall see, officials and workers also questioned factory administrators' behavior.

TABLE 4-4

Unemployment by Length of Work Experience, January-June, 1925

Previous occupational group	Years of work experience					
	None	Up to 1	1-3	3-5	5-10	10+
Industrial						
Males	.6%	2.1%	10.0%	9.0%	23.1%	55.0%
Females	1.3%	4.8%	18.5%	13.2%	30.3%	31.7%
Both	.8%	2.8%	12.1%	10.1%	24.8%	49.2%
Construction						
Males	.1%	.4%	11.0%	9.5%	28.2%	50.8%
Transport and Communication						
Males	.8%	2.5%	24.9%	17.1%	27.7%	27.6%
Females	1.8%	3.7%	35.4%	26.9%	26.3%	5.9%
Both	.9%	2.7%	25.6%	18.5%	27.5%	24.6%
Nonindustrial						
Males	1.8%	3.3%	14.6%	12.3%	24.8%	42.8%
Females	6.1%	3.4%	23.8%	22.0%	29.4%	14.6%
Both	3.5%	3.3%	18.3%	16.2%	26.7%	31.4%
Unskilled laborers[a]						
Males	33.5%	7.4%	13.6%	10.0%	13.4%	22.0%
Females	41.5%	5.0%	14.9%	10.8%	14.0%	13.8%
Both	37.0%	6.4%	14.2%	10.4%	13.6%	18.4%
All groups						
Males	14.9%	4.2%	12.8%	10.2%	20.3%	37.4%
Females	29.9%	4.7%	17.1%	13.2%	18.8%	16.2%
Both	19.9%	4.4%	14.2%	11.2%	19.8%	30.4%

SOURCE: *Trud v Moskovskoi gubernii*, 85.
a. *Chernorabochie* in the source.

Side by side on the unemployment line with skilled and experienced workers stood many unskilled and inexperienced jobseekers. Labor Exchange data for 1924/25 indicate that unskilled workers and laborers comprised half of the city's registered unemployed. That proportion remained steady throughout the decade. The competition for jobs among the unskilled was especially intense—there were only 23 job openings per 100 jobless unskilled. For those without production experience, landing a job could be extremely frustrating, and became more so as the years passed. Whereas one-fifth of the registered unemployed in early 1925 lacked production experience, a year later their ranks had swelled to one-third. The growing numbers of youths and migrants seeking their first job account for the increase.[77]

In some occupations, experience and skill are not essential job qualifications. Such was the case in the transport and communication trades. According to a 1928 study of transport workers, as many as 40 percent of them were temporary, that is, they would work for only about one year.[78] The primary reason for this high turnover was that many of the jobs (such as carriers, carters, porters, stevedores, cabbies) were the preserve of seasonal migrants. For some of these jobs, where strength was more important than skill, experience was equated with age and thereby became a liability.

Although workers had the city's highest unemployment rate, the number of jobless employees was higher. Like those of unemployed workers, the ranks of jobless employees expanded steadily throughout the decade. The two groups accounted for more than 90 percent of the city's unemployed in late 1926 (see table 4-3). In 1922 and 1923, former employees accounted for about 30 percentof the city's unemployed; by 1925 the figure had risen to about 40 percent; by late 1926, to over 50 percent.[79] Once an employee lost a job, it was very difficult to find a new one—there were only 16 job openings for every 100 unemployed employees in 1925. Even unskilled workers stood a better chance of finding a job. Soviet employees (primarily office and clerical personnel) were by far the most numerous of the jobless employees; for engineers, technical specialists, factory administrators, and high-ranking bureaucrats, employment was virtually universal.[80] Many jobless employees possessed considerable work experience—one-quarter had five to ten years experience, one-third had ten or more years experience (see table 4-4). Most lost their jobs as a result of cost-cutting policies. From 1921, Soviet agencies periodically trimmed their staffs. Among the first to be fired were those unqualified employees who had entered the state apparatus after the revolution. Political considerations forced others from their desks. As noted earlier, many employees at the end of the Civil War had politically suspicious backgrounds, a liability which often outweighed experience.[81]

Compared to workers and employees, the unemployment rate among Moscow's free professionals and private proprietors was very low—2 to 3 percent in 1926. Presumably those proprietors who were without jobs owned so little property that they could not make a living from it in spite of the high demand for virtually all goods and services provided by the private sector. Because of their close economic ties to the land, many jobless nepmen probably returned to their villages, thereby reducing that group's unemployment rate. Given the shortage of professionals, the presence of any unemployment among this group is quite surprising. The very low jobless rate among these well-to-do residents provided yet another source of worker resentment, envy, and jealousy. In the workers' state, workers bore the brunt of unemployment while these "bourgeois" prospered. But because they did not compete for the same jobs, workers tended to transfer their emotions to the areas in which the two groups engaged in direct struggle.

Once a person lost a job, how long he or she remained unemployed was often determined by gender—women remained unemployed significantly longer than did men. In 1924, the average duration of unemployment in Moscow was seven months and reportedly rose as the unemployed's ranks increased. Data from 1926 and 1927 indicate that half or more of the city's jobless males were unemployed for up to six months; another 25 percent had to endure their plight for up to one year. For the remainder, unemployment had become a chronic condition. Among females the situation was far worse—an equal proportion (38 percent) were without work for up to six months or more than one year.[82] That some women left their jobs to have a child explains in part the longer duration of female unemployment (see table 4-2). But that was not the only reason. Once again, some employers' preference for hiring males forced many women to lanquish idly. Although the data are unavailable, one assumes that the plight of unemployed juveniles was far worse.

Because unemployment is an alienating and atomizing experience, it is difficult to gauge fully how it affected its victims' attitudes. Some undoubtedly suffered from the depression, anxiety, and loss of self-esteem that results from forced idleness and the inability to adequately support oneself and family. Many sought to identify those who were

157

"responsible" for or benefitted from their plight. There were several obvious "culprits"—new workers, seasonal migrants, and eager youths. Unemployed and employed workers' resentment (and even fear) of these groups was common during the 1920s, although competition for jobs was not the only reason for these intraclass tensions. And then there was the state. Because state policies were a prime cause of unemployment and because the state provided what many unemployed believed to be inadequate assistance (although before the revolution none was offered), some jobless workers became increasingly critical of the state and occasionally attacked those offices which symbolized their plight.

According to Menzhinskii, the head of the OGPU, police officials had evidence that, in 1924, an "anti-Soviet" movement was growing among Moscow's unemployed. Unemployed workers circulated antigovernment leaflets and petitions to create committess of the unemployed. More than 3,000 of the city's jobless metalworkers attended a meeting at which they demanded speeding the pace of industrial development, reducing machine and equipment imports, restricting factory employment to one member per family, shortening the workday, and increasing unemployment assistance. Unemployed workers—many of them Red Army veterans—attacked and ransacked the Labor Exchange office in Odessa and murdered the director and several employees. Demonstrations at which they demanded jobs immediately preceded the attack. The Politburo responded to this threatening situation by forming a special investigative panel.[83]

Though usually isolated and spontaneous, the discontent continued. Four years later, Tomskii, the trade union chief, and other delegates to the Eighth Trade Union Congress spoke of acts of hooliganism and violence in which unemployed workers attacked Labor Exchange personnel and shattered files. At the same congress, young delegates complained bitterly about high rates of juvenile unemployment and sharply criticized the leadership's failure to reverse the growing crisis.[84] When the unemployed attacked the Labor Exchanges and their personnel, they were not simply attacking the symbols of their problems. As the May 1928 Moscow Labor Exchange scandal revealed, some of that agency's personnel had crassly abused their position by selling jobs and giving them to friends while the frustration and agony of many unemployed mounted. Their violence is hardly surprising. But like many desperate acts, it proved futile.

Surviving Unemployment

Before concluding this discussion of unemployment in Moscow, how the unemployed survived economically remains to be examined. One of the Labor Exchanges' responsibilities was to provide unemployment assistance in the form of cash benefits, coupons for free meals or meals at reduced prices (until 1924), temporary rent-free quarters, and exemption from taxation to those who qualified.[85] Whatever the system's shortcomings, its very existence marked a dramatic improvement over pre-revolutionary times when the state offered the unemployed no assistance.

The primary goal of unemployment assistance was to support those wage earners, in particular skilled urban workers, whose departure from their trade would be a long-term disaster. To receive unemployment assistance, applicants had to meet a three-month residency requirement and to have had previous work experience. No pretense was made of supporting recent arrivals from the countryside. Depending on their skill level and experience, an unemployed person who qualified for assistance received between one-sixth and one-half of the prevailing wage rates. At no time did the amount of aid given exceed the minimum wage. In fact, in 1927/28 the average monthly unemployment "check" was nineteen rubles eighty kopecks, or about one-third that of the minimum wage and about one-fifth that of the average worker. Initially, those who qualified for assistance only received it for six months; in mid-1927, the Commissariat of Labor extended the time limit to nine months.[86]

Because funds were meager in the early 1920s, the number of people who received unemployment assistance then was limited. As more money became available, the numbers rose. Still, fewer than half of the registered jobless ever received aid. In October 1923, only one-fifth of the city's unemployed received financial support; from 1924 on, between 24 percent and 40 percent did so. (At the beginning of 1925, 40 percent of the city's eligible unemployed received benefits; by June the proportion had dropped to 24 percent; by mid-1927, it had risen to 40 percent again. The oscillations reflect the periodic *chistki* of the Labor Exchange's rolls.) Unemployed union members could also apply for union unemployment benefits. Like the state, the unions were primarily concerned with skilled workers. This preference coupled with the unions' inability to finance a large relief program meant that only about one-quarter of the country's trade union members received union unemployment benefits.

Trade union organizations also provided special dining halls and temporary barracks lodgings for their unemployed members. The meals and lodgings are free, but the latter were generally overcrowded and tenants could only stay for up to two weeks.[87]

There existed another form of public relief for the unemployed—public works programs. In Moscow, the city soviet's Department of Labor was responsible for organizing public works and assigning personnel. The public works program began in late 1922. For the first two years, its funds and the number of participants were quite limited. In 1923, Commissar of Labor Shmidt stated: "We are not rich enough to carry them [public works—W. C.] out." In May 1923, public works programs provided work for less than 1,000 people.[88] From 1925, the number of participants grew steadily, but widely varying figures make it impossible to determine the precise number. Several sources place the number of participants at between 12,000 and 21,000 people. In 1926/27, the city Soviet claimed that 17,000 people per day took part in public work. Participants could work at such jobs for three months though some appear to have worked longer.[89]

All public work assignments were performed by *arteli* (labor collectives) that chose a leader *starosta* from among their members. Three types of collectives existed: labor, production, and trade. Labor collectives engaged in physical labor such as cleaning streets, parks, and buildings, demolishing buildings and carting off the remnants, chopping wood, and digging ditches. Production collectives were organized along occupational lines, consisted of people with comparable skills and experience, and peformed work related to their former occupation. In 1925, there were nine production collectives: weaving, construction, metalworking, leatherworking, laundering, photography, glassworking, book binding, and mechanical repairs. Such *arteli* repaired durable goods, production equipment, and even industrial plants that had been shut down. Trade collectives simply transported goods. The wages varied for each type of collective, and within each collective by the skill level of the participant. In 1927, the unskilled engaged in heavy physical labor earned one ruble ten kopecks a day; the skilled who worked in production *artels* earned one ruble eighty kopecks.

Several examples of production collectives in 1928 illustrate their differing sizes and functions. One such *artel* repaired automobiles and trucks and consisted of seventy people—54 workers, 9 employees, and 7 service personnel. In an old factory, there operated a joiners shop which repaired furniture; 277 people (248 of whom were workers) worked here.

160

At the Feniks boot factory, 720 workers, 55 employees, and 22 service personnel repaired footwear. The assignment of juveniles as apprentices and the retraining of older workers in these collectives was commonplace.[90] Production collectives comprised of unemployed juveniles also existed. For example, in 1928, there operated a paper bag factory staffed entirely by juveniles who resided in Komsomol-sponsored production homes. The workforce consisted of 259 workers, 14 employees, and 10 minor service personnel. Unemployed skilled workers taught the youths skills and production techniques.[91]

Some production collectives were obviously quite large and operated as enterprises in and of themselves. None of them produced new products and thereby avoided the charge of competing with factories that produced comparable goods and had to pay workers at the prevailing wage rates. Because many of these production collectives worked in specialized areas, the proper allocation of personnel dictated the level of success and efficiency of such operations. Such was not the case in labor collectives. According to the city soviet, "the basic principle in the organization of labor collectives . . . consisted of the interchangeable composition of the workforce."[92] Labor *arteli* only operated from May to November; production *artels* operated year round. Judging from the social composition of selected *arteli*, the personnel responsible for assigning public works jobs did not always make a strenuous effort to allocate them on an equitable basis. Thirty percent of the participants in 1924 and 1925 were women, yet they comprised about half of the registered unemployed. Juveniles fared much better. They comprised 9 percent of all *artel* members in 1924 and 12 percent in 1925; they accounted for comparable percentages of the total registered unemployed.[93]

As important as public works jobs were, they were too few and provided too little, and only temporary, financial support. Given the growing numbers of unemployed Muscovites and the meager, or complete lack of, assistance that they received, many unemployed people found it very difficult to survive economically. A 1927 study of unemployed metalworkers revealed that 57 percent of them depended upon their relatives for support; more than one-third of them depended upon their husbands. Others had to fend for themselves. Some produced handicraft items or peddled used clothes, junk, and the like. In desperation, many women became prostitutes.[94]Some people turned to crime, in particular robbery (or banditry as the Soviet press called it). In the early 1920s, as unemployment and inflation mounted, reports of armed and unarmed robbery appeared regularly in the press. In later years, crimes were reported less frequently making it difficult to form any conclusive judgements about the motives. Among those cases that were reported, there were two features common to most reports: the perpetrators were males in their twenties and most were unemployed.[95]

Given that unemployment assistance (either in outright aid or in wages from public work) could not exceed the minimum wage, jobless Muscovites standard of living was considerably lower than that of their working counterparts. The plight of families the head of which was unemployed was lamentable, but that of unemployed individuals was extremely precarious. Budget studies of selected unemployed conducted in 1924 and 1927 provide a statistical glimpse into the jobless's struggle for economic survival.[96] It is difficult to ascertain how representative the samples were; hence the evidence presented here may or may not offer a worst case scenario.

In 1924, state and union unemployment assistance programs provided a minimum of aid to a minority of people. The limits of this support system are clearly reflected in the 1924 study. Among those surveyed, public aid accounted for only 15 to 38 percent their total income.[97] Surviving on public aid was impossible. Income from the temporary work of the unemployed and their dependents augmented this assistance. Together, these sources accounted for less than half of the total income of those surveyed. To make ends meet, the unemployed depleted whatever savings and reserves that they had. But given the rampant inflation until eight months before the survey, such resources must have been limited. Finally, they sold family possessions, pawned personal items, and borrowed money from friends and family. Such practices yielded a fifth to a third of their income. Having tapped these resources, it was unlikely that they could be used again with any significant results.

Those surveyed in 1924 spent the vast majority of their income (80 to 90 percent) on food, rent, and utilities; food accounted for most (60 percent according to one study) of their expenditures.[98] Yet, the unemployed and their families consumed only two-thirds of the calories of the average working person (2,400 versus 3,600 calories). Their unbalanced diets consisted mostly of potatoes, grains, and vegetables; meat and dairy products were rarely consumed. The purchase of clothing and toiletries accounted for most of the remaining expenditures. Less than .5 percent of their income went to cultural and educational expenses; 2 to 5 percent, to the purchase of alcohol and tobacco. While some unemployed may have passed the day drinking or idling away their time, those surveyed reportedly spent an average of five hours a day visiting the Labor Exchange, their trade union, and other agencies in search of work.

By late 1927, the situation had improved but little had changed. The average income of those surveyed in Moscow had risen. State and union assistance now accounted for half of a family's and two-thirds of an individual's income. The remainder came from temporary work (13 and 10 percent respectively) and the other sources discussed above. The allocation of income was comparable to that in 1924. The diet of the average unemployed person had improved somewhat—he or she now consumed about 2,700 calories, and their protein intake increased slightly. Nonetheless, the diet remained substandard.[99] By 1927, the ranks of the unemployed had increased dramatically since 1924—perhaps doubled. The number of Muscovites suffering hardships and deprivation grew apace, but the potential for unrest increased geometrically.

Throughout the 1920s, the number of unemployed Muscovites rose steadily until by 1929 their ranks surpassed 200,000 and the unemployment rate there exceeded 20 percent. The influx of rural migrants and the economic and labor policies designed to lower production costs and to increase efficiency were the major causes of spiralling unemployment. The former was beyond the state's control. The futile attempts of rural correspondence points (*korpunkty*) to control and direct the flood of peasant migration testify to the state's limits. The latter cause was within the state's ability to change, but until 1929 few major changes occured. The labor and economic policies of the 1920s represented the continuation of the productivist policies enacted after mid-1918. Tying wages to productivity, raising output norms, and limiting the size of the labor force were among the means by which economic recovery and expansion were achieved.To advocates of the productivist position, the ends justified the means. Unemployment was an inevitable, but hopefully short-term consequence of an otherwise sound policy. While the speed with which the economy recovered vindicated and bolstered the productivists' position, the uninterrupted rise in unemployment after 1926 put them on the defensive and open to criticism by radicals who could justifiably point to the fact that the proletariat, the class on which the party and Soviet power was based, bore the brunt of unemployment. To the radicals, only a realignment of policy and a solution to the agricultural problem could alleviate the growing unemployment crisis.

The unemployment crisis wracked the proletariat. On the one hand, fear and resentment of rural migrants united urban workers against their against their "dangerous competitors." On the other hand, the crisis accelerated certain centrifugal tendencies within that class and pitted males against females, youths against their elders, and urban against new workers. What underlay both processes was that most basic of human emotions—fear, fear of losing one's job, fear of being unable to provide for one's family, fear of going hungry, fear of rejection and the doubts, anxieties, and loss of self-esteem that accompany it. The experience made a mockery of the proletariat's revolutionary dreams of economic security. While historians can measure the loss of buying power and reduced caloric intake, we are often unable to properly compute the psychological calculus that pits co-workers and neighbors against each other and drives the desperate to sell their bodies or murder officials whom they believe deny them the right to be productive, self-respecting citizens. What minimized the short-term political consequences of mass unemployment was the nature of the experience; it was very individualized and alienating. But it was never forgotten. The fear that it engendered daily divided the working class, and consciously or unconsciously helped to forge a tacit alliance between urban workers, who demanded a realization of their long-deferred revolutionary agenda, and the party's radicals in the late 1920s.

Notes

1. A. Bakhutov, "Bezrabotitsa, birzhi truda i profsoiuzy," *Vestnik truda*, 8(1924), 33-41; *Trud v SSSR, 1926-1930gg.*, 36.

2. Based on my computations from Labor Exchange data in *Ezhemesiachyi statisticheskii bulleten'*, December 1927, otd. V, tab. 4, 14. It should be noted that not all of the city's unemployed were registered at the Exchange. See the discussion below and note 10.

3. L. E. Mints, "Bezrabotitsa v dorevoliutsionnoi Rossii i SSSR," *Bol'shaia sovetskaia entsiklopedia*, 65 vols. (Moscow, 1926-1931), tom. 5, 214.

4. The Mel'nichanskii article is in *Rabochaia Moskva*, July 21, 1922; see also *ibid.*, May 16, 1922.

5. *Trud*, November 11, 1922.

6. For an example, see: *Rabochaia Moskva*, December 13, 1922; *Moskovskii proletarii*, June 22, 1924.

7. See the discussion in K. I. Suvorov, *Istoricheskii opyt KPSS po likvidatsii bezrabotitsy (1917-1930))* (Moscow, 1968), 103-104.

8. See the discussion in *Moskovskii sovet, 1917-1927*, 260-261; K. I. Suvorov, *Istoricheskii opyt*, 105.

9. *SZ*, 1925, 2/15.

10. *Rabochaia Moskva*, December 14, 1922; *Pravda*, November 30, 1922, reported that up to one-third of the registered unemployed printers in Moscow were fake registrants.

11. *Ibid.*, February 23, 1923.

12. For a discussion of the *chistka* of the rolls, see: A. Bakhutov, "Praktika birzh truda," *Vestnik truda*, 4 (1925), 49-54; *Vlast' sovetov*, 5 (1925), 6-7. The latter source states that the decision to make registration at the *Birzha truda* voluntary was accompanied by the *chistka* of the rolls. These sources place the proportion of those removed from the rolls at 55-60 percent. See also L. E. Mints, "Rynok truda v sviazi reorganizatsei Birzh truda," *Voprosy truda*, 12 (1924), 23-27. According to Mints, the number of registered unemployed in Moscow dropped by 49 percent from 106,000 in September 1924 to 54,000 in November 1924.

13. *Trud*, August 17, 1927; *Moskovskii proletarii*, July 6, 1927, 6.

14. For examples, see *Moskovskii proletarii*, December 1, 1927; February 14, February 22, 1928.

15. *Trud*, May 6, 1928; *Pravda*, May 18, 1928. An earlier article had portended this disclosure, see *Trud*, April 8, 1928.

16. *Pravda*, October 14, 1925.

17. My computations based on Labor Exchange data in *Ezhemesiachyi statisticheskii bulleten'*, January-December, 1925, otd. V, tab. 4, 14; January-December, 1927, otd. V, tab. 4, 14.

18. *Pravda*, January 17, 1922. For a discussion of the impact of demobilization, see: L. S. Rogachevskaia, *Likvidatsiia bezrabotitsy v SSSR, 1917-1930gg.* (Moscow, 1973), 85-86; K. I. Suvorov, *Istoricheskii opyt*, 69, 83, 131-132; N. P. Poniatovskaia, "Vosstanovlenie promyshlennosti i rost rabochego klassa v pervye gody NEPa," *Leninskoe uchenie o NEPe i ego mezhdunarodnoe znachenie* (Moscow, 1973), 129-135.

19. For the decree, see *SU*, 1922, 19, 209. See also K. I. Suvorov, *Istoricheskii opyt*, 132.

20. *Ekonomicheskaia zhizn'*, July 28, 1922.

21. For a discussion of the impact of these policies on unemployment, see *Professional'nye soiuzy SSSR, 1924-1926*, xix; Zavodskii, "Nasha bezrabotitsa i mery bor'by s nei," *Vlast' sovetov*, 2 (1924), 40-45.

22. In October 1921, the city soviet created a special commission to reduce the cost and improve the structure of the local bureaucracy. In 1924, a similar resolution reduced the size of the local bureaucracy by 10 to 25 percent. See: *Moskovskii sovet, 1917-1927*, 121; Aleshchenko, *Moskovskii sovet*, 223. For the Eleventh Party Conference resolution, see *KPSS v rezoliutsiiakh*, II, 304. See also Rogachevskaia, *Likvidatsiia*, 86.

23. Such was the opinion of all contemporary officials. For examples, see: *Professional'nye soiuzy SSSR, 1924-1926*, xix, 247-248; *Professional'nye soiuzy SSSR, 1926-1928*, xx; L. E. Mints, "Sovremennoe sostoianie bezrabotitsy v SSSR," *Statisticheskii obozrenie*, 3 (1927), 31-39; L. E. Mints, *Rynok truda v Rossii (za 1922g i I polovinu 1923g)* (Moscow, 1923), 26-28; A. Bakhutov, "Bezrabotitsa v SSSR i bor'ba s nei," *Vestnik truda*, 11 (1927), 38-44.

24. See the discussion of estimates in Danilov, "Krest'ianskii otkhod," 62-84.

25. L. E. Mints, "K probleme agrarnogo perenaseleniia (k voprosu o kharaktere gorodskoi bezrabotitsy)," *Voprosy truda*, 2 (1928), 15-19, estimates that the percentage of superfluous agrarian population nationally by the size of peasant holdings to be as follows: up to 2 *desiatini*—20.7 percent; *2-4 des.—33.6 percent; 4-6 des.*—20.7 percent; *6-8 des.*—11.2 percent; 8 or more *des.*—13.8 percent. According to Khriashchina, *Gruppy i klassy v krest'ianstve*, 35, as noted in K. I. Suvorov, *Istoricheskii opyt*, 73, the proportion of the superfluous rural population by the size of holdings was: landless peasants—73 percent; up to 2 *des.*—52 percent; 2-4 *des.*—46 percent; 4-6 *des.*—35 percent; 6 or more *des.*)—27 percent.

26. As quoted in K. I. Suvorov, *Istoricheskii opyt*, 72.

27. Mints, "K probleme agrarnogo perenaseleniia," 15.

28. As quoted in Carr, *Socialism*, I, 390.

29. For the April 1925 CC plenum resolution, see *KPSS v rezoliutsiiakh*, II, 116-120; for the Fifteenth Party Congress resolution, see *ibid.*, II, 433-441.

30. As quoted in E. H. Carr and R. W. Davies, *Foundations of a Planned Economy, 1926-1929* 2 vols. (New York, 1969), I, part II, 458.

31. As quoted in K. I. Suvorov, *Istoricheskii opyt, 152; see also, 70-71.*

32. *Trud*, July 1, 1925.

33. Mints, *Agrarnoe perenaselenie*, 453-460.

34. G. Belkin, "Bezrabotitsa i neorgannizovannyi trud," *Vestnik truda*, 12 (1927), 38-43. He claims that the majority of such people were hired without going through the *Birzha truda* or, if they did go through this agency, they were often hired for temporary jobs. According to S. Tarasov, "Sostoianie rynok truda i mery ego regulirovaniia v 1926/1927 khoziaistvennom godu," *Voprosy truda*, 5 (1927), 28, there was an increase in the proportion of temporary jobs procured through the exchanges.

35. Carr and Davies, *Foundations*, I, part I, 461; *Trud*, December 1, 1926.

36. *Professional'nye soiuzy SSSR, 1926-1928*, 395. Mints, *Agrarnoe perenaselenie*, 320, claims that within the CIR in 1925/26, 20 percent of the *otkhodniki* who secured industrial employment remained on the job.

37. K. I. Suvorov, *Istoricheskii opyt*, 82-83.

38. V. V. Shmidt, "Voprosy bezrabotitsy, gosnormirovaniia i okhrany truda sovtorgsluzhashchikh," *Voprosy truda*, 6 (1927), 5-12. The comments came in a speech to the All-Union Congress of Soviet Trade Employees. See also A. Isaev, "Blizhaishie zadachi po regulirovaniiu rynok truda: zadachi po regulirovaniiu gorodskogo rynok truda," *Vestnik truda*, 5 (1927), 10-15. Such preferential treatment, Isaev argued, would serve the interests of unionized urban workers.

39. A. Isaev, "Bezrabotitsa i bor'ba s nei v 1927/28 (k kontrol'nym tsifram po trudu)," *Voprosy truda*, 11 (1927), 17-28. See also, Danilov, "Krest'ianskii otkhod," 110, who places the number of *otkhodniki* in 1928/29 at a minimum of 4.3 million. See also P. Lebit, "Rabota Moskovskoi Birzhi

truda za 1925-1926g.," *Voprosy truda,* 12 (1926), 97-103. Within two months of the introduction of the free labor market, a Labor Exchange for seasonal labor was established in Moscow. Registration was voluntary and consequently the number of registrants was low. The purpose of this Exchange was to direct seasonal migrants to known job opportunites. N. Karchevskii, "Opyt aktivnogo posrednichestva Posredsezon-Biuro pri Komitete Moskovskoi Birzhi Truda," *Voprosy truda,* 11 (1925), 149-157. According to Mints, *Agrarnoe perenaselenie,* 291-293, the high unemployment in Moscow was responsible for a slight decrease in the number of seasonal migrants after 1925. See also *Pervye shagi industrializatsii SSSR, 1926-1927gg.* (Moscow, 1959), 234.

40. Isaev, "Blizhaishie zadachi," 13. Isaev places the annual number of *otkhodniki* nationwide prior to 1914 at about 5 mllion. For evidence of the increasing concern of union and labor officials over the need to regulate the labor market, see: Isaev, "Bezrabotitsa i bor'ba," 17-28; N. Aristov, "Sezonnyi rynok truda i ego regulirovanie," *Vestnik truda,* 3 (1927), 28-37; Shmidt, "Voprosy bezrabotitsy, gosnormirovaniia, i okhrana truda," 5-12.

41. *SZ,* 1927, 13/139; *SZ,* 1927, 13/132. For an April 1927 resolution "On Measures for the Regulation of Recruiting Operations," see *SZ,* 1927, 19/219.

42. For a discussion, see Carr and Davies, *Foundations,* I, part II, 460-462. Some economic organs appear to have opposed this change in policy. See L. Shastin, "Sezonnyi rynok truda v 1926/27 godu," *Voprosy truda,* 2 (1928), 48. For a discussion of these measures, see: Danilov, "Krest'ianskii otkhod," 108; Rogachevskaia, *Likvidatsiia,* 119-120.

43. For a discussion of the evolution, responsibilities and problems of *korpunkty,* see: Isaev, "Blizhaishie zadachi"; Isaev, "Bezrabotitsa i bor'ba"; Danilov, "Krest'ianskii otkhod," 106-107.

44. *Trud,* June 15, 1928.

45. For a description and photographs, see: Aristov, "Sezonnyi rynok truda," 28-37.

46. *Pravda,* March 18, 1927.

47. Aristov, "Sezonnyi rynok truda"; Karchevskii, 149-153.

48. The problem of housing will be discussed in chapter 5. But for a sample of the discussions of the problem as it affected *otkhodniki* and the unemployed, see: Lebit, "Rabota Moskovskoi Birzhi truda"; Karchevskii; *Stroitel'stvo Moskvy,* 4 (1926), 8-9; Rogachevskaia, *Likvidatsiia,* 126.

49. Serebrennikov, 57.

50. *SU,* 1922, 18/203.

51. A. G. Rashin, *Zhenskii trud v SSSR* (Moscow, 1928), vyp. 1, 8; Serebrennikov, 57; Carr, *Socialism,* I, 392.

52. *Rabochaia Moskva,* July 21, 1922. See also, *ibid.,* May 21, 1922.

53. Mints, *Rynok truda,* tab. 9, 14, places the proportion of unemployment by sex as of December 1, 1922 at: males - 38.3 percent; females - 42.9 percent; *podrostki* (both sexes) - 18.8 percent.

54. Data on female unemployment can be found in: *Moskva i Moskovskaia guberniia,* 149; *Statisticheskii spravochnik . . . 1927,* 187; *Moskovskii*

proletarii, March 8, 1926, 3. According to *Trud v Moskovskoi gubernii*, 80, the rate of unemployment among Muscovite females in 1923/24 was only about 30 percent. It is hard to explain this discrepancy. Nationally the proportion of unemployed females remained relatively constant—44.4 percent in January 1926 and January 1927. Serebrennikov, 60. For female unemployment by occupation, in 1926, see *Perepis'* . . . *1926g.*, tom. 19, tab. VI, 577. For comparable data by industrial profession, see *Moskva i Moskovskaia guberniia*, 149.

55. The lack of skills among female job-seekers surely diminished their opportunities for employment. In February 1926, two-thirds of the registered unemployed females were unskilled; in 1925, only 16 percent of unskilled females found jobs. *Moskovskii proletarii*, March 8, 1926, 3. That sexually discriminatory hiring practices continued in certain male-dominated industries is clear—in 1927, 75 percent of the unemployed metalworkers were women. *Trud*, December 1, 1927.

56. K. I. Suvorov, *Istoricheskii opyt*, 125.

57. For juvenile employment and unemployment figures, see: *Rabochaia Moskva*, October 22, 1922; *Professional'nye soiuzy SSSR, 1924-1926*, 130; *Trud v SSSR, 1924-1926* (Moscow, 1926), 6; i *Moskva i Moskovskaia guberniia*, 125, 154-155; I. Peremyslovskii, "Bezrabotitsa sredi podrostkov," *Voprosy truda*, 8-9 (1926), 39-43; A. Anikst, "Plan bor'by s bezrabotitsei na 1926g," *ibid.*, 2 (1926), 12-17; *Moskovskii proletarii*, February 7, 1927. Males appear to have comprised a slight majority of all unemployed juveniles. In using any published unemployment data for juveniles, one must be extremely cautious. Many juveniles apparently did not register at the *Birzha truda* either because they believed that they had no prospect of getting a job or because, as inexperienced workers, they were not entitled to unemployment benefits. However, juveniles who were in school and registered at the Labor Exchange were included in published unemployment figures.

58. Once again, precise statistics are lacking. For *Birzha truda* figures, see Peremyslovskii. For trade union figures, see *Professional'nye soiuzy SSSR, 1924-1926*, 123-131; *Professional'nye soiuzy SSSR, 1926-1928*, 118-125. For Moscow union figures, see *Moskovskii proletarii*, February 7, 1927. Rogachevskaia states that, according to NKT data, the absolute number of unemployed juveniles remained relatively constant in 1925-1926 and therefore the proportion of unemployed who were juveniles declined from 13.2 percent in October 1925 to 11.9 percent in April 1926. Rogachevskaia, *Likvidatsiia*, 133. This data appears to come from Peremyslovskii, but according to his absolute data the number of jobless juveniles rose. The relative decline was apparently due to a rise in the number of unemployed adults.

59. The 4.5 percent quota for *podrostki* actually represents an average; precise quotas for each branch of the economy can be found in the decree. *SZ*, 1928, 49/437. See also: *Professional'nye soiuzy SSSR, 1926-1928*, 118-119; Rogachevskaia, *Likvidatsiia*, 135-136. On the failure to attain this new, lower quota, see A. Zubov, "Sostoianie broni podrostkov v soiuznoi promyshlennosti," *Voprosy truda*, 12 (1929), 98-102.

60. K. I. Suvorov, *Istoricheskii opyt,* 74.

61. *Trud,* April 10, 1927; Anikst, "Plan bor'by," 12-17; Rogachevskaia, *Likvidatsiia,* 131-132. In 1926, only 8 percent of the *podrostki* registered at the Labor Exchanges nationwide had production experience. K. I. Suvorov, *Istoricheskii opty,* 128-129. In 1928, the city soviet allocated 2.5 million rubles for the training and retraining of workers. At that time, there were forty-one evening courses in which more than 5,000 young people were enrolled. Another 5,600 people received training in either FZU schools or courses organized in factories. What proportion of these people were *podrostki* is unclear. Aleshchenko, *Moskovskii sovet,* 369-370.

62. *Komsomol'skaia Pravda,* September 1, 1927. See also Vladimir Zenzinov, *Deserted: The Story of the Children Abandoned in Soviet Russia* (trans. Agnes Platt, Westport, Connecticut, 1975).

63. *Professional'nye soiuzy SSSR, 1926-1928,* 119.

64. For an example, see *Izvestiia tekstil'noi promyshlennosti i torgovli,* January 15, 1925, 14.

65. Carr and Davies, *Foundations,* I, part II, 473.

66. *Pravda,* December 11, 1929; Peremyslovskii, 39-43; Rogachevskaia, *Likvidatsiia,* 133; K. I. Suvorov, *Istoricheskii opyt,* 125-126.

67. See the article by Tomskii in *Pravda,* October 22, 1926. For examples, see A. S. Makarenko, *The Road to Life (An Epic of Education)* 3 vols. (trans. Ivy and Tatiana Litvinov, Moscow, 1951), esp. vol. 1. For a discussion, see Rogachevskaia, *Likidatsiia, 80; K. I. Suvorov, Istoricheskii opyt,* 125-126. See also chapter 5.

68. V. V. Shmidt, "Nashi dostizhenniia i nedostatki v oblasti regulirovaniia truda i ocherednye zadachi nashei trudovoi politiki," *Voprosy truda,* 1 (1927), 102-103; Carr and Davies, *Foundations,* I, part II, 457-482.

69. Carr and Davies, *Foundations,* I, part II, 478-482.

70. Fitzparick, "Cultural Revolution," 8-40.

71. *Trud,* November 5, 1922.

72. *Trud v Moskovskoi gubernii,* 85.

73. *Statisticheskii spravochnik . . . 1927,* 188. Unemployment among Communist Party members also increased during the decade—from 16,000 in July 1925 to 45,000 in January 1927. An unspecified majority of these were workers. K. I. Suvorov, *Istoricheskii opyt,* 80, 159.

74. *Istoriia Moskvy,* VI, 1, 297. It is unclear what criteria were used to identify these workers as skilled. The classification may have been based on the workers' own testimony. If so, there are two reasons to be suspicious about these figures. First, workers may have elevated their skill level in the hopes of securing employment. Second, many workers had their own conception of what constituted skill and may therefore have unconsciously overestimated their abilities. On workers' self-conception of skill in pre-revolutionary times, see P. Timofeev, "What the Factory Worker Lives By," in *The Russian Worker: Life and Labor under the Tsarist Regime* (ed. by Victoria E. Bonnell, Berkeley, 1983), 77.

75. *Trud,* July 14, 1927. In late 1928, Moscow SNKh ordered local labor

departments to provide for the retraining of some 10,000 unemployed skilled workers. That year the city soviet allocated 2.5 million rubles to this program. The training was to be done in conjunction with Gastev's TsIT. Aleshchenko, *Moskovskii sovet*, 369.

76. P. Lebit, "Itogi pereregistratsii bezrabotnykh v Moskve," *Voprosy truda*, 4 (1927).

77. *Trud v Moskovskoi gubernii*, 84-85. According to the Moscow soviet, almost half of the city's jobless lacked production experience. *Trud*, July 14, 1927. L. E. Mints, "Sovremennoe sostoianie bezrabotitsy v SSSR," 31-39, puts the proportion of unskilled at 55 percent in October 1926. See also Bakhutov, "Bezrabotitsa v SSSR," 38-44. On job openings, see *Statisticheskii spravochnik . . . 1927*, 36-37.

78. *Trud*, September 3, 1928.

79. *Rabochaia Moskva*, July 21, 1922, May 13, 1923; *Trud v Moskovskoi gubernii*, 85.

80. *Trud v Moskovskoi gubernii*, 80-85; *Statisticheskii spravochnik . . . 1927*, 188.

81. Carr and Davies, *Foundations*, I, part II, 483.

82. Similar patterns existed among native and migrant residents. *Perepis' . . . 1926g*, tom. 52, tab. III, 114-136; Lebit, "Itogi pereregistratsii." Rogachevskaia, *Likvidatsiia*, 77.

83. See the discussions in K. I. Suvorov, *Istoricheskii opyt*, 83-84; Rogachevskaia, *Likvidatsiia*, 80-81. Both sources cite TsGAOR, f. 5469, op. 16, ed. khr. 72, l. 137. The commission was chaired by A. M. Lezhava (Deputy Chairman of SNK RSFSR and Chairman of Gosplan RSFSR) and consisted of A. M. Bakhutov (Commissar of Labor, RSFSR), L. E. Mints (Commissariat of Labor, SSSR), S. G. Strumilin (Gosplan, SSSR), and A. M. Anikst (Gosplan, SSSR).

84. See the discussion in Dewar, 117-118; Carr and Davies, *Foundations*, I, part II, 473-482.

85. Prior to 1923, the Peoples' Commissariat of Social Insurance was responsible for the unemployment assistance program.

86. *Trud v Moskovskoi gubernii*, 392-396. The decree establishing benefits was enacted in December 1921. *SU*, 1922, 1/23. This decree abrogated a SNK decree of October 1921 which guaranteed skilled workers dismissed from state enterprises owing to a reduction of staff or the closing of an enterprise the equivalent of the local minimum wage. Unskilled workers and employees with three years of work experience and who were dismissed for the above reasons received one-third to one-half of the local minimum wage. *SU*, 1921, 68/536. For a discussion see Rogachevskaia, *Likvidatsiia*, 99-101. Until June 1927, there were two categories of aid recipients. At that time, the Commissariat of Labor created three categories: (1) skilled workers and specialists; (2) semiskilled workers and employees; (3) individuals not having a profession. The amount of aid allotments (by category) for the three was: (1) one-third of the appropriate wage rate; (2) 30 percent of the wage rate; (3) 25 percent of the wage rate. At the same

time, unemployment insurance was extended from six to nine months. That year a Politburo commission recommended that unions spend more money on unemployment aid. See *ibid.*, 124-126. See also: *Trud v Moskovskoi gubernii*, 392-396; *Trud*, August 17, 1927; April 14, 1928. *Moskva i Moskovskaia guberniia*, tab. 108, 157. The unemployed also received supplemental allowances for dependents: an additional 15 percent of the unemployed's former wage for the first dependent, 25 percent for the second dependent, and 35 percent for three or more dependents. On average, 15 to 20 percent of the city's aid recipients received supplements. This practice began in January 1925. *Moskovskii sovet, 1917-1927*, 263; Rogachevskaia, *Likvidatsiia*, 125.

87. For a discussion of barracks for unemployed residents and *otkhodniki*, see: Karchevskii; Lebit, "Rabota Moskovskoi Birzhi truda"; *Stroitel'stvo Moskvy*, 4 (1926), 8-9; Rogachevskaia, *Likvidatsiia*, 103-104, 126.

88. As quoted and noted in Carr, *Interregnum*, 52.

89. The difficulty of ascertaining precise numbers of people who held public works jobs is due to the fact that some sources only report the number of workdays worked, some provide figures for only one type of work (e.g., production work), and others provide figures for the number of people who worked on a specific day. However, since the availability of public work contracted sharply during the winter months, it is impossible to factor the latter figures. Estimates for the number of participants can be found in: A. Isaev, "Bor'ba s bezrabotinets v 1922 godu," *Voprosy truda*, 2 (1923), 26-32; *Moskovskii sovet, 1917-1927*, 263-264; Aleshchenko, *Moskovskii sovet*, 307-310, 423; P. Zavodovskii, "Itogi obshestvennykh rabot v 1924 godu," *Voprosy truda*, 4 (1925), 3-15; *Stroitel'stvo Moskvy*, 7 (1924), 17; 5 (1925), 7-9; A. Isaev, "Bor'ba s bezrabotitsei v 1924 godu," *Voprosy truda*, 1 (1925), 36-43; M. Nefedov, "Trudovaia i material'naia pomoshch' bezrabotnym v Moskve," *ibid.*, 2 (1926), 135-136; *Moskovskii sovet za desiat' let*, 25. *Trud*, April 25, 1927, 6-7, states that in Moscow in 1927 public works jobs could only be held for two months. It is unclear when the change from the three month limit occurred.

90. The three examples can be found in *Fabriki i zavody Moskovskoi oblasti na 1928-1929 god* (Moscow, 1929), 14, 20, 124; see also 48, 160. For a discussion of the work performed by such *arteli* and the wage rates for same, see: Nefedov, "Trudovaia i material'naia pomoshch'"; A. Isaev, "Kollektivy iz bezrabotnykh v Moskve," *Voprosy truda*, 2 (1926), 135-136; D. Lediaev, "Bezrabotitsa v SSSR i bor'ba s nei (1917-1927gg.)," *ibid.*, 10 (1927), 105-113; *Stroitel'stvo Moskvy*, 5 (1925), 7; *Moskovskii proletarii*, April 8, 1927, 6-7; *Moskovskii sovet, 1917-1927*, 263; Aleshchenko, *Moskovskii sovet*, 307-310.

91. For data and discussions, see: Isaev, "Kollektivy iz bezrabotnykh"; Zavodovskii, "Itogi obshchestvennykh rabot"; *Stroitel'stvo Moskvy*, 5 (1925), 7; Aleshchenko, *Moskovskii sovet*, 307-310; K. I. Suvorov, *Istoricheskii opyt*, 130. For data on the paper bag factory, see *Fabriki i zavody Moskovskoi oblasti*, 48.

92. *Moskovskii sovet, 1917-1927,* 264.

93. See note 91.

94. *Trud,* December 1, 1927; Lebit, "Itogi pereregistratsii." See also Louise Shelley, "Female Criminality in the 1920s: A Consequence of Inadvertant and Deliberate Change," *Russian History/Histoire Russe,* 9, Parts 2-3 (1982), 265-284.

95. For examples, see: *Rabochaia Moskva,* March 17, March 18, April 24, August 27, 1922.

96. The following discussion of budgets is based on: L. E. Mints, *Kak zhivet bezrabotnyi (biudzhety bezrabotnykh)* (Moscow, 1927), as discussed in Rogachevskaia, *Likvidatsiia,* 28-29. (The Mints work is a study of selected unemployed in Moscow, Leningrad, Tula, and Ivanovo-Voznesensk.) L. E. Mints, "Biudzhety bezrabotnykh," *Statisticheskoe obozrenie,* 10 (1928), 48-55 (based on a late 1927 study of selected unemployed in the same four cities). Interested readers should also consult Katomin, "Biudzhet bezrabotnogo," *Voprosy truda,* 1 (1924), 61-62 (based on a December 1922 investigation of eleven unemployed families in Ivanovo-Voznesensk).

97. The one exception to this was leather workers for whom the combined public sources accounted for three-quarters of their total income.

98. E. Zakgeim, "Pitanie bezrabotnykh," *Statisticheskoe obozrenie,* 1 (1929), 56.

99. *Ibid.,* 56-60, provides a detailed analysis of the diets of selected unemployed in 1927. His study provides an interesting complement to the Mints study of that year.

5. Daily Life in Moscow, 1921-1929

On the Bolshevik revolution's tenth anniversary, *Trud* published an article entitled "Moscow after ten years,"[1] which noted with justifiable pride the Soviet state's many accomplishments—lower death and infant mortality rates, fewer deaths from infectious diseases and tuberculosis, easily accessible medical care, the rising standard of living, and improved working conditions. Few could argue with these successes and the ways in which they ameliorated life in Moscow. But the capital was far from problem free. Annually, deepening unemployment and housing crises engulfed the city. Its apartments were overcrowded and rife with tensions; thousands were homeless. Shortages of consumer goods and municipal services complicated many residents', especially women's, lives. Life's daily problems and strains seemed minor compared to those of the 1918 to 1921 period, but they were no less real and no less irritating. In fact, precisely because the economic recovery and improvements raised hopes and expectations, some workers found the enduring problems particularly troublesome and frustrating. More important, solutions to these problems remained beyond the control of workers and, given the NEP's fiscal strictures, that of the city soviet.

Because deepening problems and mounting frustrations continually undermined improvements and successes, a ubiquitous yet rather amorphous dissatisfaction and anger tempered workers' hopes and aspirations. Outside the factories, they expressed these emotions most concretely in their complaints about housing. While they frequently criticized the city soviet for its failures and inability to overcome the shortage and poor quality of housing, workers more often vented their wrath on their well-to-do neighbors—nepmen, professionals, speculators, specialists—whom they believed prospered at their expense and who enjoyed creature comforts of which workers could only dream. The steady stream of press articles which criticized these groups' behavior and activities and the official campaigns against them heightened and legitmized workers' prejudices, attitudes and behavior. When the agricultural crisis struck in 1928, workers' standard of living began to plummet. Fear of a return to the deprivations of the 1918-1922 period heightened worker anger and made many receptive to the party's campaign against society's "bourgeois" elements—specialists, nepmen, and kulaks.[2]

While many issues divided the proletariat, the experiences of daily life outside the factory worked to unite them around common grievances and against common enemies. By examining workers' daily experiences and frustrations, we can refine our understanding of that class' attitudes and behavior. This chapter focuses on the most important of these daily realities—the standard of living, housing, family life, and relations between workers and their neighbors. In chapters 6 and 7, we will see how these experiences and attitudes affected factory life.

The Standard of Living

After years of economic collapse and deprivation, raising the workers' living standard proved to be a slow and uneven process. Until 1924, workers' standard of living improved at times and declined at others. There were several reasons for this fluctuation. One was the abandonment of natural wages at a time of hyper-inflation. In late 1920, natural wages accounted for 95 percent of the average worker's pay; the next year the proportion fell to 85 percent. During 1922, the transition to money wages intensified. By mid-1924, wages in kind accounted for only 7 percent of the average paycheck. Late that year, they were abandoned entirely.[3] Despite the steady rise in workers' nominal wages,[4] inflation often reduced their value thereby subjecting the rise in real wages to periodic reversals. Reliance on the expensive private market for many essential commodities further sapped workers' buying power.

Delayed wage payments also undermined workers' real wages. Delaying wage payments was a common practice during the early 1920s. The currency depreciation placed factory administrators in extremely awkward positions—by law their expenditures could not exceed their income, and they had to pay their workers on time. In heavy industrial enterprises that were slow to recover, the cash flow problem and shortage of capital were especially severe and intensified with the transition to cash wages. Either for lack of money or for bookkeeping purposes, many factory administrators delayed paying wages. Given the inflation rate, even a few days delay reduced workers' purchasing power. Understandably, the practice also contributed to widespread worker unrest. Nationally in 1922-1923, wage issues accounted for half of the strikes and two-thirds of the strikers. The figures for Moscow were comparable. During the summer of 1923, industrial unrest reached a peak and rumors of a general strike appear to have had some basis in fact.[5] Most strikes were wildcat strikes organized around wage issues without the knowledge or support of the unions.[6]

The situation at the AMO plant in 1922 is representative of the discontent which wage delays engendered. Early that year, the factory administration announced that it was in arrears and unable to pay the workers. This gave rise to "spontaneous meetings of workers without the knowledge of the factory committee" or the union. A wildcat strike of unspecified duration ensued. One month later, the management told the factory committee that they once again lacked the funds to pay workers. "The meeting was stormy" and the workers gave the administrators five days in which to pay them or they would again strike. Manangement came up with the money and the strike was averted.[7]

In December 1923, the party reiterated its opposition to wage delays. The Sixth Trade Union Congress in 1924 also condemned the practice because it weakened the proletariat's material position and hindered efforts to increase production. After the 1924 currency reform, the number of cases of delayed wage payments and the attendant strikes diminished, although the practice still occured as late as 1928.[8]

For these reasons, calculating the extent to which workers' standard of living rose between 1921 and 1924 is difficult. Contemporary officials were equally as confounded. At the Thirteenth Party Conference in January 1924, Tomskii, the trade union boss, claimed that real wages had risen during the previous year, but several delegates challenged his claim.[9] According to one calculation, average real wages in Moscow in October 1922 stood at more than 60 percent of the 1913 level. But according to *Trud*, workers' average real wages nationwide were less than 40 percent of the 1913 wage.[10]

After 1924, steadily rising nominal wages and the relatively stable currency and prices quickly raised workers' living standard. For all workers, the nominal wage hikes were significant. Between early 1925 and late 1928, the average Moscow worker's wage rose by about one-third.[11]

There was, however, considerable disparity from industry to industry—textile workers' wages increased by 50 percent; for printers, the figure was less than 20 percent (see appendix 7). Wages also varied with skill levels and production experience. For example, unskilled workers in 1927 earned about 70 percent of the average worker's wage,[12] whereas older, experienced, skilled workers could earn twice the average wage. To make the wage data in appendix 7 more meaningful, it should be considered in conjunction with table 5-1. As the table indicates, the majority of the country's (and presumably Moscow's) workers earned less than the average wage. Considering the shortage of skilled workers, this pattern is hardly surprising.

Real wages also rose steadily. In 1926, average real wages reached the prewar level. During the next two years, they increased significantly: in 1926/27, they exceeded the 1913 level by 15 percent; in 1927/28, they were more than 20 percent higher.[13] Even for many of those whose real wages fell below the average, their standard of living after 1926 was better than before the revolution. The free social insurance system, low-cost housing, transportation and admission to social and cultural events, and, in some cases, free education translated into greater economic security and real wages than in pre-revolutionary times.[14] The years 1925-1928 were indeed the "good years" of the NEP.[15] But the onset of the agricultural crisis in 1928 suddenly undid these gains—food prices in the private markets soared from 100 to 200 percent higher than those in state markets and in 1929 rationing was re-introduced.

Even during the heyday, however, many working-class families found it difficult to make ends meet unless more than one member worked or

TABLE 5-1

Monthly Wages of Industrial Workers Nationally as a Percent of the Average Wage

Monthly wages as a percentage of average wage	Percent of workers in each group (by year)				
	1924	1925	1926	1927	1928
Below 50%	19.8%	17.2%	15.0%	12.6%	11.6%
From 50% to 100%	41.5%	44.7%	43.2%	45.6%	46.7%
From 100% to 150%	22.8%	23.4%	24.6%	26.3%	26.3%
From 150% to 200%	9.2%	8.4%	9.8%	9.5%	9.6%
From 200% to 250%	3.7%	3.1%	3.9%	3.2%	3.1%
Over 250%	3.0%	3.2%	3.0%	2.8%	2.7%

SOURCE: Zagorsky, 176.

they had other sources of income. In 1926, approximately one-quarter of Moscow's proletarian families had two or more members working. Factory workers' families had the highest proportion of multiple wage earners. In families where the primary wage earner was unskilled or semiskilled and hence generally earned less than the average wage, the financial pressure to have family members work was greatest. Given the unemployment rate, securing work was often difficult and hence many workers' relatives engaged in petty trade, part-time and seasonal work, and occasionally speculation. Such activities were most common among low-paid workers' families.[16]

While workers' living standard rose until 1928, that of their bosses and many nepmen was much higher and rose more rapidly. In early 1925, the average worker's monthly wage was 64 rubles and that of the average employee was 108 rubles; by late 1928, the figures were approximately 95 and 150 rubles respectively (see appendix 7). But these averages conceal the very high salaries earned by some employees. Factory directors, engineers, and technical specialists were among the highest paid employees, and, in 1928, they earned average monthly salaries of 220 rubles. Some within this group of administrators earned much more, upward of 600 rubles in the case of "bourgeois" (as opposed to Communist) factory directors.[17] It was these personnel who implemented unpopular labor policies and productivity campaigns in the factory. While workers labored harder with each passing year, their wages declined relative to those of their bosses. Many nepmen also earned more than workers. In 1925/26, the average monthly income of a "bourgeois" entrepreneur (a factory owner or successful trader) was 420 rubles, while that of a "semi-capitalist entrepreneur" (a small scale producer or trader) was 100 rubles.[18]

As a class, workers earned less than any of the city's major occupational groups, significantly less in some cases. While they struggled daily to make ends meet, such "bourgeois" elements, who had been pariahs after the revolution, prospered. Their good fortune galled workers. Envy, anger, frustration, these emotions provided the backdrop against which workers and their "bourgeois" neighbors interacted.

To understand how workers spent their wages and how their living standard changed during the 1920s, let us examine a series of budget studies compiled by Soviet researchers. Table 5-2 presents the results of budget studies for workers, and in one case employees, for 1908, 1922, 1924, and 1927. Each study's sample differed. The 1908 study, which is included for the sake of comparison, was based on an investigation of workers' families in European Russia. There are two 1922 studies—for workers' families and for single workers—and three 1924 studies—for single workers, for workers' families and for employees' families. All five were conducted in Moscow. The 1927 budget comes from a three-year dynamic study of workers' families in Moscow.[19] Because the absolute amount spent on each category varied with income and, prior to mid-1924, the inflation rate distorted wages and costs, the table lists only percentages so as to allow for comparisons.

Workers' families devoted slightly less than half of their income to food. The 1922 figures reflect the expenditures for December only and are not representative of the annual average. Because of the 1921-1922 famine, until the 1922 harvest Muscovites reportedly spent upward of 95 percent of their income on food.[20] In that year, food and rationing were the main topics of factory meeting discussions,[21] and newspapers ran regular columns devoted to the famine and its consequences.[22] But even after the famine, regular newspaper articles on available food supplies underscore Muscovites' and officials' ongoing concern with food.[23]

The proportion of workers' wages spent on food varied with one's income. Throughout the 1920s, the lowest paid workers spent more than half and the highest paid workers only one-quarter of their earnings on food.[24] As real wages rose, so too did the amount of food purchased. The quality of food consumed also improved and workers' diets became increasingly well balanced as the years passed. Among working-class families surveyed in December 1922, animal products (meat, fish, and dairy products) accounted for only 9 percent of the food consumed, grains (rye, wheat, and grits) for 47 percent, and vegetables and potatoes for 42 percent. Their average caloric intake was 3,409 calories, most of which came from bread and potatoes. Two years later, the diets had changed markedly. Meat and dairy products accounted for one-fifth of the food consumed; vegetables and potatoes for one-third. Grains remained the major staple, accounting for 43 percent of their diet. But the types of grain consumed changed somewhat. Those surveyed in 1924 ate three times more wheat and 40 percent less rye than their counterparts in 1922. Because of the reduced intake of grains and potatoes, the average worker in 1924 consumed 3,250 calories. This improved diet, which provided more protein and vitamins, remained the norm until 1928.[25] Not everyone, however, ate such balanced diets, which obviously varied with income and personal preferences.

TABLE 5-2
Budget Studies for 1908, 1922, 1924, and 1927[a]

Expenditures	1 1908	2 1922	3 1922	4 1924	5 1924	6 1924	7 1927
Food	48.7%	47.1%	37.1%	44.2%	32.9%	45.5%	45.3%
Rent	17.9%	2.3%	1.9%	7.6%	4.8%	10.3%	9.4%
Fuel, electricity	2.9%	10.6%	5.7%	4.6%	2.4%	5.8%	1.4%
Household items	—	1.9%	2.0%	4.1%	3.3%	1.6%	2.9%
Clothing	12.2%	24.0%	31.6%	21.4%	27.1%	15.4%	21.4%
Alcohol, tobacco	5.4%	2.2%	2.6%	3.1%	3.8%	2.8%	5.3%
Health, hygiene	4.6%	1.1%	1.3%	1.5%	1.1%	1.1%	1.0%
Entertainment, culture	3.3%	2.1%	3.4%	2.3%	3.8%	3.8%	1.7%
Politics, trade union	1.2%	4.7%	4.8%	3.6%	4.2%	3.8%	2.5%
Aid to relatives	2.2%	—	—	1.8%	8.4%	1.5%	1.8%
Other	1.9%	4.0%	9.6%	5.8%	8.2%	8.4%	7.4%
Total	100.0%	100.0%	100.0%	100.0%	100.0%	100.0%	100.0%

a. Description of samples and sources:
   Column 1: Workers' families in European Russia, 1908; Sosnovy, 167.
   Column 2: Workers' families in Moscow, December, 1922; *Statistika truda*, 3 (February, 1923), 1-7.
   Column 3: Single workers in Moscow, December 1922; *Statistika truda*, 3 (February, 1923), 1-7.
   Column 4: Workers' families in Moscow, November, 1924; *Trud v Moskovskoi gubernii*, 250-251.
   Column 5: Single workers in Moscow, November, 1924; *Trud v Moskovskoi gubernii*, 250-251.
   Column 6: Employees' families in Moscow, November 1924; *Trud v Moskovskoi gubernii*, 255.
   Column 7: Workers' families in Moscow, January-June, 1927; R. Gindin, "Dinamika budzhet Moskovskogo rabochego poslednie tri goda," *Voprosy truda*, 1 (1928), 113-121.

In the early 1920s, workers received food from three sources—rations, state stores and cooperatives, and private markets. Although rationing continued until 1924, the size of rations declined sharply after 1922. Workers purchased 60 percent of their food in September 1923 at private markets; three years later, the proportion had declined to 38 percent.[26] Given the low cost,[27] increased quantity and improved variety of foodstuffs in state stores, workers were able to purchase more food there per ruble with each passing year and thereby to improve their diets. Then in 1927, a war scare gripped Russia.[28] Peasants, especially kulaks, responded to the scare and the worsening market situation by holding back their produce. Moscow quickly felt the effects. Food prices rose rapidly in 1928 and rationing was reintroduced early the next year. By late 1929, cereals, sugar, tea, butter, oil, herring, soap, eggs, meat, potatoes were rationed.[29] After several years of steady improvement, suddenly there was less food on the workers' tables. Once again, Muscovites were forced to turn to the private market where prices went as high as the market would bear, two to three times those in state markets. Rationing and the renewed dependence on the high priced, black market triggered memories of the Civil War. Justifiably fearful of a return to those days, many urban workers endorsed the party's collectivization and antikulak campaigns in hopes that they would alleviate the new crisis.[30] Clearly, the food situation during the 1920s was a mercurial one. The uncertainity of the early 1920s gave way to several years of steady improvement; but in 1928-1929, fear and anxiety once again punctuated workers' daily lives.

After food, the average working-class family devoted the next largest proportion of their income—more than one-fifth—to clothing. Although this marked a substantial improvement over pre-revolutionary times, workers were not necessarily better dressed. The limited availability and shoddy quality of some clothing combined to restrict the upgrading of most workers' wardrobes. The presence of more than 1,900 used clothes and junk dealers in Moscow in 1926 testifies to the considerable demand for used clothing.[31]

Prior to the revolution, rent and utilities consumed more than one-fifth of the average worker's income. In Russia in 1910, wages were lower and rents higher than anywhere in western Europe; Moscow had the country's highest rents.[32] For this reason, many workers lived in barracks and small, overcrowded apartments. After 1917, housing costs dropped dramatically, and during the 1920s, workers' rents remained very low.[33] Several factors determined an occupant's rent, the most important being his occupation. Workers received preferential treatment; their rents could not exceed 10 percent of their income. The 1928 rental scale used to determine rents in publicly owned housing fixed rents according to occupations. All other factors being equal, employees were to pay 28 percent more in rent than did workers, artisans/craftsmen (private operators) 175 percent more, professionals 324 percent more, and nonworking elements (e.g., proprietors) 934 percent more.[34] The dwelling's size and the presence (or absence) of running water, electricity, and/or sewer connections also affected the rent.[35] But the extent to which occupation-based rental scales actually determined rents is unclear. As we shall see, many workers believed that they did not.

Based on table 5-2, one might well deduce that workers in the 1920s consumed less alcohol than did their pre-revolutionary counterparts. Unfortunately, there is little other evidence to substantiate this deduction. Drunkeness and excessive alcohol consumption remained real problems in the 1920s, especially among new workers who continued the peasant custom of drinking oneself into oblivion (*zapit'*). But new workers were not that class's only drinkers, only its heartiest. Frequenting the neighborhood tavern remained a regular social ritual for many workers.

Until 1922, the state prohibited the sale of liquor, a policy initiated during World War I. Despite prohibition and the authorities' sustained struggle to curtail the number of boot-leggers (*samogonshchiki*), illegal *samogon* (home-brewed vodka, generally 25 proof) was easy to find. In 1922, the state legalized the sale of beer and wine; two years later, it did the same for hard liquor. As the availability of liquor and the number of rural migrants increased, the problem of alcohol abuse in the city became very serious. The increasing death toll there due to drunkenness testifies to the problem's dimensions. In 1923, when the production and sale of vodka were still forbidden, 16 deaths were attributed to drunkenness; in 1926, the figure soared to 144. During the 1926 Christmas holiday alone, 30 people died from excessive alcohol consumption. The proportion of patients in Moscow psychiatric clinics who received treatment for alcohol-related disorders rose from 6 percent in 1924 to 25 percent in 1925.[36] Clearly, excessive drinking was a severe problem and hence one should view with caution the data in table 5-2. Perhaps the most realistic feature of that data is that the proportion devoted that item rose steadily.

On the other hand, the small proportion of income spent on entertainment and culture masked a considerable gain. In pre-revolutionary times, many cultural activities were beyond workers' financial means. Social pressure and barriers further reduced the number of workers who attended the opera, ballet, symphony, museums, galleries and even films. After the revolution, admission prices to such cultural events were very cheap and workers and their families were encouraged to attend. Post-revolutionary Moscow also bustled with amateur and avant-garde theatrical performances in neighborhood and factory club theaters, sporting events, and the circus. How many workers actually attended such affairs is difficult to estimate.[37] When they did go out for entertainment, movies, sporting events, the circus, and local taverns appear to have been the more popular affairs. But these are impressions; a thorough study of working-class culture(s) remains to be done.

One establishment that the party and unions hoped would be a center of proletarian social and cultural life was the workers' clubs. But during the 1920s, these clubs had limited popularity. In Moscow city and *guberniia* in late 1923, there were 481 clubs with approximately 150,000 members; in 1927, the city's 181 clubs had some 100,000 members. The membership figures must be viewed with caution since many members rarely frequented the clubs or participated in their activities. Low attendance resulted from several factors—poorly defined and organized activities, poor organization, and a rowdy clientele.

In the early 1920s, the clubs' poorly organized activities resulted from a shortage of competent club officials and a strindent debate between Proletkul't and the party over the nature of club activities. Proletkul't envisioned the clubs as "forges of the new culture" and devoted its energies to organizing various types of cultural activities such as music, art and drama. The party and unions sought to focus club activities along more utilitarian lines and sponsored lectures on hygiene and politics, literacy circles, and other practical activities that might appeal to workers and serve official policy.

Younger workers (under thirty) who participated in Proletkul't cultural activities appear to have dominated the clubs' regular patrons. But many of them engaged in rowdy, disruptive behavior, and, on occasion, young "hooligans" damaged the clubs thereby forcing factory committees to form guard teams to defend their property. Rather than endure the rowdyism and antagonism of younger workers, many older workers preferred to frequent local taverns where they could socialize and drink with their peers. Considering the atmosphere at many clubs and their refusal to sell alcohol, the taverns' popularity is understandable.[38]

The budgets examined here are those of selected samples of workers. Obviously, the spending habits of the city's entire proletariat did not conform to this pattern. Low-paid workers, of necessity, devoted a larger proportion of their income to such essentials as food and utilities and spent less on entertainment and clothing. Since most workers earned less than the average wage (see table 5-1), the value of these budget studies lay in the priorities which the allocation of resources describe. One's marital status also influenced the affixing of priorities. As table 5-2 indicates, single workers devoted less money to rent and food and more to clothes and entertainment than did their married counterparts. That they devoted less of their income to rent suggests that many of the single people surveyed may have lived in factory barracks or with their parents, relatives or friends (possibly *zemliaki*).

These budget studies also mask personal preferences which made significant differences in the allocation of family income. Take the case of textile worker O. and her husband who spent 7 percent of their 1924 income (55 rubles out of 788 rubles) on alcohol and tobacco. Some people, like worker K.'s family, spent more than 50 percent of their income on food despite the fact that they kept livestock. Metalworker B. spent only 37 percent of his income on food and 11 percent on clothes, but he sent one-fifth of his earnings to his family in Vladimir.[39]

Despite their shortcomings, budget studies provide insight into workers' priorities, spending habits and standard of living. The remarkable feature about workers' spending habits during the 1920s is that they did not change. The explanation is simple. Despite the fact that after 1926 their real wages exceeded those of 1913, most of the city's proletariat remained relatively poor. Life's basic necessities—food, shelter, and clothing—consumed three-quarters of the average worker's paycheck. Granted that the quality of diet improved and the social insurance and health care systems provided a measure of security previously unknown to workers, but the quality and accessability of housing, clothing and other consumer goods remained problems. During the 1920s, workers had the lowest living standard of the city's major occupational groups. With each passing year, the gap between them widened. The improvement aside, their living standard remained a continual source of worker dissatisfaction and fueled their envy and criticisms of their relatively oppulent neighbors and bosses.

The Housing Crisis

Housing was justifiably the proletariat's most chronic grievance. They bore the brunt of the city's ever-deepening housing crisis. Their experience during the NEP stands in stark contrast to that during the Civil War when they were the chief beneficiaries of the massive housing redistribution. Squalid though they became as a consequence of the 1918-1921 economic collapse, the confiscated apartments into which workers moved represented a dramatic improvement over the barracks and basement dwellings which they had previously inhabited. Ironically, while the quality of their housing was poor, workers had more living space per capita in 1920 than they ever had or would again for several decades. Because the 1920s witnessed a reversal of the 1918-1921 experience, worker frustration became all the more intense.

As the city's population mushroomed after 1920, the amount of living space per person declined steadily and the competition for housing intensified. On the tenth anniversary of the revolution, many workers, especially those who moved to the city after 1921, lived in dwellings that more closely resembled those of pre-revolutionary times than those that they believed the revolution had promised. Although the need for housing became more acute with each passing year, until 1925 economic policy dictated that industrial restoration received the majority of available capital. Consequently, throughout the decade, housing construction and repair lagged far behind the rate of population increase. Between 1921 and 1926 the number of inhabitable apartments increased by 38 percent, but the city's population practically doubled.[40]

Worker discontent with their housing surfaced early. In May 1922, A. Rosenberg, a member of the Khamovnicheskii *raion* soviet, reported that the housing shortage had already become critical. Workers were fully justified, he stated, to demand the repair of their present dwellings and the construction of new ones. Unless these demands, endorsed by factory committees, *raion* soviets and party organizations, were met, workers' living conditions would continue to deteriorate.[41] But four months later, the editor of *Rabochaia Moskva*, Boris Volin, wrote that the city soviet had too few resources to meet the demand for housing construction and repair. He agreed that the situation was very poor, but counseled workers to be patient.[42] Workers paid little heed and their complaints mounted. In October, the city soviet responded to their criticisms and demands by creating an Extraordinary Housing Commission. The commission's first act was to order that 10 percent of the city's living space be made available to housing associations (*zhilishchnye tovarishchestva*) which were organized at the workpace. This "new" living space was to be distributed to those in need of housing on a priority basis: workers and employees without adequate housing were the first priority; the registered unemployed, the second priority.[43]

Many residents were reluctant to give up part of their dwellings. For example, the Uritskii factory's housing association encountered resistance from two recalcitrant apartment dwellers. One was a professional who lived with his wife and fourteen-year-old daughter in a five-room apartment; the other, a nepman whose three member family also occupied five rooms. The association dismissed both protests and allocated one of the professional's large rooms to three workers and their spouses.[44] By November 1, the Extraordinary Commission announced that the 10 percent levy had resulted in 11,341 "new" rooms which were occupied by some 21,000 people.[45] Unfortunately, the levy did little to reduce the growing demand for housing. What it did do was expose some of the housing inequities that existed. While three workers' families shared one subdivided room, the professional's family lavished in four rooms. This case was no exception.

By 1924, there was public discussion of "the housing hunger, the housing catastrophe."[46] The next year, a trade union official lamented that Moscow's living space was filled "to the point of overflowing" (*do otkaza*).[47] These were not exaggerations. With each passing year, the amount of living space per person declined—from 9.3 square meters in 1920 to 5.5 square meters in 1927—and the average number of inhabitants per apartment increased—from five in 1920 to nine in 1926.[48] As the demand for housing outstripped construction, the populations of factory barracks swelled, apartments were subdivided with increasing frequency, the renting of corners became more common, and many homeless people were forced to sleep in corridors, storerooms, sheds, kitchens, bathhouses, and even asphalt cauldrons. For those who refused to live in such conditions, the only alternative was to live outside the city and commute as much as fifteen kilometers to work.[49]

While rapid population growth and inadequate construction were the prime reasons for Moscow's housing crisis, they were not the only reasons. In fact, the city's population in 1923 was 25 percent smaller than in 1917; yet the number of apartments had diminished by only 18 percent. True, much of that housing was in disrepair and of substandard quality. But what made the crisis worse was the city soviet's desire to place workers in decent apartments and not have to reopen the accursed barracks that had housed so many before the revolution. As the data in table 5-3 indicate, at least until 1923 the soviet's housing policy produced some success. The average amount of living space per person that year was slighly greater than in 1912. Nonetheless, overcrowded housing remained a reality of Moscow life. In 1923, more than one-half of the residents lived in apartments with two occupants per room; another third lived in apartments with three to five people per room. Less than 10 percent had the luxury of having a room to themselves.[50]

But the success of the soviet's policy was limited. Although many

TABLE 5-3
Results of the Housing Redistribution
in Moscow, 1912-1923

Size of accommodation	Percent of the population	
	1912	1923
One room or more	7.1%	8.6%
1/2 to one room	31.2%	54.7%
1/4 to 1/2 room	57.3%	31.8%
Less than 1/5 room	4.5%	4.9%

SOURCE: Sosnovy, 15.

Moscow workers had more living space than they did before 1917, as a class they had the least amount of living space. That inequity remained true throughout the decade. In 1927, the average amount of living space per person (in square meters) was: workers—5.6; artisans—5.9; employees—7.0; professionals—7.1.[51] The types of dwellings in which workers lived varied widely. The 1918-1921 redistribution primarily benefitted those workers who resided in Moscow during those years. The 10 percent levy benefited those workers who returned to Moscow in 1921-1922. After that, the number of workers forced to live in factory barracks, corners of apartments, sheds and other substandard dwellings grew annually. Everything was different, but little had changed in the area of housing.

To illustrate how crowded Moscow housing was during the 1920s, consider the following examples. But first, a word of caution. Relative to most workers, especially the most recent arrivals, the housing described below was comfortable, even spacious. In 1922, warehouseman V. lived in a one-room apartment in an old wooden house with his wife, two daughters, and, for at least part of the year, his mother-in-law. The apartment had 13 square meters of living space and one window. The furnishings were meager: a bed, a couple of tables and stools, and a kerosene primus stove. Late the next year, the family moved to a newly renovated apartment, which also had one room (18.6 square meters) and one window. The parents slept in the bed and the children slept on the floor.[52]

During the first half of 1924, textile worker O., her husband, and two children lived in a one-room apartment in a two-story house shared by four families. Their apartment had only 7.7 square meters of living space and one window. The family had two cots; the mother and daughter slept in one, the father and son in the other. They moved in 1925 to a somewhat larger and cleaner one-room apartment. The room was large enough for both O. and her husband to have their own corners. Two chairs, stools, and tables were the only furniture in the apartment.[53]

The apartments occupied by the American journalist Louis Fischer, his wife, and two children were not much better. Like many Muscovites, the Fischer's moved often in hopes of getting better housing. Their first apartment belonged to the AMO factory and was formerly an old age home for noble ladies. The Fischers occupied one room and shared a huge communal kitchen from which food was constantly stolen. They then moved into an apartment in the former mansion of Kharitenko, tsarist Russia's sugar king. The building did not have a kitchen, but there was a room with a cold water tap that three families shared. As was common practice at the time, everyone cooked on kerosene primus stoves. The Fischer's third apartment was located in a ten-room, two-story house occupied by seven families. The communal kitchen had neither gas nor hot water nor electricity nor shelves. Each night the primus stoves had to be removed, otherwise they would have been stolen. There was one small bathroom, but the tenants used the tub for washing laundry, galoshes, kerosene cans or for dyeing clothes. They bathed at work or in one of the city's many public baths.[54]

To fit such cramped conditions, it follows that most families' furniture was quite simple. That of workers V. and O.'s discussed above was typical. Stools were more common than chairs and beds were scarce. Surveys conducted in 1923 and 1924 found an average of three people per bed in Moscow. Those without beds slept on the floor, tables or makeshift plank beds. It was common for very young children to sleep in open drawers.[55] Such conditions inspired the following popular little tune:

> In Moscow we live as freely,
> as a corpse in his coffin.
> I sleep with my wife in the dresser,
> My mother-in-law sleeps in the sink.[56]

The furnishings of a family's apartment reflected not only their economic condition but often provide insight into its members' values. Many working-class families had portraits of Lenin and/or Marx or revolutionary posters on the walls, but it was not uncommon to find them next to an iconostasis. For example, in weaver P.'s one-room apartment was an iconostasis of four icons. Next to it hung several revolutionary posters.[57] Unfortunately, it is difficult to determine the extent to which the juxtaposition of icons and revolutionary posters represented the inhabitants' conflicting worldviews or a syncretic culture which, like the *dvoeverie* of medieval Russia, was devised to avoid friction.

During the early 1920s, workers also demanded an improvement in the quality of their housing. The deterioration of dwellings during the Civil War had turned many apartments into spawning areas for infections and epidemic diseases. To identify and cleanse such dwellings, in 1921 the city soviet organized volunteer health sections and public clean-up campaigns. Some 2,500 such sections existed by 1923 and their activity proved to be crucial in the struggle against epidemics. But cleaning dilapidated, substandard housing and repairing and improving that housing were two different activities. The latter proceeded extremely slowly.

The slow rate of repairs resulted from two factors—the lackadaisical attitude of some residents toward housing maintenance, and the shortage of capital. Beginning in 1920, city leaders sought to shift the responsibility for repairing apartments to the residents. Laws passed in 1920 and 1921 required residents to maintain sanitary housing and to make certain repairs. Failure to do so could result in civil, and possibly criminal, punishments.[58] These laws remained in force throughout the decade. The legislation was an attempt not only to ameliorate housing conditions, but also to inculcate citizens with a sense of responsibility and respect for public property. These values were conspicuously absent among some residents. The fact that housing was very cheap (rent free until 1922) and did not belong to the occupants "has killed the economic interest of the dwellers" who often mistreated their dwellings or failed to maintain them.[59] In 1922, the Petrograd soviet lamented "the insuperable difficulties in fighting the psychology of the man in the street (*obyvatel'*) who looks upon national property as belonging to nobody and therefore at times aimlessly destroys it."[60] Surely the same problem existed in Moscow.

The disrepair of housing in the early 1920s testifies to the consequences of years of neglect. At factory meetings and in the press, workers constantly complained about overcrowding and the need to repair walls, windows, floors, stairs, ceilings, and water and heating systems. They recognized that the lack of capital hampered the repair process, but that in no way lessened the stridency of their demands. Frustrated by the slow pace, some workers stole factory goods and supplies with which to repair their apartments. Although discontent over the disrepair diminished somewhat after 1925, complaints continued to appear in the press.[61]

Even if residents had adhered to the letter of the law, overcoming their housing's disrepair was beyond their financial means. Unfortunately, it was also beyond the city soviet's means. Until 1924, the inflation rate placed severe fiscal strictures on the soviet, which, in accordance with national policy, gave priority to industrial recovery and the restoration of municipal utilities. Funds for housing repair were simply insufficient to meet the demand. In 1923, the city soviet allocated less than one-tenth of the amount spent in 1913 for housing repair. This meager sum barely made a dent in the problem.[62]

Nor was the soviet in a position to build enough new housing. No large scale housing construction took place in Moscow before 1923 and few housing units were built in 1924. Of the new housing built in 1923/24, 60 percent was built by private investors and cooperatives. Until the establishment in 1925 of a bank to finance municipal housing, the city lacked access to the credit necessary to construct the requisite new housing. The bank's creation marked a turning point in municipal housing construction. After 1925, the city soviet and state agencies built more than 80 percent of all new housing.[63] Still, insufficient capital limited new construction. According to Gosplan, from 1923 to 1926 less money was spent on urban housing construction than was spent in pre-revolutionary Russia in one year.[64] During these years, 167,000 people moved into new housing, but the population grew by more than 500,000.[65] Worker anger was justified.

While worker discontent helps to explain the decision to build more housing, the major reason for the policy change was the realization that the housing crisis impinged on worker productivity, undermined the labor force's stability, and thereby limited economic growth. On this, workers and officials agreed. At factory committee and production meetings, workers stridently complained that the shortage and poor quality of housing made it difficult to get enough sleep, fostered illnesses, and thereby contributed to increased absenteeism. For workers who lived in such conditions, an efficient utilization of their workday was impossible.[66] In 1926, the party passed several resolutions which described the housing situation as "catastrophic" and called on all party and state organs to "attach great significance to housing in view of the fact that the further growth of industry, increases in labor productivity and better living conditions are hampered by the housing crisis."[67] The impact that the problem had on economic and industrial development was clearly stated in a July 1926 Central Committee and Central Control Commission resolution. "The housing issue remains one of the most critical issues in the daily lives of workers, without a satisfactory solution to the housing problem it will be impossible to raise the workman's standard of living. Indeed, the growing housing crisis hampers the development of industry by lowering the productivity of labor and preventing the employment of the increased workforce that is needed."[68]

With the First Five-Year Plan's approach, the importance of and need for more and better housing grew commensurately. In response, in January 1928, the Central Executive Committee and Sovnarkom issued a resolution "On housing policy," which called for increasing the tempo of construction and repairs, strengthening and developing housing cooperatives, exploiting the available housing fund in a more rational manner, and attracting private capital.[69] But the demand for housing continued to outstrip its supply.

Expressions of sympathy and resolutions were unable to solve the mounting crisis. Nor did the press's hailing of each new building as a victory quiet growing worker discontent.[70] As late as 1928, officials could do little but point to their limited accomplishments and new policies with sheepish pride and counsel workers to continue to be patient. Such was the tone of the discussion on the housing crisis at the Third Plenum of VTsSPS in February 1928.[71] The plenum had little else to offer.

Not only was the amount of housing construction during the NEP inadequate, but what was built was often of inferior quality. A 1927 city soviet investigation of newly constructed housing revealed a host of problems. Many floors, doors, and windows were made from unseasoned wood and poor quality materials, and within a short time they warped or split, often rendering them useless. So poorly designed were many buildings that some rooms were accessible only through other rooms, making their use as individual apartments difficult and annoying to the residents. Other problems among the long "series of shortcomings" included unnecessarily congested stairwells, inadequate insulation from street noise, the absence of sufficient baths and ventilation systems, and the construction of excessively large rooms that had to be subdivided. For lack of funds, the construction of creches, day-care centers, and rooms for collective use in apartment buildings had to be deferred.[72]

Given that demand far outstripped housing construction and renovation, many workers turned to their factories in search of a place to live. Many of the city's larger factories, such as Dinamo, AMO, Trekhgornaia and Serp i molot, owned reasonably decent apartment buildings. But factory adminstrators often preferred to use these dwellings to attract skilled workers and *spetsy*. Those apartments available to other workers were quickly filled in the early 1920s. To their newest workers, the factories offered only a place in their barracks.[73] Precisely what proportion of the city's proletariat lived in factory barracks is unclear. Two facts appear certain: the number grew with each passing year, and the majority of them were new workers from the villages.

Despite attempts by factory and union activists to maintain certain standards of quality and cleanliness in the barracks, the conditions there were reminiscent of those in pre-revolutionary times. In 1928, *Trud* described one barracks:

> The long narrow room has only one window, which cannot be opened. Some of the panes are broken and the holes plugged with dirty rags. Near the doorway is an oven which serves not only for heating but for cooking as well. The chimney spans the entire length of the room from the doorway to the window. The smell of fumes, of socks hung to dry, fills the room. It is impossible to breathe in the closeness of the air. Along the walls are crude beds covered with dirty straw ticks and rags, alive with lice and bugs. The beds have almost no space between them. The floor is strewn with cigarette butts and rubbish. About two hundred workers are housed here, men and women, married and single, old and young—all herded together. There are no partitions, and the most intimate acts are performed under the very eyes of other inhabitants. Each family has one bed. On one bed a man, a wife and three children live, a baby occupies the "second floor"—a cot hanging over the bed. The same toilet is used by men and women.[74]

Living in these overcrowded and unsanitary barracks affected workers in many ways. They got less sleep and became ill more often than those who had better dwellings. Consequently, they had higher absenteeism rates and were less productive than the average worker. One worker put the problem succinctly: "Those who work poorly live in barracks . . . only improved conditions will permit the improvement in productivity."[75]

While the effect of barracks' life on worker productivity concerned officials, they also worried about the barracks' political climate. Many new workers who lived there clung to peasant habits and values. To the distress of officials religion pervaded barracks life. At least until the mid-1920s, priests had almost unrestricted access to worker barracks, and they distributed religious leaflets and read the Bible to tenants. Some barracks held public prayer services, and icons were common ornaments. To counter the church's influence, local party leaders enlisted party and Komsomol members to conduct antireligious work in the factories and barracks. These activists blended the struggle against illiteracy with that against god by teaching people to read from Marx, Lenin, and Darwin. Lectures, readings, movies, and radio listening circles were other common campaign methods.

The attack on religion and traditional patterns of peasant behavior created tensions in the barracks. The most prominent was that between generations—between the often irreverant and the disrespectful youth and Komsomol members, and recent, more conservative arrivals from the villages who clung to traditional beliefs in the face of a bewildering new world of work and ideas. Tensions between the sexes, especially between spouses, also existed. The overcoming of illiteracy and the sense of independence that came with work and a regular income created in some women a growing dissatisfaction with their secondary role in conjugal situations. In other instances, party and Komsomol members had serious disagreements with their nonparty spouses and relatives who abhorred the new secular values adopted by one of their own. Unions and the Komsomol also worried that barracks life also had a "pernicious influence" on the young and contributed to their demoralization and "backward development."[76] Barracks life was obviously a physical and emotional strain that frustrated official goals and adversely affected their residents.

Divided though they often were on many issues, all workers were united in their demands for better housing. The types of housing in which the proletariat lived varied widely. Most urban workers and long-time residents lived in the subdivided apartments confiscated between 1918 and 1921 from the former bourgeoisie and aristocracy. As overcrowded, poorly equipped and rundown as these apartments were, they were a marked improvement over these workers' pre-revolutionary housing and offered families a measure of privacy if not comfort. For new workers who lived in factory barracks, the contrast with pre-revolutionary times was less obvious, and the hardships experienced there made daily life an arduous affair. The Civil War redistribution had held out the hope to workers that the new government would provide them with decent housing. While the city soviet tried to live up to that expectation, the NEP's economic policies ensured that the quality of workers' housing deteriorated. This was not the policies' intention, but it was their undeniable effect.

The Homeless and Crime

As much as workers who resided in apartments or barracks had reason to complain, they enjoyed a privilege not shared by all residents—they had a place to live. For thousands of Muscovites, the search for housing was a daily ordeal. As early as September 1922, a letter to the editor of *Rabochaia Moskva* stated that "masses of people pass the night on the streets." In view of the approaching winter, the author proposed the construction of overnight lodgings. Such a suggestion, he noted, had the support of many party members and particularly the members of the Workers and Peasants Inspectorate (Rabkrin). Three days later, the paper announced the opening of a temporary home for unemployed youths from the countryside. Opened on the Komsomol's initiative and with the support of the Labor Exchange, the dwelling housed one hundred people. Shortly thereafter, the soviet opened an overnight barracks for other homeless residents.[77]

As the number of homeless Muscovites increased, so too did the number of overnight barracks. By 1929, the city operated eight such dwellings. Table 5-4 indicates the steady growth in the number of night lodgings and inhabitants. Although the influx of *otkhodniki* caused the number of admissions to oscillate seasonally, the steadily increasing number of registrants during the "off-season" suggest that the majority of those lodgings' tenants were city residents or those seeking to establish residence there.[78] The municipally operated night lodgings listed below were not the only temporary lodgings in Moscow. As noted above, the Komsomol provided overnight lodgings for homeless youth. The construction workers union did the same for seasonal builders; in 1928, eight such barracks housed 29,000 *otkhodniki*.[79]

The conditions in overnight barracks were worse than those in factory barracks. Despite regulations which stipulated that they meet certain sanitary requirements and possess certain amenities of life, the shortage of capital and uncaring attitudes of the temporary tenants meant that these ideals were rarely met. Some barracks lacked separate facilities for men and women, and most were extremely overcrowded, dirty and lacked hot water, laundry facilities, and litter baskets. The dining areas were especially unsanitary and often strewn with garbage. The food and dining conditions were often so horrible that few tenants ate there. At one lodging only four of the 120 tenants ate in the dining hall.[80]

So large was the city's homeless population that the increasing num-

TABLE 5-4
Number of Monthly Registrants at Moscow's Night Lodgings:
Selected Months, 1925-1928

Date		Number of lodgings	Number of admissions	Males	Females
Jan.	1925	3	89,414	61,621	11,000
Apr.	1925	3	82,276	51,268	10,985
Jul.	1925	4	95,115	32,065	10,405
Oct.	1925	4	113,154	31,093	10,890
Jan.	1926	4	113,449	35,816	11,701
Apr.	1926	4	108,792	28,693	10,866
Jul.	1926	5	120,039	106,908	13,131
Oct.	1926	6	149,365	135,014	14,351
Jan.	1927	6	112,252	94,492	17,760
Apr.	1927	6	137,400	121,170	16,230
Jul.	1927	6	218,363	203,082	15,281
Oct.	1927	6	216,545	191,498	17,046
Jan.	1928	6	174,887	157,568	17,319
Apr.	1928	8	204,464	182,191	22,273
Jul.	1928	8	216,402	192,984	23,418
Oct.	1928	8	223,464	199,363	24,101

SOURCE: *Ezhemesiachyi statisticheskii bulleten'*, Jan. 1925-Mar. 1928, tab.
XV, 21; Apr. 1928-Dec. 1928, tab. XXI, 45.

a. It is unclear in the source why the sum of male and female registrants from
January 1925 to July 1926 does not equal the total number of registrants.

ber of night lodgings were unable to accommodate them. When the
weather permitted, many people slept in parks, public gardens, ceme-
teries, streets, and along the river banks. During the winter months, they
sought shelter in abandoned or partially constructed buildings, train
stations, sheds, bathhouses, and even asphalt cauldrons. The unemployed, *besprizorniki* (homeless orphans), and recent migrants comprised
the vast majority of the homeless population, although some permanent
workers also populated their ranks.

From this group came the largest number of criminals.[81] Leaving
aside professional criminals, evidence of whose nefarious activities is too
sparse to allow for discussion, the most visible of the city's criminals
were the *besprizorniki*, the orphaned and runaway children for whom
criminality was both a game and means of survival. The chaos between
1914 and 1922 produced far too many of these tragic victims, many of
whom moved to Moscow because the opportunities there were greatest.
Precisely how many *besprizorniki* lived in the city is difficult to deter-

mine since many were transients and avoided all contacts with official-
dom. Their ranks grew most dramatically during the Civil War and
famine years. Yet as late as 1928, *besprizorniki* continued to flock to
Moscow.

Left to their own devices, they formed gangs that offered them
protection and enhanced their criminal activities. The boys specialized
in theft; the girls, in theft and prostitution. The gangs created their own
communal organizations and systems for the division of their spoils.
They lived where they could—in sheds, asphalt cauldrons, parks, abandoned buildings or boats, or, if they had some money, in night shelters.
Many used the wall of *Kitaigorod*, in the city's center, as their central
base and organized there a type of dormitory appointed with furniture
made of bits of wood and junk. In their social milieu, the use of drugs
(especially cocaine) and alcohol were everyday occurences, and children
as young as five indulged and stole so that they could purchase more.[82]

Orphaned girls frequently turned to prostitution. In 1927, more
than one-quarter of the prostitutes arrested in Moscow were under eighteen years of years, some were as young as twelve. While some became
prostitutes to sustain themselves, others did so to support their drug
habit. Almost three-quarters of those arrested in 1924 regularly used
cocaine, opium, or morphine.[83] Many other women also became prostitutes. While some did so for personal reasons that will forever remain
secret, many resorted to prostitution in order to survive. Unemployment,
the lack of financial support, and the need to sustain their families left
them no choice. Women of the street practiced their trade quite openly
in several parts of town, Tverskaia and Trubny squares being the best
known. In the former, the sidewalks swarmed with teenage prostitutes;
in the latter, the trade was less brisk and males in search of whores had
to frequent one of several large tenements, in the corridors of which hung
the sweet spell of opium and where next to the doors were tacked photographs of the "fair occupant in the scantiest of costume." Those who
operated out of these shabby tenements had a distinct advantage over
their competitors—they had a bed. The housing shortage forced the
others to ply their trade in hallways, alleys, backyards, and on park lawns
and benches.[84]

Despite the efforts of the police, party, and state agencies to eliminate crime, prostitution, and drug use and to reduce the number of
besprizorniki, all remained common features of Moscow life. Considering the deepening housing and unemployment crises, this is hardly surprising. But the conspicuous presence of criminals, prostitutes, and drug

195

users adversely affected the quality of life there. Because most thefts, robberies, muggings, and rapes occurred at night, men and women alike worried about venturing out alone after dark. The large numbers of homeless who passed the night in public places only heightened these anxieties. Parents were also greatly concerned for their children. This was particularly true of the parents of unemployed juveniles, who out of idleness or for want of excitement fell in with *besprizorniki* gangs and took to drinking and drug use.[85]

Family Life

Workers' relatively low wages and their overcrowded living conditions imposed severe strains on them and their families and adversely affected their lives. While daily frustrations, anxieties, and uncertainities punctuated the lives of all family members, women often bore the heaviest burden. The most obvious example of this was their role in the division of family labor.

Legally, men and women were equal. But at home, as on the job, traditional, patriarchial attitudes held sway. Shopping, cleaning, cooking, and child-care were, according to most Russian males, women's work. That many women also held full-time jobs turned most days into an exhausting experience. The scarcity of household conveniences, municipal services, electricity, refrigeration, and running water forced women to devote long hours each day to household chores. For want of refrigeration, women had to shop virtually every day, an exercise that often required traveling from store to store and waiting in queues. Because cooking on portable primus stoves turns even a simple meal into a long ordeal, cooking also consumed much time. So too did cleaning the apartment and washing clothes. Less than one-fifth of the city's apartments had running water, and hence water for cleaning and cooking had to be carried from communal taps, pumps (usually located outside), or from the river or open canals.[86] According to time-budget studies conducted in 1931, women who worked full-time jobs spent an additional five hours a day on domestic chores and child-care. This left two or three hours a day at most for personal sanitation, politics, or self-improvment. Males, on the other hand, devoted only two hours a day to domestic chores and child-care.[87]

The personal and social costs engendered by overcrowded housing conditions and the demands of daily life are difficult to estimate, but data on crime in Moscow suggest that they were substantial. Between

1923 and 1927, the crime rate among females rose more rapidly than did that of males. While males were more likely to commit crimes of property or hooliganism (often associated with drunkeness), females were more commonly arrested for attacks on people. During those years, the number of women arrested for assault and battery increased by five times; those arrested for murder and "shocks, blows, and attacks on individuals" by six times. As a proportion of all crimes, those against people soared from 10 to 40 percent. People who lived in one room or less and those without permanent residences were the most apt to commit crimes. Spouses, relatives, and neighbors were their most common victims.[88]

Of the 202 cases of hooliganism that came before Moscow's Peoples' Courts in the mid-1920s, 25 percent of them were directly attributed to the acute housing problem. Many of those convicted were housewives, mostly workers' wives, who were found guilty of starting fights over an apartment or kitchen.[89] Petty though the issues may seem, they provide a measure of the frustration and hostility that the strains of daily life induced.

Crime statistics measure only people's most dramatic reactions to their conditions. A host of minor problems also eroded their patience and civility. For example, consider the problems caused by so simple a device as a doorbell. Because they were formerly one-family residences, many of Moscow's apartment buildings had only one doorbell for all of the residents. So as to avoid confusion, each apartment was assigned a doorbell code usually determined by the number of rings. It goes without saying that such a system is fraught with the potential for error and, in some cases, mistakes or misuse precipitated fights and arguments.[90]

Daily frustrations and hardships could not help but affect the stability of workers' families. Judging from the city's divorce rate, the impact was significant. Unfortunately, the nature of the data prohibits identifying the reasons for divorce and that rate among workers. But so steeply did the city's divorce rate rise that it seems inconceivable that the strains and quarrels of daily life did not contribute to its increase. In 1921, there were 5,790 divorces; in 1927, 19,421 divorces; and in 1929, 23,745 divorces.[91]

The 1920s remains the decade of the easy divorce.[92] After 1926, the "postcard divorce" made the dissolution of marriage especially easy. The "postcard divorce" operated in the following manner. If either spouse wished to divorce the other, that person simply went to the ZAGS office (*Zapiski aktov grazhdanskogo sostoianiia*, which registered all marriages and divorces) and filled out a postcard announcing that the marriage had been terminated. The divorced, and possibly unwitting, spouse received the announcement in the mail several days later.[93]

But divorce did not always end a couple's relationship. Because of the housing shortage, many divorced couples were forced to remain room-mates. When one of them remarried or took a lover, the situation could become extremely awkward. Indeed, just such a situation formed the basis of the popular contemporary film "Bed and Sofa" in which two workers contend for the love of one's wife and the right to her bed. Then there was the case of a ballerina who surprised her husband by bringing home a new husband after divorcing the former husband in the morning. Since he could find no other housing, the rejected male had to occupy a corner in his former wife's "honeymoon suite."[94]

Economic insecurity and overcrowded housing affected even the happily married. Nowhere is this more graphically illustrated than in the city's rising abortion rate. In 1920, the Soviet government legalized abortions performed by trained doctors in approved hospitals and clinics. During the 1920s, more and more women elected to have abortions. The number of registered abortions per 100 births rose from 19.6 in 1923, to 31.4 in 1925, to 55.7 in 1926.[95] While some women chose abortion to terminate an unwanted pregnancy or for medical reasons, more than half of those who received abortions did so because they lacked the financial resources to support a child. Low wages, unemployment, and the shortage of housing space were major considerations for women who sought abortions.[96]

While some party members regarded the rising abortion rate as "massive" and "horrifying," others accepted it and argued that the women's reasons for electing the operation were real and justifiable.[97] On one fact, all agreed. The abortion law marked a significant improvement over the pre-revolutionary situation, when abortions were illegal and untrained doctors, midwives, and nurses clandestinely performed them in unsanitary conditions, situations that often resulted in infection, permanent bodily injury, or death. During the 1920s, the number of women who died from abortions, contracted postoperative ailments, or reported to hospitals with incomplete abortions contracted steadily.[98]

The lowest average wages of the city's major occupational groups, the least amount of housing space per person, a rapidly rising crime rate directly attributable to these conditions, and the personal frustrations and anxieties that accompanied these depressing phenomena, these were the realities with which the Moscow working class struggled daily. To be sure, these were not items on that class's revolutionary agenda. What made the experiences especially galling was that their bosses and other well-to-do residents did not endure such hardships. On the contrary, they prospered and frolicked during the NEP. Their success and happiness only further angered workers. It is against this backdrop that we examine workers' relations with their neighbors.

Workers and Their Neighbors

As a result of the 1918-1921 housing redistribution and soviet control of housing assignments, class-based residency patterns in Moscow were much less obvious than before the revolution. Prior to 1917, aristocratic and bourgeois residents dominated the neighborhoods within the Sadova ring, the center of the city. Workers and petty bourgeois residents dominated the areas beyond that ring and in Zamoskvoretskii *raion* across the Moscow River from the Kremlin. By 1926, the situation had changed considerably. Employees dominated the center of the city, but the proportion of workers living there had increased and that of former aristocrats and bourgeois had declined. Beyond the Sadova ring and in Zamoskvoretskii, workers comprised the largest group (and in some neighborhoods a majority) of residents, but the proportions of employees, professionals, and nepmen had all increased.[99]

Although muted, class-based residency patterns endured, often for very practical reasons. Factory barracks were situated in Zamoskvoretskii and other predominantly working-class districts beyond the Sadova ring. So too were the major factories. To avoid a long daily commute, many workers preferred to live in these neighborhoods. The employees who worked in center city preferred to live near there for the same reason. Nonetheless, during the 1920s, the city's neighborhoods housed a more heterogeneous mixture of social classes than ever before. But proximity and familarity did not contribute to social harmony. On the contrary, they often fanned the flames of class conflict.

In these more socially integrated neighborhoods, workers, employees, specialists, and nepmen often lived under the same roof.[100] Articles in and letters to the press indicate that class tension ran high in some buildings and occasionally conflicts erupted. Worker resentment of their well-to-do neighbors, whom they believed did not pay a commensurately higher rent, was the primary cause of such tension. From the press, one gets the definite impression that these "bourgeois" became the symbol of and scapegoat for the deep frustrations and anxieties caused by years of material deprivation. This appears to have been the result that the press wanted. Newspaper reports, cartoons, and letters to the editors critical of nepmen and other "bourgeois" elements were especially prominent in 1921-1922 and after 1925, when the official antinepman campaign began. While such coverage kept the nepmen's more nefarious activities in the public eye, workers had their own reasons for resenting and distrusting those entrepreneurs. Many nepmen made their fortunes on the Civil War black market and, during the NEP, they charged high prices for their goods. That they prospered at the workers' expense could not but exacerbate worker animosity. Apartment houses were often the front line in this guerrilla class war. A few examples best illustrate these points.

The major complaint of workers at the former Al'shvang textile factory in 1922 was their deplorable housing conditions. Their overcrowded apartment building desperately needed repairs, but there was no money available. Equally as infuriating to the workers was the fact that some 400 workers shared half of the building, while nepmen occupied much of the other half. These nepmen had more living space and earned more money than the workers; yet they reportedly paid approximately the same rent.[101] At an apartment which housed many printers, a similar problem existed. The workers occupied 60 percent of the apartments; other workers, "speculators, professionals, etc." inhabited the rest. Many of these "speculators, professionals, etc." were allegedly quite rich; yet they paid what the workers considered a less than equitable rent. To end this unfair practice, the workers vowed to use the press to expose the income of "such elements" in the hopes that social pressure would force them to pay their fair share.[102] At another apartment building, tensions between workers and nepmen took the form of struggle for control of the building's administrative board. A series of disputes between the two classes over how the building should be run eventually resulted in the creation of "two administrations" (*pravleniia*): one composed of workers; the other, of nepmen.[103]

These expressions of hostility also reflected many workers' perception of what was just. The relative wealth (real or perceived) of some "bourgeois" enabled them, so workers believed, to secure better housing. While these people were able to turn the period's economic problems to their advantage, workers bore an inordinate burden of the drive for economic recovery and growth. It was these social elements, not workers, who were benefiting from the NEP and the hardships of others. There was little justice in such a situation.

The press seized on this grassroots tension and took every opportunity to intensify it. The constant coverage given to the high prices charged by private traders, the substandard working conditions in private factories, and the creature comforts that wealthy nepmen enjoyed kept these "class enemies" in the public eye. Antinepmen cartoons often accompanied these articles. In an August 1922 cartoon, a very plump nepman wearing a top hat is inflating a balloon on which is printed the word "bread." The caption reads "Who will win?" (*Kto-kogo?*)[104] Some cartoons depicted nepmen in swank private cafes; others showed private owners who possessed two sets of account books and who ignored worker demands.[105] Whatever the situation, nepmen were portrayed as enemies of the people. In fact, in one cartoon speculators and shopkeepers joined priests, former tsarist policemen, and bootleggers as the five avowed enemies of Soviet power.[106] But the press also equated nepmen with politically suspect employees. A 1922 cartoon portrayed a plump bourgeois dressed in a fancy, three-piece suit, two-tone shoes, and a yachting cap. He wore a big grin and looked like a pig. The accompanying article warned that his kind could be found everywhere—in factories, trusts, and offices—and that all must struggle against his views.[107] To many workers, the accusation had considerable basis in fact.

The social activities and night life of the city's well-to-do reinforced their popular image. Like workers, they had their preferred nightly haunts. At the best (or worst depending on one's viewpoint) of these nightspots, black-tied waiters served wealthy customers sumptuous meals (even during the famine) and fine vintage wine. Here customers could enjoy live entertainment and gamble away the profits made by legal or illegal commercial ventures.[108] Nightly, they passed the time living for the moment and worrying little about what the next day would bring. A description of the "Bar" clearly conveys the extent to which such establishments satisfied the clientele's long-repressed desires.

> Then, there was a restaurant called "Bar" not far from the Savoy Hotel. In the winter of 1921-22 it sold good, simple meals in one large dining-room where there was music in the evenings. The following summer "Bar" blossomed out with small private dining-rooms in sheds in a back-yard. It simultaneously acquired upstairs premises by remodeling a derelict hotel, and an era of naughtiness began. At first clients who took a girl friend or two to one of the private dining-rooms would receive a modest hint from the waiter that there were rooms upstairs if they were in no hurry to go home. Then "Bar" started a cabaret and it was understood that the artists

were ready to solace the evening of a lonely N.E.P.-man, and would doubtless not refuse to spend the night with him. By the fall of 1922, "Bar" was doing a roaring trade as a snappy restaurant, night club and brothel all in one. The sale of wine and beer became legal that year, but at "Bar" there were vodka and liquours as well. In the winter of 1922-23 they went further and cocaine and heroin were to be had, for a price, by clients in the know. A merry little hell it was in the spring of 1923. . . .[109]

Eventually, "Bar" was shut down, not because of its profilgate activities but for tax evasion. It was not the only such establishment in town; other night spots offered comparable attractions and several openly operated casinos. While local authorities may not have condoned the decadence which permeated gambling houses and night clubs, such establishments had little trouble getting licenses so long as they paid part of their receipts to the city soviet. A description of the largest casino in Moscow, the Praga, illustrates the activities and clientele which characterized such haunts.

The biggest gambling establishment was a place called Praga at the corner of the Arbat Square. In the main outer room there were two roulette tables both with zero and double zero, two baccarat tables and a dozen games of *chemin de fer*. Banks at baccarat frequently ran as high as $5,000, a dozen different currencies were used, from bundles of Soviet million notes to hundred-dollar bills, English five- and ten-pound notes, and most surprising of all, no small quantity of gold, Tsarist ten-rouble pieces, English sovereigns, and French twenty-franc coins. As in France, there was an "inner *cercle prive*," where only baccarat was allowed and play was higher, with banks of $25,000 or $30,000.

It was a strange sight, this Praga, in the center of the world's first Proletarian Republic. Most of the men looked like what they were, the low-class jackals and hangers-on of any boom, with fat jowls and greedy vulpine features; but there were others of a better class, former nobles in faded broadcloth and Red Army soldiers in uniform, back from fighting Moslem rebels in Central Asia or from "liquidating" Makhno's anarchist movement in the Ukraine, eager for Moscow's fleshpots and a flutter at the tables. A smattering, too, of foreigners, fixers, agents and the commercial vanguard of a dozen big firms attracted by Lenin's new policy of Concessions, hurrying to find if the report was true that Russia might again become a honey-pot for alien wasps. And women of all sorts, in an amazing variety of costumes, mostly daughters of joy whom N.E.P. had hatched in flocks, noisy and voracious as sparrows. Later in increasing number the wives and families of N.E.P.-men, the new profiteers, with jewels on their stumpy fingers and old lace and ermine round their thick red necks. And one night I saw a grand dame of the old regime, spare and prim in a high-necked gild frock that she had worn maybe at the Court of Queen Alexandra of England. . . . But the high-born lady took readily to commerce and found, she said, genuine satisfaction in the whirl of exchange, intrigue, and petty *combinazione* that was N.E.P. This night at Praga she opened a bank at *chemin de fer* with two English ten-pound notes, "passed" seven times with impassive countenance, then left the game with the equivalent of 1,000.[110]

After the heady years of the early 1920s, such haunts came under increasing surveillance and harassment by local authorities. The second half of the decade witnessed their gradual demise and that of their clientele. As in the early 1920s, publicly expressed worker resentment accompanied the later years' antinepmen campaign. Worker-nepmen conflicts over housing continued. For example, a Komsomol member wrote to *Pravda* complaining about the mounting tension between workers and nepmen in his apartment building and expressing the fear that fights might well break out.[111] Workers at the Svoboda factory in 1928 were irate because the "large and small bourgeois" in their building had substantially better living conditions than they did.[112] Cartoons conveying the wealth and illegal activities of nepmen continued to appear regularly. In one cartoon, the frame was split. On one side, a well-dressed nepman and his bejewelled girlfriend in a fur coat are shopping in a well-stocked private store where the temperature was set at 68 degrees. On the other, a group of poorly dressed workers are waiting in line in an understocked, cold cooperative.[113]

The antinepman campaign reached its peak in 1929 when state agencies began to exile them from Moscow. This time, workers benefited at the nepmen's expense by moving into the apartments of those exiled. Precisely how many working class families moved into these confiscated apartments is unclear. One late 1929 report claimed that more than 700 apartments formerly occupied by nepmen had been allotted to workers' families.[114] To workers, the policy was undoubtedly a good one. After years of complaints about and struggles with nepmen, they had been vanquished. Their dens of inequity had been closed, their market profiteering somewhat curtailed, and their coveted apartments given to workers. But the benefits were limited and short-lived. The nepmen's demise in 1928-1929 paralleled a decline in the workers' standard of living. The number of confiscated apartments given over to workers were too few to make a dent in the housing crisis that deepened with the onset of the Five-Year Plan in 1929 and the attendant rapid population growth.

No single statement can convey the complexity of workers' daily lives outside the factory during the NEP. Although subject to reversals until 1925, their standard of living improved until late 1928 when rationing returned and the gains slowly accrued were quickly wiped out. Even during the period's good years, workers remained the lowest paid of the city's major occupational groups. Their housing was also inferior and got worse as the decade progressed. Urged on by the party and press, frustrated workers lashed out at their more prosperous and comfortably housed neighbors.

There was no quintessential working-class experience during these years. Skilled and experienced urban workers earned higher wages and generally had better apartments than did new workers whose recent arrival and lack of skills and experience translated into lower wages and factory barracks housing. But the differences between workers paled in comparison to those between workers and nepmen, "speculators, professionals, etc." When it came to wages, housing, and the other daily realities that defined their lives beyond the factory gates, workers were far more united than they were divided. Interestingly, what united workers outside the factory were issues and realities that resulted from the application of NEP policies. Yet within the factory, as we shall see, the consequences of those policies often divided workers. Not until the late 1920s, when workers' "enemies" became those of the party, were the experiences and frustrations of factory and daily life joined. When that occurred, workers moved quickly to assert their long-deferred revolutionary agenda.

Notes

1. *Trud*, November 10, 1927.
2. These issues will be discussed in chapter seven and the conclusion. See also, Fitzpatrick, "Cultural Revolution."
3. The following table lists the form of wage payments from 1920 to 1922.

Year	Money	Rations	Work clothes	Communal services
1920	6.9%	36.8%	25.7%	30.6%
1921	13.8%	41.0%	13.5%	31.7%
1922	32.0%	48.6%	—	19.4%

Source: *Ekonomicheskaia zhizn'*, November 22, 1922.

Aleshchenko, *Moskovskii sovet*, 305, claims that by the end of 1922 natural wages in Moscow's metal, garment, chemical, food processing, leather and printing industries accounted for only 4 percent of the total wage package. In textiles, the figure was 24 percent. See also, "Voprosy zarabotnoi platy i NKT," *Voprosy truda*, 2 (1924), 12-17; *Statisticheskii ezhegodnik, 1922-1923*, vyp. 1, chast' IV, tab. 8-2, 224; International Labour Office, *Industrial and Labour Information (Russian Supplement)* 5 vols. (Geneva, 1922-1923), V, 1 (June 5, 1923), 8; S. Zagorsky, *Wages and Regulations of Conditions of Labour in the U.S.S.R.* (Geneva, 1930), 97; *Istoriia Moskvy*, VI, 1, 254.

4. According to the Commissariat of Labor, the average monthly wage of an industrial worker in 1921 equalled one-quarter of the 1913 wage. In 1922, the proportion rose to one-third; the next year, to three-quarters. Whether average nominal wages surpassed the 1913 level in late 1924 or 1925 is open to debate. But given that wages in certain industries, notably textiles, lagged behind most others, average nominal wages probably did not exceed prewar levels until late 1925. For discussions, see: *Trud v Moskovskoi gubernii*, 146-151; *Torgovo-promyshlenaia gazeta*, May 12, 1922; *Vestnik metallopromyshlennosti*, 10-12 (1922), chast' II, 23; *Moskovskii sovet za desiat' let*, 22.

5. For a discussion of this unrest, see Issac Deutscher, *The Prophet Unarmed, Trotsky: 1921-1929)* (New York, 1929), 106-107.

6. In one-third of the cases, the strikers' demands were met; an equal proportion went unsatisfied. A. Stopani, "Eshche ob osebennostiakh nashikh zabastovok," *Voprosy truda*, 7-8 (1924), 38-42; L. Edvard, "Trudovye konflikty v pervyi polovine 1923g.," *ibid.*, 10-11 (1923), 60-67; A. Stopani, "Promyshlennye konflikty na mestak," *ibid.*, 1 (1923), 29-31; *Rabochaia Moskva*, May 19, 1922; *Moskovskii sovet, 1917-1927*, 256-257.

7. Shikheev, 62.

8. *Professional'nye soiuzy, 1924-1926*, 245-246; *Professional'nye soiuzy, 1926-1928*, 358-359; Zagorsky, 89-92.

9. Carr, *Interregnum*, 78, 123-138. Many trade unionists feared that the transition to money wages at a time of high inflation would lower the workers' standard of living. *Trud*, September 14, 1922.

10. According to *Trud*, November 6, 1927, the average real wage as a percentage of that in 1913 was: 1918—40.9 percent; 1919—30.8 percent; 1920—30 percent; 1921—31.6 percent; 1922—37.2 percent; 1922/23—57 percent. See also *Statisticheskii ezhegodnik, 1922-1923*, vyp. 1, chat' IV, tab. VIII-1, 224-225.

11. A. P., "Zarabotnaia plata rabochikh i sluzhashchikh Moskovskoi gubernii v 1927/28," *Voprosy truda*, 12 (1928), 111-116.

12. *Trud*, July 23, 1927.

13. *Professional'nye soiuzy, 1924-1926*, 245-246; *Professional'nye soiuzy, 1926-1928*, 358-359.

14. G. Polliak, "Zarabotnaia plata i potreblenie," *Statisticheskoe obozrenie*, 3 (1929), 56; Zagorsky, 187-189.

15. This was how worker number 17 described 1925-1928. See Jay (Janusz) K. Zawodny, *Twenty-six Interviews with Former Soviet Factory Workers*

(deposited in Hoover Library, Stanford University, 1954) (citation suggested by Zawodny).

16. In 1926, the proportion of working-class families in Moscow with two or more working members was as follows:

Family size	Factory industry	Artisan industry	Railroad
2 people	27.0%	23.4%	18.6%
3 people	27.3%	19.9%	20.6%
4 people	30.4%	21.2%	20.9%
5 people	33.7%	21.4%	23.1%
6 people	35.5%	26.3%	27.0%
7 people	36.1%	23.4%	29.8%
8 people	33.0%	40.5%	28.4%
9 people	32.1%	25.0%	30.9%
10 people	30.5%	46.2%	28.0%

Source: *Perepis'* . . . *1926g*, tom. 55, tab II, 128-129.

For an example of a budget of a working-class family in which both spouses worked, see Kabo, *Ocherki*, 47-51. On supplemental income, see: *Ekonomicheskaia zhizn'*, November 22, 1922; Polliak, "Zarabotnaia plata," 47-68. According to a Sovnarkom report, in the fall of 1923, upward of one-fifth of all Muscovites engaged in speculation and other private economic activities. Trifonov, *Klassy*, 70-71.

17. For a discussion of employees' salaries, see: Zagorsky, 140-151; Rashin, *Fabrichno-zavodskie*, 39-64; A. P., "Zarabotnaia plata," 111-116; B. Miliutin, "Voprosy sotsial'nogo strakhovnaia v resheniiakh VII s"ezda soiuzov," *Vestnik truda*, 2 (1927), 26-28; *Moskva i Moskovskaia guberniia*, 180; Lampert, 136.

18. L. F. Morozov, *Rezhaiushchii etap*, 10.

19. These budget studies have their weaknesses, the most important being that it is often difficult to ascertain the sample investigated. Second, they do not take into account activities which can not be evaluated in monetary terms, such as the free health and social insurance system. Finally, there is no indication that those surveyed reported income other than that earned in wages. Interested readers should also consult the following budget studies (listed in chronological order): F. Markuzon, "Biudzhet Moskovskogo rabochego v dekabre 1922 goda," *Voprosy truda*, 5-6 (1923), 40-47; *Statisticheskii spravochnik* . . . *1924-1925*, vyp. 1, chast' IV, tab. 32, 240; *Trud v Moskovskoi gubernii*, 239; *Trud v Moskve i Moskovskoi gubernii v 1924-1925gg.* (Moscow, 1926), 97-102; N. Gumilevskii, "Biudzhet sluzhashchego k nachale 1925 goda," *Voprosy truda*, 7-8 (1925), 80-89; N. Shesterkina, "Kak zhivet rabochie," *Moskovskii proletarii*, May 14, 1926, 4-5; V. Il'inskii, *Biudzhet rabochikh SSSR* (Moscow, 1927); G. S. Polliak, "Dinamika rabochego biudzheta (noiabr' 1926-noiabr' 1927g)," *Statisticheskoe obozrenie*, 5 (1928), 44-56; *Trud v SSSR, 1926-1930*, 52-53. See also the sources listed in table 5-2.

20. E. O. Kabo, *Pitanie russkogo rabochego do i posle voiny: po statisticheskim materialam, 1908-24* (Moscow, 1928), 46.

21. For an example of discussions at the Oborona factory, see *Rabochaia Moskva*, February 17, 1922.

22. For example, see *ibid.*, February 17, February 22, 1922.

23. For examples, see: *Pravda*, April 10, 1925; *Trud*, December 9, 1926.

24. Kabo, *Pitanie*, 46; Polliak, "Zarabotnaia plata," 60.

25. Kabo, *Pitanie*, 47-71, 79-82. For a discussion of the pre-revolutionary diet, see *ibid.*, and Pisarev, *Narodnonaselenie*, 128-129. For the composition of 1921 rations, see *Statisticheskii spravochnik 1921*, vyp. 1, 425. See also *Professional'nye soiuzy SSSR, 1924-1926*, 230-232.

26. *Rabochaia Moskva*, March 23, 1923; *Trud*, July 5, 1927. At the cooperative of the Paris Commune factory, the worker-correspondent reported that the better quality and lower prices of some goods in the private market weakened the effectiveness of the cooperative. *Rabochaia Moskva*, March 7, 1923. For worker complaints over the lack of a factory cooperative and dependence on the private market, see *ibid.*, March 9, 1923.

27. In Moscow in 1923 and 1924, the cost of fifteen basic food products in state store equalled about 25 percent of the average workers' family income. Sosnovy, 149.

28. For a discussion of the 1927 war scare, see Alfred G. Meyer, "The War Scare of 1927," *Soviet Union/Union Sovetique*, 5, 1 (1978), 1-25.

29. *Pravda*, February 21, 1929; Schwarz, 136; *Istoriia Moskvy*, VI, 1, 327.

30. This will be discussed in the conclusion. See also Lynn Viola, "The '25,000ers': A Study in a Soviet Recruitment Campaign during the First Five-Year Plan," *Russian History/Histoire Russe)*, 10, 1 (1983), 1-30.

31. For a discussion of clothing, see N. Ognyov, *The Diary of a Communist Schoolboy* (trans. Alexander Werth, New York, 1928). On the number of used clothes and junk dealers, see *Perepis' . . . 1926g.*, tom. 19, tab. IV, 276-409.

32. Michael F. Hamm, "The Breakdown of Urban Modernization: A Prelude to the Revolutions of 1917," *City in Russian History*, 196.

33. Rents were abolished in January 1921 and re-introduced in 1922. *SU*, 1922, 30/349. The re-introduction of charges for municipal services occurred in September 1921. *Ibid.*, 1921, 62/445.

34. In the Soviet Union, living space includes only living rooms, dining rooms, and bedrooms and excludes kitchens, bathrooms and corridors. The rental charge in Moscow rose from 20 kopecks per square meter in 1924/25 to 30 kopecks in 1925/26 to 38 kopecks in 1927/28. *Stroitel'stvo Moskvy*, 5 (1927), 1-2; 10 (1927), 5; Sosnovy, 149.

35. According to a report published in *Rabochaia Moskva*, February 19, 1922, rents were fixed at: 60 kopecks per square *sazhen'* for apartments without plumbing or sewer services; 75 kopecks per square *sazhen'* for dwellings without sewer services; 90 kopecks per square *sazhen'* for dwellings with both water and sewer services. One *sazhen'* equals 12.7 cubic yards.

36. Data on alcohol related deaths and disorders can be found in *Moskovskii proletarii*, April 27, 1928, 15-16.

37. For examples of the amount spent by workers' families on entertainment, see Kabo, *Ocherki*, 29-121.

38. Membership figures for workers' clubs in Moscow can be found in:

Trud v Moskovskoi gubernii, 338-340; *Moskva i Moskovskaia guberniia,* 78-79; *Statisticheskii spravochnik . . . 1927,* 93. The problems of workers' clubs in the early 1920s are discussed in John Hatch, "The Politics of Mass Culture: Workers, Communists and Proletkul't in the Development of Workers' Clubs, 1921-1925," *Russian History/Histoire Russe* (forthcoming). Interested readers should also see: *Moskovskii proletarii,* October 14, 1926, 33-34; September 30, 1926, 6-7; *Pravda,* April 12, 1923; July 23, August 27, 1924.

39. Kabo, *Ocherki,* 29-39, 103, 107. See also *Istoriia Moskvy,* VI, 1, 297.

40. According to a report in *Rabochaia Moskva,* February 19, 1922, there were 163,651 apartments in Moscow in late 1921. See also, *Statisticheskii ezhegodnik, 1922-1923,* vyp. 2, chast' XVII, tab. 4, 195. According to the 1923 census, there were 189,496 inhabited apartments in 1923. *Perepis' 1923g.,* chast' I, tab. II, 36. In 1926, the number had increased to 226,052. *Staticheskii spravochnik . . . 1927,* 22-23. This source gives the 1923 figure as 192,004. Renovation rather than construction accounted for the increase in the number of inhabited apartments.

41. *Rabochaia Moskva,* May 13, 1922.

42. *Ibid.,* September 6, 1922. Articles similar in tone to that discussed in the text appeared periodically. For examples, see *Pravda,* January 30, March 6, 1925.

43. *Rabochaia Moskva,* October 8, 1922. The government also sought to deal with the severe housing problem by demunicipalizing some housing. An August 1921 decree charged local soviets with reviewing which municipalized housing could be returned to former owners. Only buildings with less than five apartments could be demuncipalized and only on the condition that the owners completed repairs within one year and set aside ten percent of the living space for assignment by the local Soviet. As one author put it, this partial demunicipalization was "simply a call for help directed to everybody, including former owners, to repair crumbling houses." Alexander Block, "Soviet Housing—The Historical Aspect: Some Notes on Problems of Policy—II," *Soviet Studies,* 3, 3, (January, 1952), 239. See also, Alfred J. DiMaio, *Soviet Urban Housing: Problems and Policies* (New York, 1974), 12.

44. *Rabochaia Moskva,* October 20, 1922.

45. *Ibid.,* November 3, 1922.

46. P. Kozhanyi, "Zhilishchnyi vopros," *Voprosy truda,* 10 (1924), 56.

47. I. Resnikov, "Voprosy zhilishchogo stroitel'stva'," *Vestnik truda,* 3 (1925), 29. See also, *Stroitel'stvo Moskvy,* 2 (1924), 1-7, especially 3.

48. *Vsia Moskva, 1929,* otd. 1, 19; *Moskovskii sovet, 1917-1927,* 363; *Goroda soiuza SSSR,* 100; *Statisticheskii spravochnik . . . 1927,* 18-23. See also A. Gibshman, "Zhilishchnyi fond i zhilishchnye usloviia nashikh gorodov," *Statisticheskoe obozrenie,* 7 (1928), 76-84.

49. See the report from Trekhgornaia factory stating that some of the workers lived in sheds in the summertime. *Rabochaia Moskva,* September 21, 1922. See also: *ibid.,* September 12, 1922; *Trud,* November 16, 1927, January 29, 1928.

50. *Perepis'1923g.,* vyp. III, tab. V, 186.

51. *Trud*, March 1, 1928; Leon Trotsky, *The Real Situation in Russia* (New York, 1928), 47; Sosnovy, *Housing*, 121, A 1929 study of a limited number of Moscow metal and textile workers indicates that the amount of living space per person dwindled rapidly as the influx of peasant migrants intensified in 1928 and 1929. The surveyed textile workers occupied 4.5 square meters and the metalworkers, 4.85 square meters of living space in early 1929. K. and Sh., "Zhilishchnoe polozhenie tekstil'shchikov," *Statisticheskoe obozrenie*, 6 (1929), 60-65.

52. Kabo, *Ocherki*, 99-101.

53. *Ibid.*, 29-33. See also, *ibid.*, 35-39, 69-71, 75-80.

54. M. Fischer, *Lives*, 34-46.

55. S. G. Strumilin, "Domashnyi byt v svete inventar'ev," *Izbrannye proizvedeniia* 5 vols. (Moscow, 1963-1968), III, 250-275; Kabo, *Ocherki*, 176. To enable workers to buy furniture, the city soviet passed a resolution in December 1927 that provided easy credit to workers for its purchase. *Trud*, December 15, 1927.

56. M. Fischer, *Lives*, 21.

57. Kabo, *Ocherki*, 54-61.

58. See the discussion in: Hazard, 9; Block, "Soviet Housing - II," 235-236; DiMaio, 12.

59. I. G. Koblents, *Zhilishchnoe pravo* (Moscow, 1924), 38-39.

60. As quoted in Alexander Block, "Soviet Housing—The Historical Aspect: Some Notes on Problems of Policy—I," *Soviet Studies*, 3, 1 (July, 1951), 14.

61. There are many examples of such complaints, but for a reasonable selection, see: *Rabochaia Moskva*, March 23, April 7, September 30, 1922; June 18, 1923; *Pravda*, April 18, 1925; *Trud*, January 29, 1928. On worker theft, see *Rabochaia Moskva*, March 20, 1923.

62. *Stroitel'stvo Moskvy*, 2 (1924), 1-7.

63. The following table lists new housing construction in Moscow. The figures are in millions of rubles.

Builder	1923/24	1924/25	1925/26	1926/27
City soviet	3.0	15.7	31.3	40.0
State organs	1.5	4.9	6.5	7.0
Cooperatives	4.2	8.2	14.8	17.0
Private	2.0	3.0	2.0	2.0
Number of occupants of new housing:	11,000	31,000	55,000	70,000

Source: *Stroitel'stvo Moskvy*, 10 (1927), 6.

See also: *Ibid.*, 11 (1925), 6; 7 (1925), 1-4; 4 (1926), 1; 11 (1926), 4-5; *Vsia Moskva, 1929*, otd. 1, 19.

64. Sosnovy, 65. See also, *Moskovskii sovet, 1917-1927*, 358. One measure of the slow pace of housing construction during the NEP is that those areas beyond the Sadova ring which prior to 1917 had been the fastest growing areas of the city were until 1926 the slowest growing districts. Vydro, 12; *Statisticheskii spravochnik . . . 1927*, 18-23.

65. *Stroitel'stvo Moskvy*, 10 (1927), 6; 11 (1925), 6.

66. S. V. Antronov, "Odin iz itogov proizvodstvennykh konferentsii tekstil'noi promyshlennosti," *Izvestiia tekstil'noi provmyshlennosti i torgovli,* November 15, 1926; V. Safronov, "Proizvodstvennye konferentsii po Moskve i Moskovskoi gubernii," *Vestnik truda,* 11 (1925), 176-179; Iakov Rysko, "Zhilishchnyi vopros v metallopromyshlennosti," *Vestnik truda,* 11 (1925), 39-49; *Trud,* January 19, 1928; *Pervyi shagi,* 483-499.

67. *Direktivy KPSS i sovetskogo pravitel'stva,* I, 588-590; I, 573.

68. *Ibid.,* I, 588. Vs. Il'inskii, "Kvartirnoe dovol'stvie personala tsenzovoi promyshlennosti SSSR v 1923-27gg.," *Statisticheskoe obozrenie,* 8 (1928), 49, echoed the thrust of this resolution: "The apartment issue in contemporary industrial conditions is a production issue. Without a solution to it, there may be no solution to the issue of the development of industry."

69. *Direktivy KPSS i sovetskogo pravitel'stva,* I, 796-804; *Trud,* January 5, 1928.

70. For examples, see: *Pravda,* January 8, April 23, May 6, 1925; *Trud,* July 7, December 28, 1927. For data on new housing construction, see: *Moskva i Moskovskaia guberniia,* tab. 153, 228; *Stroitel'stvo Moskvy,* 10 (1927), 6-7; *Moskovskii sovet, 1917-1927,* 364-367. See also, Anatole Kopp, *Town and Revolution: Soviet Architecture and City Planning, 1917-1935* (trans. Thomas E. Burton, New York, 1970), 138. For a survey of housing construction on a *raion* by *raion* basis, see *Stroitel'stvo Moskvy,* 10 (1926), 1-4.

71. *Trud,* March 1, 1928.

72. *Trud,* November 17, 1927. See also, *Moskovskii sovet, 1917-1927,* 366-367, and the discussion of building materials by Harold L. Alt, *American Engineers in Russia,* box 2.

73. For examples, see: *Rabochaia Moskva,* March 11, September 21, 1922; *"Dinamo,"* II, 92, 133; *Istoriia . . . Likacheva,* 81, 124; Lapitskaia, *Byt,* 127-131; *Stroitel'stvo Moskvy,* 4 (1924), 25.

74. *Trud,* March 17, 1928. See also, *Moskovskii proletarii,* March 27, 1924, 7, for a description of barracks.

75. Antronov.

76. For examples, see: S. Lapitskaia, "Byt rabochikh staroi i novoi fabriki," *Bor'ba klassov,* 6 (1933), 88-106; Lapitskaia, *Byt,* 128-136; A. Poselianina, "Leninskii prizyv (Moskovskii zavod 'serp i molot')," *Bor'ba klassov,* 1 (1934), 145-146. *Trud,* May 22, 1927. See also note 66.

77. *Rabochaia Moskva,* September 3, September 6, 1922.

78. Data from the 1926 census indicate that the January 1927 figure listed in table 5-4 is accurate. *Perepis' . . . 1926g.,* tom. 56, tab. XV, 208. See also the comparable estimates in M. Teodorovich, "Zhilishchnye usloviia i prestupnost' v Moskve," *Statisticheskoe obozrenie,* 10 (1928), 89-94.

79. For a discussion and description, see *Trud,* August 25, 1927; April 21, 1928.

80. *Trud,* August 25, 1927; April 8, April 21, 1928.

81. Teodorovich, 89-94. See also note 49.

82. For a discussion of *besprizorniki,* see: *Trud,* September 21, 1928;

Komsomol'skaia Pravda, August 30, 1927; January 7, 1928; *Moskovskii sovet, 1917-1927*, 94; Aleshchenko, *Moskovskii sovet*, 327, 429; Zenzinov, 9-183. For discussions of *besprizornik* life and stories of children who successfully escaped it and became upstanding citizens, see *Moskovskii proletarii*, January 15, 1926, 7-9; February 3, 1926, 20-22; Makarenko. On their lives and criminal activities, see M. N. Gernet, *Prestupnost' i samoubiistva vo vremia voiny i posle nee* (Moscow, 1927), 107-108, 154-155. See also Jennie A. Stevens, "Children of the Revolution: Soviet Russia's Homeless Children (*Besprizorniki*) in the 1920s," *Russian History/Histoire Russe*, 9, Parts 2-3, (1982), 242-246. A very interesting fictional account of these waifs and their activities can be found in Vyacheslav Shishkov, *The Children of the Street: Life in a Commune of Russia's Besprizorniki* (trans. Thomas A. Whitney, Royal Oak, Michigan, 1979).

83. According to the police records of arrested prostitutes in 1924, 37.3 percent were 25 or younger and 17.4 percent were 20 or younger. Comparable figures for 1926/27 were 76.1 percent and 46.3 percent respectively. Of 573 investigated prostitutes in 1924, 410 were drug addicts. M. N. Gernet, "K statistike prostitutsii," *Statisticheskoe obozrenie*, 7 (1927), 86-89. See also: Gernet, *Prestupnost'*, 154-155; Zenzinov, 75-76; Duranty, 147-148; Reswick, 259-262; Dreiser, 81.

84. As quoted in Duranty, 148; Gernet, "K statistike prostitutsii," 86-89; Reswick, 259; Shelley, 269-277.

85. For example, see *Trud*, July 15, 1927.

86. Norton T. Dodge, *Women in the Soviet Economy: Their Role in Economic, Scientific and Technical Development* (Baltimore, 1966), 97. A 1927 investigation of the city's housing discussed the absence of utilities and conveniences. *Trud*, November 16, 1927. Data on water and sewer systems can be found in: *Perepis' 1923g.*, vyp. 1, tab. XII, 138; vyp. III, tab. VI, 216; *Moskovskii sovet za desiat' let*, 40; *Goroda soiuza SSSR*, 22.

87. As discussed in Kingsbury and Fairchild, *Factory*, 249-250. So burdensome was the responsibility for chores during the late 1920s and early 1930s that groups of five workers would hold down four jobs and rotate the responsibility for domestic chores. Iu. Larin, *Zhilishche i byt'* (Moscow, 1930), as discussed in Kopp, 107. For an example of the division of labor at home, see Kabo, *Ocherki*, 63-65.

88. M. Teodorovich, 89-94. For crime statistics for Moscow, see *Moskva i Moskovskaia guberniia*, 100-112; *Statisticheskii spravochnik . . . 1927*, 94-101; Shelley, 265-284. Housing conditions affected people in more subtle ways. For example, a 1928 study conducted by two public health workers in Moscow revealed that among those investigated, most of whom were between the ages of 16 and 25, there was a marked reduction in sexual activity from what would be considered normal for someone in that age group. The study by B. B. Kogan and M. S. Lebedenskii, *Byt rabochego molodezhi po materialam anketnogo obsledovaniia* (Moscow, 1929) is discussed in Stephen P. Dunn and Ethel Dunn, "The Study of the Soviet Family in the USSR and in the West," *Slavic Studies Working Paper #1* (Columbus, Ohio, 1977), 10-12. I have been unable to obtain the original.

89. Sosnovy, 218. See also, *Pravda*, February 9, 1928; M. Fischer, *Lives*, 63.

90. *Ibid.*; Sosnovy, 213.

91. In those years cited in the text, there were 19,683, 26,211 and 30,302 marriages respectively. *Statisticheskii spravochnik . . . 1927*, 12-13; *Moskovskaia oblast': statisticheskii spravochnik po raionam Moskovskoi oblasti* (Moscow, 1931), 22-23. The changing marital patterns of the city's population are clear from the following table.

MARITAL PATTERNS OF THE MOSCOW POPULATION,
1902, 1920, AND 1926 (in percents)

Sex and marital status	1902	1920	1926
Males:			
Single	39.4%	26.4%	32.3%
Married	56.8%	49.5%	64.2%
Widowed	2.8%	3.0%	1.9%
Divorced	.1%	.5%	1.2%
Unknown	.8%	20.7%	.4%
Females:			
Single	34.3%	34.9%	28.8%
Married	44.2%	41.9%	50.9%
Widowed	20.5%	20.1%	16.7%
Divorced	.3%	1.0%	3.3%
Unknown	.6%	2.1%	.3%

Sources: Bradley, "*Muzhik* and Muscovite," 470; Vydro, 23; *Perepis' . . . 1926g.*, tom. 36, tab. I, 72.

92. For a historical perspective on divorce, see Peter Juviler, "The Family in the Soviet System," *The Carl Beck Papers in Russian and East European Studies*, 306 (1984).

93. For a discussion of divorce in the 1920s, see David and Vera Mace, *The Soviet Family* (New York, 1964), 213-221.

94. Reswick, 232-233.

95. For the 1920 abortion decree, see N. A. Semashko, *Health Protection in the U.S.S.R.* (London, 1934), 82-84. It is reprinted in Rudolf Schlesinger, ed., *The Family in the U.S.S.R.* (London, 1949), 144. According to Semashko, 84-88, there were 6.4 abortions per 100 live births in 1911. In 1934 and 1935, the figures were 271 and 221 respectively. The 1936 abortion law severely curtailed access to abortions. See Schlesinger, *Family*, 269-279; Lorimer, 127. According to *Aborty v 1925 godu* (Moscow, 1927), 31, the abortion rate in Moscow in 1925 was 27.

96. More than one-fifth elected abortions because they did not want the child; 13 percent of the women suffered from medical problems. *Aborty v 1925*, 45. For comparable data from the Dostoevskii abortion clinic, see Schlesinger, 176. See also: Kingsbury and Fairchild, *Factory*, 152-154; Alice W. Field, *Protection of Women and Children in Soviet Russia* (London, 1932), 83.

97. For a discussion, see H. Kent Geiger, *The Family in Soviet Russia* (Cambridge, Mass., 1968), 73.

212

98. Semashko, 84-88; Schlesinger, 172-173; *Aborty v 1925*, 29-51.

99. Bradley, "*Muzhik* and Muscovite," 267, notes a certain degree of class integration in Moscow around the turn of the century. But, in no way does his evidence deny the existence of class-based patterns of residency. On patterns of residency in the 1920s, see Iagolin, 85-88.

100. *Perepis'...1926g.*, tom. 56, tab. XV, 208; *Moskva i Moskovskaia gubernii*, tab. 156, 233. See also the article in *Moskovskii proletarii*, March 24, 1924, 9, which discusses the problem of the mixing of social groups in *dom kommuny*.

101. *Rabochaia Moskva*, April 22, 1922.

102. *Ibid.*, September 16, 1922. I have been unable to find a follow-up article on the results of this tactic. See also *ibid.*, April 26, September 16, 1922.

103. *Ibid.*, February 13, February 23, 1923.

104. *Ibid.*, August 16, 1922.

105. *Ibid.*, September 17, October 8, 1922.

106. *Ibid.*, October 13, 1922.

107. *Ibid.*, September 7, 1922. For other examples, see: *ibid.*, September 11, 1923; *Trud*, September 19, 1922, September 4, 1927. According to Markoosha Fischer, folk tunes and songs about nepmen were very popular in Moscow during the period. M. Fischer, *Lives*, 21.

108. See the discussion of a lavish party hosted by a speculator who made a "killing" by the illegal sale of sugar during the 1921/22 famine. Duranty, 140-144.

109. *Ibid.*, 146-147.

110. *Ibid.*, 145-146.

111. *Pravda*, January 30, 1925.

112. *Trud*, January 29, 1928.

113. *Ibid.*, February 20, 1924. See also *ibid.*, September 4, 1927.

114. *Rabochaia Moskva*, November 24, December 12, 1929. My thanks to Lynn Viola for bringing these articles to my attention.

6. The Drive for Productivity

Control over production was high on the proletariat's revolutionary agenda. To secure it, they moved quickly in late 1917 and 1918 to enact workers' control. But their attempts to assert local control ran into opposition from the predominantly productivist party leadership. The two viewed workers' control differently. Workers and party radicals perceived it as an end in itself and as a means toward increasing worker influence over their lives. Productivists saw it as a means to an end and as a counterbalance to one-man management. In early 1920, the productivists dealt the final blow to the workers' valiant effort. The organizational and political contours of factory life had been fixed. Responsibility for factory operations and the implementation of official policies there rested with factory directors and managerial personnel. The powers of factory committees were limited to checking and verifying management's performance. The productivists had won. But workers' desire to assert control over production remained alive.

Having consolidated their control over production, party leaders moved to enact their labor and economic policies, the primary goal of which was to raise productivity. Toward this end, they sought to tie wages to productivity, to establish production norms, and to improve labor discipline. The economic collapse of 1918-1921 had destroyed all hopes of raising productivity. But the foundations of Soviet labor policy had been laid. Whereas the introduction of the NEP marked a decisive break with many of War Communism's policies, save for ending labor militarization, such was not the case with labor policy. In fact, during the NEP these policies were extended, and the drive to raise worker productivity steadily intensified. Factory managers implemented these policies which denied workers any formal control over production. The way in which managers did so angered workers.

Many realities tempered the drive. The most important of these were the shortage of skilled and experienced workers, the growing number of inexperienced and undisciplined workers, substandard factory conditions, antiquated and inefficient machinery, and until the mid-1920s, chaotic wage mechanisms. To ensure that workers' rights, health, and safety would not be violated in the drive for productivity, the state enacted the 1922 Labor Code. While that code stipulated that wages must be tied to productivity, required workers to meet minimum production norms to receive the minimum wage, and prescribed the means by which output norms were to be established, it also sought to protect workers' from exploitation. It clearly stated the workers' rights and the protection which they were due. The Labor Code mandated the eight-hour workday, required a weekly rest period of no less than forty-two continuous hours, placed limits on the amount of overtime, fixed rates of pay for overtime work, forbade the employment of children under fourteen and limited the workday of juveniles (ages fourteen to eighteen) to six hours, and defined the factory and work conditions necessary to protect the health and safety of workers. It also empowered trade unions, factory committees, and labor inspectors to expose violations of the law and to protect workers' health and safety.[1]

On paper, the 1922 Code was the world's most progressive and comprehensive labor legislation. It demonstrated the party's belief that increases in productivity were not to be achieved by exploiting workers. With the establishment of socialism, the cruel exploitation of the proletariat for the enhancement of a few people's greedy desires had been abolished forever. But as we shall see, the factory directors and managerial personnel who had to enact the state's productivist policies and obey the Labor Code frequently ignored, and at times blatantly violated, the latter to achieve the former. This was especially true in the early 1920s.

Precisely because factory managerial personnel might disregard or even callously ignore workers' rights, the Tenth Party Congress had assigned unions a dual role. On the one hand, they were to enforce the workers' state's policies and laws that, *ipso facto*, could not violate workers' rights. On the other hand, unions were to protect workers from management's misapplication of policies and violations of the Labor Code. The dual role that unions were expected to play was difficult enough in the abstract. But in the early 1920s, most union leaders viewed increased worker productivity as the means to restoring industry and

215

improving work conditions. Only higher productivity would generate the capital necessary to make the factories safe places to work. Wittingly or unwittingly, unions and managers became *de facto* allies. With the unions' function of marshaling management compromised and the institutional restraints on management thereby weakened, factory directors and their support personnel frequently violated the spirit and letter of the Labor Code and related policies. Not until mid-1924 did the union leadership come to the conclusion that they had the priorities reversed, that better conditions and safer machinery were the surest way to higher productivity. Management's behavior did not change as quickly.

Raising productivity and lowering production costs were the central tenets of labor and economic policy, but they were not obsessions perceived by the country's productivist leaders as the shortest route to the realization of some Marxist utopia. As during the Civil War so too in the early 1920s, pressing realities dictated these priorities. By 1921, the nation's economy had virtually ground to a halt. Restive workers vociferously demanded that their material well-being be improved. Food, fuel, clothing, and other essential goods were in short supply. To meet the workers' demands and to realise socialism's material promises, economic recovery had to be achieved. How was this to be done? Who would bear the brunt of the cost of recovery?

Instituting the NEP provided a partial answer to the first question. But having embarked on the NEP, answering the second question proved more difficult and divisive. That question was at the heart of the political debates that divided the party in the 1920s.[2] Ideally, party leaders hoped that the proletariat and peasantry would share the cost of recovery. But it soon became obvious that the proletariat would bear a disproportionate share of the burden. There were several reasons for this.

The first was that hungry workers desperately needed food. Given the failure of requisitioning, the state had instituted a free market. The reality of the market was simple. If the peasantry was to be induced to sell its produce, industry had to produce goods that the peasantry needed and, above all, could afford. Economic officials hoped that, by purchasing peasant produce at prices low relative to those of manufactured goods, the peasantry would help to pay for the costs of recovery. It was via pricing mechanisms that the burden of recovery would be distributed. Although illiterate, peasants were not dumb. Those who could afford to do so realized that, by withholding their produce (or selling it to a private trader who paid more for it), they could force up the price. When they did so, as during the 1923 "scissors crisis" and in 1927/28, the impact was dramatic. Both events underscored just how much the urban standard of living depended upon the peasantry.

Higher worker productivity and lower production costs were also necessary to hasten capital accumulation. If economic recovery was to be achieved quickly, if economic expansion was to occur, if worker demands for better housing and consumer goods were to be met, and if the party's and proletariat's dream of a socialism of abundance were to be realized, capital was essential. Because it eschewed the means employed by capitalists to accumulate capital, the Soviet state had to rely on internal resources. Raising productivity became an important—and easily verifiable—avenue to capital accumulation.

We have already discussed some of the economic policies' consequences—mass unemployment and the slow rate of housing repair and construction. Let us now turn our attention to the economic and labor policies' effects on Muscovites' working lives. The policies designed to raise productivity both united and divided workers. On the one hand, they resented the way in which factory administrators enforced those policies. As the drive for greater productivity intensified, so too did the deterioration of worker-management relations. On the other hand, the policies enacted frequently pitted groups of workers against one another.

How the drive for productivity was implemented and its impact on the fabric of factory life provide the focus for the rest of this study. This chapter will discuss the policies and the ways in which they affected the industrial working class. This is best accomplished by dividing the NEP into two periods: 1921-mid-1924, mid-1924-1929. In the first period, the spectres of inflation and economic instability and the legacies of the Civil War frequently frustrated attempts to raise productivity and improve wages and conditions. In the latter period, the "good years" of the NEP, rapid economic growth and the implementation of new policies reduced some problems and created new ones. Chapter 7 will focus on how workers overcame their divisions, united against management, and utilized production meetings to press their demands for improved conditions and greater control over production.

Wages and Productivity (1921–Mid-1924)

Immediately after the Tenth Party Congress's decision to embark on the NEP, state and union officials began to enact wage mechanisms consistent with the principle of linking wages to productivity. The first steps were cautious and simply reiterated this long-sought and often-ignored principle. Two April 1921 Sovnarkom decrees are representative of these early efforts. The first urged local organs to introduce simplified wage scales that allowed workers to see the relationship between wages and productivity. The other introduced bonuses in kind for factories that achieved their production quotas.[3] A September 1921 Sovnarkom decree reaffirmed yet again that wages must reflect productivity and that the link between the two must be made clear to workers. But it rejected the principle of egalitarianism and mandated that any wage system must provide enough flexibility to allow management to reward work initiative. Nonetheless, it demanded that all workers, regardless of their productivity, be guaranteed the minimum wage. Wages could be paid in whatever form was deemed appropriate—food, consumer goods, housing, clothing, and other products and services.[4] (Although rationing ended in 1921, the payment of wages in kind continued into 1924.) Then, in November 1921 the government significantly amended the September decree when it announced that workers would only receive their full wages if they met their minimum output quota. All pretense that workers' jobs would ensure their social maintenance was dropped. To earn a decent income, workers had to be productive. The 1922 Labor Code turned this principle into law.[5]

But the enunciation of principles and their implementation in an orderly manner were two distinct processes. Although wages were supposed to reflect productivity, in the early 1920s, they increased at a much faster rate than did productivity. The relationship between the two varied from industry to industry and even within industries. Therefore, the following figures must be viewed as representative of the trend. In Moscow's metal industry in 1922/23, average output per worker stood at 41 percent of the 1913 level, while the average monthly wage was 56 to 82 percent higher, depending on the currency used. In the textile industry in 1923/24, productivity was 17 percent higher than the year before, but wages had increased by 43 percent. According to the Moscow Sovnarkhoz, the average industrial worker's wage increases exceeded those of productivity by 31 percent during the last quarter of 1923.[6] Between October 1922 and March 1924, the average wage rose by 80 percent, while productivity rose by 24 percent.[7] Whatever the precise figures, there can be no doubt that until late 1924, differing wage mechanisms, inflation, the condition of industry, and worker unrest united to frustrate official attempts to tie wages to productivity.

To introduce order into the existing and chaotic wage mechanisms and to fix the relative value of skills and experience, VTsSPS approved a new, seventeen-grade wage scale in 1922. Grades one to nine applied to workers and set the ratio of the lowest to highest paid workers at 1:2.7. Grades ten to seventeen applied to administrative and technical personnel; the ratio here being 2.7:5. This was the ideal. The wage scale did not establish wages *per se*, rather it fixed the wage increments between workers who possessed different skill levels and years of experience.[8] A number of factors combined to undermine the wage scale's intent.

Collective agreements were one of the most important factors. Collective bargaining, which began on an industry-by-industry basis after February 1922, created two common problems in the area of wages. The first was that, despite Sovnarkom's insistence that governmental agencies had the exclusive power to determine wage scales,[9] collective agreements often resulted in different industries setting their own wage scales. Second, different rates of recovery among industries meant that the workers in two industries who had comparable skills and experience would earn radically differing wages. The city's consumer industries (with the exception of the textile industry) were the chief beneficiaries of collective agreements in the early 1920s. Because their products were in great demand and the capital required to restore and expand production was less than that demanded by heavy industries, most consumer industries recovered more quickly than heavy industries. Hence, factory directors there were more willing to conclude collective agreements that increased their workers' wages. The reverse was true in industries such as metals and transport that were slow to recover and required large sums of capital to do so.

The extent to which collective agreements undermined official attempts to reward skill and experience are clear. In September 1922, the average wages in Moscow's food processing industry, which traditionally had been low paying, exceeded those of usually high-paid metalworkers.[10] That same year, "girl workers in the tobacco factories packing cigarettes were getting more than a coal hewer or fitter."[11] Needless to say, their relatively low wages angered experienced metalworkers, skilled fitters and others who shared their fate. To redress the inequities, in 1924 VTsSPS recommended that the wages of workers in consumer industries be held down, while those of workers in heavy industries be raised.[12]

That some workers received piece-rate wages and others time-based (hourly or daily) wages further undermined attempts to tie wages to productivity. What proportion of Moscow workers received piece-rate wages in the early 1920s is unclear. But nationally in 1923, more than 40 percent of the workforce did so; by mid-1924, that proportion rose to 60 percent.[13] But the presence of both time-based and piece-rate wages in the same industry created a series of problems. In some cases, output norms were set low thereby enabling piece-rate workers to earn higher wages than their co-workers who had the same skills, experience, and level of productivity, but earned hourly wages. To equalize the wages and reduce the discontent of workers earning hourly wages, compensatory bonuses often had to be paid to them.[14] The potential for disincentive in such a system is obvious.

Precisely how output quotas were determined is unclear. According to the 1922 Labor Code, factory administrators and unions officials were to jointly determine the quotas. In some cases, foremen recommended those norms; in others, rate-setting bureaus (TNBs) performed that task. When foremen set them, practical experience was usually the guide. When TNBs performed this function, they were supposed to take into account the maximal utilization of the machinery, the enterprise's technical equipment and capacity, and average worker output at each skill level.[15] Given the factories' dilapidated condition in the early 1920s, attempts to set realistic output norms were quixotic. TNBs often encountered "enormous difficulties," not the least of which were the conflicts that broke out between rate-setters (*rastsenshchiki*) and workers who resented shop- and factory-wide norms. That the rate-setters' work was often of very low quality compounded the problem and further angered workers.[16] Nevertheless, attempts to establish and raise output quotas continued apace. In 1923 and 1924, output norms in many of the city's factories were increased. At Dinamo, output norms were raised by 15 to 25 percent; in the textile industry, by 10 to 20 percent.[17]

Other factors served to strain the desired relationship between wages and productivity. Until the stabilization of the currency in 1924, inflation wreaked havoc with real wages. While nominal wages rose steadily from 1921, the inflation rate frequently meant that real wages declined. This was especially true in 1923. The managerial practice of delaying wage payments further undermined efforts to raise real wages. Pressure to increase productivity while their buying power was subject to reverses angered many workers who demanded that their wages be raised. The problem was at the root of much of the labor unrest during the 1921-1924 period.

And then there was the shortage of skilled labor. Luring sufficient numbers of skilled workers back to the factories after 1920 proved to be a difficult task. Many skilled and experienced workers had died between 1914 and 1921. Others had taken up positions in the union, party or state bureaucracy. To convince skilled, former workers to return to work, some factories sent recruiters to the villages. But these efforts proved insufficient to reduce the shortage.[18] At the Moskovskii proletarii factory, there were 50 percent fewer skilled workers in 1924 than before the war.[19] According to a spokesman at the 1922 metal industry congress, "Cadres of skilled workers have grown scarce" and were but a small proportion of the total workforce. Consequently, the raising of factory productivity was difficult. "It is essential," he continued, "to avert the catastrophe of a completely lifeless *(obeskrovlennyi)* workforce in the metal industry." The situation was equally as dire in the textile industry.[20] In view of this shortage, factories had no choice but to hire unskilled workers whose lack of experience, skills, and labor discipline restrained the rate at which productivity rose. The inundation of the workforce by new workers increased annually until by the late 1920s union leaders complained that the "working class is being diluted by large numbers of people from other classes, especially from the villages."[21]

The lack of labor discipline among workers, especially new workers, manifested itself in a variety of ways. Leaving one's machine(s) to strike up a conversation or smoke a cigarette, arriving late to work (or leaving early), arriving drunk or drinking on the job, and not coming to work at all were accepted habits among many new workers. As their ranks within the workforce increased, these problems, especially drunkenness on the job, intensified. Factory administrators and party, Komsomol, and union activists struggled to improve labor discipline and to instill the rudiments of a work ethic in undisciplined workers. But their success was slow and uneven.

Their battle to reduce drunkenness proved to be a Sisyphian one. Some workers continued to arrive at work drunk; others continued to drink during work from bottles smuggled in and hidden in machinery, garbage cans and rafters. A large still was actually found in the Sokol'niki machine works in 1923.[22] Despite a concerted antialcohol campaign carried on in the press, at public lectures, and in factory committee meetings, the problem endured. Drunkenness remained a prime cause of absenteeism, especially on "blue Mondays." In 1926, more than 10 percent of the workforce in many factories was absent on Mondays. Drunkenness also caused many industrial accidents. In Moscow in the first half of 1928, there were 9,605 reported alcohol-related illnesses or accidents; 80 percent of the victims were workers.[23]

Efforts to reduce absenteeism proved more successful. In 1921/22,

Moscow workers did not show up for one-third of the workdays.[24] This figure represents a citywide average; in some industries and enterprises, the situation was far worse. Consider the case of the metal industry. Of 105 reporting factories, two had absentee rates in excess of 50 percent; two, absentee rates of 30 to 50 percent; and fourteen, absentee rates of 16 to 30 percent. Six months later the situation had actually deteriorated—of 156 factories, the figures were three, eighteen, and forty-six respectively.[25] In time, the average proportion of workdays missed declined, from 17 percent in 1924/25 to a low of 7.6 percent in 1926/27.[26] The improvement resulted from a confluence of external factors—the levying of fines for unauthorized absence, the gradual improvement in the material condition of workers, and the sharp rise in unemployment—rather than from the internalization of discipline, although that process also occurred.

There were many reasons why one might miss work. Some, such as illness or organizational work, were legitimate. Over time, the number of days missed for the latter reason declined dramatically; those missed for illness did so slowly. These reasons aside, many workers simply never showed up for work; sometimes they offered an excuse, sometimes not. The problem of unauthorized absence was especially acute among those workers with strong ties to the land, who frequently extended weekend visits to their village or summer vacations that they usually took during the sowing, haymowing, or harvest times.[27] That landowning workers were major contributors to the high absentee rate is clear from the results of a study conducted by the city textile trust, which revealed that when peasant-workers took their holidays, the absenteeism rates dropped.[28]

The problem of labor indiscipline evoked concern from state and union officials and managerial personnel alike. For them, the problems stood as an obstacle to raising productivity. But given the steady influx of new workers into factories, the future offered little hope for labor discipline improving dramatically. Experienced and disciplined workers also resented new workers' behavior, especially when it had an adverse impact on their productivity, wages, and safety. Ignoring safety rules, carelessly operating machinery, engaging in horse-play, drinking, and other undisciplined behaviors threatened all workers' safety and served to divide them.[29]

But labor indiscipline was not always rooted in ignorance nor the exclusive domain of new workers. In some cases, it may well be that tardiness, the taking of unauthorized breaks, and slowing the pace of production were some workers' ways of asserting a measure of control over their pace of work and "getting back" at management. Such was apparently the case at one unidentified factory where the factory committee reported that younger workers were relatively more productive because, unlike their elders, they did not leave their machines to converse or smoke during "traditional," as opposed to authorized, breaks.[30] Unfortunately, limited evidence prohibits making this subtle, but important distinction. Nor should the hypothesis be blown out of proportion. The fact remains that the number of inexperienced and untrained new workers entering the factories grew annually, and the problem of labor indiscipline mounted.

While penalizing workers remained the most common and direct way to temper poor work habits, efforts were also made to instill better work habits by educating and training workers. The most systematic of these was that conducted by the Central Institute of Labor (TsIT). Founded in late 1920, TsIT devoted its energies to studying the scientific organization of labor (*nauchnaia organizatsiia truda* or NOT). Inspired by the research and ideas of Frederick W. Taylor, the institute, headed by Aleksei Gastev, spent most of its time conducting research to discover optimal work methods. Although devoted to extending Taylor's research so as to raise productivity, the institute's advocates, including Lenin, drew a sharp and careful distinction between Taylorism as applied in capitalist enterprises, which utilized his work to exploit workers for the sake of greater profits, and the Soviets' use of his research to ease the burden, while simultaneously increasing the productivity, of labor. The NOT movement's goal was to harmonize the work process in order to raise the productivity of—but not increase the exploitation of—workers. To accomplish this, the institute conducted time-motion studies in its labs and in factories. Given that the latter often preceded the raising of output norms, they were not very popular with some workers. Nor did older, skilled workers appreciate Gastev's belief that theirs were craft skills which should be eliminated by mechanization and a stricter division of labor.[31]

In addition to its research activities, TsIT actively tried to educate workers on ways to increase productivity. Toward this end, it sponsored worker training courses at which workers were instructed on how to coordinate the pace of their work and the machine(s), how to minimize mistakes and accidents, and how to overcome impediments to production. How many of Moscow's workers attended such courses is difficult to say, but they were most popular with younger workers. Complementing these training courses were NOT circles organized in the factories.

The circles' purpose was to involve managerial and technical personnel, party and union activists, and workers in discussions of and ways to improve production and raise productivity. In Moscow and other cities, the organization and focus of these circles gave rise to debates among NOT supporters. Gastev and his allies perceived them as forums at which optimal production methods would be disseminated to workers and technical personnel. His rivals argued that workers' experience and knowledge of factory affairs were important resources and that, rather than being passive recipients of information and advice, workers should be actively involved in efforts to determine ways to raise productivity. The debate over the structure and activities of NOT circles mirrored that between the productivists and radicals, the central point of contention being the role and active involvement of workers. In this debate, Gastev and his productivist supporters carried the day.[32]

Alongside NOT circles were production propaganda circles. Organized by the All-Russian Bureau of Production Propaganda in late 1920, they also sought to involve factory administrators, technical specialists, party and union activists, and workers in discussions of ways to raise productivity and to improve production. They organized factory tours to explain how the factory's shops were integrated, offered lectures on production issues, sought to elicit worker suggestions on how to improve production, and encouraged worker-inventors.[33]

Neither NOT nor production propaganda circles succeeded in attracting wide worker participation. Managerial and technical personnel dominated most such circles. Rather than being forums at which worker opinions and suggestions were elicited, they were formal academic affairs at which those in attendance listened to reports and lectures by administrative personnel on how to raise productivity.[34] Many workers viewed them as but another means to intensify labor, and they stayed away from them. According to a March 1924 report on NOT circles, few workers knew about the circles' activities or results and fewer attended them. Production propaganda circles experienced the same fate.[35]

Labor Conditions and Labor Protection (1921–Mid-1924)

Another impediment to raising worker productivity was the condition and productive capacity of industry. Before the revolution, the conditions in most factories were poor, unhealthy, and often dangerous. Lighting and ventilation systems were inadequate, ceilings were low, and windows were few and poorly located. Factories were often overcrowded, and many machines were dangerously close together. Decent toilet and dining facilities were rare. After seven years of neglect, deterioration, and lack of investment, the conditions of all factories in 1921 were abysmal.[36] The cessation of hostilities brought little immediate improvement. Given the shortage of capital, official demands to balance books (and hopefully show a profit), and the inflation rate, many industrial managers deferred all but the most essential repairs and improvements. Though understandable, the decision was a short-sighted one that served to slow productivity's rise.

Workers had many reasons to be dissatisfied with their working conditions and their complaints filled the daily press. They complained that most machinery needed repair, that walls and support beams were weak and unsafe, that structural defects in ceilings and basements caused flooding which in turn sped the rusting of machinery. Substandard technical and mechanical conditions existed in virtually all factories. In some cases, workers realized that lack of capital delayed efforts to repair their workplaces; but in most, they accused factory administrators of neglect. Workers in both the state and private sector expressed their grievances.[37]

When workers complained that poor working conditions hindered their efforts to raise productivity, they were not exaggerating. A 1924 study revealed that many of Moscow's factories were in substandard condition and desperately needed repairs—in the textile industry, the proportion was 25 percent; in the metal industry, 40 percent. One can only imagine the state of industrial enterprises during the previous three years. Not only were conditions poor, but much of the machinery and technical equipment in the city's factories was outdated. For example, a 1924 investigation of the Iakhromskii textile factory revealed that two-thirds of its machinery was twenty to fifty years old. Nor was that plant atypical.[38] Antiquated machinery and substandard conditions meant that many machines and even shops frequently had to halt production for repairs. At one Moscow machine-building plant, such problems forced the factory to be idle for 25 percent of the average workday in 1924.[39] Given these conditions, strictly tying wages to productivity made a mockery of any rational and equitable wage policy and invited worker unrest.

Many factory managers used the demands and constraints imposed upon them by official policies to violate those clauses of the Labor Code that sought to protect workers from exploitation. Their attitudes toward factory repairs and workers' rights and safety betrayed their narrow and often crass interpretation of official policies and laws and their frequent disregard for workers' well-being. The extent of the problem is clear from the following examples. A 1922 investigation of 900 enterprises in Moscow revealed that many employers violated the legislation guaranteeing the continuous weekly rest period and supplementary holidays for workers in unhealthy industries. Infractions relating to child labor were five to six times higher than before the NEP.[40] Employers also frequently ignored regulations regarding working hours, overtime, and minimal safety standards. In 1924/25, substandard sanitary conditions accounted for one-third of all labor violations. Poor sanitary and working conditions contributed to a deterioration of the workers' health as well as productivity. Investigations of textile factories revealed that poor conditions resulted in high incidences of respiratory ailments, especially tuberculosis.[41]

Although Labor Code violations were commonplace in state enterprises during the early NEP, private enterprises were especially flagrant violators. The reasons for this range from private owners' contempt for all Soviet legislation, to lack of capital, to the fact that workers in private enterprises were less well-organized and less aware of their rights than their counterparts in state-owned enterprises. Workers in private enterprises complained about poor lighting and ventilation, unsanitary workshops, and dangerous machinery. That textile workers in the private sector had higher incidences of job-related diseases such as tuberculosis, rheumatism, and eye injuries than did workers in state enterprises testifies to the poor conditions there. Whereas violations of the eight-hour day and the employment of underage workers declined steadily in state enterprises, private owners flaunted such laws. Workers in some private factories had to work ten- and fifteen-hour days with no overtime pay. Violations of laws governing night work and the employment of young children were common. At one private sugar factory where the majority of workers were females ages fourteen to twenty, the workday ran from 9:00 am to midnight.[42] Some owners required their workers to live at the workplace and, in some instances, locked out workers who returned after the established curfew.[43] Not all owners acted with such contempt for the law, but the number of enlightened nepmen appear to have been few. Conditions in private artisan shops were even worse.[44]

To curtail such behavior, the Labor Code empowered trade unions, factory committees, and labor inspectors to expose substandard conditions and violations of the law and to protect workers' health and safety.

Harsh penalties existed for violations.[45] But until 1924, most union leaders, like managers, were preoccupied with wage and productivity issues and paid inadequate attention to ensuring that working conditions met legal specifications. When they did attempt to improve conditions, the factory directors' claim that they lacked the capital to do so blunted their efforts. Without their union's active support, factory committees themselves had little leverage with which to correct violations and to improve conditions. Unfortunately, workers received little more than verbal support from labor inspectors who were few in number and often of low quality. Although three-quarters of the city's labor inspectors were party members, their influence was less than that of factory directors who claimed that lack of capital and the demands of recovery limited their ability to improve conditions.[46]

Dismal and unsafe work conditions not only limited worker productivity, they also caused large numbers of industrial accidents. Because data on industrial accidents were admittedly poor,[47] those cited below should be treated as minimum figures. In Moscow *guberniia* in 1922/23, there were more than 9,000 reported industrial accidents, at least 25 of which were fatal. By 1924/25, the number had risen to more than 25,000, 86 of which were fatal.[48] During these years, the accident rate per thousand workers exceeded that of the tsarist period, though by how much varies widely depending on the source. According to the Moscow Department of Labor, the accident rate rose from 15 accidents per thousand workers between 1914 and 1917, to 35 in 1919, and to 108 in 1923/24. But another study claimed that the accident rate per thousand workers in selected textile factories only increased from 24.4 in 1912 to 26 in 1924, though in some factories the accident rate had quadrupled. Both studies agree that close to half of the accidents resulted from the failure of factory administrators to institute the legally mandated safety equipment and to ensure that the plant's machinery was safe. Upward of one-third were the fault of workers, particularly inexperienced and poorly trained workers many of whom were recent arrivals from the villages.[49]

Despite the fact that violations of the Labor Code were common and resulted in accidents, deaths, and on occasion strikes, during the early 1920s unions considered the issue of labor protection secondary to increased productivity. When forced to choose between the implementation of party policy and the demands of their constituents, unions frequently chose the former. That party members increasingly dominated union leadership positions played no small role in this choice.[50] Not until late 1924 was there a pronounced shift in policy. One author attributes this shift to industry's restoration and growth, the strengthening of its financial base, improvements in workers' material conditions, the opening of new enterprises and repairing of old ones, and a growing concern with labor protection issues.[51] Undoubtedly all of these improvements contributed to this change, but the latter, particularly among workers and some union activists, proved decisive.

In the course of 1924, pressure grew within union ranks to pay serious attention to labor protection. The number of articles on labor conditions and protection in union newspapers and journals increased significantly. The articles' common line of argument was that improving working conditions and devoting greater attention to labor protection would result in higher productivity and hasten the rate of industrial recovery.[52] By late 1924, the logic of the argument and pressure from below convinced union officials of the need to balance their priorities. Various union conferences and the Sixth Trade Union Congress passed resolutions which not only linked wage increases to productivity, but which also linked increases in productivity to improved labor conditions and protection.[53] Although slow in coming, the unions' new policy heralded a period of improved labor conditions and protection.

Political Implications of the Early NEP

Worker unrest had ushered in the NEP and remained a perennial aspect of Muscovite life during its early years. Unfortunately, sparse evidence prohibits a comprehensive discussion of the dimensions of worker discontent. But the reasons for it are clear. With the shift from a policy of social maintenance to an open labor market in an inflation-riddled market economy, worker attitudes shifted accordingly. Whereas in 1920-1921, hungry workers demanded food and an improvement in their abject standard of living, in the early 1920s they coupled demands for economic improvement with the growing belief that the exploitation of the pre-revolutionary period was being re-instituted in a new guise. The signs were everywhere—rising unemployment, demands for increasing productivity, fluctuating real wages, and the restoration and strengthening of managers' and specialists' powers—and workers used what power they had to struggle against them.

Workers had several weapons at their disposal. The most powerful was the strike. According to the Moscow *Guberniia* Trade Union Council, the number of strikes increased from 32 in 1923 to 49 in 1924. But, strikes as a proportion of all labor disputes (*konflikty*) declined—from 4 percent in 1923 to 1.8 percent in 1924/25. It is difficult to ascertain these figures' accuracy. Because wildcat strikes without the union's or factory committee's knowledge or approval were common in the early 1920s,[54] one suspects that the 1923 figure is low.

A wave of wildcat strikes swept the industrial centers in August and September 1923. What triggered that unrest was a sales crisis caused by the state's raising of manufactured goods' prices. Peasants reduced their purchases thereby creating an overproduction and cash-flow crisis in industry. Unemployment rose, wage payments were delayed, and real wages declined. Fearful of a weakening of their economic position, workers reacted sharply. According to one report, "economic questions . . . are agitating the working masses . . . Hostile elements have reared their ugly heads. . . . In a series of large enterprises in Moscow and other cities there has been observed a revival of agitation hostile to us, especially in enterprises with lower wages. Evil demagogy on questions of wages has suddenly increased in these months." Rumors of a general strike circulated in Moscow,[55] but no such strike occurred. In fact, it appears that rarely, if ever, did strikes involve more than individual factories.

Although data on strikes may underestimate their numbers, two facts regarding labor disputes are clear: violations of collective agreements triggered virtually all stikes; and increasingly workers eschewed the strike and carried their grievances to the assessment and conflict commissions, conciliation chambers, and labor arbitration courts established by the unions to adjudicate labor disputes. In 1923, there were 799 labor disputes in Moscow city involving 185,217 workers; the next year, the figures were 1,481 and 253,908 respectively. Undoubtedly, one reason why workers' appealed their grievances with increasing frequency was that, in the majority of cases, the adjudicating organs ruled in their favor or negotiated a satisfactory compromise.[56] Clearly, workers' increasing use of these bodies after 1921 to redress grievances hastened the routinization of industrial conflict. As that process accelerated, strikes diminished as a proportion of labor conflict.

Conflicts over the negotiation or interpretation of collective agreements were common in the early 1920s. In 1923, they accounted for almost 70 percent of all disputes and 82 percent of all participants. Their importance waned the following year, accounting for 40 percent and 75 percent respectively. The contested issues are listed in table 6-1.

Given the inflation rate, confusing wage mechanisms, and practice of delayed wage payments, one could anticipate that wages would be the

TABLE 6-1
Disputed Issues in Collective Agreements

| | 1923 | | 1924 | |
Issue	Number	Percent	Number	Percent
Wages	564	42.2%	544	50.6%
Assignments	360	27.0%	242	22.5%
Hiring and firing	131	9.8%	103	9.6%
Labor Protection	121	9.0%	99	9.2%
Other	160	12.0%	87	8.1%
Total	1,336	100.0%	1,075	100.0%

SOURCE: *Trud v Moskovskoi gubernii*, 426.

single most disputed issue. Nor, in light of workforce reductions and poor working conditons, are the presence of hiring and firing and labor protection in the table surprising. The prominence of assignments deserves note. Assignments here refer not to job assignments, but rather assignments to professional, technical and cultural education courses or to rest homes and sanatoria. At issue was how many such assignments would be made and how workers would be chosen.[57]

Workers also frequently appealed specific violations of collective agreements and the Labor Code. In fact in these two years, the proportion of all disputes triggered by such violations almost doubled—from 31 percent to 60 percent. Once again, wages led the way. In 1923, wage issues accounted for 36 percent of all Moscow labor disputes and involved 55,000 workers. The next year, the number of disputes jumped by 40 percent, accounted for 46 percent of all disputes, and involved more than 100,000 workers.[58] What proportion of these resulted in strikes is unclear, although one suspects that the AMO strike over delayed wages (discussed in chapter 5) was not an isolated event. Because wages and production norms were intimately connected, the raising of output norms often sparked wage disputes. Given the poor condition of machinery and factories, the raising of output quotas in 1923 and 1924 often meant that workers had to labor harder to compensate for inefficient machinery; yet they believed that they were not duly compensated. Rather than enduring what they perceived as increased exploitation, they frequently staged wildcat strikes. So angered were Serp i molot workers at management's raising of output norms (apparently in violation of the collective agreement) that party and nonparty workers staged a wildcat strike.[59]

While wages and resentment over the intensification of labor were the most common causes of labor disputes, the implementation of other labor and economic policies also raised workers' ire. Particularly important was the firing of workers, which in 1923 and 1924 accounted for one-quarter of all complaints. Disputes over management's disregard for labor protection trailed a distant fourth as a proportion of all conflicts, but in 1924 they involved 60 percent of all individuals who appeared before arbitration organs. This high proportion suggests that entire shops and possibly factories lodged protests against substandard conditions and inadequate labor protection.[60]

Incomplete though the evidence is, there can be little doubt that between late 1920 and mid-1924, the working class seethed with discontent. This was especially true in 1923, when rumors of a general strike circulated in Moscow. No such strike occurred. Factory and shop strikes occurred, but unrest centered on specific grievances and was very localized. Wages, work, and their discontents were at the root of the unrest. There is little evidence that workers organized beyond the factory gate. Nor did the party, unions, or factory committees urge them to do so. The productivist-oriented party leadership and party-dominated union leadership viewed the task of restoration and increased productivity as the period's primary objectives. Given that the application of official policies and the consequences of inflation were the proletariat's major grievances, one hardly expects the party and unions to give form to and organize worker discontent. Rather, they urged workers to "work within the system" by taking their grievances to the appeal boards created to right the wrongs committed by management. Increasingly, workers followed their advice. They did so not because the party and unions had proved themselves once again to be the workers' natural allies. They had not yet. In fact, between 1920 and 1924, worker participation in the party and unions fell to an all-time low.[61] The breach between the party and workers, between unions and workers, remained wide until 1924.

This is not to suggest that the mass of workers had become antiunion or antiparty. Most supported the revolution and its ideals. What they demanded was that these organizations protect workers and strive to fulfill the workers' revolutionary agenda and the revolution's promises, as workers interpreted them. In short, they demanded that the workers' state manifest itself in concrete ways. The NEP's policies of rationalization, tying wages to productivity, reducing costs, intensifying labor, and one-man management were not the means by which workers hoped to enact their revolutionary agenda. They were the problems. They smacked of a return of the old order. What spared the party from feeling the full force of workers' discontent was that the NEP, by its very nature, absolved the party from direct responsibility for many of the problems of factory and economic life. Impersonal market forces increasingly determined the course of the economy.

Hence management became the object of much worker discontent and the breach between the two widened. Armed with official policies demanding increased productivity, lower production costs, and greater efficiencies, managerial personnel often wantonly disregarded the Labor Code and workers' needs and grievances in pursuit of these goals. While the period's policies created hardship and discontent among workers, it was the way in which management implemented them that proved especially galling. But save for strikes and appeals to grievance and arbitration boards, until 1926 workers had no trustworthy forums in which to express their displeasure and "settle the score" with management. Until then, worker discontent with management simmered.

Discontent with the NEP's principles and policies was not confined to the proletariat. These issues also deeply divided the Communist Party itself. The Workers Opposition's defeat in 1921 proved a major setback for the party's radicals who hoped to give workers greater control over production and management and greater influence in the party. Although defeated, supporters of the Workers' Opposition continued to press their demands and their attempts to carry their message to workers. In July 1921, a Workers'-Peasants' Socialist Party formed in Moscow. Led by a former Gorodskoi *raion* Communist Party committee member, V. L. Paniushkin, this party espoused workers' control and criticized the non-worker character of the party and state. This party's size is difficult to determine but it apparently had supporters in Gorodskoi *raion*, not a working-class district but one of the centers of Workers' Opposition support.[62] Late 1921 also witnessed the appearance of another leftist group—the Workers' Truth. In a journal of the same name, the group—composed mostly of intellectuals—attacked the NEP as a return to capitalism with all its attendant class antagonisms. They were especially critical of the rift between the new industrialists (factory managers, specialists, the heads of trusts) and workers and between the party and workers.[63]

The most significant heir to the Workers' Opposition was the Workers' Group, composed primarily of workers or ex-workers and led by one active and two expelled party members. Like its predecessors, the Workers' Group condemend the authority of bourgeois managers and specialists and espoused workers' control of industry. It further condemned the suppression of worker and trade union democracy and the growing bureaucratism of society. To supporters of the Workers' Group, the NEP, with its elevation of productivity to new heights and its reducing of workers' power to new lows, stood for the "new exploitation of the proletariat."[64]

Precisely how much influence these groups (or Mensheviks and SRs) had among Moscow workers is difficult to ascertain. One western historian claims that many workers and rank and file party members listened to the arguments of these groups with "open or sneaking sympathy."[65] Although the documentation to support this assertion is sparse, the similarity between the various oppositions' platforms and workers' views suggest that such sympathy may have existed, assuming of course that workers knew of these groups. The role that these oppositions played in the labor strife of the early 1920s is equally as problematic. Some of their supporters apparently played an active role, but again lack of evidence prohibits a precise analysis. What is known is that members of the Workers' Group were debating whether or not to call for a general strike in the summer of 1923 when the OGPU arrested about twenty of its leaders, thereby effectively ending the group's organizational influence.[66]

The labor and political unrest of the early 1920s reverberated throughout the party and contributed to the appearance of the Left Opposition. In its "Platform of the 46," the opposition presented a scathing denunciation of the NEP's priorities, party economic policy (which they decried as "casual, unconsidered, and unsystematic") and the increasing stultification of party and worker democracy. After attacking what they perceived as the failure of currency policy, the "incorrect credit policy," pricing policy and the "inequalities in wage payments which provoke natural dissatisfaction among the workers," the opposition called for "extensive, well-considered, planned, and energetic measures" to avert a deepening of the economic crisis. It also demanded that some of the burden of recovery be taken off the workers' shoulders and placed on the peasantry. That the critique of economic policy found in the "Platform of the 46" attracted party stalwarts as diverse as Trotsky, Bubnov, and Kaganovich caused considerable concern within the leadership.[67]

Although the Moscow City Party Committee's leadership (and the country's trade union leadership) supported the party line and its three leaders—Zinoviev, Kamenev, and Stalin—throughout the 1923-1924 crisis, many party members supported the opposition. In some of the city's party cells, a majority did so. About one-third of the garrison's party cells supported the "Platform of the 46." So widespread was criticism of the party leadership among the troops that discussions among military cells were halted. Many party and nonparty youth received the opposition enthusiastically. The Komsomol's Central Committee and most Komsomol cells in the city endorsed the Platform as did many student cells. Workers' reaction to the opposition was mixed. In some large factories, the opposition leaders were received enthusiastically; in others, they found little open support. About 80 percent of the factory cells supported the party line.[68] The Left Opposition was defeated.

From the available evidence, it is extremely difficult to ascertain which oppositon supporters endorsed which of their criticisms. The platform itself consisted of two distinct aspects—an attack on economic policy and an attack on the internal party situation. Many of the forty-six signators, for example Kaganovich and V. Iakovlev, agreed with the assessment of the economic ills but disavowed the critiques of the party.[69] If this was the case among the forty-six, it was surely true among the population at large, many of whom found the intraparty situation of little interest.

Worker support for the party line in the struggle with the Left Opposition, in many cases, was probably less an endorsement of party policies than it was a rejection of Trotsky, the opposition's leader. Party agitators and spokesmen who addressed workers undoubtedly reminded them that it was Trotsky who advocated the total militarization of labor and the trade unions in 1920-1921. Although the "Platform of the 46" expressed considerable concern over, and at times outright rejection of, the prevailing labor policies, the critical presentation of the platform and Trotsky's earlier views on labor by party agitators may well have proved decisive in convincing most workers to endorse the party line. Because few factory workers belonged to the party at the time, many workers' knowledge of the platform was limited to the presentations of party agitators.

Taken as a whole, the support given to the various opposition groups and the labor unrest in 1921-1924 sent a clear signal to the party leaders—remedy the economic ills or face the consequences. But to the party's productivist leaders, only the systematic and thorough application of existing policies would ensure rapid recovery and the meeting of workers' economic demands. Although some minor policy modifications did occur in 1924, the principles remained unaltered. In fact in late 1924, the party leadership pressed its productivist policies with new vigor.

Wages and Productivity (Mid-1924–1928)

After several years of worker unrest and disappointments in attempts to tie wages to productivity, the stabilization of the currency in the second quarter of 1924 offered party leaders the opportunity to launch a new campaign to raise productvity. The first salvo came in August 1924 when the party's Central Committee plenum passed a resolution "On wage policy." After noting that past wage increases had outstripped productivity, the resolution announced that "the watchword for the day should become: increase the productivity of labor, expand production. . . ." Toward this end, the resolution urged the realization of several "concrete measures": a more rational organization of labor and production; the raising of output norms to achieve the maximal utilization of machinery and the workday; the establishment of a systematic process for the upward revision of output norms; the establishment of proper relations between workers and technical personnel; the encouraging of inventions; the further concentration of industry; the standardization of products of mass consumption so as to lower costs; and improved economy of materials, fuel and overhead costs. The Central Committee called on all party, state and trade union organs to ensure that wage increases reflect those of productivity.[70] The resolution marked the beginning of the rationalization campaign, the goals of which were identical to those noted in the resolution. That campaign and its 1926 successor, the regime of economy, set the tone of factory life for the late 1920s.[71]

The Sixth Trade Union Congress held that November endorsed the Central Committee's resolution and passed one of its own stating that: "The class-wide task of the proletariat and the immediate material interests of each worker demand the heightened (*zaostrennyi*) attention of the unions to the problems of raising the productvity of labor."[72] The same congress introduced a new seventeen-grade wage scale designed to impose order on the chaotic wage situation. Consistent with official concerns to increase productivity, the ratio between the highest and lowest paid workers widened by one-third. The new wage scale proved to be much more successful than its 1922 counterpart. Yet some problems remained. For example, bonuses and supplemental pay continued to be paid to hourly wage workers in order to equalize their earnings and those paid on a piece-rate basis.[73]

According to the Central Committee, the surest way to raise productivity was to intensify labor. This would reduce production costs per worker and enable enterprises to lay off superfluous workers. Two methods were employed. The first was to raise output norms. The second was to increase the number of machines which workers operated. There were two phases in the drive to intensify the workday: in 1924-1925 and in 1927-1928. Although increasing the number of machines which workers operated occurred in many industries, the shift was most dramatic in the textile industry where production costs were very high. Until late 1924, the vast majority of textile workers operated only one or two machines. In September of that year, several Moscow textile plants shifted weavers and spinners to three looms or spindles on an experimental basis. Two months later, VSNKh instructed the Textile Trust to adopt the practice for all workers. The change was dramatic. In January 1925, only 99 weavers nationwide operated three or four looms; about 200,000 spinners tended an equal number of spindles. By July, the respective figures were 33,628 and 3.3 million. Sixty percent of the city's weavers worked under the new system by the end of 1925. Productivity increased by 66 percent.[74]

Many workers reacted angrily to the change. Some staged strikes in protest; others presented their grievances to appeal boards. In 1924 alone, 70,000 textile workers were involved in labor disputes. They accounted for 40 percent of all city workers involved in disputes.[75] Irate workers complained that "the party had renounced the communist program (and) the principles of Karl Marx,"[76] and asserted that there was no difference between the old owners and the new workers' government.[77] Despite the groundswell of unrest, officials and management stood their ground. In fact, in 1927/28, the number of machines which workers operated increased yet again. And as earlier, the change came first and in its most pronounced form in the textile industry. By the end of 1928, virtually all of Moscow's textile workers operated three or four machines. Then, as in 1925, worker response was quick and negative. Wildcat strikes occurred and the number of complaints registered with assessment and conflict commissions rose steeply.[78]

Not all workers reacted hostilely to the change. Worker-communists, Komsomol members, and young workers were among the first to volunteer to tend more machines or be shifted to higher piece-rates.[79] While worker-communists may have volunteered in response to party discipline, young workers did so willingly and enthusiastically. Many youths, whose ranks diminished steadily as a proportion of the workforce, were graduates of TsIT courses and technical schools, where they had learned more efficient and productive work methods. For young workers, the transition to more intensive forms of labor offered new opportunities. They were young and adaptive enough to learn new methods or work more machines. By working harder and more efficiently, they could improve their wages, status and job security. In this environment, their training and lack of traditional production skills proved to be an advantage. Successful performance of their jobs also brought them to the attention of foremen and party activists whose recommendation might qualify them for promotion or enable them to enter a training program or technical school and thereby increase their skills and social mobility. In short, the transition offered them opportunities for advancement.

Willingness to adopt more intensive forms of labor was not the only example of young workers' different attitude toward work and productivity. They also actively participated in a series of production campaigns, the most notable being socialist competition, production exchanges and invention exchanges. The Komsomol spearheaded these campaigns, which began in the late 1920s and reached their peak of popularity during the First Five-Year Plan. The purpose of socialist competitions was to raise labor productivity in a shop or factory. To accomplish this, Komsomol activists organized competitions on an intrafactory or, more commonly, interfactory basis to achieve a desired goal such as reducing absenteeism, breakage or waste or increasing output.[80] The purpose of production and invention exchanges was to share worker inventions and production "secrets" and practices which had raised productivity. These exchanges usually occured between two or more factories in the same industry.[81]

The most notable and controversial of Komsomol and youth production activities was the organization and extension of shock work (*udarnichestvo*). Despite union officials' pleas that raising productivity was to be accomplished by "systematic, practical work" and not by shock (*udarnyi*) campaigns,[82] young workers displayed an eagerness to organize and participate in such campaigns. Their willingness reflects their enthusiasm over the perceived advantages—personal or ideological—of such activities and their support for the Komsomol.[83] Although not practiced on a wide scale until 1929, shock work first appeared in Moscow in late 1926 and grew steadily during the next two years.[84]

The stated goals of shock work did not differ significantly from those of the contemporary productivity campaigns. They included the development of more intensive work methods, the rationalization of production, the raising of skill levels, the maximum utilization of inventions, and the struggle against old work habits.[85] What distinguished them was the means utilized to achieve these goals. Whereas managerial and technical personnel imposed new work routines, output norms and other changes to achieve the productivity campaign's goals, young workers who participated in shock work set their own personal goals. In some cases, they organized production or shock brigades (*udarnaia brigada*) in a shop and competed to achieve new productivity goals. At other times, they worked alone and engaged in production competitions with fellow workers in their or other shops. Although it is difficult to ascertain the number of Muscovite shock workers prior to 1929, their ranks swelled annually. The initiators of and most active participants in shock work were urban workers in their twenties. Many were party and Komsomol members and politically active. Unskilled, new workers with ties to the land and older, skilled workers were least likely to participate in shock work.[86]

Older workers viewed such "norm-busting" with resentment, even fear. They resented being forced to work harder. Less energetic and nimble and more reluctant to abandon old work habits than were young workers, for them the speed-up translated not into new opportunities, but into exhaustion with insufficient reward. Their young co-workers enthusiasm for raising productivity and intensifying labor threatened to alter the traditional pace of work and further reduced any control over production that they had. The rationalization of production that accompanied the intensification also angered older workers. That process often took the form of a sharper division of labor that reduced the value of some skills. Together with increasing mechanization, the trend in industry was toward the elimination of some traditional skills. Consequently, the campaign to rationalize and intensify labor threatened the status of many older, skilled workers whose shared experiences, long-standing relationships, and threatened skills fostered a generational collective solidarity.

Their hostility to these changes is understandable. So too is their resentment of younger workers and others who enthusiastically embraced the change. As young workers (individually or collectively) strove to intensify labor, "conflicts and confrontations" between the generations mounted.[87] Many new workers also resisted the drive to rationalize and intensify production. But their reasons differed from those of older, skilled workers. What new workers resented was being forced to work harder and adopt a labor discipline that was alien to many of them. In this way, policies designed to raise productivity created divisions and raised tensions between workers.

Although they stimulated divison and labor discontent, the policies designed to raise productivity by intensifying labor succeeded. Worker productivity rose markedly in 1925; in 1926, it exceeded the prewar level. In its report to the 1928 Trade Union Congress VTsSPS credited the rehabilitation of factories and machinery and the rationalization and intensification of production with raising labor productivity during the previous two years.[88] In the textile industry, this was undoubtedly the case. Thanks to labor intensification, the rate of wage growth slowed relative to that of productivity. Increases in productivity in 1926/27 exceeded those of wages for the first time since the revolution; comparable increases occurred during the following year.[89] The sharp rise in textile workers wages in 1925-1928 (see appendix 7) resulted not from an official desire to equalize wages, but from higher productivity. The same was true in the metal industry. From 1925 on, the policy enunciated in 1924 bore fruit.

A steady rise in both nominal and real wages accompanied the rise in worker productivity. The gains were especially marked from 1926 to 1928. But, despite the improvement, wages continued to provoke considerable concern among workers. From 1924 on, disputes over wage issues accounted for the vast majority of the nation's strikes—86 percent of those in 1926 and 77 percent of those in 1927.[90] The majority of wage-related strikes were over established output norms—hardly a surprising fact in the midst of the rationalization campaigns. Data on the number of strikes and strikers in Moscow is too fragmentary to allow for any meaningful analysis. But national-level data on strikes suggests that, although the number of strikes rose from 1925 to 1928, the number of strikers and duration of strikes declined. The reduction in the numbers of strikers in state industry was the most dramatic.[91] Most strikes were apparently wildcat strikes organized without the union's or factory committee's knowledge or approval. In 1928, Tomskii, the trade union chief, blamed these strikes on the fact that "trade unions have paid inadequate attention to the needs of the masses, to their being detached from the masses, and showing contempt for the small matters of workers' lives."[92] Although it had narrowed, the breach between workers and unions remained.

Factory Conditions and Labor Protection (Mid-1924-1928)

Accompanying rising wages and productivity from mid-1924 was a steady improvement in factory and workshop conditions. In general, by

239

1926 the conditions in most factories had been restored to their pre-revolutionary condition—a vivid reminder that the inheritance from the old order imposed severe constraints. The shortage of capital throughout the decade meant that restoring, rather than improving, work conditions was the norm. The construction of new workshops and factories did occur,[93] but until the First Five-Year Plan, the pace of new construction was slow. Consequently, as late as 1928, the majority of the city's industrial enterprises were overcrowded, the lighting and ventilation systems remained inadequate, and the productive machinery was outdated and in poor condition.[94] In new shops and factories or in renovated plants, the conditions of work improved markedly—new machinery, better lighting, and modern ventilation systems were installed as were cafeterias and washrooms.[95]

The improvement in factory conditions was by no means universal, nor was it achieved without a struggle. Private owners once again appear to have been the most reluctant to improve work conditions either because they were short of capital or nervous about the political climate and therefore hesitant to invest in any but the most essential repairs. Complaints about poor working conditions and violations of the Labor Code frequently appeared in the press.[96] While it is difficult to gauge the extent to which conditions in private enterprises improved or deteriorated, the prominent press coverage given private employers' illegal behavior, together with the mounting antinepmen campaign, served to reinforce many workers' negative attitudes toward these entrepreneurs. In an effort both to extend their influence and to improve conditions there, unions devoted increasing attention in the late 1920s to organizing workers in private factories. A 1926 VTsSPS directive urged union activists in private enterprises to ensure that owners provided decent working conditions and adhered to labor laws and to establish and increase the power of factory committees there.[97]

While unsatisfactory conditions in private enterprises received prominent press coverage, unsafe conditons continued to exist in state enterprises as well. The extent to which this was the case is underscored by the fact that more than one-third of all industrial accidents in 1928 resulted from bad working conditions such as poor lighting, inadequate ventilation, improper utilization of the workplace, and defective machinery and instruments. Another 25 percent were due to "inattention to issues of technical safety" (either by workers or management) or a lack of protective equipment or clothing.[98]

The primary rationale used by state factory directors to explain their hesitancy to improve factory conditions was financial. Beginning with the 1924 rationalization campaign, factory directors were under increasing pressure to reduce costs and accumulate capital. Despite the arguments of union and state officials that better working conditions and improved labor protection resulted in greater productivity, fewer accidents and less absenteeism,[99] managers found it easier and cheaper to delay improvements in the factory's physical plants. The demands of the rationalization campaign provided them with a financial excuse for deferring repairs. Such was the case at a Moscow chemical plant where the labor inspector demanded that a defective machine be repaired. Management refused. As a result, a worker was killed.[100] Workers and union activists frequently complained at factory committee and production meetings that factory directors were cutting costs at the expense of workers' safety and health.[101] Still, the problems endured.

The conditions of work and machinery varied from industry to industry. In the city's textile industry, conditions continued to be considerably worse than in others. Not only were the physical plants of most textile factories old and in need of basic repairs, but half or more of the machinery was outdated and prone to breakdown.[102] For example, between 1924/25 and 1925/26, the proportion of idle work-time industrywide soared. In the former year, the average worker was idle for one-half day per work year; in the latter day, the figure was 4.3 days. Forty percent of this time was devoted to repairing machines; another 23 percent to cleaning machines, a task normally conducted after the workday. The irony is that as the pace of production increased so too did the frequency of breakdowns. For workers on piece-rates, breakdowns meant a loss of income and hence deepened their resentment of managers who were quick to intensify labor but slow to repair the machinery necessary to productivity. A particularly acute problem in this industry was ventilation. Throughout the late 1920s, union officials and workers alike complained that the ventilation systems in many plants were inadequate, a threat to workers' health, and a detriment to increased productivity.[103] Considering the problems that they faced daily, the rising productivity of textile workers was all the more remarkable.

Although work conditions in some industries and factories remained substandard and dangerous, the overall improvement translated into a decline in the proportion of strikes and labor disputes over conditions.[104] One major reason for the improvement was the changed attitude of unions and the Commissariat of Labor towards work conditions and labor protection. Whereas before 1924, both gave top priority to raising productivty, after mid-1924 they continually pressed management to improve conditions and pay greater attention to worker safety. They argued that this was a *quid pro quo* to greater productivity. V. V. Shmidt succinctly stated the changed attitude in 1926: "For us labor and union officials—W. C. the question of labor protection is now the fundamental issue."[105]

Despite the support that some union and state officials gave to workers' struggles to ameliorate the decrepit and substandard inheritance of the old regime, other responsible officials were less obliging. Officials in the Commissariat of Labor complained that many commissariats and trusts devoted too little attention to factory conditions and labor protection. In some cases, these agencies condoned or turned a blind eye to the failure or refusal of factory administrators to obey the appropriate laws or to fulfill the conditions of collective agreements because they perceived the accumulation of capital as the over-riding need.[106] Among those criticized for their negligence were the city's labor inspectors. According to Rabkrin, the Moscow City Labor Protection Office suffered from serious deficiencies. Rabkrin investigators charged that labor inspectors had not been systematic in their duties nor had the office fully utilized its labor inspectors. Many inspectors put insufficient pressure on economic agencies and factories to spend the funds designated by collective agreements for improving conditions and labor protection. Likewise, the struggle against overtime work had been "insufficiently energetic"; there were even cases where inspectors failed to report such work.[107]

Despite such enduring problems, citywide there was a general improvement in labor protection in the late 1920s. Laws regarding working hours and rest periods were obeyed with increasing frequency, and there was a systematic lowering of overtime work and the proportion of workers performing such work. The amount of money devoted to improving conditions, sanitation, and safety rose steadily.[108] As frustrating as the pace of improvements was, overall it was steady.

The amelioration of work and safety conditions should not be interpreted to mean that industrial accidents declined in numbers. Such was not the case. The industrial accident rate rose from 1925; despite some oscillations, the fatality rate declined. Nationally, that rate jumped by 9 percent between 1926 and 1928. The accident rate in Moscow appears to have risen at a comparable rate.[109] Throughout the decade, the proportion of accidents due to workers remained significant. In 1928, one-fifth of all industrial accidents were the fault of workers; worker

242

ignorance of safety measures and managerial reluctance to institute them also accounted for many accidents.[110] The problem was particularly acute among new workers fresh from the villages. According to one contemporary observor, the influx of unskilled, undisciplined and poorly trained new workers accounted for the increased number of industrial accidents. The metal, woodworking and construction industries, which had the highest proportion of new and seasonal workers, also had the highest accident rates.[111]

For new workers in 1928 as in 1923, unfamilarity with machinery, bad work habits, and poor labor discipline combined to produce industrial accidents. But new workers were not the only victims of their mistakes. They also put their co-workers in danger and fueled tensions between them and disciplined and experienced workers. Urban workers' resentment of the consequences of new workers' behavior coupled with the growing competition for jobs and new workers "infiltration of production" served to divide the city's workers.[112] But paralleling that division was a common mounting worker antipathy toward management. Management's refusal or reluctance to repair dangerous conditions or institute safety precautions and its relentless insistence that workers be more productive without providing the proper machinery and equipment with which to do so symbolized to workers management's disdain for them. Divided though they often were, when the opportunity availed itself, workers would unite in a wholesale assault on management.

The Seven-Hour Workday

Throughout the NEP, numerous problems plagued the Soviet economy— relatively low rates of production and productivity, underutilization of industrial equipment, a shortage of consumer goods, and unemployment among others. In an effort to overcome these problems, just prior to the tenth anniversary of the Bolshevik revolution the government announced its intention to introduce the seven-hour workday. A joint commission composed of representatives from the Commissariat of Labor, VTsSPS, and VSNKh prepared for the transition to the shorter workday.[113] The transition first occurred on an experimental basis in the textile industry, the goods of which were in short supply and high demand. Several of the plants chosen for experiment were in Moscow.

Many union, labor, and party officials viewed the shorter workday as the culmination of Soviet labor policy. Articles written before the change commenced abounded with enthusiastic prognoses. Although the

243

workday would be shorter, workers' wages were not to be reduced. Hence Soviet policies would differ from capitalist policies that sought to lower the standard of living of workers. The shorter day would allow workers more time for culture, education, leisure, and physical exercise. The new policy would also speed the realization of the rationalization campaign's goals by allowing for the introduction of the three-shift system (to begin at 4:00 a.m. and end at 1:00 a.m.) and thereby provide for a better utilization of machinery and the workday, an expansion of production, and a reduction of costs. It would also create new jobs, and thereby slow or even reverse mounting unemployment. To ensure the rationalization of production, greater productivity and lower costs, labor was to be further intensified by increasing the number of machines that workers operated. In this way, they hoped that daily worker output would not decline. Officials also envisioned a reduction in the amount of damaged materials and improve the quality of goods since the number of substandard products was greatest in the final hour of work.[114]

Despite this optimism, the joint commission realized that significant problems had to be addressed. Among these were the issues of wages and production norms, labor protection, night work for women, and the quality of the soon-to-be hired workers. But soon after the implementation of the new policy in the twenty-four "trial" factories in January–February 1928, the problems' dimensions became apparent.

One of the most significant problems proved to be the workforce itself. Because of a shortage of skilled and experienced workers, many of those hired (in some factories, as many as half) were new workers fresh from the villages. Like their counterparts who joined the working class throughout the decade, these raw peasant recruits lacked labor discipline, had high rates of absenteeism and tardiness, and drank on the job. A considerable proportion of those hired were the children of workers, some of whom had technical training. Many—if not most—of the newest workers were women.

The influx of so many unskilled and inexperienced workers (upward of 20,000 workers joined the workforce during the experiment's first months) had an adverse impact on productivity. During the first six months of the seven-hour day, the "trial" factories' productivity actually declined and the proportion of substandard products rose. New workers were not the only reason for this situation. The adjustment to more intensive forms of labor was difficult for many older, skilled workers who were angered by the change. As in earlier years, young workers "show(ed) themselves as the vanguard in relation to the transition to the intensification of work." Many of the younger workers apparently volunteered to operate four machines.[115]

The structure of the new shifts also angered some workers. While some worked a full seven-hour shift, others had to work two three-and-a-half hour shifts with seven hours off in between. This schedule was designed to provide workers with free time during the day so that they could rest, attend classes, or pursue leisure activities. But most workers used the time to do chores and often returned to the second shift tired. The Textile Workers Union protested the split shift and the Commissariat of Labor ruled in the union's favor. Nonetheless the practice continued.[116] The expansion of night-work created further problems. The number of child-care centers did not expand commensurate with the workforce, a shortage that complicated and disrupted many families lives. Likewise, the growing demand for housing meant that many workers either had to find accommodations in already overcrowded factory barracks or had to commute long distances. In either case, they often got insufficient sleep, a condition that further spurred the accident rate and lowered productivity.[117]

The inadequate preparation devoted to technical questions meant that most of the factories were not prepared to operate around-the-clock. The lighting was often inadequate and contributed to high accident rates on the late shift.[118] Much of the outdated machinery was incapable of being worked continuously and frequently broke down. Problems with ventilation became especially acute. Because of inadequate ventilation systems, temperatures rose constantly over the course of the day reaching as high as ninety-seven degrees Fahrenheit in one plant, and the air became increasingly dense with dust and fiber.

Taken together, these problems temporarily reversed what officials deemed the proper relationship between wages and productivity. Not until 1926/27 had increases in textile workers' productivity exceeded those of wages. The seven-hour day was supposed to widen that gap even more. But during the experiment's first six months, disruptions in production resulted in wages rising at a faster rate. Only in late 1928 was the proper relationship restored. Buoyed by this, policymakers moved to introduce the new workday in other industries. Again lack of proper preparation and the influx of new workers caused disruptions and problems comparable to those in the textile industry.[119] Throughout the post-1929 years, the three-shift system gradually expanded. The seven-hour day remained on the books until 1940, but in practice the experiment died a quiet death during the First Five-Year Plan. Its abandonment apparently reflected the leadership's disappointment with its unsatisfactory economic results.

The optimism that preceded the seven-hour day proved premature. The hasty transition meant that insufficient preparatory work was devoted to personnel training and organizational and technical issues. Had it been, the problems probably would have been foreseen and addressed. Instead, the rush to production spelled confusion for one of the more progressive proposals of its time. What was the reason for such haste, especially in light of the fact that virtually no mention of the reform appeared before the October 1927 announcement? Solomon Schwarz has stated that "today there can be no doubt that the purpose was to play off the new reform against the leftist opposition within the CPSU."[120] If he is referring to the Left Opposition that faced imminent expulsion from the party, this explanation seems incomplete. Undoubtedly other factors played a role, such as the leadership's heightened optimism after two years of steady postrecovery growth, the promise of increased production of lower cost textile goods that could be traded with the peasants at a time when they were withholding their produce from the marketplace, and the possibility of realizing both the productivists' desire for greater productivity and production and the radicals' desire to lessen the workers' burden and ease the unemployment crisis.

Although halting in the early 1920s, the productivists' relentless campaign yielded positive results. Recovery was achieved by 1926 and, during the next two years, industrial production and productivity continued to increase. The speed with which the economy overcame destruction and chaos emboldened delegates to the Fourteenth Party Congress in 1925 to embark on preparations for a planned economy and socialist industrialization. Two years later, the next congress reaffirmed that policy. The seven-hour day symbolized the party's optimism.

But the policies that induced recovery and growth also strained the fabric of factory life. While some workers criticized the state and its policies, virtually all of them resented management's application of those policies and its disregard for workers' complaints, safety, and well-being. The rift between the two continually deepened. While workers occasionally resorted to the strike and increasingly took their grievances to arbitration boards and courts, such behavior was designed to address only specific complaints. Yet worker discontent with mananagement was much broader and deeper than any single complaint or set of complaints. Not until the creation of factory production meetings did workers have a forum in which to vent their antipathy for management. As we shall see, in the late 1920s these meetings became battlegrounds on which workers attacked management. In the process, they threatened to destroy the fabric of factory life and pressed once again for the fulfillment of their revolutionary agenda.

Before that assault could begin, workers had to overcome the divisions between them which productivist policies had created. Urban workers' resentment of new workers' "infiltration of production" at their co-workers' and family members' expense, of their careless and undisciplined behavior, of their inundation of Moscow, and of the strains that it produced on the quality of life, these were real and deep divisions. So too were those between enthusiastic young workers and their elders, and between patriarchal males and their female co-workers. Resentment, jealousy, and petty disputes riddled Moscow's industrial proletariat. Deep though these divisions were, the prospect of revenging management and asserting a measure of control over production proved strong enough to overcome them. But workers did not accomplish this by themselves. The Communist Party led the way.

Notes

1. For the 1922 Labor Code, see *SU*, 1922, 70, 903.

2. For a discussion, see Alexander Ehrlich, *The Soviet Industrialization Debate, 1924-1928* (Cambridge, Mass., 1960)

3. *SU*, 1921, 27, 154; *SU*, 1921, 28, 156. In July 1921, Sovnarkom issued a decree on collective payment of wages in money and kind for employees. First enacted in Moscow and Petrograd, the decree instructed the appropriate commissariats to ensure that adequate supplies of money and products be allotted. To receive the supplies, institutions had to reduce their personnel by 50 percent, reduce absenteeism and increase productivity. *Ibid.,* 1921, 55, 336.

4. *Ibid.,* 1921, 67, 513.

5. For a discussion of the amendment, see Dewar, 88.

6. *Vestnik metallopromyshlennosti,* 7-9 (1924), 158-159; *Izvestiia tekstil'noi promyshlennosti i torgovli,* 2 (January 15, 1926), 11; *Ekonomicheskaia zhizn',* August 9, 1927; A. Bakhutov, "Voprosy zarabotnoi platy i proizvoditel'nost' truda," *Voprosy truda,* 12 (1924), 27-33; N. K. Akinshina, "Statistika proizvoditel'nosti truda v promyshlennosti SSSR v pervye gody sovetskoi vlasti (1918-1925gg.)," *Ocherki po istorii statistiki SSSR* 2 vols. (Moscow, 1957), II, 268-296.

7. *Istoriia Moskvy,* VI, 1, 304. This source claims that the average wages of metalworkers rose by 120 percent, while their productivity rose by 86 percent. Deutscher, *Soviet Trade Unions,* 100, claims that nationally wages

rose by 90 percent and productivity by only 23 percent. See also: Strumilin, *Zarabotnaia plata,* 1-88; Zagorsky, 115.

8. See the discussion in Bergson, 137-193 passim.

9. In April 1921, Sovnarkom gave VTsSPS the exclusive right to handle all questions related to wage scales. *SU,* 1921, 37, 138. In late 1922, that power was given to the Commissariat of Labor. *SU,* 1922, 66, 871; 1922, 79, 999.

10. *Rabochaia Moskva,* December 27, 1922. According to L. E. Mints, *Rynok truda v Rossii (za 1922g i I polovina 1923g)* (Moscow, 1923), 34, the average wages of the city's metalworkers equaled those of food processing workers in 1922 and were slightly higher in 1923. The same pattern existed in Leningrad. A comparison of the monthly wages of metalworkers by profession in 1908, 1923, and 1924 provides further evidence of the unequal rates at which wages were raised. *Trud v Moskovskoi gubernii,* 188.

11. As quoted in Carr, *Interregnum,* 72.

12. Zagorsky, 132-133. The effect of VTsSPS's action is conveyed by the following table:

AVERAGE WAGES OF WORKERS IN SELECTED MOSCOW INDUSTRIES, 1913, 1924, AND 1925 (in prewar goods rubles)

Industry	1913	1st 1/2 1924	1st 1/2 1925
Metals	34.35	28.99	38.08
Textiles	22.05	19.93	23.87
Chemicals	23.50	24.30	33.00
Foods	20.80	26.14	33.00
Leather	26.08	32.63	42.14
Printing	34.08	34.93	38.08

Source: *Trud v Moskovskoi Gubernii,* 147.

13. The proportion paid on this basis varied considerably from industry to industry, the range running from two-thirds of the metalworkers to less than one-quarter of the printers in 1924. Petrochenko and Kuznetsova, 33-34. See also Carr, *Socialism),* I, 402-403, 416-447.

14. Dewar, 91, 133-135; Sorenson, 215.

15. Petrochenko and Kuznetsova, 75-76.

16. *Ibid.,* 70; *Trud,* November 21, 1923.

17. Aleshchenko, *Moskovskii sovet,* 285, states that output norms in city industries were raised as follows: food processing - 7 to 35 percent; leather - 20 percent; textiles - 10 to 20 percent; metal - 9 percent. *"Dinamo,"* II, 9. See also: G. Veinberg, "Promyshlennost', zaplata i proizvoditel'nost' truda v leningradtsev," *Vestnik truda,* 2 (1925), 87-88; Petrochenko and Kuznetsova, 68.

18. *"Dinamo,"* II, 66; A. Poselianina, "Vosstanovlenie zavoda 'Serp i molot'," *Bor'ba klassov,* 7-8 (1934), 189.

19. *Moskovskii proletarii,* September 28, 1924, 13.

20. *Vestnik metallopromyshlennosti,* 10-12 (1922), 11. See also: N. Aristov, "K voprosu o krizise v kvalifitsirovannoi rabochei sile v SSSR," *Voprosy truda,* 7-8 (1925), 41-48; *Izvestiia tekstil'noi promyshlennosti i torgovli,* 36-37 (October 15, 1925), 1.

21. *Trud*, September 27, 1929. For discussions of the hiring of new workers and its consequences in specific factories, see: *"Dinamo,"*) *II, 66; Bogdanovskii, 177-178; Poselianina, 193.*

22. *Rabochaia Moskva*, May 12, 1923.

23. *Trud*, August 17, 1928; G. Polliak, "Nevykhody na rabotu po dniam nedeli," *Statisticheskoe obozrenie*, 4 (1927), 48-57; I. Tolstopiatov, "Truddistsiplina i proguly," *Voprosy truda*, 1 (1929), 21-25; I. G. Eremin, "Trudovaia distsiplina v tekstil'noi promyshlennosti," *Izvestiia tekstil'noi promyshlennosti i torgovli), 3 (1929), 3-5; Moskovskii proletarii), July 28, 1926, 11-12; March 14, 1928, 2.

24. *Statistika truda v promyshlennykh zavedeniiakh* (Moscow, 1923), tab. III, 25; *Moskovskii sovet, 1917-1927, 255.* For national figures by union, see *Statisticheskii ezhegodnik, 1921* (Moscow, 1922), chast' III, tab. III, 214-217.

25. *Vestnik metallopromyshlennosti*, 10-12 (1922), chast' II, 24. The second set of figures in the text was for June and the higher rates of absenteeism were probably the result of worker-peasants extending their vacations in the village.

26. *Moskovskii sovet, 1917-1927, 255.* See also: M. Katel, "Rabochee vremia promyshlennykh rabochikh SSSR," *Vestnik truda*, 5 (1925), 102-115; *Moskva i Moskovskaia guberniia*, tab. 110, 158-159. For metal industry figures for 1922-1923, see *Vestnik metallopromyshlennosti*, 4-8 (1923), 65.

27. Katel, 102-115; *Vestnik metallopromyshlennosti*, 10-12 (1922), chast' II, 24; *Moskovskii proletarii*, June 1, 1924. At the Napilnik factory, the workers' desire to return to the village was so great that in order to have a factory meeting during the summer months, the factory gates had to be locked. *Ibid.*

28. *Izvestiia tekstil'noi promyshlennosti i torgovli*, June 7, 1921, 11.

29. At production meetings, urban workers, who dominated the forums, frequently complained about the problems caused by labor indiscipline. *Pervyi shagi*, 302-304, 335-341; *Dokumenty trudovoi slavy*, dok. 27, 50-51.

30. *Moskovskii proletarii*, September 28, 1924, 13.

31. On the raising of output quotas after a time-motion study, see *"Dinamo,"* II, 9. On NOT activities, see: Bailes, "Alexei Gastev"; Sochor; Traub; Lieberstein; Petrochenko and Kuznetsova, 3-44; and the documents in *Nauchnaia organizatsiia truda, proizvodstva i upravleniia: sbornik dokumentov i materialov, 1918-1930gg.* (Moscow, 1969) (Hereafter abbreviated as *NOT*).

32. Sochor has a good discussion of the debate and participants.

33. E. B. Genkina, "Voznikovenie proizvodstvennykh soveshchanii v gody vosstanovitel'nogo period (1921-1925)," *Istoriia SSSR*, 3 (1958), 63-89.

34. *NOT*, 213-221.

35. *Ibid.*, 221; Genkina, "Voznikovenie proizvodstvennykh soveshchanii," 68-71.

36. For reports of factory inspectors, see *Ekonomicheskaia zhizn'*, September 20, 1920. For descriptions of factory conditions and the workforce in pre-revolutionary times, see Von Laue, "Russian Labor," 51-65; "Russian Peasants," 61-80.

37. For examples, see *Rabochaia Moskva*, February 21, February 22, June 21, August 22, 1922; May 4, 1923.

38. Matiugin, *Moskva*, 76-77. At the AMO plant in late 1923, inadequate machinery and a shortage of tools hindered production. Shikheev, 63.

39. Bakhutov, "Voprosy zarabotnoi platy," 27-33.

40. *Ekonomicheskaia zhizn'*, September 10, 1922. The Inspectorate of Labor Protection, which conducted the investigation, was responsible to the Moscow *Guberniia* Trade Union Council.

41. B. Markus, "Voprosy okhrany truda v tekstil'noi promyshlennosti (k nachalu 1927/28 goda)," *Voprosy truda*, 2 (1928), 23-40; M. Nefedov, "Okhrana truda moskovskikh rabochikh v 1924-1925g.," *Voprosy truda*, 2 (1926), 136-143; I. Zhavoronkov, "Polozhenie rabochikh v l'nianoi promyshlennosti," *Izvestiia tekstil'noi promyshlennosti i torgovli*, 15-16 (May 12, 1925).

42. *Rabochaia Moskva*, February 21, 1922.

43. *Moskovskii proletarii*, July 27, 1924. See also: *Rabochaia Moskva*, February 21, October 6, October 31, November 1, 1922; Trifonov, *Ocherki*, 121; Trifonov, *Klassy*, 91-92.

44. For examples, see *Rabochaia Moskva*, June 21, October 25, 1922.

45. For penalties for violations of labor protection laws, see *SU*, 1922, 30, 369; 31, 373.

46. Data on the number and composition of labor inspectors can be found in *Moskovksii sovet, 1917-1927*, 265; V. Shmidt, "Perspektivy blizhnaisnei raboty N.K.T.," *Vestnik truda*, 5-6 (1924), 40-48.

47. Akache, "Registratsiia neschastnykh sluchaev," *Voprosy truda*, 8-9 (1926), 25-27.

48. *Moskovskii proletarii*, May 14, 1926, 6-7, gives the figure as 9,000; *Moskovskii sovet 1917-1927*, 267 gives a figure of 9,884.

49. *Izvestiia tekstil'noi promyshlennosti i torgovli*, 6 (February 28, 1925), 24; Nefedov, "Okhrana truda," 136-143. An article in *Moskovskii proletarii*, May 14, 1926, 6-7, states that in 1922/23 55 percent of the industrial accidents were the fault of workers. In an effort to stem the rise in industrial accidents, the Moscow *Guberniia* Council of Trade Unions established "safety circles" in which workers were encouraged to identify unsafe conditions and to pass safety techniques on to inexperienced workers.

50. Edwin B. Morrell, "Communist Unionism: Organized Labor and the Soviet State" (unpublished Ph.D. dissertation, Harvard University, 1965), 40-43, cites data from an unpublished Soviet candidate's dissertation to support this contention.

51. Nefedov, "Okhrana truda," 136-143.

52. For examples, see: *Moskovskii proletarii*, October 12, December 7, 1924; February 15, 1925; A. Kats, "Povyshenie proizvoditel'nost' i okhrana truda," *Vestnik truda*, 11-12 (1924), 89-95. An interesting barometer of the shift toward greater concern with labor protection is the number and proportion of articles in *Voprosy truda* concerned with the issue. See "Nash otchet chitateliam," *Voprosy truda*, 1 (1926), 4-7; *ibid.*, 1 (1927), 3-9.

53. See the report on the Sixth All-Russian Congress of Textile Workers in *Izvestiia tekstil'noi promyshlennosti i torgovli*, December 16, 1924, 14-15.

54. *Trud v Moskovskoi gubernii*, 420-423. In one-third of the cases, the demands of strikers were completely satisfied; an equal proportion went unsatisfied. Stopani, "Eshche," 38-42; Edvard, 60-67; Stopani, "Promyshlennye konflikty," 29-31; *Rabochaia Moskva*, May 19, 1922; *Moskovskii sovet, 1917-1927*, 256-257. According to VTsSPS, a majority of strikes occured against the union's will and union organs were estranged from their members and demands. *Professional'nye soiuzy SSSR, 1922-1924, 230.* The following table lists national strike figures.

NUMBER OF STRIKES AND STRIKERS NATIONWIDE, 1922-1927

Year	Number of strikes		Number of participants	
	State	Private	State	Private
1922	446	99	192,000	—–
1923	381	135	165,000	—–
1924	151	111	42,800	6,056
1925	99	94	34,000	3,349
1926	200	120	32,000	8,894
1927	396		20,000	

Source: Mary McAuley, *Labour Disputes in Soviet Russia, 1957-1965* (Oxford, 1969), 15; *Professional'nye soiuzy, 1922-1924*, 229.

55. *Izvestiia TsK*, August-September 1923, 11-12, as quoted in Daniels, 209-210. See also Issac Deutscher, *The Prophet Unarmed, Trotsky: 1921-1929* (New York, 1959), 106-107.

56. *Trud v Moskovskoi gubernii*, 423-425. See also: Stopani, "Eshche," 38-42; Edvard, "Trudovye konflikty," 60-67; Stopani, "Promyshlennye konflikty," 29-31. For a discussion of these arbitration bodies and their activities, see: *Trud v Moskovskoi gubernii*, 420-434; McAuley, 9-35. According to VTsSPS, assessment and conflict commissions were "one of the most important and accessible organs to the working masses in the enterprises." *Professional'nye soiuzy, 1922-1924, 224.*

57. *Trud v Moskovskoi Gubernii*, 427. Nationally, 56 percent of all labor disputes, representing 80 percent of the participants, were over changes in collective agreements. *Professional'nye soiuzy, 1922-1924, 226.*

58. *Ibid.*, 423. In 1923, there were 249 such disputes involving 32,737 participants; the next year the figures were 896 and 62,716 respectively. Nationally, 60 percent of the strikes, representing 72 percent of the strikers, were over wages. *Professional'nye soiuzy, 1922-1924, 230.*

59. A. Poselianina, "Leninskii prizyv (Moskovskii zavod 'Serp i molot')," *Bor'ba klassov*, 1 (1934), 142-145.

60. *Trud v Moskovskoi gubernii*, 420-423.

61. This issue will be discussed in chapter 7.

62. *Moskovskie bol'sheviki v bor'be s pravym i "levym" opportunizmom 1921-1929gg.* (Moscow, 1969), 35-37.

63. For a discussion, see: Carr, *Interregnum*, 79; Dobb, 334; Sorenson, 177.

64. The Workers' Group had some 200 members in Moscow. The leaders of this group were Miasnikov (who was expelled from the party in 1922 for

continued factional activity), Kuznetsov (who was expelled at the Eleventh Party Congress as one of the leaders of the Workers' Opposition splinter group which published the "Declaration of the 22"), and Moiseev (a prominent leftist). Vl. Sorin, *Rabochaia gruppa ("Miasnikovshchina")* (Moscow, 1924).

65. Deutscher, *Prophet Unarmed*, 108.

66. Sorin, 97-112.

67. The "Platform of the 46" can be found in Leon Trotsky, *The Challenge of the Left Opposition, 1923-1925* (New York, 1975), 397-403.

68. Carr, *Interregnum*, 327; Rigby, 118-130; Deutscher, *Prophet Unarmed*, 116-117, 125, 132, 302; Stephen F. Cohen, *Bukharin and the Bolshevik Revolution: A Political Biography, 1888-1938* (New York, 1973), 234. According to *Moskovski bol'sheviki*, 70, there was considerable support for the Left Opposition in Krasnopresnenskii, Khamovnicheskii, Baumanskii and Zamoskvoretskii districts. While these districts had a large number of educational institutions and military garrisons, the first three also had a considerable number of factories.

69. See the qualifiers amended by the signators, Trotsky, *Challenge*, 402-403.

70. *Direktivy KPSS i sovetskogo pravitel'stva*, I, 488-491.

71. See also the discussion in chapter 7.

72. Bakhutov, "Voprosy zarabotnoi platy," 27-33; Petrochenko and Kuznetsova, 37; "VI Vsesoiuznyi s"ezd professional'nykh soiuzov: rezoliutsii," *Vestnik truda*, 11-12 (1924), 235-255; in particular, see "Po tarifno-ekonomicheskii rabote soiuzov," 238-241.

73. Dewar, 133-135; Sorenson, 215.

74. *Ekonomicheskaia zhizn'*, July 19, 1925, November 17, 1927; *Izvestiia tekstil'noi promyshlennosti i torgovli*, December 1, 1925.

75. *Trud v Moskovskoi Gubernii*, 431-432.

76. Iu. I. Suvorov, *Bor'ba kommunisticheskoi partii za povyshenie effektivnosti proizvodstva v oblasti promyshlennosti (iz opyt khoziaistvennoi deiatel'nosti Moskovskoi partiinoi organizatsii v 1925-1928gg.)* (Iaroslavl', 1972), 29 (hereafter abbreviated as Suvorov, *Bor'ba*).

77. Such was the opinion of some workers at the Trekhgornaia factory. Lapitskaia, *Byt*, 128-129.

78. *Professional'nye soiuzy, 1926-1928*, 363-364; *Dokumenty trudovoi slavy*, dok. 63, 100. For a discussion of the change, see Suvorov, *Bor'ba*, 35-37.

79. For examples, see: *Dokumenty trudovoi slavy*, dok. 63, 100; *Moskovskii proletarii*, February 3, 1925. According to Rodionova, 173-175, the first workers to make such changes voluntarily were those young workers who had joined the party during the Lenin levy.

80. *Pervye shagi*, 450-455; *Politicheskii i trudovoi pod"em*, 99-109; *Dokumenty trudovoi slavy*, dok. 50-58, 85-95. See also *Komsomol'skaia Pravda*, February 2, June 27, 1928.

81. Suvorov, *Bor'ba*, 81-82; *Ocherki istorii moskovskoi KPSS*, 437.

82. L. Ginzburg, "Proizvoditel'nost' truda i perspektivy zarabotnoi platy," *Vestnik truda*, 1 (1925), 107-112.

252

83. For examples, see *Ocherki istorii moskovskogo organizatsii VLKSM* (Moscow, 1976), 200. For examples of Komsomol-organized shock brigades in factories, see: Kurkhantanov, 92; *Gorodnoe zvanie—il'ichevtsy po zalam muzeia zavoda imeni Vladimir Il'icha* (Moscow, 1970), 65.

84. K. A. Basurmanov, "U zastavy il'icha," *Iunost' nasha Komsomol-'skaia: dokumental'nye materialy, ocherki i vospominiia iz istorii Komsomola Kalinskogo raion goroda Moskvy, 1917-1970* (Moscow, 1970), 111, claims that the first shock brigade was formed at the Dinamo plant in late 1926.

85. See the discussion in Kukushkin and Shelestov, 55-57. For examples of what qualified as early shock work, see the biography of a shock worker in N. Adfel'dt, "Master ressornogo tsekha," *Bor'ba klassov*, 3-4 (1931), 74-75.

86. *Pervyi shagi*, 441-450; *Professional'nye soiuzy SSSR, 1926-1928gg.*, 123; *Ocherki istorii moskovskogo KPSS*, 451; Popov, "Ot pervogo kommu-nisticheskogo subbotnika," 24; Suvorov, *Bor'ba*, 80-82; Petrochenko and Kuznetsova, 114-117. On the composition of shock workers, see: Rashin, *Sostav*, 135-137, 169-170; *Professional'nye soiuzy SSSR 1926-1928*, 124.

87. For a discussion of such conflicts at the AMO plant, see Shikheev, 66. For an emigre worker's view of the same, see the report of worker no. 13 in Zawodny. For similar observations by American engineers and visitors to Russia, see the reports of C. R. Cady and Gordon Fox, *American Engineers in Russia*, box 2; William Reswick, *I Dreamt Revolution* (Chicago, 1952), 259.

88. *Professional'nye soiuzy, 1926-1928*, xviii; Petrochenko and Kuznet-sova, 79-94. The work of TNBs played a role in increased productivity. For a discussion of the work of the TNB at the Livers Factory, see Nikolai Kozlov, "T.N.B. na Moskovskoi kruzhevnoi fabrike 'Livers'," *Izvestiia tekstil'noi pro-myshlennosti i torgovli*, (December 31, 1926), 23.

89. *Ibid.*, 15-18 (August-September, 1927), 30-34; G. Demirchoglian and Ia. Kvasha, "Proizvoditel'nost' truda v tekstil'noi promyshlennosti SSSR," *Statisticheskoe obozrenie*, 9 (1927), 50-57; *Moskva i Moskovskaia guberniia*, 164-165.

90. *Professional'nye soiuzy, 1926-1928*, 358-359.

91. *Ibid.; Professional'nye soiuzy, 1924-1926*, 245-246.

92. As quoted in Deutscher, *Soviet Trade Unions*, 77.

93. For examples, see *Pravda*, August 10, September 7, 1927; November 10, 1928.

94. *Trud*, July 7, 1928.

95. For a discussion of the improvements at the Proletarskii trud factory since 1924, see *Trud*, April 3, 1928. See also the interview with worker number 17 in Zawodny.

96. For examples, see: *Pravda*, April 24, November 3, 1925; *Trud*, March 25, May 30, 1928.

97. The directive can be found in *ibid.*, December 3, 1926.

98. I. Tolstopiatov, "Bol'she vnimaniia okhrane truda," *Voprosy truda*, 5 (1929), 18-24. See also the report by Lebedev to the Seventh All-Union Congress of Textile Workers in *Izvestiia tekstil'noi promyshlennosti i torgovli*, 20 (May 31, 1926), 9-12.

99. For example, see S. Kaplun, "Rezhim ekonomii i okhrana truda," *Voprosy truda*, 5-6 (1926), 16-22.

100. Tolstopiatov, "Bol'she vnimaniia," 18-24.

101. This will be discussed in chapter 7.

102. Suvorov, *Bor'ba*, 66, states that 45 to 60 percent of the country's textile equipment was in poor condition or outdated.

103. M. Romanov, "Proizvoditel'nost' truda, zarabotnaia plata i izderski na rabochuiu silu v khlopchato-bumazhno promyshlennosti," (part 1), *Izvestiia tekstil'noi promyshlennosti i torgovli*, (July 1-15, 1927), 19-24; (part II), *ibid.*, 15-18 (August-September, 1927), 30-34. See also, Markus, "Voprosy okhrany truda," 33-40; Suvorov, *Bor'ba*, 66; *Izvestiia tekstil'noi promyshlennosti i torgovli*, 20 (May 31, 1926), 9-12.

104. *Professional'nye soiuzy, 1926-1928*, 358-361. There was a brief rise in 1927.

105. V. V. Shmidt, "Regulirovanie truda stroitel'nykh rabochikh," *Voprosy truda*, 2 (1926), 3-11; M. Nefedov, "Okhrana truda," 136-143.

106. A. Bakhutov, "Voprosy regulirovaniia truda v RSFSR," *Voprosy truda*, 1 (1927), 49-54. This is a stenographic copy of his report to the Seventh All-Union Trade Union Congress.

107. N. Aristov, "Nedochety v rabote Moskovskogo GOT v oblasti okhrany truda (po materialam MRKI)," *ibid.*, 5 (1928), 110-111.

108. Markus, "Voprosy okhrany truda," 33-40; Tolstopiatov, "Bol'she vnimaniia," 18-24.

109. The national figures were 138.5 and 151.2 respectively and are from Tolstopiatov, "Bol'she vnimaniia," 18-24. For Moscow rates, see P. Lebit, "Promyshlennyi travmatizm v Moskovskoi gubernii," *Voprosy truda*, 1 (1929), 107-108. Beginning in 1927, *Voprosy truda* began reporting industrial accidents and fatalities on a regular basis. For these rates, interested readers should consult this journal.

110. Lebit, 107-108.

111. D. Shneer, "Travmatizm na Moskovskikh postroikakh," *Voprosy truda*, 9 (1928), 117-118. In 1927, the accident rate in the construction industry was 223 per 1,000 workers. In industry, the accident rates in RSFSR industries ranged from 34.4 to 40.8 per 1,000 workers. *Voprosy truda*, 1 (1928), 175; 7-8 (1928), 310.

112. Tolstopiatov, "Bol'she vnimaniia," 18-24.

113. For the resolution, see *SZ*, 1927, 61, 613. For a discussion of the joint commission, see *Professional'nye soiuzy, 1926-1928*, 416-417.

114. For examples, see: B. Markus, "K voprosu o semichasovom rabochem dne," *Voprosy truda*, 12 (1927), 3-15; V. Shmidt, "O semichasovom rabochem dne v tekstil'noi promyshlennosti," *Izvestiia tekstil'noi promyshlennosti i torgovli*, 12 (1927), 1-3; T. N. "K voprosu vvedeniia semichasovogo rabochego dnia na tekstil'nykh fabrikakh," *ibid.*, 3 (1928), 21-22; *Moskovskii proletarii*, January 7, January 14, 1928, 6-7.

115. B. Markus, "Nekotorye predvaritel'nyi itogi osushchestvleniia semichasogo rabochego dnia," *Voprosy truda*, 6 (1928), 10.

116. *Trud*, January 12, October 1, 1928.

117. *Komsomol'skaia Pravda*, February 28, 1928.

118. *Trud*, November 7, December 12, 1928.

119. This discussion is based on the following sources: Markus, "Nekotorye predvaritel'nyi itogi"; A. Vinnikov, "Pervyi itogi i perspektivy provedniia semichasovogo rabochego dnia," *Voprosy truda*, 2 (1929), 46-55; "Nekotorye itogi perekhoda predpriatii na semichasovoi rabochii den'," *ibid.*, 9 (1929), 90-92; N. Vasil'ev, "Ratsionalizatsiia proizvodstva i voprosy truda," *ibid.*, 1 (1929), 26-31; M. Nestorov, "Semichasovoi rabochii den' na fabrikakh vtorogo khlopchutogo bumazhnogo tresta," *Izvestiia tekstil'noi promyshlennosti i torgovli*, 7 (1928), 23-28; G. Tsypkin and A. Goldberg, "Predvaritel'nye itogi perekhod na semichasovoi den'," *Statisticheskoe obozrenie*, 11 (1928), 30-35; *Torgovo-promyshlennaia gazeta*, June 6, 1928; *Moskovskii proletarii*, April 7, 1928, 5-6; June 14-21, 1928, 3-4; October 28, 1928; *Direktivy KPSS i sovetskogo pravitel'stva*, II, 856-859. For a discussion of the problems at the Krasnyi Bogatyr' rubberworks, see: A. Sorkin and S. Bondarchuk, "Zavod 'Krasnyi Bogatyr' (Moskva)," *Voprosy truda*, 9 (1929), 90-92; *Moskovksii proletarii*, October 28, 1928. See also Schwarz, 259-268.

120. Schwarz, 260n.

7. Opening Pandora's Box: Mobilization and Worker Activism

By early 1921, party leaders had defined the contours of factory politics and relations. The responsibility for administering the factory and implementing economic and labor policies there rested with the factory director. His power underscored the productivist leadership's conviction that an administrative hierarchy was essential to proper industrial management and to the successful realization of the policies designed to boost production and productivity. But the factory director was not to be the equivalent of the pre-revolutionary factory owner who ruled his property like the tsar ruled his subjects. He was not an owner, but a manager whose charge was to administer the factory in accordance with party and state policy.

While in theory Soviet factories were organized on the principle of one-man management, the real administrative structure was often different. The factory director was usually a Communist (or Red) director who, because of his party membership, was appointed to ensure that policies were carried out properly. But most directors lacked sufficient technical education and expertise, a deficiency which made them very dependent on the chief engineer or technical director and his staff of technical specialists (*spetsy*). The vast majority of technical personnel were "bourgeois" specialists, that is, they were neither Communists nor of proletarian background. It was precisely because these essential personnel were "bourgeois" that the director was a party member. But amidst the drives for industrial recovery and productivity, factory directors often deferred to their technical staff whose knowledge (real or alleged) of production gave them real power. Because the delineations between the Red director, chief engineer, and technical staff were often blurred, this study uses the terms management or managerial personnel when referring to those people who implemented and enforced policy.

A myriad of policies—from the Labor Code to specific directives on any given issue—carefully circumscribed, on paper at least, the director's and all managerial personnel's power and behavior. There also existed (or was supposed to exist) institutional restraints on management. The most important of these were the unions and their organs in the factory, the factory committee. As we have seen, the unions were expected to play a dual role. They were to aid management in executing policies designed to raise production and productivity and to protect workers from any exploitation that might result from management's improper implementation of policy. Factory committees were to concentrate their energies on similar activities. The roles assigned to management, unions and factory committees were designed to provide a system of institutional checks and balances that, if properly carried out, would both hasten industrial growth and the realization of the "proper" relationship between one-man management and workers' control. Such was the theory.

The reality proved to be quite different, especially in the early 1920s. By 1920, the disintegration of the proletariat and the economy had severely weakened the factory committees that, when they functioned at all, concentrated their energies on procuring the food and fuel necessary for survival and averting the ever-imminent total collapse of production. The militarization of labor and strengthening of managerial powers in 1920 provided the *coup de grace* to the political power of factory committees. Alienated from their restive constituents, the unions too were ineffectual.

Unrestrained by these institutional checks, many industrial managers interpreted the relentless calls for more production, higher productivity, and lower costs in their own myopic way. Their violations of the Labor Code and collective agreements and their reluctance to improve working conditions in the early 1920s undermined all attempts to maintain the "proper" relationship between one-man management and workers' control and angered workers and party radicals. The strikes, labor disputes, and the Workers Truth's, Workers' Group's, and above all Left Opposition's scathing denunciations of party economic policy and demands for greater worker control over management placed the party's productivist leadership under considerable political pressure. The latter had created a system of checks and balances to protect workers and institutionalize their power. But in the early 1920s, the party and unions did little to enforce that system. The primacy given to economic recovery had tilted the balance in favor of unrestrained managerial behavior and nullified workers' control.

In 1923/24, the party leadership sought to restore the balance in a way which would not compromise their demands for greater productivity. Production meetings and conferences were designated the means to that end. Organized and administered by the unions and factory committees, production meetings were to be forums in which workers and management would cooperate in discovering ways to increase production and lower costs. This was to be accomplished not simply by devising ways to increase worker productivity but also by exposing the shortcomings and failures of management. The meetings would hopefully achieve several goals simultaneously. They would tap workers' knowledge of factory affairs and their creative energies in the drive to realize economic policy. They would establish the system of checks and balances. And they would blunt oppositionists' criticisms that the productivist leaders had turned their backs to workers. With the creation of production meetings, the party opened a second front in its battle to realize its economic policy.

Although slow in gaining legitimacy, by the late 1920s, production meetings became arenas in which workers attacked management and sought to reassert a measure of control over factory life. They took on a dynamic of their own and, in 1928-1929, threatened to destroy the fabric of factory life. The assault on management was not the only only significant result of these meetings. So too was the re-emergence of the Communist Party's power and influence in the factories. But its success was the unions' failure. No discussion of production meetings can be complete without first examining the relationships between workers, unions, and the Communist Party.

Unions

Until 1924, the "breach between the masses and the unions" of which Vyshinskii spoke in early 1921 did not diminish significantly. True, workers increasingly turned to the unions' grievance and appeal boards to adjudicate disputes with management. But such behavior served workers' immediate interests. That most strikes occurred without the factory committees' or unions' sanction and often caught union officials unaware underscores how divided workers and unions were. The unions active participation in raising worker productivity while they simultaneously turned a blind eye to substandard and dangerous working conditions angered workers and explains why workers showed little interest in union activities in the early 1920s.

From 1923, the unions' slogan was "closer to the masses" *(blizhe k massa)*.[1] But their failure to pay closer attention to many issues that concerned workers gave the slogan a hollow sound. Until late 1923, many workers expressed their dissatisfaction by quitting their union. For example, only 10 percent of Moscow's metalworkers belonged to the union in early 1923. In hopes of realizing their slogan, from late 1923 unions launched a campaign to expand their membership. By April 1924, the metalworkers union boasted that 95 percent of their potential constituents were union members. The membership of all others unions also grew steadily. But new membership among the unemployed and students exceeded that of employed people by three and eight times respectively.[2] To those two groups, union membership held the promise of a variety of benefits, but apparently many employed workers adopted a more cynical view.

The rise in union membership did not mean that workers viewed the unions as more effective or legitimate. Union leaders were well aware of this and demanded that discussions of ways to improve union-worker ties were to be the major item on the agendas at union conferences and congresses in 1924.[3] The renewed attention that unions began to pay to factory and work conditions in 1924 heralded a change in union behavior. From 1924, unions struggled to balance their production and protection roles.

The gulf between the unions and their constituents in the early 1920s evidenced itself in another way—low rates of worker participation in factory committee meetings. The exodus of talented organizers, the subjugation of unions to the party, the militarization of labor, and the reinstitution of one-man management during the Civil War years, all served to restrict and severely weaken factory committees. VTsSPS itself admitted that this condition resulted from the committees' subjugation by the party during the post-1918 years. From 1920 to 1924, many factory committees were moribund. In those factories where the committees remained alive, meetings were held infrequently and the few workers in attendance were passive. Attendance rates of 15 to 20 percent appear to have been the norm. In factories with a high proportion of new workers, the rate was even lower. At one factory, it was necessary to lock the gates prior to Friday meetings to keep the worker-peasants from skipping the meeting and returning to the village.

When they were called, factory committee meetings generally consisted of reports and speeches devoted to the importance of raising productivity. The method of electing committee members also contributed to worker disillusionment. The union, party cell, or factory committee itself usually chose the candidates whose number equalled the number of positions. Nominees had to secure unanimous approval to be elected. Given the absence of union democracy, many workers simply turned their backs on the committees.[4]

From 1924 to 1929, union ties to their constituents strengthened, but workers' participation in union activities continued to be selective. Workers increasingly used union-established appeals proceedures to seek redress of their grievances, in large measure because many of workers viewed them, especially the assessment and conflict commissions, as likely to rule in their favor.[5] This undoubtedly helped to enhance unions' image among workers. The unions' greater attention to ameliorating work conditions and fostering greater labor protection also served them well, as did the priority given to union members for admission to sanatoriums, the reduced rent charged members, the greater opportunity for technical education, and a variety of other material benefits.[6] Together with the expansion of the workforce, these factors accounted for a 55 percent increase in the number of unionized workers in Moscow between 1924 and 1928.[7]

But tensions still plagued union-worker relations. As during the early NEP, union leaders found it difficult to transmit resolutions, appeals, and ideas to their members.[8] One reason for this was that many of these proclamations urged workers to improve productivity and labor discipline. Unions continued to be active organizers and executors of the campaigns to raise worker productivity. Union officials and conferences approved policies that implemented such unpopular policies as the extension of piece-rates, the raising of output norms, and increasing the number of machines operated by workers. The close cooperation between union leaders and managerial personnel on a wide range of production issues did little to enhance the popularity of unions. Throughout the 1920s, strikes continued to occur without the unions' knowledge or support. Nor were workers impressed by the fact that, as Tomskii stated, unions paid "inadequate attention to the needs of the masses, to their being detached from the masses, and showing contempt for the small matters of workers' lives."[9]

Union officials were sensitive to the problems. Many openly admitted the tenuous ties of unions to workers, the need to strengthen those ties, the lack of trade union democracy, the poor quality of union activists, and the bureaucratism of union proceedings.[10] One way in which unions hoped to remedy some of these problems was to expand the range of union democracy. Toward this end, in July 1925 VTsSPS issued a directive on extending worker participation in factory committee elections. The directive called for the elimination of undemocratic methods of factory committee elections. The nomination of candidates and their election at open meetings replaced the submission of lists of candidates. Unanimous approval of candidates was no longer necessary. The directive also urged greater accountability of factory and shop committees to workers, more active penetration *(proniknovenie)* of committees into factory life, regular and less bureaucratic meetings, and systematic attempts to involve workers in union work.[11] The call for greater union democracy, which probably reflected an attempt to blunt workers' and the various opposition groups' criticisms of unions, was well received by workers.

During the factory committee elections in 1926, most unions implemented new electoral proceedures. At shop- or factory-level meetings, workers nominated candidates after a report on the activities of the outgoing committee. Press reports on the elections suggest that the number of nominees exceeded the number of positions. The elections took place at a second meeting. The new electoral proceedures resulted in a sharp rise in worker participation. Factory committee attendance rates ranged from 30 percent to 85 percent. The proportion of nonparty workers elected to committees rose substantially; in some factories, they comprised the majority of the new committees.[12] As we shall see, the increased attendance and participation by workers in factory committee activities was part of a general rise of worker activism in the late 1920s.

Without demeaning the unions' efforts to become "closer to the masses," their success was mixed. So long as they continued to cooperate with management in the drive to raise productivity, many workers carefully, and at times suspiciously, scrutinized union behavior. Because unions remained executors of party policy, when workers sought to effect change and flex their political muscle, they turned to the party. As one worker put it, in the factory the party, not the union was the "real god."[13]

The Communist Party

As was true of worker-union relations, those between the party and working class in the early twenties were tenuous. By 1921, the party, which in 1917 had attracted to its ranks large numbers of workers at the bench and which had built its power base in factory committees, had few production workers on its rolls. While some factories may have had several dozen party members, few were production workers; most were managerial personnel.[14] Overall workers by social origin accounted for only 45 percent of the party in 1921, but less than one-fifth were workers engaged in production. This "de-proletarianization" of the party came under attack from various opposition groups in the early 1920s. The 1921 party purge *(chistka)* was, in part, a response to these criticisms. Yet until the 1924 Lenin levy *(Leninskii prizyv)*, production workers accounted for a minority of the party which called itself the vanguard of the proletariat.

The paucity of workers within its ranks caused considerable agonizing within the party from 1921 to 1923. While some members, especially the various left oppositions, wanted to expand the party's proletarian ranks, Lenin warned that many of those who worked in factories were actually petty bourgeois who would weaken the party's proletarian character. He cautioned that the mass admission of workers might alienate the party from the peasant population and lead to the creation of two parties. He argued that "at the present time the proletarian policy of the party is not determined by the character of its membership but by the enormous individual prestige enjoyed by the small group which might be called the Old Guard of the party."[15]

Despite Lenin's warning, the party majority's desire to expand its proletarian constituency prevailed. By late 1923, the condition of party cadres was critical. Most were bogged down in administrative duties that overtaxed them and contributed to a general state of exhaustion. For this reason, a December 1923 resolution noted the pressing need for "the recruitment of new party members from among workers at the bench." The stress on recruiting workers into the party served three purposes. First, it would ease the burden carried by existing party members. It would also serve to increase the proportion of proletarian members and, hopefully, to bridge the gulf between workers and the party. Finally, expanding the number of worker-communists would weaken the various opposition groups' criticisms and strengthen the triumvirate's position in its battle with the Left Oppostion. In Moscow, the party leadership's position carried a majority of factory cells in the struggle with that opposition. They undoubtedly hoped that expanding the number of workers would further strengthen their support at the factory level. Three days before Lenin's death in January 1924, the Thirteenth Party Conference passed a resolution calling for the recruitment into the party of "no less than 100,000 new members who are genuine proletarians." Formally initiated after Lenin's death, the Lenin levy continued into late 1924. During that year, some 25,000 workers joined the Moscow City party organization, the size of which grew from 53,100 to 88,300. The same year the ranks of the city Komsomol swelled from 28,394 to 57,677. Textile, metal, and railroad workers accounted for about 60 percent of the new party members.[16] The size of many factory cells grew dramatically. In many larger factories, such as Dinamo, Serp i molot, AMO, Pervaia Sittsenabivnaia, Trekhgornaia, and Osvobozhdennyi trud, party cells more than doubled in size and the proportion of worker-communists increased significantly. At Serp i molot, the proportion was 18 percent; at AMO, 13 percent.[17] The Lenin levy also transformed the social composition of the city party organization. By the end of 1924, two-thirds of its members were workers by social origin and 48 percent workers at the bench.[18] In 1925, a second Lenin levy occured; in October 1927, yet another—to celebrate the revolution's tenth anniversary. By October 1928, the size of the city party organization had grown to more than 150,000.[19]

Many of the new worker-communists (*lenintsy*) had considerable production experience (*stazh*). According to a late 1927 Moscow party committee report, 24 percent of its proletarian members had up to three years of production experience, 35 percent had three to eight years experience, and 41 percent had more than eight years experience. At Serp i molot, the majority of workers who joined the party had ten to fifteen years of experience. Urban workers in their twenties and thirties dominated the *lenintsy*'s ranks. What they lacked as a group was education. In 1927, only 3 percent had some higher education, 18 percent had some middle-level education, and 58 percent had some elementary education. Presumably, the remainder had no formal education.[20] To remedy the lack of formal education and political education in particular, the network of party schools, Marxist circles, political courses and other party educational institutions expanded considerably during the post-Lenin levy years.[21]

Given the breach between the workers and party and worker discontent with official policies in the early 1920s, why did workers join that party in such large numbers in 1924? Some did so simply because they shared the party's politics and vision of the future. Others joined because they wanted to be politically active and affect the development of policy. While participating in unions and soviets allowed one to be active, these organs executed rather than created policy. It was the party that developed policy and was the "real god." It was also the only political party. To engage in politics meant coming to an accomodation with the limits of political life. Only by working within those limits would one be able to affect change. Surely the minor gains that strikes and other diffuse manifestations of discontent had secured were clear to many workers.

Also the parameters of political life were widening in 1924. After several years of refusing to admit new members and focusing almost exclusively on raising productivity, the party's line had begun to shift. In late 1923, it began to criticize management and created production meetings. Troubled though it was, the country's economic condition was improving and, as it did, it enhanced the party's stature. To those who desired to be politically active, these shifts portended greater opportunities to influence policy. Finally, party membership offered the surest avenue to upward mobility, either within or outside of the factory. Whatever their motives, thousands joined the party and Komsomol. As the economy improved and party policies became increasingly critical of management, thousands more workers did so. But as the unions' experience indicates, sheer numbers did not guarantee that the breach between the party and workers would disappear. To understand how the party succeeded in placing itself in the vanguard of the proletariat, let us examine production meetings.

Production Meetings, 1923-1926

The creation of production meetings and conferences came in response to a November 1923 instruction (tsirkular) published by VSNKh, VTsSPS, and the Council of Labor and Defense (STO). The document began by noting that reducing the cost and price of industrial products was "the most fundamental and urgent task facing the economy." It continued:

> The high cost and inflated prices of industrial products are determined to a significant extent by *the incompetence of management* in the industrial sphere, and particularly in the commercial sphere. Therefore it is the duty of trade union organizations to conduct a systematic and resolute struggle against deficiencies in our economy. . . . In this struggle trade union organizations should display a maximum of initiative and determination, they should carefully scrutinize and supervise developments in enterprises and should render maximum assistance to economic organs in the improvement of economic organization.[22] (Emphasis added.)

Toward this end, the document urged the creation of production meet-ings (*soveshchanii*) and conferences (*konferentsii*) of enterprise and trust administrators and worker delegates. At these meetings, responsible offi-cials and worker delegates were to present reports on the "condition of work in the enterprise and trust" and to exchange ideas on ways to improve production and lower costs. Economic problems and cases of mismanagement revealed at these (or any other meetings) were to be forwarded to higher union officials.[23]

A February 1924 Central Committee directive also urged party cells to organize production meetings in factories and production conferences in economic trusts and union organs, at which workers, unions, and management would discuss methods to hasten the implementation of party economic policies.[24] From May on, calls for the creation of pro-duction meetings came from a variety of union and state agencies and convocations.[25] Although similar in many ways to production propa-ganda and NOT circles, production meetings differed in one important respect—they provided forums in which the "incompetence of manage-ment" could be exposed. Most workers had few doubts about their man-agers' "incompetence." What they questioned was how real the opportunity to expose it would be.

Production meetings had two purposes. The most explicit was that they were to be the forums at which workers' suggestions and criticisms could be used to increase productivity, to lower costs, and to expose and to correct the problems created by the "incompetence of management." (Toward the same end, the Twelfth Party Congress ordered the reorgani-zation of Rabkrin.) But production meetings were to act as a corrective to mismanagement, not as competitors with management. On this point, the November 1923 document was quite explicit: there was to be "mutual assistance between economic and trade union organs."[26] Pro-duction meetings were also vehicles by which the "proper" relationship between one-man management and workers' control could be estab-lished. They did not limit the managers' power, rather they sought to actively engage workers in overseeing and verifying managerial behavior and to hasten worker-management cooperation. After several years of worker unrest that was often sparked by management's misapplication of policies, establishing "proper" worker-management roles and relations was politically necessary.

The organization of production meetings proceeded slowly in 1924. Not until September of that year did VTsSPS present a clearly formulated position on their purpose and composition. According to VTsSPS, "production meetings, representing one of the major forms of mass union economic work in enterprises, pursue the goal of involving the masses of workers in the interests of production, improving and developing production" in close collaboration with management. The issues that production meetings were to address echoed those listed in other party and union directives designed to raise productivity: the utilization of materials and fuel; the conditions of instruments, tools and machinery; the rationalization of production and the workforce; issues relating to wages and norms; waste; and the organization of administration. Meetings were to be composed of "active workers" chosen as delegates by shop and factory level meetings, administrative and technical personnel, and conscious workers who voluntarily attended. The document concluded by reiterating that "production meetings should not interfere in the administrative and technical activities of the factory administration."[27]

While the stated purposes of production meetings were clear, other factors explain the timing of their appearance. One was that, until late 1923, the drive to reduce industrial costs had fallen almost exclusively on workers. Management's implementation of these policies—and the policies themselves—had generated considerable discontent among workers and party radicals. Involving workers in attempts to force management to share the burden of the cost of recovery held out the promise of not only reducing industrial costs, but also of diffusing grassroot unrest. Secondly, these meetings would help to resuscitate factory committees, many of which were moribund in 1923. By making these former organs of worker democracy responsible for the organization and conduct of production meetings, factory committees were given a new, albeit circumscribed, reason for existence. In this way, the creation of production meetings and the revitalization of factory committees could be used to counter criticisms that the party stifled worker democracy and shunned the creative energies and initiative of conscious workers. Under the direction of trusted party and union activists, these meetings would ensure that worker criticisms could be aired and funneled in less threatening, even constructive, directions. Worker participation might even hasten the realization of economic goals.

As the content of the September 1924 VTsSPS directive clearly indicates, the rationalization campaign of 1924-1926 provided the goals toward which production meetings were to orient their work. The August 1924 Central Committee resolution "On wage policy" (discussed in the previous chapter) had first enunciated the campaign's goals. Simply stated, the resolution called for increasing labor productivity by means of intensifying and rationalizing labor and production. It urged all factory production meetings and commissions to implement the policy. Taken together, the rationalization campaign and the organization of production meetings formed the basis of the party's two-pronged strategy to restore the economy and raise productivity.

It is worth dwelling for a moment on the meaning of this dual strategy. The contradiction inherent in it was that, while the drive for labor intensification meant greater sacrifices by the working class, the call for production meetings seemed to be an attempt to enlist workers in their own undoing. But from the leadership's viewpoint, it was more than a case of trying to have one's cake and eat it too. In fact, the party leadership was deeply divided over a number of issues. While productivists might have preferred a straight-forward drive for labor intensification as the shortest route to economic recovery, they would have been open to attack by the radicals' argument that the proletariat was forced to bear all of the costs of recovery. The production meetings would diffuse this criticism by giving the drive for labor intensification the appearance of worker support. Likewise, those radicals who saw the democratization of socialist restoration and reconstruction as the primary goal could not ignore the problem of economic recovery, itself a fundamental issue for workers. For radicals, the production meetings offered the possibility of creating a groundswell of worker activism in the guise of mobilizing the forces of economic recovery. Thus, the call for production meetings could enjoy deceptively wide support within the leadership. But whose agenda would prevail remained to be seen.

The organizational structure of production meetings paralleled the administrative hierarchy found throughout the economy. Within the factory, there existed both shop- and factory-level meetings, although the former were rare until late 1925. At shop production meetings, participants elected a production commission usually comprised of three members. They also elected shop representatives to work with the factory production commission. The latter bodies, the size of which varied from three to seven members, were either appointed by the factory committee or elected at an open meeting. Both commissions were responsible for organizing and planning meetings.[28] There also existed production conferences that were convened in the trusts or at city or *guberniia* union convocations.

In 1924, few production meetings were held. Although the number increased throughout 1925, they could hardly be described as widespread. During the former year, it appears that production conferences in trusts or at city or *guberniia* union convocations were more common than factory production meetings.[29] According to one source, production conferences and meetings occurred in only forty-four enterprises in the whole *guberniia* during the first year of their existence.[30] Regardless of the level at which they were convened, the types of participants and nature of discussions were remarkably similar. Data on thirty-four conferences in 1924/25 indicate that about 40 percent of the delegates were party or Komsomol members. Administrative and technical personnel, foremen, and union officials also attended in large numbers, but such was not the case with nonparty workers.[31]

The agendas of and discussions at conferences were quite homogeneous. Taking their lead from the goals outlined in official resolutions, the issues discussed included: calculating output norms; better utilization of the workday; mechanization; organizational questions; wages; reasons for waste and breakage; and, on occasion, issues of workers' daily lives, especially housing. While discussions of these issues did occur, most of the time appears to have been devoted to the presentation of reports by enterprise directors, technical personnel, and union officials.[32] The formal nature of such meetings at the factory level meant that they resembled the scholastic NOT worker circles more than they did forums for the exchange of ideas on how to improve production.

At both the trust and factory level, these meetings suffered from a wide range of problems and incurred the criticisms of party and trade union officials. According to a 1925 party resolution, one reason for the slow growth of production meetings was the failure of many party organizations and trade unions to give sufficient attention to them. To a certain extent the party's inattention probably reflected the slowness with which new cadres, who joined the party during the Lenin levy, were being trained and the fact that seasoned party veterans were overworked. That the quality of cadres was a problem is clear from another major shortcoming of production meetings—the poor quality of planning and reports. The meetings' formal structure did little to interest workers and the reports appear to have frustrated even the most zealous of those in attendance. Not only were many reports poorly prepared and difficult to understand, but frequently the reporters were unable to answer questions about them. To make matters worse, many reports did not address major issues of interest to those in attendance. Industrial managers also criticized these meetings. One factory director, after stating that he was not opposed to them in principle, claimed that the workers' low educational level doomed them to failure. Another viewed them as a "waste of working time."[33]

Not surprisingly, these meetings failed to attract wide worker participation, although the evidence does suggest that attendance rose slightly during 1925.[34] Aside from their organizational problems, the major reason for the low attendance rates was the workers' perception that they were but another means of intensifying their labor. Despite the calls to use them to correct management's deficiencies, the topics of discussion and pleas that workers cooperate with management made many workers skeptical. Aside from the leaders, those who did attend often were passive, even inattentive. One observer attributed this lack of interest to the workers' narrow concerns: "The experience of production conferences has shown that in many cases workers were primarily interested in the productivity of *their* shop, *their* department" (emphasis in original). Only when issues that related to their shop were discussed would workers participate. Otherwise "they remained passive." Even when they did participate, their comments centered on petty conflicts and questions of a personal nature.[35]

To overcome this "shop consciousness" (*tsekhovschina*) some factories organized factory exhibits and tours of the various facets of production in order to give workers insight into how their work affected the rest of the factory. For example, at the Trekhgornaia textile factory, party and union activists organized an exhibition of the stages of production, from the processing of the raw cotton to the completion of a product. They presented and explained tables and diagrams and organized tours of the shops. Some factory commissions organized shop-level production meetings to complement factorywide meetings. The number of shop meetings and rates of attendance at them increased steadily during the second half of 1925. In fact, shop meetings accounted for most of the rise in overall attendance. However, they were not organized on a systematic basis until 1926.[36]

This "democratization" of production meetings did not occur without a price. Although shop meetings were more popular among workers and allowed them to express their suggestions and grievances in a familiar environment, the expansion of their numbers reinforced "shop consciousness" and perspectives as well as the hierarchial divisions of authority within the factory. While they may have allowed for broader participation in the struggle with mismanagement, shop meetings reduced to a minimum any possibility of a factorywide alternative to one-man management.

269

Throughout 1924 and 1925, the number of suggestions put forward by workers at these meetings also increased.[37] The vast majority of these centered on the revelation and elimination of such problems as excessive waste, cleaning garbage from the factory floor, the repair or construction of ventilation systems, and improving lighting. In some cases, more substantial changes such as the mechanization of certain labor intensive tasks, fuel economy or the re-arranging of machines on the shop floor so as to ensure a more efficient flow of operations were suggested and implemented. The posting of "defect registers" (*defektivnye vedomosti*) in shops became common.[38] But, there is little evidence to indicate that workers put forth ideas that would have involved an intensification of labor. Rather their ideas centered on improving production and conditions so as to ease their workload.

Two other concerns occupied the workers' attention at these meetings—housing and relations with administrative and technical personnel. Workers in attendance complained that their and their co-workers living conditions ranged from poor to abysmal. Many lived in overcrowded apartments or factory barracks; others had to commute considerable distances to work. Delegates agreed that the conditions and commute both contributed to high rates of absenteeism and tardiness and lower productivity.[39] Criticisms of trust and factory administrators took two forms. The more passive were discussions of the bureaucratism of administrative organs; the more threatening took the form of verbal criticisms of specific managerial personnel. One union official complained that such incorrect relations and attitudes toward these personnel hindered the production meetings' effectiveness.[40] But, such criticisms were less frequent and much milder in 1924-1925 than they would become in the near future. Like the proverbial tip of the iceberg, they provided a glimpse of a much larger and deeper problem.

Among production meetings' prescribed goals were the raising of production and productivity and reducing the problems caused by mismanagement. Production and productivity increased substantially in 1924 and 1925, but the role of such meetings in achieving these goals appears to have been minimal. Most of the increase resulted from policies imposed from above—the raising of output norms, extension of piece-rate wages, and increasing the number of machines tended by workers. Nor were the meetings very successful in improving the labor discipline of workers, particularly new workers from the villages. Their failure to do so restrained the rate at which productivity rose. As one commentator put it: "The campaign to raise the productivity of labor in 1923-1925 did not justify its hopes."[41] The meetings also had limited success in the struggle against mismanagement.

But this first phase in the evolution of production meetings was not without significance. During 1924-1925, factory and shop level organizational structures came into existence, and party and union activists gained valuable experience. What was lacking was a belief by workers that production meetings were forums at which they could with safety candidly express their opinions on the root causes of industry's problems. During the next few years, production meetings gained that reputation.

Production Meetings, 1926-1928

The Fourteenth Party Congress's decision in December 1925 to embark on a course of socialist industrialization marked a turning point in the drive for productivity. The need to lower production costs, to increase production and to hasten the accumulation of investment capital intensified. This renewed emphasis manifested itself in February 1926 with the VSNKh order heralding the introduction of the new phase of the campaign for increased productivity—the regime of economy.[42] In April, the Central Committee and Central Control Commission issued an appeal to all party members entitled "On the struggle for the regime of economy," which noted the historic decision of the recent party congress, the realization of which depended on the accumulation of capital. But unlike capitalist states, it continued, the country had to rely on internal sources for capital. Therefore, it was necessary to wage a resolute struggle against waste, unnecessary expenditures, and all forms of inefficiency. The appeal charged party members to implement several concrete tasks so as to ensure success: to draw all soviets, unions, cooperatives, and other social organizations into the struggle; to expose examples of waste and ineconomy in the press; to make managers accountable to the working masses for the reduction of costs; to reduce the size of commissariats' and trusts' bureaucracies; to raise labor productivity; to reduce absence and idle work time; and, to strengthen the rationalization campaign. Rabkrin and the Central Control Commission were responsible for monitoring the campaign. In June, a Sovnarkom and USSR Central Executive Committee resolution transformed the appeal into law.[43]

Managers were quick to use the regime of economy to cut costs. But as before, they often did so in ways which violated the spirit and letter

271

of the law. Workers complained that managers economized by closing workers' clubs, reducing the number of lights and extending the distance between them, laying off workers, neglecting to repair and improve factory conditions, and not issuing protective clothing.[44] In August, a joint Sovnarkom, Central Committee, and Central Control Commission report condemned management's crass and often illegal behavior which "seriously harmed the welfare of workers." "These ugly acts are made worse by the fact that they have been carried out *while* excessive bureaucratic staffs have been retained in administrative bodies, *while* there has been an impermissable protection of 'higher ranks,' . . . *while* bonuses have been issued to these 'higher ranks,' *while* there have been masked increases in pay for 'higher officials' in the form of endless official journeys and the issuance of advances that are not repayable" (emphasis in original). The report reiterated that "the aim of the regime of economy is not to reduce, but continuously to improve the material and cultural level of the working class." Party members who did not combat these abuses were subject to expulsion. The following month the Moscow party committee echoed this criticism and urged party cadres to struggle resolutely to advance the regime of economy.[45] The more strident criticisms of management set a new tone for production workers and emboldened them to air their grievances.

Party and union organizers were slower to implement the regime of economy and many viewed it as a short-term measure. These activists' shortcomings came under attack in the August report that criticized those who viewed the regime as a shock campaign rather than an integral part of economic policy. Party leaders were equally critical of cadres who, to date, had failed to involve the working masses in the campaign. Production conferences and meetings were to play an important role in the campaign, but party and union activists had been insufficiently energetic in convening these forums. Party members who did not properly combat the abuses of the campaign were subject to expulsion. In short, the regime of economy's early successes were too few.[46] The criticism had its effect for, as one historian put it, the campaign began "with a new force" in September 1926.[47]

Production meetings during 1926-1928 differed from those in previous years in two major respects: worker attendance at and participation in production meetings increased significantly; so too did worker criticisms of factory administrative personnel. The demands of the regime of economy played a significant role in the change. By imploring workers to expose the "incompetence of management" and factory activists to lead the drive, official policy provided workers' grievances with legitimacy and backing. But as the criticisms mounted and expressions of animosity deepened, all hopes that workers and managers would cooperate in the drive to lower costs dissolved. Production meetings began to take on their own dynamic. Rather than staying within their official guidelines, they became battlegrounds on which workers attacked their bosses.

Ascertaining precise participation rates in production meetings from 1926 is difficult given significant disparities between the sources. According to one estimate, only 6 percent of the national workforce attended factory or shop-level meetings in 1925/26. At the end of 1926, the proportion rose to 10 percent; in 1927, it reached 15 percent. However, the Moscow *Guberniia* Trade Union Council put the *guberniia* wide participation rate at 21 percent in 1926 and 24 percent in the first half of 1927. Ninety percent of the participants were workers; the remainder were administrative and technical personnel. Many workers who attended were party and union *aktiv*. Most were in their twenties and thirties, had considerable production experience, and were skilled or semiskilled. Urban workers dominated the production meetings' leaders and participants. Until late 1928, few new workers attended the meetings.[48]

These estimates are averages and disguise the very different participation rates between industries and between factories within industries. Metal and textile workers had the highest participation rates. This was especially the case in large factories. For example, 30 to 40 percent of the workers at Trekhgornaia, Dinamo and Serp i molot in 1927 reportedly attended the meetings. In other industries, for example, the leather industry, the participation rates were much lower. Shop meetings were better attended than factory meetings. In some factories, such as Serp i molot, attendance rates at shop-level meetings reached upward of 75 percent.[49]

There were several reasons why textile and metal workers had much higher participation rates. In these industries, especially in the large factories, much of the work was mechanized and a majority of workers received piece-rate wages. The long-standing conflict between workers and management over the fixing of output norms and piece-rate wages was especially pointed there. Likewise, increasing the number of machines that workers operated had an amplified effect in these industries given the nature of production technology and the high proportion of antiquated and inefficient machinery in them. Both industries had high unemployment rates, a reality that angered workers. In both, a growing proportion of workers were forced to live in overcrowded factory barracks or to commute long distances. In short, deep frustrations over the conditions of labor and daily life fueled worker discontent.

Finally, after the 1924 Lenin levy, a larger proportion of workers in these industries belonged to the Communist Party. Textile, metal, and railroad workers accounted for about 60 percent of the city's new party members (*lenintsy*).[50] During 1924, party cells more than doubled in size in the larger metal and textile factories; mass worker enrollments in the party in 1925 and 1927 increased the size of party cells even more.[51] The infusion of large numbers of party *aktiv* into the factories played a significant role in increased attendance at production meetings. Party leaders had implored their comrades to play an active role in productivity campaigns and in production meetings. This was to be done in cooperation with union activists. Although unions and factory committees were responsible for factory production meetings' organization and performance, the low attendance at and the lackluster performance of these meetings in the early years resulted in the unions coming under increasing fire. Throughout 1926 and 1927, party and union leaders alike complained that many of the production meetings' and conferences' shortcomings were due to union activists' inadequate performance. Many of them failed to organize meetings, to appreciate their significance, to attract workers to them, to properly plan them, and to take seriously the suggestions of participants.[52]

Into this partial organizational void stepped the party and its cohort of new members. Whereas in 1923, worker-communists were in short supply, by 1927 they existed in most factories—and in all large factories—in substantially larger numbers. Although criticized occasionally for their shortcomings, the emphasis from 1926 was on mobilizing cadres to use production meetings to implement the regime of economy. The urgings and threats by party leaders and local committees added further impetus. Whether the quality of these cadres was better than their union counterparts is unclear, but they had two distinct advantages—the party's organizational backing and its political prestige. Under the direction of the party and the *lenintsy* in particular, production meetings entered a new phase.

While worker passivity at production meetings remained an enduring problem in some factories, active participation rose substantially. Worker-communists took the lead, although they were a minority of those who attended meetings and conferences.[53] After 1926, Komsomol members and young workers also had high participation rates. However, women had disproportionately low rates of participation.[54]

Of the problems discussed at meetings, the condition of equipment received more attention than any other. Workers complained that the machinery was old and worn-out: "The machines began to work under serfdom, but they must live under socialism."[55] Likewise, they criticized the shortage and poor conditions of tools and instruments. How, workers asked, could they be expected to be more productive when the machines and instruments with which they worked were of such poor quality? Such equipment made idle time and waste inevitable. The low quality of supplies and raw materials compounded the problem. In addition to criticizing conditions and management's sloth at improving them, workers also put forth suggestions for improving production. They offered ideas for reorganizing the shop floor, mechanizing certain aspects of production, improving lighting, saving fuel, and reducing waste. The savings which resulted from such suggestions were often quite substantial.[56] But, as in earlier years, most such suggestions centered on improving the workplace so as to ease the workload rather than on intensifying labor. One union official stated: "The broad strata of workers will express interest in production meetings only in such cases when they see that they combat not only the defects of production, but ease work and improve the conditions of work. . . ."[57]

From late 1926 on, workers also devoted considerable attention to the problem of labor discipline. These discussions suggest a significant tension between politically active urban workers and new workers. The former dominated the ranks of proletarian party members and participants at production meetings; few of the latter were politically active or expressed interest in the meetings. As the drive to raise productivity intensified, the lack of labor discipline and the sloppy work habits of new workers posed an increased burden for the more disciplined urban workers and, in some cases, endangered them. Although the evidence is insufficient to reconstruct the discussions, it suggests that new workers' indiscipline coupled with their "infiltration of production" at the expense of urban and young workers played significant role in the mounting tension between the two groups.[58]

What distinguished production meetings in 1926-1929 from those held earlier was that workers increasingly used them to vent their hostility toward and grievances with factory administrators and technical specialists (*spetsy*). Expressions of hostility were not new to Russian factories. They had existed before the revolution and during 1917-1919

275

workers often verbally—and sometimes physically—assaulted "bourgeois" technicians and managers. The tensions endured after 1919, but the shift to one-man management and constant appeals by party, state and union officials to cooperate with these former "class enemies" in the name of restoring production muted the confrontations, if not the level of antipathy.[59] Since recovery was the top priority, union and party cadres who shared worker resentment toward management were hamstrung and unable to do more than appeal to arbitration and conciliation boards.

Despite the repeated appeals to expose mismanagement and to reduce production costs by streamlining factory bureaucracies, success in achieving these goals was minimal until 1926. In that year, the campaign to reduce the size and to improve the accountability of trust and factory administrations began in earnest. One reason was the party's widening public campaign against mismanagement and unscrupulous managerial behavior. The aforementioned August 1926 condemnation of abuses committed by factory administrators was part of the campaign as was the resolution of the Seventh Trade Union Congress in 1926 which stated: ". . . the struggle with bureaucratism can only be accomplished by the wide active participation of professionally organized workers and employees. Production conferences and commissions in enterprises . . . are the best forum for involving the wide working mass in the activities of . . . improving the organization of enterprises . . . ."[60] The congress called for a further reduction in the size and cost of economic administrations. Throughtout 1926-1929, articles appeared in the union press urging the use of production meetings to achieve these goals.[61]

The revelations of Rabkrin investigations also contributed to the mounting criticisms of mismanagement and bureaucratism. The Central Committee's appeal on the regime of economy had charged Rabkrin with implementing the campaign. Under the direction of Peoples' Commissar Ordzhonikidze, national and local Rabkrin investigators actively ferreted out and exposed cases of waste and mismanagement. Rabkrin investigated the organization and efficiency of a wide array of offices. The studies, which were widely reported in the press, revealed that among managerial and clerical personnel tardiness was very widespread, that work habits were poor, and that few agencies had created systems of control designed to improve the discipline and efficiency of their staffs. In some cases, the problems were even more acute than among workers.[62] Coming as they did at a time when managers were driving workers to be more productive, efficient and disciplined, yet were reluctant to improve conditions that would make achieving these goals possible, these revelations confirmed many workers suspicions, fueled their hostility toward managerial personnel, and emboldened them to launch their own attack.

An August 1927 Sovnarkom resolution further encouraged workers and party cadres to expose factory administrative personnel's shortcomings. The resolution called for reducing administrative and management expenditures by a minimum of 20 percent by simplifying administrative structures and reducing staffs and wasteful expenditures.[63] Although aimed at reducing bureaucratic costs and bureaucratism in general, workers and many rank and file party cadres interpreted the law in their own particular way.

What accounts for the more urgent tone in the drive against mismanagement? Quite possibly, it was a scapegoating technique used to deflect criticisms from the regime's policies to those who executed them. If successful, it would help to identify the party as workers' prime protector without compromising official demands for higher productivity. But this was not the only reason. The fact remains that many managerial personnel were either incompetent or improperly implemented state policies. Because the costs of their behavior fell most heavily on workers, their poor performance was both an economic and political issue. There was probably no single reason for this new tone which both productivists and radicals could support. It appealed to the former by focusing renewed attention on cost reductions and capital accumulation without compromising their insistence on higher worker productivity. And it appealed to the latter by more vigorously imploring workers to restrain managerial power and by distributing more equally the burden of the cost of capital accumulation. For both, the potential political losses were minimal and the potential gains substantial.

By 1926, then, workers were bringing to production meetings deepening senses of frustration, hostility, and anger. Over the past few years, the growth of their living standard had been slow and subject to reverses. During the same period, official labor policy demanded continually higher worker productivity. Yet management, which was quick to demand greater productivity and fire workers, was slow to improve their work conditions that would ease their burden, reduce the accident rate, and make higher productivity possible. Legitimizing workers' rising hostility toward their bosses was the mounting public campaign by the party, unions and state agencies to expose and reduce managerial abuses and inefficiency. This campaign together with that against bureaucratism and Rabkrin's public reports worked to create a climate of official opinion that condoned, even encouraged, criticism of industrial management.

What pushed this rather narrow campaign for improve managerial efficiency far beyond those bounds was the support given to angry workers by the *lenintsy*. Unlike most of their predecessors for whom party membership was often synonomous with promotion out of the factory and into the bureaucracy, the majority of new party members were workers who remained at their job. While the party attempted to break down its newest members' "shop consciousness" and to inculcate in them, among other things, a less Manichean and more dialectical view of the respective roles of workers and managers in industrial production, these new worker-communists continued to share with their co-workers a deep antipathy toward managerial personnel. The increasing frequency with which party members urged participants at production meetings to criticize such personnel indicates that these new communists took the appeal to reduce administrative costs and bureaucratism very seriously.[64] That failure to expose and correct cases of bureaucratism and management's violations of the labor laws could result in expulsion from the party provided further impetus for them to do so. Often cajoled into attending production meetings by party and union activists, beginning in 1926 workers arrived there to find these co-workers, cloaked in the status and protection that their newly acquired party membership afforded, criticizing management and technical personnel.

During 1926-1928, workers at production meetings expressed their anger and frustration with their bosses and *spetsy* with increasing frequency and virulence. Workers and management each resented the way in which the one treated the other. Managers complained that workers lacked labor discipline, spoke to them rudely, showed no respect, and displayed little evidence of a willingness to cooperate. Workers countered these charges by arguing that "it is not only us who are rude but so are they [managers—W. C.] . . . foremen are especially rude." Workers resented that their bosses treated them in a condescending manner reminiscent of pre-revolutionary interpersonal relations. This condescension manifested itself in ways other than daily interaction. They complained that technical personnel ignored production meetings called by the factory committee, but when the director gave an order for such a conference, "all are present" (*vse nalitso*). They also resented the fact that managers and specialists belittled workers' knowledge and ignored their suggestions, but then "appropriated the workers' own recommendations" for improving production. That managers and *spetsy* demanded a better utilization of the workday, higher productivity and a reduction of waste without properly understanding the problems of or limits of the machinery and tools angered workers. One textile worker at a production meeting stated: "You say that we are poor workers, but our answer to you is that you are poor bosses. . . . The director never goes through the departments, he never sees what machines framers work on. . . . The result of this is that workers and production both suffer."[65]

Workers' complaints extended beyond the factory gates. Those workers who lived in factory barracks criticized managers for neglecting to improve the living conditions there. They were quick to link these conditions with managerial complaints about the quality of production and rates of productivity. One worker stated: "You demand a better utilization of the workday, but look at the horrible conditions of life in the barracks."[66] Surely the high salaries, better housing, and more opulent life-style of their bosses only intensified these criticisms.

While verbal complaints rose in number and intensity, so too did the incidence of threats against and physical assaults on managers and especially *spetsy*. At the Dzerzhinskii factory in 1927, technical personnel lived in fear of assault and rarely ventured into the shops alone. When the director of the Sverdlov factory made his round of the shops, he came upon a female worker who, in the presence of a large number of workers, said: "I will mangle your snout, so that your wife and children won't know you."[67] The union official who reported the incident attributed the deterioration of factory personnel relations to the influx of new workers who lacked respect and labor discipline and who were often drunk when such confrontations occurred. To a certain extent, this was no doubt the case. That skilled workers were sometimes the objects of new workers' hostility lends credibility to this explanation. But many workers, urban workers and new workers alike, each for his/her own reasons, harbored deep antipathy toward his/her supervisors and could point to official policy to justify expressing it. In fact, what is most significant about the workers' growing antimanagement sentiment was that it provided a common ground on which workers could stand united.

Then in March 1928 news of the Shakhty affair broke. The affair centered on the alleged sabotage of the coal industry by several German and fifty Russian engineers. Both before and during the six-week trial in May and June, the press prominently discussed these "bourgeois specialists" conspiracy with foreign agents and former capitalist mine owners to weaken the Soviet coal industry in preparation for foreign, capitalist

intervention. Among the acts of sabotage committed by these "bourgeois" *spetsy* were "unnecessary waste of capital, lowering the quality of
production, raising the cost of production" and undermining the working and safety conditions of workers. Given the similarity between the
charges and demands of prevailing policy, which they improperly executed, many *spetsy* and other managerial personnel must have wondered
if they too qualified as saboteurs. Such was surely the desired effect of
the trial. Krylenko, the prosecutor, "gave full rein to the resentment of
workers towards their supervising engineers" by quoting workers' state-
ments that these *spetsy*) persecuted them and were the "vampires of the
working class."[68] During the trial, more than 100,000 spectators, many
of whom were workers and party and Komsomol members, attended.
For those unable to attend, the daily press provided detailed coverage.
All but four of the accused were found guilty.

The evidence suggests that the Shakhty trial was a show trial organized by Stalin and his supporters to justify their mounting political
campaign against "bourgeois" specialists, managerial incompetence and
their political rivals. Whether or not the accused were guilty is irrelevant
to this study. The trial's importance rests in the fact that it confirmed
many workers' belief that their bosses too were "vampires of the working
class" and enemies of the workers' state. The trial was not a revelation;
it was proof.

The trial was also of profound political importance. It ignited a new
wave of specialist-baiting and conflicts with manangement and temporarily destroyed many specialists' and managers' power to control workers' behavior. It thereby created a new opportunity for workers to assert
some control over their productive lives. However, united though they
were against management, different groups of workers had different conceptions of how best to achieve that goal. Urban workers, who dominated the factory committees and production meetings, sought to use
those institutions to regain some of their lost power. New workers did
so by working the way they saw fit. The result of their behavior was a
sharp deterioration of labor discipline that undermined the efforts of
urban workers.

Finally, the trial forged a tacit alliance between workers, party radicals and other party members who, in 1928-1929, demanded a change
in state policy. For workers and radicals, the trial provided the proof that
their accusations and criticisms of "bourgeois" managers and specialists
were legitimate. For Stalin and his supporters, it provided a rationale
with which to criticize those who had endorsed and defended the use of

these *spetsy*. The workers finally had some powerful, if only temporary, allies.

On June 3, 1928—while the Shakhty trial was still underway—the Central Committee issued an appeal to all party members and workers entitled "On the development of self-criticism." The appeal stated: "The problems of the reconstruction period [post-1925-W. C.] . . . will not be resolved without courage, decisiveness, and the consistent introduction of the masses into the affairs of socialist construction, the verification and control of the whole apparatus on the part of these millions, (and) the cleansing of unfit elements [from the apparat-W. C.]." The appeal went on to speak of the importance of criticism and self-criticism (*kritika-samokritika*) in the revitalization of production meetings and the struggle against bureaucratism, the definition of which had taken on a new and broader meaning in the aftermath of the Shakhty affair, the contemporaneous Moscow Labor Exchange corruption scandal, and the onset of the cultural revolution.[69]

Although the official watchword of the *kritika-samokritika* campaign was "do not look at the individual" (*ne vziraia na litsa*)—that is, focus on the performance not the personality of the person being criticized—the atmosphere of the times did little to discourage the the settling of scores or the attacking of supervisors perceived by workers as class enemies.[70] Class animosity, vindictiveness, and jealousy appear to have motivated participants in criticism and self-criticism sessions as much as, and in some cases more than, an objective assessment of the situation at hand. The tone of the campaign in the factories can be easily gleaned from the following appeal addressed to workers at the Serp i molot plant: "the slogan of self-criticism . . . is a call to workers in all branches, all organs of the proletarian dictatorship . . . to strengthen the struggle of the mass of workers with bureaucratism, ineconomy, sloppiness, and the arrogant attitudes of bosses (*chinovniki*) to workers' inquiries."[71]

The criticism and self-criticism campaign created new problems for production meeting organizers. Official policy demanded that production meetings should be forums in which workers' participation acted as a corrective to mismanagement while, at the same time, workers and managers cooperated in the struggle to increase productivity and reduce costs. But, during the second half of 1928, it was the former charge which attracted most participants' attention. The official campaign against bourgeois *spetsy* begun in 1928 unleashed such a wave of worker denunciations of theirsupervisors that, in November of that year, a

Pravda editorial complained that all specialists and managers were being treated like class enemies.[72] In this atmosphere, the other purpose of production meetings—to reduce costs in cooperation with management—was neglected, and in some cases rejected. Production commissions proved unable to properly direct the rising tide of worker discontent and to restore labor discipline. Whether their inability to accomplish the former reflects their sympathy with workers' grievances, their inability to control the meetings, or their confusion in the face of seemingly contradictory official policy is unclear.

The All-Union Review

In late 1928, production meetings veered sharply away from their officially charted course and became battlegrounds in a mounting class war. By so doing, they compromised the meetings' intended purposes. To correct the deficiences of production meetings and those responsible for their organization, *Pravda* announced in October 1928 an All-Union review (*smotr*) of production meetings. The stated purposes of the review were: to expose the shortcomings of production meetings and the poor direction of these meetings by union and party organizers; to invigorate these meetings; to involve all workers in the meetings; and to persuade factory and trust administrators, managers, and union and party organizers to develop "a more attentive attitude to production meetings." The review was to be a "mass campaign" to evaluate and eliminate the problems of production meetings. To accomplish this, all enterprises were to organize review commissions at the shop and factory level. Members of the commissions were to include representatives of the party organization, factory committee, the editorial collegium of the factory newspaper (*stengazet*), production commissions, and the engineering and technical personnel. The review commissions were charged with involving the mass of workers in the review process.[73]

The review, which began in October 1928 and was to be completed by March 1929, suffered from some of the same problems that plagued earlier production meetings. One of the major problems was organization. Throughout January and early February 1929, *Pravda* ran numerous articles that criticized the bureaucratism and lack of planning by those organs responsible for the review. Among those singled out for criticism was the Moscow *Guberniia* Council of Trade Unions and its newspaper, *Rabochaia Moskva*. To remedy the problem, *Pravda* called for a "massive verification" (*proverka*) of review commissions in the capital. The purpose of the *proverka* was to purge the "wreckers" of the review—"economic administrators, trade unionists, and party members not aiding in the review work."[74] Throughout the review campaign, articles in *Pravda* repeatedly criticized the failures and shortcomings exhibited by review's union organizers. Individual factories in which the review proceeded too slowly or in an unsatisfactory manner also came under fire.[75] But the most virulent denunciations were reserved for those factories in which review commissions existed only on paper: "The inactivity of review commissions is the worst form of bureaucratism, it is bureaucratism by the organizations created to struggle with bureaucratism." Such behavior was "sabotage."[76]

The review commissions proved unable to focus on the task at hand, that is, evaluating production meetings, apparently because those in attendance interpreted the review meetings as an expanded version of production meetings. Criticisms of managerial and technical personnel punctuated workers' discussions and suggestions of production problems, factory and shop organization, lack of proper tools and instruments, and conditions of daily life. *Pravda* complained about such wide-ranging discussions and admonished its readers: "This is incorrect . . . review commissions are not registrars but military organs" charged with a specific duty.[77]

When discussions did focus on the problems of production meetings, workers' criticisms often focused on economic administrators, managers and *spetsy*. One worker asked, what was the point of the review? The real problem with "our production meetings," he stated, was the "negligent attitude of economic administrators (*khoziaistvenniki*)." Other workers complained about specialists who either did not care about production meetings and therefore did not attend them or, if they did attend, were unprepared. As was the case in the past, workers also criticized managerial personnel for ignoring suggestions put forth by workers at production meetings: "in three years they have not carried out one suggestion." Workers perceived, probably quite correctly, that the major concern of managers was the plant's industrial and financial plan.[78]

One of the goals of the review was to involve as many workers as possible, ideally all workers. Judging from published reports, worker participation was very high, ranging from 40 percent in some factories to 100 percent in others. Once again, Moscow's textile workers and metalworkers were among the most active.[79] One reason for the high and widely varying rates of participation appears to have been the extent of organization. In well-organized factories, party and union activists and the factory newspaper not only explained the review's purpose and disseminated the meetings' results, they also pressured workers to attend.[80] Another reason for increased participation appears to have been the workers' perception of the review's purpose. If the wide-ranging topics of discussion are a reliable indication of workers' perceptions, many workers saw the review as a forum for assessing production life and relations in general. And then there were specific issues such as the introduction of the seven-hour, three-shift workday and its attendant problems in the textile industry.

Finally, the unleashing of worker discontent and attacks on managerial personnel temporarily muted the differences between urban and new workers and semiproletarians and by so doing, encouraged the latter two groups to attend the meetings. When groups of workers joined forces, whether in 1928-1929 or in 1917-1918, they were volatile and powerful allies. What gave that alliance its power was their mutual antipathy toward management. But what limited its' power were the allies' different demands and perspectives. In 1928-1929 as in 1918, new workers' labor indiscipline undermined urban workers efforts to extend their power.

Although the review campaign's stated purpose was to review and to invigorate production meetings, the contemporaneous cultural revolution, mounting and officially sanctioned class war, struggle against bureaucratism, attacks on the "right deviation" in the party and unions, party purge (*chistka*) of 1929, and onset of the First Five-Year Plan raises a host of questions about the role of the review campaign in the wider upheavals in the party and society. A full treatment of the period is beyond the scope of this work, but two observations deserve note.

First, the review of production meetings was an integral part and a reflection of the general upheavals in Soviet society. It was a struggle against "bourgeois enemies," such as economic administrators managers and specialists as well as party and union activists, whose negligence, formalism, or bureaucratism frustrated the realization of party policy and the initiative of conscious workers. Workers played an active role in this struggle. To use the parlance of the period, the review was another front in the battle against the enemies of the party line. Second, party leaders who organized the campaign employed a tactic common to the entire period—appealing to the masses over the heads of officials responsible for the execution of policy so as to identify those elements in the factory (or society at large) who obstructed the realization of party policy and promises. In so doing, these leaders often unleashed the wrath of frustrated workers.

One aspect of the review deserves special note. The unions were responsible for production meetings. Yet it was the unions, and VTsSPS in particular, which were the big losers in the review. Not only were union leaders often labeled defenders and propagaters of the "right deviation" within the party, but the review also laid much of the blame for the production meetings' and review's shortcomings on the doorstep of union leaders and activists. Given the splits within the party leadership at the time, it is unclear to what extent this was one of the review's purposes. Like production meetings, the review probably attracted a wide spectrum of supporters who saw it as a means of confronting, if not rectifying, an equally wide array of problems.

The purposes of production meetings were to correct the deficiencies of management and to raise productivity. Judged by this criteria, the meetings were not very successful. The mounting attack on management did not eliminate mismanagement and gave rise to labor indiscipline. The increased productivity during the late 1920s resulted more from the implementation of labor policy than from worker input. But to state that rank and file party members or workers subverted the intent of the party leadership regarding the role of production meetings would be facile. It is unlikely that production meetings satisfied anyone: leaders, activists, managers, or workers. The direction which the meetings and review ultimately took was probably less the product of any hidden agenda on the part of party leaders and activists than an authentic expression of the widespread worker discontent over long-standing grievances—grievances which many activists shared. In the process, the uneasy social balance in the factories was destroyed.

Production meetings were initiated in 1923-1924 to overcome managerial "incompetence" and to realize the "proper" relationship between one-man management and workers' control. They failed to achieve either. Although they were to be forums in which workers' organs would cooperate with management in enacting official policies, until 1926 deep-seated worker suspicions over the meetings' purposes coupled with poor leadership and organization undermined their legitimacy, limited their size, hampered theireffectiveness, and virtually precluded cooperation between workers and managers. By 1928-1929, emboldened by their *lenintsy* co-workers' example, the official campaigns against "bourgeois" specialists, managerial incompetence and bureaucratism, and the Shakhty trial, workers pushed the meetings beyond their prescribed purposes and transformed them from forums for cooperation into battle-grounds in a mounting class war. This was not the party leadership's original intention, but it was the logical consequence of its policies. Having unleashed the workers' discontent, restraining it proved difficult.

The result was escalating chaos in the factories in 1928-1929. Often fearful of even venturing into shops at a time when they were the state's and workers' enemy, many "bourgeois" specialists temporarily lost or abdicated their control over production. Paralyzed by the contradictory demands to increase production and to unmask "bourgeois" sabotage and by growing worker militance, many factory directors often did nothing. Workers' unwillingness to defer to their bosses undermined all hopes of establishing the "proper" balance between them. The deterioration of labor discipline among new workers undermined urban workers' efforts to strengthen their institutional power. In the late 1920s as in 1917-1918, the temporary alliance between politically active, disciplined, urban workers and undisciplined, new workers against their common enemy—"bourgeois" managerial personnel—transformed factory relations and disrupted production. But by unleashing workers' discontent, the party unconsciously spurred labor indiscipline at a time when the realization of the Five-Year Plan demanded greater labor discipline.

To overcome these problems, the party moved simultaneously on several fronts. Throughout 1929, the party leadership conducted a sustained campaign to enforce the "proper" application of one-man management. The campaign culminated in a Central Committee special resolution that called for the "establishment and consolidation of one-man management (*edinonachalie*)."[81] But as the contemporaneous All-Union review of production meetings indicates, the September resolution's purpose was not to transform factory directors into dictators, but to create the "proper" relationship between one-man management and workers' control. The successful application of these policies would reverse both the deterioration of factory relations and labor discipline. So too would the proper implementation of the simultaneous campaigns to intiate mass shock work and socialist competitions, the goals of which were to increase labor productivity and discipline. But in the highly charged atmosphere of the cultural revolution, class war, and the First Five-Year Plan, and the high degree of mobility which accompanied each, the realization of these goals remained beyond the party leadership's reach.

Although in the process it had unleashed forces which it had not always desired or intended, on balance the party emerged from 1928-

1929 with renewed power and influence in the factories. It was the party not the unions which had reinvigorated factory politics and led the workers' assault on managerial personnel. The party had once again placed itself in the vanguard of the proletariat. But in 1928-1929 as in 1917-1918, workers had proven more radical than the party and had often pushed it beyond its intended role. Then as earlier, the workers' and party leadership's agendas overlapped. But rooted as they were in different historical and political experiences, they were not identical.

Party-worker relations in the late 1920s were not the only area that provides a sense of historical *déjà vu*. Precisely when there emerged from the proletariat a valuable and respected cadre of factory leaders, other processes drained their ranks. Beginning in 1928-1929, the mass exodus of workers from the factories into educational institutions, factory administrative positions, and party, union and state bureaucratic positions siphoned off those leaders precisely at the time when workers most needed them to successfully press their demands. In 1928-1929 as in 1917-1920, individual workers' upward mobility weakened the working class' ability to enact their revolutionary agenda.

Notes

1. *5-i gubernskii s"ezd Moskovskikh profsoiuzov* (Moscow, 1923), 6.

2. The proportion of Moscow metal workers who paid union dues rose from 10 percent on October 1, 1923 to 43 percent on January 1, 1924 to 95 percent by April 1, 1924. *Moskovskii proletarii*, May 25, 1925, 5.

3. *Trud v Moskovskii gubernii*, 272-280, especially 274; *Moskovskii proletarii*, May 11, 1924, 1; January 10, 1926, 2-3.

4. The lack of worker participation at meetings is discussed in *Professional'nye soiuzy, 1924-1926*, 67-68; *Moskovskii proletarii*, March 27, 1924, 2. On the factory meeting lock-up, see *ibid.*, June 1, 1924. The factory was the Napilnik plant.

5. See the discussion in chapter 6 and Lampert, 33-34. For a different assessment of the assessment and conflict commissions, see the interview with worker no. 19 in Zawodny.

6. For a discussion, see Sorenson, 193.

7. *Moskva i Moskovskaia guberniia*, 130-131; *Statisticheskii spravochnik . . . 1927*, 184-185.

8. See the report of Mel'nichanskii to the 8th All-Union Congress of Textile Workers in *Izvestiia tekstil'noi promyshlennosti i torgovli*, 4 (1928), 27-29.

9. As quoted in Deutscher, *Soviet Trade Unions*, 77.

10. For example, see: *Moskovskii proletarii*, February 3, 1926, 10-11; *Trud*, December 17, 1926; *Professional'nye soiuzy, 1924-1926*, VIII-IX.

11. *Professional'nye soiuzy, 1924-1926*, VII-IX.

12. For discussions and examples of elections, see *Moskovskii proletarii*, April 14, May 21, July 7, July 28, 1926. See also: *Professional'nye soiuzy, 1924-1926*, 64-67; Dewar, 151.

13. Worker no. 19, Zawodny.

14. For example, in early 1924, there were only fifty communists at the Krasnyi proletarii factory and few worked in production, N. Marmershtein, ed., *Slavnye traditsii: K 100-letiiu zavoda "Krasnyi proletarii" imeni A. I. Efremova* (Moscow, 1957), 113-114. At Serp i molot, there were 107 party members, twenty of whom did not work at the factory but in other organizations. Most of the remaining members were administrators. Poselianina, "Leninskii prizyv," *Bor'ba klassov*, 1 (1934), 142-143. Both of these were large factories; the situation in smaller plants was surely no better.

15. As quoted in Bettleheim, *Class Struggles in the USSR, First Period*, 322; see the discussion on 311-325. See also Carr, *Bolshevik Revolution*, I, 311-319. This discussion of the Lenin levy is based on Rigby, 110-131. See also: *KPSS v rezoliutsiiakh i resheniiakh s"ezdov, konferentsii i plenumov TsK*, 4 vols. (Moscow, 1954-1960), I, 771-778; S. L. Dmitrenko, "Sostav mestnykh partiinykh komitetov v 1924-1927gg.," *Istoricheskie zapiski*, 79 (1967), 77-108, esp. 78-89. In January 1924, workers by occupation accounted for only 18.8 percent of party members; workers by social origin accounted for 44 percent. Rigby, 116.

16. *Moskovskaia gorodskaia i Moskovskaia oblastnaia organizatsiia KPSS v tsifrakh* (Moscow, 1972), 37, 46-47, 182-183; *Ocherki istorii moskovskoi KPSS: 1883-1965* (Moscow, 1966), 408-409, 431.

17. "*Dinamo*," II, 95; Poselianina, "Leninskii prizyv," 142-143; *Istoriia . . . Likacheva*, 114, 131; Kurkhantanov, 90; Bogdanovskii, 172; *Imeni Voitovicha* (Moscow, 1962), 44; *Moskovskii proletarii*, March 1, 1925, 21; Rodionova, 152-156; Suvorov, *Bor'ba*, 7-8.

18. *Ocherki istorii moskovskoi KPSS*, 410; Rodionova, *Gody napriazhennogo truda*, 156.

19. *Moskovskaia gorodskaia i Moskovskaia oblastniia organizatsii*, 46-47; *Ocherki istorii moskovskoi KPSS*, 408-409, 431; F. M. Vaganov, *KPSS v bor'be za uskorenie tempov sotsialisticheskogo stroitel'stva (1927-1929gg)* (Moscow, 1967), 98-99. From late 1924 until the end of the decade, the proportion of workers by social origin and occupation remained about the same—two-thirds and 48 percent respectively. During the October 1927 *Prizyv*, more than 12,000 workers from the bench joined the Moscow party organization. *Moskovskaia gorodskaia i Moskovskaia oblastniia organizatsiia*, 38.

20. *Ibid.*, 79, 84; *Politicheskii i trudovoi pod"em rabochego klassa SSSR (1928-1929gg.)* (Moscow, 1956), 38-39.

21. *Ocherkii istorii Moskovskoi KPSS*, 411; Rodionova, 54, 156-158; Suvorov, *Bor'ba*, 16.

22. *Profsoiuzy SSSR*, II, 338-339.

23. *Ibid.*, II, 339-340.

24. *Direktivy KPSS i sovetskogo pravitel'stva*, I, 442-445. Production

meetings were held at the shop or factory level; production conferences were those held at trust, union or interunion levels at which delegates from numerous enterprises were in attendance.

25. See the appeal from VSNKh and the Central Committee of the All-Russian Textile Syndicate in *Izvestiia tekstil'noi promyshlennosti i torgovli*, August 20, 1924, 6. For the VTsSPS resolution on producton meetings in enterprises, see *Trud*, September 23, 1924. For the TsKK-RKI instruction on the program for production meetings, see *ibid.*, August 12, 1924. Carr, *Socialism*, I, 427n.

26. *Profsoiuzy SSSR*, II, 339.

27. *Ibid.*, II, 353-355; *Trud*, September 23, 1924.

28. On the size and functions of producton commssions, see Mikhail Dynnik, "Proizvodstvennye soveshchaniia i NOT," *Vestnik truda*, 4 (1925), 90; Petrochenko and Kuznetsova, 64; Pav. Ioffe, "Proizvodstvennye soveshchaniia v 1-m polugodii 1926/27 khoz. goda," *Vestnik truda*, 12 (1927), 77, states that the average size of factory producton commissions nationwide was 13 members and that of shop production commissions was "half as big." Workers accounted for 62 percent of the members of factory commissions and 70 percent of those on shop commissions; technical personnel accounted for 26.5 percent and 18.5 percent respectively.

29. For a discussion of production meetings in the pre-1925 years, see: Genkina; V. Noskresenkaia and L. Novoselov, *Proizvodstvennye soveshchaniia—shkola upravleniia (1921-1965gg.)* (Moscow, 1965), 3-32; I. P. Ostapenko, *Uchastie rabochego klassa SSSR v upravlenii proizvodstvom (Proizvodstvennye soveshchaniia v promyshlennosti v 1921-1932gg.)* (Moscow, 1964), 17-59. For examples of union conferences, see: *Moskovskii proletarii*, May 25, 1924, 6-7; *Torgovo-promyshlennaia gazeta*, December 3, 1924; *Dokumenty trudovoi slavy*, dok. 38, 64-66; Safronov, "Proizvodstvennye konferentsii po Moskve," 176-179; Dynnik, 90-98; L. S. Rogachevskaia, "Rabota proizvodstvennykh soveshchanii v pervye gody industrializatsii (1926-1927)," *Istoricheskie zapiski*, 57 (1956), 255.

30. Matiugin, *Moskva*, 69, claims that as many as 32,000 participants had attended production meetings in Moscow by February 1925. This figure seems high considering the constant laments over the low level of participation. According to Rabkor (worker correspondent) reports in *Moskovskii proletarii*, August 31, 1924, 7, workers wanted to participate in production meetings but in many factories there were none.

31. Safrononv, "Proizvodstvennye konferentsii po Moskve," 176-179.

32. *Ibid.*; Dynnik, 90-98; *Ocherki istorii moskovskoi KPSS*, 436-437. These were among the topics recommended for discussion by a September 1924 VTsSPS resolution on production meetings. The resolution can be found in *Trud*, September 23, 1924.

33. *Direktivy KPSS i sovetskogo pravitel'stva*, I, 508-512. See also: V. Safronov, "Kak proshli proizvodstvennye konferentsii v Moskve," *Vestnik truda*, 2 (1927), 151-153; Lampert, 33.

34. Figures on the number in attendance at factory and shop level meetings vary. For example, Matiugin, *Moskva*, 69, claims that by February 1925

there had been 545 meetings with some 35,000 in attendance. Rodionova, 168-170, puts the number of conferences and meetings in 1925 at 850 and claims that there were more than 50,000 in attendance. According to Aleshchenko, *Moskovskii sovet*, 284, there were about 600 meetings and conferences with more than 65,000 in attendance. Rogachevskaia, "Rabota proizvodstvennykh soveshchanii," 255, puts the number of meetings in 1925 at 371 with 34,000 in attendance. Whether the above estimates of those in attendance represent the total number of participants or individuals is unclear. Given complaints about the low level of worker participation, I suspect that the figures represent total participants. For national (and some Moscow) figures, see *Professional'nye soiuzy SSSR, 1924-1926*, 65-76.

35. Dynnik, 90-98. The same observation was made by Gr. Faingold in an article entitled "Ne tol'ko slushaite, no i govorite" in *Moskovskii proletarii*, March 27, 1924, 2. However, Faingold was referring to factory committee meetings.

36. Dynnik, 90-98; *Professional'nye soiuzy SSSR, 1924-1926*, 73-76. See also Suvorov, *Bor'ba*, 20. According to *"Dinamo,"* II, 97, there were thirteen shop meetings held from April to June 1924 with the attendance at each ranging from 80 to 160.

37. See note 34 for sources.

38. For examples of suggestions and changes at the former Tsindel' textile plant, see Petrochenko and Kuznetsova, 63. For examples of the same at the Trekhgornaia textile plant, see A. Popov, "Ot pervogo kommunisticheskogo subbotnika—k stakhanovskomu dvizheniiu," *Bor'ba klassov*, 12 (1935), 23. For the same at the AMO plant, see: *Istoriia . . . Likacheva*, 132. For the same at Dinamo, see: *"Dinamo,"* II, 90; *Moskovskii proletarii*, March 27, 1924, 4. For the same at Moskabel' (former Russkabel'), see N. Khrestin, *Vyskokoe napriazheniie (Moskovskii kabel'nyi zavod)* (Moscow, 1962), 46-47. For the same at Serp i molot, see Petrochenko and Kuznetsova, 83. See also: *Moskovskii proletarii*, September 21, 1926, 22; Rodionova, 169-170.

39. For example, see: *"Dinamo,"* II, 90; Safronov, "Proizvodstvennye konferentsii po Moskve," 176-179. See the discussion in chapter 6.

40. *Moskovskii proletarii*, March 27, 1926, 4-5; and Dynnik, 90-98; both make special note of the tensions. However, Safronov, "Proizvodstvennye konferentsii po Moskve," 176, claims that at no conference—as opposed to factory or shop meeting—were there demagogic speeches or attacks on administrators (*khoziaistvenniki*).

41. *Izvestia tekstl'noi promyshlennosti i torgovli*, April 20, 1926.

42. *Torgovo-promyshlennaia gazeta*, February 24, 1926.

43. *Direktivy KPSS i sovetskogo pravitel'stva*, I, 578-583, 585-587. For a discussion of the regime of economy, see I. Suslov, "Za rezhim ekonomii," *Moskovskii proletarii*, June 17, 1926, 2.

44. For examples, see: Safronov, "Kak proshli," 151-154; Suvorov, *Bor'ba*, 64; Petrochenko and Kuznetsova, 81.

45. The report was entitled "On the successes and insufficiencies of the campaign for the regime of economy." *Direktivy KPSS i sovetskogo pravitel'stva*, I, 590-597, esp. 594; *Dokumenty trudovoi slavy*, dok. 43, 71-74.

46. *Direktivy KPSS i sovetskogo pravitel'stva*, I, 594-595.

47. Suvorov, *Bor'ba*, 44.

48. For national estimates, see Rogachevskaia, "Rabota proizvodstvennykh soveshchanii," 269. The figures for Moscow can be found in *Dokumenty trudovoi slavy*, dok. 27, 50-51. Comparable rates of attendance in 135 textile plants can be found in Suvorov, *Bor'ba*, 22.

49. *Dokumenty trudovoi slavy*, dok. 23, 43-44; dok. 27, 50-51; *Professional'nye soiuzy SSSR, 1926-1928*, 68-69; *Pervyi shagi industrializatsii SSSR, 1926-1927gg.* (Moscow, 1959), 335-341, 372-376; *"Dinamo,"* II, 124-125; Rogachevskaia, "Rabota proizvodstvennykhsoveshchanii," 270; Suvorov, *Bor'ba*, 22.

50. *Moskovskaia gorodskaia i Moskovskaia oblastnaia organizatsiia*, 37, 42-47, 182-183; *Ocherki istorii moskovskoi organizatsii*, 408-409, 431. For discussions of the impact of the Lenin levy in specific factories, see: *"Dinamo,"* II, 95; Poselianina, "Leninskii prizyv," 142-143; *Istoriia . . . Likacheva*, 90; V. Bogdanovskii, *Imeni Vladimira Il'icha* (Moscow, 1962), 172; Khrestin, 44; *Imeni Votovicha* (Moscow, 1969), 129. See also: *Moskovskii proletarii*, March 1, 1925; *Politicheskii i trudovoi pod"em*, dok. 9, 38-39.

51. *Moskovskaia gorodskaia i Moskovskaia oblastnaia organizatsiia*, 38, 46-47; *Ocherki istorii moskovskoi organizatsii*, 408-410, 431.

52. *Direktivy KPSS i sovetskogo pravitel'stva*, I, 666-672; *Moskovskii proletarii*, January 10, March 15, June 9, July 28, 1926. V. Safronov, "Chto pokazlo obsledovanie proizvodstvennykh soveshchanii i komissii v Moskvy," *Vestnik truda*, 1 (1927), 94-96.

53. *Dokumenty trudovoi slavy*, dok. 23, 43-44; dok. 48, 81-84; *Pervyi shagi*, 372-376, 410-418; Safronov, "Kak proshli," 151-154.

54. *Pervyi shagi*, 375, puts the rate of attendance by youth at 40 to 45 percent of all factory youth.

55. *Ibid.*, 338.

56. *Ibid.; Dokumenty trudovoi slavy*, dok. 23, 43-44; dok. 29, 53; dok. 30, 53-54; dok. 32, 55; *"Dinamo,"* II, 124; *Ekonomicheskaia zhizn'*, October 14, 1925; Rogachevskaia, "Rabota proizvodstvennykh soveshchanii," 273.

57. *Izvestiia tekstil'noi promyshlennosti i torgovli*, April 20, 1926.

58. *Pervyi shagi*, 302-304, 335-341, 483-499; *Dokumenty trudovoi slavy*, dok. 27, 50-51; Rogachevskaia, "Rabota proizvodstvennykh soveshchanii," 267.

59. For a discussion of these tensions, see: Bailes, *Technology and Society*, 44-69; Lampert, 12-37.

60. As quoted in B. Kozelov, "Osnovaia direktiva VII s"ezda," *Vestnik truda*, 1 (1927), 5-6.

61. For example, see: *ibid.*, 5-14; *Moskovskii proletarii*, July 20, 1927.

62. V. Novikov, "O trudovoi distsipline," *Voprosy truda*, 10 (1926), 3-6; Ia. Morozov, "Trudovaia distsipline v Moskovskikh uchrezhdeniiakh," *ibid.*, 7 (1927), 117-120; S. N. Ikonnikov, *Sozdanie i deiatel'nost' ob"edinennykh organov TsKK-RKI v 1923-1934gg.* (Moscow, 1971), 175-214.

63. *SZ*, 1927, 53/542.

64. For an example of such behavor at Serp i molot, see Poselianina, "Leninskii prizyv," 145.

65. Antronov, 2.

66. *Ibid.*

67. I. Tolstopiatov, "Truddistsiplina i proguly," 21-25. For representative discussions of mounting tensions and the reasons for them, see: V. Safronov, "Kak proshli," 151-153; Antronov; *Pervye shagi,* dok. 33, 335-341; dok. 50, 373-374; dok. 62, 417-418; *Politicheskii i trudovoi pod"em,* dok. 73, 124-126; A. Stopani, "Nashi zadachi v bor'be s biurokratizm," *Voprosy truda, 2 (1927), 3-7; I.* Maizel, "Massovaia ekonrabota soiuzov (k itogam VII s"ezda profsoiuzov," *Vestnik truda,* 3 (1927), 69-75; Bailes, *Technology and Society),* 44-94 passim.

68. As quoted in Bailes, *Technology and Society,* 91-92. For a discussion of the Shakhty trial, see *ibid.,* 69-94.

69. *Pravda,* June 3, 1928; Fitzpatrick, "Cultural Revolution," 8-40.

70. *Pravda,* November 11, 1928.

71. *Politicheskii i trudovoi pod"em,* dok. 73, 124-126. See also, *ibid.,* dok. 23, 57-58; dok. 31, 66-69. For a discussion of the campaign at the AMO plant, see *Istoriia . . . Likacheva,* 145-148.

72. *Pravda,* November 11, 1928.

73. *Ibid.,* October 25, October 28, 1928; January 3, January 16, 1929.

74. *Ibid.,* January 8, February 3, 1929.

75. For examples, see *ibid.,* January 3, January 4, January 11, January 18, January 31, February 8, March 1, 1929.

76. *Ibid.,* January 6, January 11, 1929.

77. *Ibid.,* January 4, January 9, January 12, 1929; *Politicheskii i trudovoi pod"em, dok. 78, 132-133; dok. 81, 135-137.*

78. *Pravda,* January 12, February 14, 1929.

79. For examples, see: *ibid.,* January 8, March 1, March 2, March 5, 1929; *Politicheskii i trudovoi pod"em,* dok. 72, 123-124; dok. 77, 129-131; dok. 81, 135-137; dok. 90, 155-156.

80. *Pravda,* January 27, January 30, 1929; *Politicheskii i trudovi pod"em,* dok. 89, 153-155.

81. For a discussion of one-man management in 1928-1929, see Hiroaki Kuromiya, "Edinonachalie and the Soviet Industrial Manager, 1928-1937," *Soviet Studies,* 36, 2 (April 1984), 185-204.

8. Thoughts on Changing Relations between the Working Class and Party

Collectivities do not partition their historical experience according to the metronomic time of the calender, but according to some deeper, qualitative, psychological sense of time. For Moscow's workers, the 1920s actually began in mid-1921 with the end of the War Communism and the Civil War; it ended in early 1929 amidst the frenzied outbursts of the First Five-Year Plan era. It is less easy to characterize the salient qualities that gave the period its psychological unity, the way in which Moscow workers remembered it. This is because, during the 1920s, itself a period of transition, the working class underwent significant changes. Continually inundated by new workers and subjected to centrifugal and centripetal forces set in motion by the demands and frustrations of daily life and official policies, it was often deeply divided over some issues and united around others.

Two broad themes emerge, however. The first is the unfolding of class consciousness of Moscow's workers from the Civil War to the First Five-Year Plan. The term class consciousness means more than the general tautology that classes, being composed of conscious human beings, display a class consciousness. Rather, the term is used as Marx used it when he wrote of a class being conscious first "of itself" as a class and then "for itself," that is, conscious of its distinctive interests and role. The 1920s began with the destruction of this latter form of consciousness and presents the story of its re-emergence as a political force.

The second theme, which is intertwined with the first, is the vicissitudes in the relations between Moscow's working class and the party. The revolutionary agenda of the working class and that of the party, springing as they did from different historical and experiential sources, remained qualitatively different. But by no means were they exclusive;

293

on the contrary, they intersected on key items. As the class consciousness of Moscow's workers re-emerged and as they began to articulate their revolutionary agenda more precisely, these qualitative differences and outward similarities came more and more to the fore, especially in the latter half of the 1920s. The subsequent integration of the agendas in 1928-1929 heralded the end of one era and the beginning of another.

Under the political leadership of the Bolsheviks, the triumph of 1917-1918 had led workers from a consciousness of the need to defend their rights as workers to the brink of a vision of themselves as the shapers of a new society, if not a new civilization. An undifferentiated hopefulness and confidence had permeated and galvanized the class as a whole.

The chaos of the Civil War years destroyed that hopefulness and confidence and turned their dreams of a socialism of abundance into nightmares of poverty, misery, disease and near-starvation. Whereas workers collectively experienced the euphoria of revolution, they often struggled individually to overcome the chaos and desperation of the Civil War years. Those bitter years left deep scars on those Muscovites who endured them. They also left legacies that profoundly affected factory and urban life during the 1920s.

With the disintegration of Moscow's revolutionary working class of 1917-1918 came the dissolution of its consciousness and revolutionary solidarity. Shorn of its leaders, transformed in its composition, and forced into the daily struggle for individual survival, working class consciousness gave way to individual strategies hastily fashioned to overcome the immediate situation. When unrest erupted in early 1921, workers offered little evidence of class consciousness. Their primary demand—food—reflected the collective demand of hungry individuals. Condemnations abounded, but gone was the ability manifested just a few years earlier to articulate clearly their broad demands and to organize themselves to achieve them. Moscow's working class in 1921 was not only quantitatively different from that of 1917-1918, it was also qualitatively different.

As the economic situation deteriorated during 1918-1921, so too did worker-party relations. Animated by a sense of its historic mission and the need to preserve the revolution, the party vainly sought to arrest the economic collapse by asserting increasingly centralized control. At the point of production, War Communism translated into relentless calls for undernourished workers to raise production and the replacing of the workers' vision of workers' control with unrestrained one-man management. Because well-intentioned regulations designed to ameliorate deepening crises accomplished little, and often exacerbated the problems, the party's revolutionary rhetoric sounded ever more hollow. Because it had tied itself to a diastrous policy, the party assumed *de facto* responsibility for the crisis.

By early 1921, Moscow's workers had yet to repudiate the revolution, if only because so many of them had become its accomplices. But the historic partnership with the Bolsheviks that had produced the victory of 1917 was over. A profound breach separated the former allies and a deep alienation replaced the precocious class consciousness of 1917-1918.

In 1921, the task of economic restoration commenced. To hasten recovery, the state implemented a series of policies designed to reduce production costs, maximize industrial productivity and efficiency, and speed capital accumulation—*khozrachet,* industrial concentration, forced staff reductions, the withdrawal of industrial subsidies, tying wages to productivity, raising output norms, and increasing the number of machines which workers operated. By 1925/26, these policies restored the economy to prewar levels. This was the NEP's great achievement. But success had its price. Fewer workers labored in the city's factories. Unemployment soared. Once-productive adults found themselves idle and hard-pressed to make ends meet. Much of a generation of youth watched helplessly as their dreams for productive lives slipped away. Many women, welcomed by employers in 1918-1921, found the doors to productive futures slammed in their faces. Only the doors to their small, overcrowded apartments remained open and what entered was not hope, but endless sources of anxiety, gnawing realities that drove increasing numbers of them to lash out in frustration.

Pressured to work more intensively, groups of workers found themselves pitted against one another. New workers' lack of labor discipline endangered and frustrated the more experienced and disciplined workers. As more and more new workers infiltrated production, tensions between them and urban workers mounted. Older, skilled workers resented the steady intensification and division of labor and those younger workers who actively embraced these processes.

Divided though they were over certain issues, other aspects of factory and daily life worked to unite workers or groups of workers. The slow, uneven improvement in wages until mid-decade angered virtually all workers and gave rise to wildcat strikes and escalating numbers of labor disputes. So too did the slow rate at which factories, shops, machinery, and equipment improved. What made the slow pace especially galling was that ameliorating these conditions was essential to meeting demands for higher productivity. Underlying these common grievances was workers' resentment of their bosses. Seemingly always willing to cut costs and quick to raise production norms, factory managers were slow to make the necessary improvements, heed workers' suggestions, and give them the respect they deserved. As the housing crisis deepened, frustrated workers turned against their "bourgeois" neighbors—nepmen, specialists, professionals—whose relative comfort stood as a vivid reminder of revolutionary hopes dashed. Fueled by the inequities at home and at work and the press coverage given them, the embers of class war smoldered in workers.

Because it was simultaneously divided and united over important issues, expressions of worker discontent remained amorphous, diffuse, and poorly articulated in the early 1920s. Although they resorted to wildcat strikes and carried their disputes to arbitation and grievance boards, these tactics addressed only specific problems. Work and its discontents generated considerable unrest, but the increasing routinization of industrial conflict dealt only with the symptoms of deeper problems. What workers lacked in the early 1920s was a legitimate and powerful political arena in which to expose what some viewed as the root causes of their and their factories' problems.

In spite of these deepening divisions, the economic recovery of the early 1920s released Moscow's working class from the necessity of concentrating on the immediate struggle for daily survival. Out of that breathing spell a consciousness of its own distinctive class interests slowly began to emerge. Given time and a modicum of stability, the workers' revolutionary agenda would also again emerge.

Likewise, their alienation from the party was lessening. The simple fact was that things had improved, and substantially so since 1921. Equally as important was that the NEP by its very nature had absolved, to a certain degree, the party from direct responsibility for many of the problems of factory and economic life. In contrast to the party's direct control of the economy during War Communism, impersonal market forces increasingly determined the course of the NEP economy. The "boss," not the party, became the personified focus of Moscow workers' economic discontent.

For its part, the party had weathered the storm. The menacing unrest of early 1921 had evaporated in the economic warming that followed the adoption of the NEP. But the NEP was not a happy solution for the party. Even the most cursory reading of Marx revealed that many NEP policies could only inflame working-class discontent. Regardless of whether one took a radical or gradualist position on the issue of the pace of socialist transformation, further alienating the workers was a dangerous course for a party that had come to power on an almost exclusively working-class base of support. Furthermore, there were growing disagreements within the party as to whether NEP policies could generate sufficient internal investment to sustain steady economic development and what the social costs of those policies were. And there was the painful paradox of the world's toughest-minded socialists defending the NEP as a suitable instrument of socialist transformation. Regardless of where one stood on these issues, one political reality had to be faced: the party's historic alliance with the working class had to be strengthened.

The turning point came in 1924-1925. The Lenin levy in 1924 offered workers admission to the most powerful political institution, the "real god." Many urban workers availed themselves of these new opportunities. There was good reason for them to do so. By 1924, any workers who had overcome their own residual sense of alienation and distrust of the party could see membership as attractive. Those who were doing well under NEP found spokesmen in the party for their position, as did those who were or were becoming disenchanted with it. The party offered the most powerful means of influencing policy and continued to assert the fundamentally special role of the working class in socialist construction. Perhaps most important, many workers were beginning to see the party as a possible ally in their growing struggle with their bosses.

The historic alliance began to re-form on a tentative basis. Over the next three years, the working class and party would, in effect, engage in negotiating its terms. Unlike 1917, it was to be no whirlwind courtship and speedy marriage. The qualitatively different revolutionary agendas of the working class and the party prevented that. The party's agenda continued to spring from the calculus of high policy and its historic mission, a set of equations in which the party's own capacity to mobilize the working class' energies remained the great unknown. The workers' unfolding agenda had its origins in the dictates of daily life and labor, though increasingly they came to realize that their agenda could not be fulfilled in isolation from the larger problems confronting the nation. Thus, the period 1925-1928 was one of a gradual convergence toward agreement, a period in which both sides were of necessity learning from each other.

The mid-1920s were also a psychological turning point. As recovery quickened and daily survival seemed assured, workers' expectations rose. Calls for socialist industrialization and the beginning of large-scale construction projects further raised those expectations. Workers had played the leading role in the recovery. Gradually, the simple desire for a job, any job, gave way in the mild prosperity of these years to the demand for a right to a job and firmer guarantees of economic security. Gradually, the diffuse discontent with factory affairs gave way to confident demands for a greater role in determing their productive lives. Expectations were rising. Consciousness was crystallizing. Agendas were being articulated.

The place where the differences between the two agendas came into clearest collison, the place where neither side could back down, was at the point of production. For the party, economic development was the key to the socialist revolution's and Soviet state's survival; whether gradual or radical in tempo, economic development demanded increased output and labor productivity. Here, the workers' active participation was vital. For workers, the way in which development was achieved determined the quality of their lives and defined the limits of their power as a class. The issue was not whether to be more productive, but how would higher productivity be achieved and who would decide. The productivists' position, which had given rise to much unrest, was unsatisfactory to workers. The radicals' position, according to which productivity was intertwined with the democratization of production, offered hope.

To elicit worker participation in exposing the "incompetence of management" and restoring the "proper" relationship between one-man management and workers' control, production meetings were organized. While they were relatively quick to join the party and Komsomol, workers were slower to expose their bosses' "incompetence." Their reticence stemmed not from any doubts they had about their bosses' performance, but from doubts about the real function, power, and effectiveness of production meetings. After all, without the firm support of the party or union, a worker's accusation or criticism might cost him his job at a time when too few employment opportunities existed. Not until 1926 did production meetings win the workers' trust. As their legitimacy grew, thanks to the party's mounting campaign against managerial incompetence and bureaucratism, production meetings became forums in which increasing numbers of workers united, under the *lenintsy*'s leadership, to fan the embers of class war. With the Shakhty trial and the ensuing criticism-self-criticism campaign, the meetings became vehicles for pressing local demands and, more important, arenas in which working-class consciousness crystallized into a more general set of revolutionary demands. In the process, the embers turned to flames and spread quickly.

Increasingly, workers' behavior in production meetings dismayed the party's productivists who had hoped that the meetings would serve the limited function of fine-tuning production. Party radicals, on the other hand, found in production meetings substantiation for their objections to the NEP and provided them with a most powerful weapon.

In 1928-1929, the party and workers, especially urban workers, reforged the old alliance of 1917-1918, but this time with a difference. The generalized euphoria experienced by the working class in 1917-1918 had been reshaped by the often bitter experiences of the ensuing years into specific attitudes and demands. Some workers found in the party certain policies that addressed the substance of their demands, and some in the party found in workers' demands substance that could be translated into policy. As through a glass darkly, in the outlines of the societal transformations that began in 1928-1929 can be found the urban workers' revolutionary agenda as shaped in the 1920s.

Nineteen-twenty-eight marked the beginning of a period of revolutionary transformation comparable in importance to that of 1917-1918. Collectivization fundamentally realigned the contours of agrarian life and methods of cultivation. The First Five-Year Plan destroyed the semicapitalist economy of the NEP and introduced a centrally planned economy designed to ensure large-scale industrialization and rapid economic growth. The cultural revolution sought to destroy the remaining vestiges of "bourgeois" influence and power. Toward that end, nepmen and kulaks were stripped of their economic power; "bourgeois" intellectuals and technical specialists experienced political attacks from the party, state, workers, and their self-proclaimed allies. Thousands of workers were admitted to educational institutions to create a new Soviet intelligentsia that would be politically reliable and thereby free the country of its dependence on "bourgeois" elements. Part and parcel of these changes was the victory of Stalin and his supporters over Bukharin and his supporters in the struggle to control the party and thereby to determine policy formulation.

Known as the "second," "third," or "Stalin" revolution, until recently western historians have portrayed the transformations of this period as a "revolution from above."[1] In one sense, this is true; the changes resulted from the initiation of new policies. The term "revolution from above" implies that the party imposed these changes on an unwilling populace. But, this period also witnessed a "revolution from below" in which many groups actively participated and which evidenced deep continuities between the pre- and post-1928 years.[2] To ask which "revolution" anticipated or precipitated the other is to skirt the most important issue. What makes the period distinctive is that the "revolution from above" and the "revolution from below" interacted, reinforced, and pushed each other along unforeseen lines. Their symbiotic rather than their causal relationship is what gave the "second revolution" its power and appeal.

Which Moscow workers welcomed and actively participated in the "second revolution" and why? Complete answers to these questions would take us far beyond this study's scope. But some tentative answers and thoughts are in order.

Workers participated in several aspects of the 1928-1931 cultural revolution. Within the factories, their most visible activity was specialist-baiting and attacks on "bourgeois" managerial personnel. By virtue of their party membership and leadership in factory committee and production meetings, urban workers provided the direction and impetus to the assault. It was the *lenintsy* urban workers who instilled in their co-workers the confidence that criticisms of these personnel were safe, even desirable. Komsomols and young workers also played an active role. For those urban workers old enough to have participated in factory revolutionary activities in 1917-1918, the campaign to expose managerial "incompetence" and restore the "proper" balance between one-man management and workers' control offered them the opportunity to enact an important item on their revolutionary agenda—a degree of control over production. In the late 1920s as a decade earlier, many were undoubtedly convinced that they were capable of doing as good, if not a better job than their bosses. For worker-Komsomols, whose knowledge of 1917-1918 came from the press, books, and tales of revolutionary heroics, the goal was the same, but the motivations somewhat different. For these young iconoclasts, the cultural revolution offered the opportunity to re-enact those stormy, heroic days, to create socialism, and to banish from the factories and society those "bourgeois" who frustrated the realization of revolutionary dreams and denied many of their generation the right to productive lives.[3]

Workers actively participated in another aspect of the cultural revolution—the mass migration from factories to educational and training institutions where they studied to become engineers, technical specialists, managers, foremen, the core of the new Soviet intelligentsia.[4] These new opportunities provided the avenues to upward mobility and greater economic status and security that many workers desired. It also appealed to their desire to transform the dictatorship of the proletariat from a political abstraction into reality.

Among those who remained in the factories, young and Komsomol workers took the lead in initiating shock work and socialist competitions, integral aspects of labor policy during the Five-Year Plan. For these workers, who during the late 1920s had been in the vanguard of those who adopted more intensive labor techniques, these campaigns to raise productivity and improve production allowed them not only to put into practice more efficient work methods learned in technical schools but also to improve their and the country's general economic well-being. Their successful performance provided the proof that socialism was superior to capitalism, a superiority that many held as a tenet of faith.[5] Shock work and socialist competitions, therefore, became endowed with an importance of historic proportions. But as such competitions increased, so too did older, skilled workers' resentment of those who participated in them.

Many urban workers also activley participated in the collectivization campaign. There were several reasons why they did so. During the 1920s, competition between urban workers and migrants for permanent and seasonal employment mounted steadily. As urban unemployment increased, so too did urban workers desire to remove the root cause of the problem. The few futile efforts made prior to 1929 failed to appease urban workers' demands that their right to a job be given priority. What compounded the tension between the two was the peasantry's ability to significantly affect the urban standard of living by withholding their produce. The most dramatic example of this power came in 1928-1929 when peasants, incited to new fears by the 1927 war scare and resentful of the widening of the scissors, withheld their produce. The shortage of food in Moscow and other urban areas resulted in the dispatching of urban food teams to the villages and the re-introduction of rationing in early 1929.[6] To peasants, the food detachments conjured up images of the Civil War requisitioning teams. Understandably, many peasants, either actively or passively, resisted the new policy. To urban workers, the shortage of food and re-introduction of rationing also conjured up images of a horrible past, one they were determined not to relive. To forestall that grisly possiblity, many urban workers volunteered for food collection and collectivization teams.

One barometer of the growing strains between urban workers and the peasantry was the decline of urban support for *shefstvo* (patronage) societies. The first *shefstvo* organizations in Moscow appeared during

the famine of 1921-1922. At that time, *raion* Soviets, some large factories, and Red Army garrisons "adopted" villages in the famine-stricken
Chuvash Autonomous *oblast'*. Each month one day's wages were collected and the proceeds purchased food to be sent to the region and paid
for temporary or permanent adoption of Chuvash children.[7] Such organizations were temporary.

In January 1923, Lenin proposed the creation of permanent *shefstvo*
societies composed of urban workers. The societies' purpose was to
involve workers in the arduous task of hastening the cultural and material
development of the villages.[8] True to Lenin's wishes, many factories
"sponsored" specific villages. By mid-1925, membership in Moscow
shefstvo societies approached 150,000. Workers comprised 60 percent
of the members. Only one-third of the members belonged to the party,
but of those *lenintsy* and Komsomol members were particularly active.
For most, membership was a passive affair and consisted of monthly
contributions. Those who were active devoted part of their vacations or
free time to conducting cultural and educational work in the villages.
The opening of reading rooms, literacy circles, and schools were common
activities. Members also provided economic assistance, such as repairing
machinery or training peasants to do so and helping to organize cooperatives. Until 1927, *shefstvo* societies appeared to be an important means
of realizing the *smychka*.

During 1927-1928, as unemployment reached 20 percent in Moscow and a new agricultural crisis reared its head, membership in *shefstvo*
societies declined sharply. Worker resistance to the training of peasants
and providing economic asistance to the villages mounted at a time when
the struggle for urban jobs and food intensified and the hard-won
improvements in workers' standard of living were undermined. Urban-
rural relations entered a new phase. With the onset of collectivization
and the decree "On *shefstvo* work," which called for those societies to
devote their energies to "the socialist transformation of the countryside,"
membership in the faltering *shefstvo* societies increased markedly.[9]
Between 1928 and mid-1930, thousands of urban workers volunteered
in response to the party's plea for cadres to implement its new policies
in the countryside.

That many urban workers supported a solution to the rural question is clear from their active involvement in the movement of the
"25,000ers." In response to the party's call for 25,000 of the "most
advanced workers" to participate in the collectivization of the countryside, more than 70,000 workers volunteered. The social profile of the

"25,000ers," 6,600 of whom were from Moscow city and *oblast'*, resembles quite closely that of the urban worker activists who organized and participated in production meetings. Most were urban-born workers who had "no connection of any sort with the countryside" and who had more than ten years of production experience. A majority (70 percent) were party members; another 9 percent belonged to the Komsomol. A variety of considerations motivated these volunteers, but virtually all saw the movement and policy of collectivization as essential to improving Soviet life and defending the regime against the rural class enemy—the kulak.[10]

Given worker, especially urban worker, support for and participation in the cultural revolution, specialist-baiting, shock work, socialist competitions, and collectivization—all of which were policies embraced by Stalin and his supporters in their struggle with Bukharin and the "right deviation"—what conclusions can be drawn about working-class support for the sharp changes in policy that began in 1928? Until more research is devoted to worker-party relations during this tumultuous period, no firm conclusions can be drawn. But given that worker antipathy toward "bourgeois" specialists and managerial personnel, urban workers' demands for a solution to the rural problem, worker unrest over the consequences of many NEP policies, and young worker participation in shock work and socialist competitions antedated the battle between the Stalin and Bukharin camps, anyone who seeks to answer the above query might do well to carry another with them into their research— who led whom? Did Stalin and his supporters skillfully exploit workers' discontent and hopes to provide themselves with the mantle of proletarian legitimacy in their struggle with the "right deviation"? Or did workers' discontent dictate the inclusion of important items in, and therefore in part the content of, the platform which Stalin and his supporters fashioned? Whichever proves to be the more accurate assessment, in broad outline, the policies initiated in 1928-1929—the expansion of opportunities for worker expression and mobility, the expansion of the economy and greater job opportunities, the attacks on workers' rivals and "enemies," the unleashing of many youths' production enthusiasm, and a solution to the rural problem—addressed the revolutionary demands of many workers, especially urban workers. They may not have been pleased by the ultimate outcome of these policies, but at their inception, the policies held out the promise of solving many pressing problems that plagued workers' lives.

History is a dialectical process. Nowhere is this clearer than in

1928-1929. During that brief period, worker consciousness and class solidarity re-emerged. And yet almost immediately that solidarity began to give way to new intraclass tensions. The movement of many workers, who had articulated anew that class's revolutionary agenda, from the factory to the classroom deprived factories of some of their best leaders. Collectivization drove a wedge between urban workers and those who retained land in and social and economic ties to the villages. It also precipitated new waves of rural-urban migration which flooded the factories and construction sites with new workers. As demands for increased productivity and labor discipline mounted, intraclass tensions deepened. The material hardships and shortages of the early 1930s generated new discontent. In short, the policies enacted to solve the problems of the 1920s generated the problems of the 1930s. Worker consciousness and worker-party relations changed accordingly.

Notes

1. For examples, see: Leonard Schapiro, *The Communist Party of the Soviet Union* (New York, 1971), 365-402; Issac Deutscher, *Stalin: A Political Biography* (New York, 1967), 294-344; Stephen F. Cohen, *Bukharin and the Bolshevik Revolution: A Political Biography, 1888-1938* (New York, 1975), 270-336.

2. See the essays in Fitzpatrick, *Cultural Revolution.*

3. On the motivations of youths, see Fitzpatrick, "Cultural Revolution."

4. Fitzpatrick, *Education and Social Mobility.*

5. On these campaigns and attitudes, see: Schwarz, 188-193; and the reports in *American Engineers in Russia.*

6. R. W. Davies, *The Socialist Offensive: The Collectivization of Soviet Agriculture, 1929-1930* (Cambridge, Mass., 1980), 39-202; Lewin, *Russian Peasants,* part II. On food team members' attitudes and behavior, see Lynne Viola, "Notes on the Background of Soviet Collectivization: Metal Workers Brigades in the Countryside, Autumn 1929," *Soviet Studies,* 36, 2 (April 1984), 205-222.

7. Matiugin, *Moskva,* 126-127.

8. *Pravda,* January 4, 1923.

9. For discussions of *shefstvo* work and membership, see: A. S. Sulianov, "Shefskaia pomoshch' rabochego klassa derevne v podgotovke sotsialisticheskogo preobrazovaniia sel'skogo khoziaistva (1925-1929gg.)," *Rol' rabochego klassa v sotsialisticheskom preobrazovanii derevnii v SSSR* (Moscow, 1968), 5-60; Aleshchenko, *Mosovskii sovet,* 352-353; *Ocherki istorii Moskovskii KPSS,* 416-417, 440; Rodionova, 195-198. For examples of factory *shefstvo* societies, see: *"Dinamo,"* II, 105-112; *Istoriia . . . Likacheva,* 126-127; Bogdanovskii, 160; *Imeni Voitovicha,* 133.

10. Lynne Viola, "The '25,000ers'."

Appendices

Appendix 1

Price Index for a Standard Ration
of Goods, 1913-1924

Date		Price index
1913		1.00
1914		1.01
1915		1.30
1916	Jan.	1.56
	Apr.	1.68
	Jul.	2.08
	Oct.	2.58
1917	Jan.	3.15
	Apr.	3.84
	Jul.	7.73
	Oct.	8.71
1918	Jan.	27.80
	Apr.	61.40
	Jul.	123.20
	Oct.	129.20
1919	Jan.	288.00
	Apr.	349.00
	Jul.	861.00
	Oct.	1,590.00
1920	Jan.	4,570.00
	Apr.	6,740.00
	Jul.	12,130.00
	Oct.	12,700.00
1921	Jan.	26,900.00
	Apr.	54,300.00
	Jul.	79,000.00
	Oct.	80,000.00
1922	Jan.	371,000.00
	Apr.	3,264,000.00
	Jul.	4,927,000.00
	Oct.	9,476,000.00
1923	Jan.	20,746,000.00
	Apr.	37,700,000.00
	Jul.	121,759,000.00
	Oct.	624,200,000.00
1924	Jan.	5,400,000,000.00

SOURCE: *Statistika truda,* December 1, 1922,
4; March 3, 1923, 14; May 5, 1923, 8;
September 9, 1923, 7; September 7-9, 1924, 8.

Appendix 2

TABLE A-2
Death and Infant Mortality Rates in Moscow, 1913-1929

Year	Number of deaths per thousand	Number of deaths of children under one year per 1,000 live births
1913	23.1	—
1914	23.0	—
1915	24.0	303
1916	23.0	342
1917	23.7	355
1918	29.9	322
1919	45.4	330
1920	36.3	230
1921	25.5	248
1922	29.0	244
1923	14.4	167
1924	16.1	182
1925	13.6	137
1926	13.6	135
1927	13.6	133
1928	12.6	—
1929	12.9	—

SOURCES: Robert Kuczynski, *The Balance of Births and Deaths* 2 vols. (Washington, 1931), II, 15; Frank Lorimer, *Population*, 115-119; *Statisticheskii spravochnik* . . . 1927, 12-13; Vydro, *Naselenie*, 22.

Appendix 3

Table A-3
Birth Rates in Moscow, 1913-1929

Year	Number of births per 1,000 inhabitants
1913	32.2
1914	31.0
1915	26.9
1916	22.9
1917	19.6
1918	14.8
1919	17.4
1920	21.4
1921	30.7
1922	25.6
1923	31.0
1924	30.9
1925	31.7
1926	29.6
1927	25.6
1928	22.7
1929	21.7

SOURCES: Kuczynski, *Balance*, II, 10-27; Lorimer, *Population*, 33; *Statisticheskii spravochnik . . . 1927*, 12-13; Vydro, *Naselenie*, 22.

Appendix 4

TABLE A-4
Sexual Composition of Moscow
by Age Groups, 1917-1926

Females per 1,000 males

Age group	Nov. 1917	1918	1920	1923	1926
0-9	1,033	1,028	1,033	1,004	980
10-19	919	947	1,043	1,059	1,115
20-29	1,028	1,180	1,008	935	1,054
30-39	984	987	912	886	955
40-49	804	857	1,016	906	861
50-59	1,046	1,066	1,313	1,213	1,162
60-69	—	—	—	—	2,004
60 and older	1,933	1,995	2,426	2,274	—
70 and older	—	—	—	—	3,475

SOURCE: Vydro, *Naselenie*, 23.

TABLE A-5
Occupational Structure of Moscow, 1912, 1918, 1920, 1923, and 1926

Occupation	Absolute number					Percent of active population				
	1912	1918	1920	1923	1926	1912	1918	1920	1923	1926
Workers	406,293	597,511[a]	205,427	219,059	293,205	40.2%	65.2%[a]	37.2%	26.6%	27.8%
Employees	235,670		233,375	275,419	354,615	23.3%		40.5%	33.4%	33.6%
Domestics	99,000	67,342	46,828	14,335	42,355	9.8%	7.4%	8.5%	1.7%	4.0%
Free professionals	10,501	39,918	6,125	10,300	6,752	1.1%	4.4%	1.1%	1.2%	.6%
Proprietors with wage labor	38,138		713	5,053	6,288	3.8%			.6%	.6%
Proprietors with family or artel members' labor	65,906	93,619[a]	30,776	5,857	20,479	6.5%	10.2%[a]	5.6%	.7%	1.9%
Self-employed	—			64,453	73,455	—			7.8%	7.0%
Family members helping proprietors	—		3,172	6,707	13,541	—		.6%	.8%	1.3%
Others	124,425	29,705	35,202	127,997	114,939	12.3%	3.3%	6.4%	15.5%	10.9%
Unemployed	30,095	89,003	—	94,953	130,298	3.0%	9.7%	—	11.5%	12.3%
Total	1,010,048	917,098	551,618	824,083	1,055,927	100	100.2%[a]	99.9%[a]	99.8%[b]	100.

SOURCE: *Trud v Moskovskoi gubernii,* 2; *Krasnaia Moskva,* 140; *Moskovskii sovet 1917-1927,* 180; *Perepis' 1923g,* chast' II, tab. II, 222-232; *Perepis' . . . 1926g,* tom. 19, tab. I, 118.

[a]Data for these years were not categorized and represent totals only.
[b]Due to rounding of figures.

Appendix 6

TABLE A-6

Composition of the Moscow Working Class, 1918, 1923, and 1926

Types of worker	1918	1923	1926
All workers	305,861	219,059	293,205
Workers in rural economy	312	837	1,521
Industrial Workers	136,409	128,375	172,239
Miners	2,480	32	50
Metalworkers	20,805	39,165	40,373
Wood workers	1,997	7,342	5,709
Paper workers	1,680	857	2,276
Printers	12,087	12,678	16,743
Textile workers	40,372	18,050	32,800
Garment workers	15,514	14,340	9,967
Leather workers	2,339	7,122	6,132
Food and tobacco workers	17,323	11,857	13,360
Chemical workers	14,992	4,969	8,210
Mineral workers	—	587	1,201
Construction workers	71	8,658	4,261
Power plant workers	169	2,725	3,600
Local transport workers	5,314	—	4,182
Others	1,266	—	23,375
Workers in artisan industry	—	—	13,782
Construction workers	12,696	—	12,903
Railroad workers	11,901	14,784	30,595
Other transport workers	23,959	26,659	20,371
Workers in trade & credit	—	—	10,702
Institutional workers	—	—	13,038
Other workers	121,394	48,483	18,054

SOURCES: *Perepis' 1918g.*, tab. VII, 12-13, tab. IX, 16-17; *Perepisi 1923g.*, chast' II, tab. II, 222-232; *Perepis' . . . 1926g.*, tom. 19, tab. III, 287-290; Grunt, "Moskovskii proletariat," 67-111.

Appendix 7

TABLE A-7
Average Monthly Wages and Salaries of Industrial Workers and
Employees in Moscow, 1925 and 1928 in Rubles

Industry	Workers			Employees		
	Jan. 1925	Dec. 1928	Percent increase	Jan. 1925	Mar. 1928	Percent increase
Stone and Earth	59.28	98.27	66.6%	113.96	191.53	68.1%
Mining	77.09	102.70	33.2%	114.77	130.84	14.6%
Metals	69.77	97.82	40.2%	107.50	145.79	35.6%
Machine-building	75.87	113.01	50.0%	119.04	160.74	35.0%
Chemical	66.19	95.82	44.8%	108.14	154.26	42.6%
Food/Beverage/ Tobacco	64.26	97.39	51.6%	94.14	145.03	54.1%
Leather	84.54	114.83	35.8%	118.34	146.08	23.4%
Cotton	46.31	66.37	43.3%	94.78	125.98	32.9%
Wool	44.29	69.76	57.5%	103.97	136.38	31.2%
Silk	46.80	71.18	52.9%	92.56	119.93	29.6%
Other Textiles	54.73	87.57	60.0%	102.15	137.15	34.3%
Garment (includes Toiletry)	54.03	87.50	62.0%	100.48	137.94	37.3%
Printing	78.42	93.20	18.8%	116.93	164.56	40.7%
Power	88.68	115.60	30.4%	123.00	154.38	25.5%
Others	70.86	96.07	35.6%	111.13	145.14	30.6%
Average	63.75	—[a]	—[a]	107.67	149.18	—[a]
Gap between high and low wage	44.39	49.23		30.44	71.60	

SOURCE: *Ezhemesiachyi statisticheskii bulleten'*, Jan. 1925, otd. V, tab. 2, 12-13; Mar. 1928, otd. V, tab. 2, 12-13; Dec. 1928, otd. III, tab. 2, 13.
[a]Not computed in source.

Bibliography

PRIMARY SOURCES

Censuses

TsSU, *Itogi Vserossiiskoi gorodskoi perepisi 1923g.* 4 vols. Moscow, 1924-
1927.
————, *Itogi perepisi naseleniia 1920g.* Moscow, 1928.
————, *Vserossiiskaia promyshlennaia i professional'naia perepis' 1918g.*
Moscow, 1926.
————, *Vserossiiskaia promyshlennaia i professional'naia perepis'1918g.:
predvaritel'naia svodka dannykh.* Moscow, 1920.
————, *Vsesoiuznaia perepis' naseleniia 1926g.* 56 vols. Moscow, 1928-1933.
————, *Vsesoiuznaia perepis' naseleniia 1926.: predvaritel'nye itogi.* 3 vols.
Moscow, 1927.
————, *Vserossiiskaia perepis' promyshlennykh zavedenii 1920g.* 15 vols.
Moscow, 1921-1927.

Statistical Publications

*Ezhemesiachyi statisticheskii bulleten' po gorodu Moskve i Moskovskoi gub-
ernii.* Moscow, 1924-1928.
*Fabrichno-zavodskaia promyshlennost' gor. Moskvy i Moskovskoi gubernii,
1917-1927gg.* Moscow, 1928.
Kontrolnii tsifri po truda na 1929-1930. Moscow, 1930.
Materialy po tekushchei promyshlennoi statistike za 1919 i 1920. Moscow,
1920.
Mints, L. E., ed., *Voprosy truda v tsifrakh: statisticheskii spravochnik za
1927-1930gg. (k XVI s''ezdu VKP(b)).* Moscow, 1930.
*Moskovskaia oblast': statisticheskii spravochnik po raionom Moskovskoi
oblasti.* Moscow, 1931.

Moskva i Moskovskaia guberniia: statistiko-ekonomicheskii spravochnik, 1923/24-1927/28. Moscow, 1929.

Moskva i Moskovskaia oblast' 1926/27-1928/29: statistiko- ekonomicheskii spravochnik po okrugam. Moscow, 1930.

Sereda, S. P. et al., eds., *Universal'nyi spravochnik tsen.* Moscow, 1928.

Statisticheskii ezhegodnik g. Moskvy i Moskovskoi gubernii 1914-1923gg. Moscow, 1925.

Statisticheskii ezhegodnik g. Moskvy i Moskovskoi gubernii 1924-1925gg. Moscow, 1927.

Statisticheskii ezhegodnik g. Moskvy i Moskovskoi gubernii za 1926g. Moscow, 1928.

Statisticheskii spravochnik g. Moskvy i Moskovskoi gub. 1927g. Moscow, 1928.

Statisticheskii spravochnik SSSR za 1928g. Moscow, 1929.

Statistika truda v promyshlennykh zavedeniiakh. Moscow, 1922.

Trud v Moskve i Moskovskoi gubernii v 1924-1925gg. Moscow, 1926.

Trud v Moskovskoi gubernii v 1923-1925gg.: sbornik statisticheskikh materialov. Moscow, 1926.

TsSU, *Finansovoe polozhenie domovogo khoziaistva gorod Moskva po kategoriam domovladedenii).* Moscow, 1927.

————, *Materialy uchet professional'nogo sostava personala fabrichno-zavodskoi promyshlennosti SSSR v 1925g.* Moscow, 1928.

————, *Samoubiistva v SSSR, 1922-1925gg.* Moscow, 1927.

————, *Samoubiistva v 1925 i 1926gg.* Moscow, 1929.

————, *Sostoianie pitaniia gorodskogo naseleniia SSSR v 1925/26 s/kh godu.* Moscow, 1927.

————, *Sostoianie pitaniia gorodskogo naseleniia SSSR, 1914-1924.* Moscow, 1926.

————, *Statisticheskii ezhegodnik, 1918-1920.* 2 vols. Moscow, 1921.

————, *Statisticheskii ezhegodnik, 1921.* Moscow, 1922.

————, *Statisticheskii ezhegodnik, 1922-1923.* Moscow, 1924.

VTsSPS, *Trud v SSSR: statisticheskii spravochnik za 1924-1925gg.* Moscow, 1926.

————, *Trud v SSSR, 1926-1930gg.: spravochnik.* Moscow, 1930.

Newspapers and Journals

Ekonomicheskaia zhizn'
Istoriia proletariata SSSR
Izvestiia tekstil'noi promyshlennosti i torgovli
Komsomol'skaia Pravda
Moskovskii proletarii
Partiinoe stroitel'stvo
Pravda
Rabochaia Moskva
Statistika truda
Stroitel'stvo Moskvy

316

The New York Times
Torgovo-promyshlennaia gazeta
Trud
Vestnik metallopromyshlennosti
Vestnik truda
Vestnik statistiki
Vlast' sovetov
Voprosy truda

Documents

5-i gubernskii s"ezd Moskovskikh profsoiuzov. Moscow, 1923.

XIV S"ezd Vsesoiuznoi Kommunisticheskoi Partii (B): stenograficheskii otchet. Moscow, 1926.

Dekrety sovetskoi vlasti. 10 vols. Moscow, 1957-1959.

Direktivy KPSS i sovetskogo pravitel'stva po khoziaistvennym voprosam. 4 vols. Moscow, 1957-1958.

Dokumenty trudovoi slavy moskvichei, 1919-1965—iz istorii bor'by za razvitie kommunisticheskikh form truda: sbornik dokumentov i materialov. Moscow, 1967.

Kostomarov, G. D., ed.,

Kommunisticheskie subbotniki v Moskve i Moskovksoi gubernii v 1919-1920gg. Moscow, 1950.

KPSS v rezoliutsiiakh i resheniiakh s"ezdov, konferentsii i plenumy TsK. 4 vols. Moscow, 1956-1960.

Krasnyi Arkhiv. 106 vols. Moscow, 1922-1941.

Moskovskaia gubernskaia konferentsiia professional'nykh soiuzov (14-15 Sentiabr' 1921). Moscow, 1921.

Moskovskie bol'sheviki na zashchite sovetskoi stolitsy v 1919g.: sbornik dokumentov. Moscow, 1947.

Nauchnaia organizatsiia truda, proizvodstva i upravleniia: sbornik dokumentov i materialov, 1918-1930gg. Moscow, 1969.

Organizatsionnyi vopros na tret'em gubernskom s"ezde profsoiuzov (10-14 Maia 1921g.) (izvlecheniia iz stenogrammy). Moscow, 1921.

Partiia v bor'be za vosstanovlenie narodnogo khoziaistva, 1921-1925: dokumenty i materialy. Moscow, 1961.

Pervye shagi industrializatsii SSSR, 1926-1927gg. Moscow, 1959.

Politicheskii i trudovoi pod"em rabochego klassa SSSR (1928-1929gg.). Moscow, 1956.

Professional'nye soiuzy SSSR, 1922-1924gg.: otchet V.Ts.S.P.S. k VI s"ezdu professional'nykh soiuzov. Moscow, 1924.

Professional'nye soiuzy SSSR, 1924-1926gg.: otchet V.Ts.S.P.S. k VII s"ezdu professional'nykh soiuzov. Moscow, 1926.

Professional'nye soiuzy SSSR, 1926-1928gg.: otchet V.Ts.S.P.S. k VIII s"ezdu professional'nykh soiuzov. Moscow, 1928.

Profsoiuzy SSSR: dokumenty i materialy. 4 vols. Moscow, 1963.

Rabochii klass sovetskoi Rossii v pervyi god diktatury proletariata: sbornik dokumentov i materialov. Moscow, 1964.

Resheniia partii i pravitel'stva po khoziaistvennym voprosam. 14 vols. Moscow, 1967-1983.

Sed'moi s"ezd Rossiiskoi Kommunisticheskoi Partii. Moscow, 1924.

Sobranie uzakonenii i rasporiazhenii rabochego i krest'ianskogo pravitel'stva, 1917-1924. Moscow, 1917-1924.

Sobranie zakonov i rasporiazhenii rabochego i krest'ianskogo pravitel'stva. Soiuz Sovetskikh Sotsialisticheskikh Respublik, 1924-1928. Moscow, 1924-1928.

Uprochenie sovetskoi vlasti v Moskve i Moskovskie guberniia: dokumenty i materialy. Moscow, 1958.

Secondary Sources

Aborty v 1925 godu. Moscow, 1927.

Adfel'dt, N., "Master ressornogo tsekha," *Bor'ba klassov,* 3-4 (1931), 74-75.

Akache, "Registratsiia neschastnykh sluchaev," *Voprosy truda,* 8-9 (1926), 25-27.

Akhinshina, N. K., "Statistika proizvoditel'nosti truda v promyshlennosti SSSR v pervye gody sovetskoi vlasti (1918-1925gg.)," in *Ocherki po istorii statistiki SSSR.* 2 vols. Moscow, 1957.

Aleshchenko, N. M., "Moskovskii sovet v 1918-1920gg.," *Istoricheskie zapiski,* 91 (1973), 81-112.

———, *Moskovskii sovet v 1917-1941gg..* Moscow, 1976.

Aluf, A., "Profsoiuzy i krest'ianstvo," *Vestnik truda,* 1 (1925), 47-54.

American Engineers in Russia. Unpublished Collection, Hoover Library, Stanford University.

Anderson, Barbara, "Female Labor Participation, Migration, and Marital Status in Leningrad and Moscow," Paper presented at the conference "Mother and Child in Pre-Revolutionary Russia," University of Illinois, Urbana, Illinois, October 21-23, 1976.

———, *Internal Migration during Modernization in Late Nineteenth Century Russia.* Princeton, 1980.

———, "Internal Migration in a Modernizing Society: The Case of Late Nineteenth Century European Russia." Ph.D. dissertation, Princeton University, 1973.

———, "Who Chose the Cities? Migrants to Moscow and St. Petersburg Cities in the Late Nineteenth Century," in *Population Patterns in the Past.* Ed. Ronald D. Lee. Princeton, 1977.

Anderson, Michael, *Family Structure in Nineteenth Century Lancashire.* Cambridge, England, 1971.

Anikst, A., *Organizatsiia rabochei sily v 1920 gody.* Moscow,1920.

———, "Plan bor'by s bezrabotitsei na 1926g.," *Voprosy truda,* 2 (1926), 12-17.

Antonova, K. I., "Bor'ba rabochikh tsentral'nogo-promyshlennogo raiona za khleb v 1918 gody," in *Iz istorii bor'by trudiashchikhsia Moskvy i Moskovskoi oblasti za ustanovlenie sovetskoi vlasti i sotsialisticheskoe stroitel'stvo: sbornik trudov.* Moscow, 1977.

Anweiler, Oskar, *The Soviets: The Russian Workers, Peasants and Soldiers Councils, 1905-1917.* Translated by Ruth Hein. New York, 1975.

Aristov, N., "K voprosu o krizise v kvalifitsirovannoi rabochei sile v SSSR," *Voprosy truda,* 7-8 (1925), 41-48.

―――, "Nedochety v rabote Moskovskogo GOT v oblasti okhrany truda (po materialam MRKI)," *Voprosy truda,* 5 (1928), 110-111.

―――, "Sezonnyi rynok truda i ego regulirovanie,"*Vestnik truda,* 3 (1927), 28-37.

Avrich, Paul, *Kronstadt 1921.* New York, 1974.

―――, "Russian Factory Committees in 1917," *Jahrbücher für Geschichte Osteuropas,* 11, 2 (June 1963), 161-180.

―――, "The Bolshevik Revolution and Workers Control in Russian Industry," *Slavic Review,* 22, 1 (March 1963), 47-63.

Azrael, J., *Managerial Power and Soviet Politics.* Cambridge, Mass., 1966.

Babun, F., "Komsomol zavoda 'Serp i molot'," in *Iunost' nasha Komsomol'skaia: dokumental'nye materialy, ocherki i vospominaniia iz istorii Komsomola Kalinskogo raion goroda Moskvy, 1917-1970.* Moscow, 1970.

Baevskii, D. A., *Rabochii klass v pervye gody sovetskoi vlasti (1917-1921gg.).* Moscow, 1974.

Bailes, Kendall, "Alexei Gastev and the Soviet Controversy over Taylorism, 1918-1924," *Soviet Studies,* 29, 3 (1977), 373-394.

―――, *Technology and Society under Lenin and Stalin: Origins of the Soviet Technical Intelligentsia, 1917-1941.* Princeton, 1978.

Baker, Anita B., "Deterioration or Development: The Peasant Economy of Moscow Province Prior to 1914," *Russian History/Histoire Russe,* 5, 1 (1978), 1-23.

―――, "Stagnation and Change in Peasant Agriculture in Pre-1914 Moscow Province," Paper presented at 2d New England Slavic Association Conference, Cambridge, Mass., April 15-16, 1977.

Bakhutov, A., "Bezrabotitsa, birzhi truda i profsoiuzy," *Vestnik truda,* 8 (1924), 33-41.

―――, "Bezrabotitsa v SSSR i bor'ba s nei," *Vestnik truda,* 11 (1927), 38-44.

―――, "Praktika birzh truda," *Vestnik truda,* 4 (1925), 49-54.

―――, "Voprosy zarabotnoi platy i proizvoditel'nost' truda," *Voprosy truda,* 12 (1924), 27-33.

Barker, G. R., *Some Problems of Incentives and Labor Productivity in Soviet Industry.* London, 1955.

Basurmanov, K. A., "U zastavy il'icha," in *Iunost' nasha Komsomol'skaia.*

Bater, James H., "Some Dimensions of Urbanization and the Response of Muncipal Government: Moscow and St. Petersburg," *Russian History/Histoire Russe,* 5, 1 (1978), 46-63.

―――, *St. Petersburg: Industrialization and Change.* Montreal, 1976.

Belkin, G., "Bezrabotitsa i neorgannizovannyi truda," *Vestnik truda,* 12 (1927), 38-43.

Benet, Sula, ed., *The Village of Viriatino*. Trans. by Sula Benet, New York, 1970.

Bergson, A., *The Structure of Soviet Wages*. Cambridge, Mass., 1944.

Berkman, Alexander, *The Bolshevik Myth (Diary 1920-1922)*. London, 1925.

Bettelheim, Charles, *Class Struggles in the USSR, First Period: 1917-1923*. Trans. by Brian Pearce. New York, 1978.

———, *Class Struggles in the USSR, Second Period: 1923-1930*. Trans. by Brian Pearce. New York, 1978.

Billik, V. I., "V. I. Lenin o sushchnosti i periodizatsii sovetskoi ekonomiki politiki 1917-1920gg. i o povrote k nepu," *Istoricheskie zapiski*, 80 (1967), 126-169.

Block, Alexander, "Soviet Housing—The Historical Aspect: Some Notes on Problems of Policy," (Part I), *Soviet Studies*, 3, 1 (July 1951), 1-15; (Part II), 3, 3 (January 1952), 229-257.

Bogdanov, V. V., *Kul'tura i byt naseleniia tsentral'no-promyshlennoi oblasti*. Moscow, 1929.

Bogdanovskii, V., *Imeni Vladimira Il'icha*. Moscow, 1962.

Bogoslovskii, S., "Fizicheskoe razvitiie promyshlennykh rabochikh i sluzhashchikh," (*chast'* I), *Statisticheskoe obozrenie*, 8 (1927), 88-93.

———, "Sostoianie zdorov'ia promyshlennykh rabochikh i sluzhashchikh," *Statisticheskoe obozrenie*, 12 (1927), 91-98.

Bol'shakov, A. M., *Derevnia 1917-1927*. Moscow, 1927.

———, *Sovetskaia derevnia*. Leningrad, 1924.

Bonnell, Victoria E., *Roots of Rebellion: Workers' Politics and Organizations in Petersburg and Moscow, 1900-1914*. Berkeley, 1983.

———, ed., *The Russian Worker: Life and Labor under the Tsarist Regime*. Berkeley, 1983.

Borders, Karl, *Village Life under the Soviets*. New York, 1929.

Bradley, Joseph Crane, Jr., "*Muzhik* and Muscovite: Peasants in Late Nineteenth Century Urban Russia." Ph.D. dissertation, Harvard University, 1977.

———, "Patterns of Peasant Migration to Late Nineteenth Century Moscow: How Much Should We Read into Literacy Rates?." *Russian History/Histoire Russe*, forthcoming.

Brinton, Maurice, *The Bolsheviks and Workers' Control*. London. 1970.

———, "Factory Committees and the Dictatorship of the Proletariat," *Critique*, 4 (1975), 78-86.

Broderson, Arvid, *The Soviet Worker: Labor and Government in Soviet Society*. New York, 1966.

Brodskii, N. L. et al., *Krest'ianii v XX veke*. Moscow, 1925.

Brower, Daniel, "Labor Violence in Russia in the Late Nineteenth Century," *Slavic Review*, 41, 3 (1982), 417-431.

Brown, Emily Clark, *Soviet Trade Unions and Labor Relations*. Cambridge, Mass., 1966.

Bryant, Louise, *Mirrors of Moscow*. New York, 1923.

320

Buck, Pearl, *Talk about Russia with Masha Scott*. New York, 1945.

Bunyan, James, Ed., *The Origins of Forced Labor in the Soviet State, 1917-1921: Documents and Materials*. Baltimore, 1967.

Bychkov, L., "Moskovskii Komsomol v grazhdanskoi voine," *Bor'ba klassov*, 7-8 (1934), 176-182.

Carr, E. H., *The Bolshevik Revolution, 1917-1923*. 3 vols. Middlesex, 1966.

———, *The Interregnum, 1923-1924*. New York, 1954.

———, *Socialism in One Country, 1924-1926*. 2 vols. London, 1973.

——— and R. W. Davies, *Foundations of a Planned Economy, 1926-1929*. New York, 1969.

Chamberlin, William Henry, *The Russian Revolution, 1917-1921*. 2 vols. New York, 1965.

Chapman, Janet G., *Real Wages in Sovet Russia*. Cambridge, Mass., 1963.

Chastnyi kapital v narodnom khoziaistve SSSR. Moscow/Leningrad, 1927.

Cherniak, N., *Partiinaia organizatsiia i sotsialisticheskoe sorevnovanie*. Moscow, 1948.

Clark, Colin, *A Critique of Russian Statistics*. London, 1939.

Cohen, Stephen F., *Bukharin and the Bolshevik Revolution: A Political Biography, 1888-1938*. New York, 1973.

———, "Stalin's Revolution Reconsidered," *Slavic Review*, 32, 2 (June 1973), 264-270.

Conquest, Robert, *Industrial Workers in the U.S.S.R.*. New York, 1967.

Dadykin, A. P., ed., *Formirovanie i razvitie sovetskogo rabochego klassa, 1917-1961*. Moscow, 1964.

Dallin, David, "Between the World War and NEP," in *The Mensheviks from the Revolution of 1917 to the Second World War*. Ed. Leopold H. Haimson. Chicago, 1974.

Daniels, Robert V., *The Conscience of the Revolution: Communist Opposition in the Soviet Union)*. *New York, 1960*.

Danilov, V. P., *"Krest'ianskii otkhod na promysly v 1920-kh godakh,"* Istoricheskie zapiski, 94 (1974), 55-122.

———, *Sovetskaia dokolkhoznaia derevnia: sotsial'naia, struktura, sotsial'nye otnosheniia*. Moscow, 1979.

Davies, R. W., *The Socialist Offensive: The Collectivization of Soviet Agriculture, 1929-1930*. Cambridge, Mass., 1980.

Day, Richard B., *Leon Trotsky and the Politics of Economic Isolation*. Cambridge, 1973.

Demirchoglian, G., Kvasha, I., "Proizvoditel'nost' truda v tekstil'noi promyshlennosti SSSR," *Statisticheskoe obozrenie*, 9 (1927), 50-57.

Deutscher, Issac, *The Prophet Armed, Trotsky: 1897-1921*. New York, 1965.

———, *The Prophet Unarmed, Trotsky: 1921-1929*. New York, 1965.

———, *Soviet Trade Unions: Their Place in Soviet Labor Policy*. London, 1950.

———, *Stalin: A Political Biography*. New York, 1967.

Dewar, M., *Labor Policy in the U.S.S.R., 1917-1928*. London, 1956.

DiMaio, Alfred John, *Soviet Urban Housing: Problems and Policies.* New York, 1974.

Dmitrenko, S. L., "Sostav mestnykh partiinykh komitetov v 1924-1927gg.," *Istoricheskie zapiski,* 79 (1967), 77-108.

Dobb, Maurice, *Russian Economic Development Since the Revolution.* New York, 1928.

Dobrodomov, A. A., ed., *Moskva za 50 let Sovetskoi vlasti, 1917-1967.* Moscow, 1968.

Dobrotvor, N., "Moskovskie rabochie v prodotriadakh," *Bor'ba klassov,* 7-8 (1934), 182-188.

Dobrovol'skii, E. N., *Daesh avtomobil': dokumental'naia povest'.* Moscow, 1971.

————, *Tri izmeneniia.* Moscow, 1977.

Dodge, Norton T., *Women in the Soviet Economy: Their Role in Economic, Scientific and Technical Development.* Baltimore, 1966.

Dohan, Michael R., "The Economic Origins of Soviet Autarky, 1927/28-1934," *Slavic Review,* 35, 4 (December, 1976), 604-635.

Dorokhova, G. A., *Raboche-krest'ianskaia inspektsiia v 1920- 1923gg..* Moscow, 1959.

Dreiser, Theodore, *Dreiser Looks at Russia.* New York, 1928.

Drobizhev, V. Z., Sokolov, A. K., Ustinov, V. A., *Rabochii klass Sovetskoi Rossii v pervyi god proletarskoi diktatury (Opyt strukturnogo analiza po materialam professional'noi perepisi 1918g.).* Moscow, 1975.

Dunn, Stephen P. and Dunn, Ethel, *The Peasants of Central Russia.* New York, 1967.

————, "The Study of the Soviet Family in the USSR and in the West," *Slavic Studies Working Papers.* No. 1, Columbus, Ohio, 1977.

Duranty, Walter, *I Write as I Please.* New York, 1935.

Dva mesiatsia rabotei V. I. Lenina: ianvar'-fevral' 1921. Moscow, 1934.

Dvinov, Boris, *Moskovskii sovet rabochikh deputatov, 1917-1922: vospominaniia.* New York, 1961.

Dynik, Mikhail, "Proizvodstvennogo soveshchanii i NOT," *Vestnik truda,* 4 (1925), 90-98.

Edvard, L., "Trudovye konflikty v pervyi polovine 1923g," *Voprosy truda,* 10-11 (1923), 60-67.

Ehrlich, Alexander, *The Soviet Industrialization Debate, 1924-1928.* Cambridge, Mass., 1960.

Engelstein, Laura, *Moscow, 1905: Working Class Organization and Political Conflict.* Stanford, 1982.

Fabriki i zavody Moskovskoi oblasti na 1928-1929 god. Moscow, 1929.

Fedor, Thomas, *Patterns of Urban Growth in the Russian Empire.* Chicago, 1975.

Field, Alice W., *Protection of Women and Children in Soviet Russia.* London, 1932.

Fischer, H. H., *The Famine in Soviet Russia, 1919-1923: The Operations of the American Relief Administration.* New York, 1927.

Fischer, Louis, *Men and Politics: Europe Between the Two World Wars*. New York, 1966.

———, *Machines and Men in Russia*. New York, 1932.

Fischer, Markoosha, *My Lives in Russia*. New York, 1944.

Fitzpatrick, Sheila, "Cultural Revolution and Class War," *Cultural Revolution in Russia, 1928-1931*. Ed. Sheila Fitzpatrick. Bloomington, Ind., 1978.

———, ed., *Cultural Revolution in Russia, 1928-1931*. Bloomington, Ind., 1978.

———, *Education and Social Mobility in the Soviet Union, 1921-1934*. Cambridge, 1979.

G., A., "Moskovskaia obshcheugolovnaia prestupnost' v period voennogo kommunizma," in *Prestupnik i prestupnost'*. Ed. E. K. Krasnushkina, G. M. Segal, Ts. M. Feinberg. Moscow, 1927.

Gaister, A., *Rassloenie sovetskoi derevni*. Moscow, 1928.

Gaponenko, L. C., *Rabochii klass Rossii v 1917 godu*. Moscow, 1970.

Geiger, H. Kent, *The Family in Soviet Russia*. Cambridge, Mass., 1968.

Genkina, E. B., "Voznikovenie proizvodstvennykh soveshchanii v gody vosstanovitel'nogo period (1921-1925)," *Istoriia SSSR*, 3 (1958), 63-89.

Gernet, M. N., "K statistike prostitutsii," *Statisticheskoe obozrenie*, 7 (1927), 86-89.

———, *Prestupnost' i samoubiistva vo vremia voiny i posle nee*. Moscow, 1927.

Gibshman, A., "Zhilishchnyi fond i zhilishchnye usloviia nashikh gorodov," *Statisticheskoe obozrenie*, 7 (1928), 76-84.

Gimpel'son, E. G., "Rabochii klass v upravlenii promyshlennost'iu v pervye gody Sovetskoi vlasti (noiabr' 1917-1920)," *Istoriia SSSR*, 2 (1977), 4-16.

———, "Sotsial'no-politicheskie izmeneniia v sostave rabochego klassa v pervye gody Sovetskoi vlasti," *Rabochii klass—vedushchaia sila Oktiabr'skoi sotsialisticheskoi revoliutsii*. Moscow, 1976.

———, "Zarabotnaia plata i material'noe obespechenie rabochikh v 1917-1920gg.," *Istoricheskie zapiski*, 87 (1971), 57-90.

Ginzburg, L., "Proizvoditel'nost' truda i perspektivy zarabotnoi platy," *Vestnik truda*, 1 (1925), 107-112.

Gladkov, Fyodor V., *Cement*. Trans. by A. S. Arthur and C. Ashleigh. New York, 1971.

Glezerman, G., *Likvidatsiia ekspluatatorskikh klassov i preodolenie klassovykh razlichei v SSSR*. Moscow, 1949.

Gliksman, Jerzy G., "The Russian Urban Worker: From Serf to Proletarian," in *The Transformation of Russian Society: Aspects of Social Change Since 1861*. Ed. Cyril E. Black. Cambridge, Mass., 1960.

Goldman, Emma, *My Disillusionment in Russia*. New York, 1970.

Goodey, Chris, "Factory Committees and the Dictatorship of the Proletariat (1918)," *Critique*, 3 (1974), 24-47.

———, "Factory Committees and the Dictatorship of the Proletariat: Additional Notes," *Critique*, 5 (1975), 85-89.

Gordon, Manya, *Workers Before and After Lenin*. New York, 1941.

Gorodnoe zvanie — il'ichevtsy po zalam muzeia zavoda imeni Vladimir Il'icha. Moscow, 1970.

Grigorenko, Petro G., *Memoirs.* Translated by Thomas Whitney. New York, 1982.

Gregor, Richard, ed., *Resolutions and Decisions of the Communist Party of the Soviet Union: The Early Period, 1917-1929.* vol. 2 of 4 vols. Gen. ed. Robert H. McNeal. Toronto, 1974.

Grunt, A. Ia., *Moskva 1917-i: Revoliutsiia i contrrevoliutsiia.* Moscow, 1976.

———, "Moskovskii proletariat v 1917g. (K voprosu o chislennosti, sostave i territorial'noe razmeshchenii), *Istoricheskie zapiski,* 85 (1970), 67-111.

———, *Pobeda oktiabr'skoi revoliutsii v Moskve.* Moscow, 1961.

Gumilevskii, N., "Biudzhet sluzhashchego k nachale 1925 goda," *Voprosy truda,* 7-8 (1925), 80-89.

———, *Biudzhet sluzhashchikh v 1922-1926.* Moscow, 1928.

Hajnal, J., "European Marriage in Perspective," in *Population and History.* Eds. D. V. Glass and D. E. C. Eversley. London, 1965.

Hamm, Michael F., "The Breakdown of Urban Modernization: A Prelude to the Revolutions of 1917," in *The City in Russian History.* Ed. Michael F. Hamm. Lexington, Kentucky, 1976.

———, ed., *The City in Russian History.* Lexington, Kentucky, 1976.

Harrison, Marguerite E., *Marooned in Moscow: The Story of an American Woman Imprisoned in Russia.* New York, 1921.

Hatch, John, "The Politics of Mass Culture: Workers, Communists and Proletkul't in the Development of Workers' Clubs, 1921-1925," *Russian History/Histoire Russe.* Forthcoming.

Hazard, John N., *Soviet Housing Law.* New Haven, 1939.

Iagolin, B., "Rozhdaemost' po g. Moskve v sviazi s sotsial'nym sostavam naseleniia," *Statisticheskoe obozrenie,* 10 (1928), 85-88.

Ignat'ev, G. S., *Moskva v pervyi god proletarskoi diktatury.* Moscow, 1975.

Ikonnikov, S. N., *Sozdanie deiatel'nost' ob"edinennykh organov TsKK-RKI v 1923-1934.* Moscow, 1971.

Il'inskii, V., *Biudzhet rabochikh SSSR v 1922-1926g.* Moscow, 1928.

Il'inskii, Vs., "Kvartirnoe dovol'stvie personala tsenzovoi promyshlennosti SSSR v 1923-1927gg.," *Statisticheskoe obozrenie,* 8 (1928), 45-50.

Imeni Voitovicha. Moscow, 1969.

International Labor Office, *Industrial and Labour Information(Russian Supplement).* 5 vols. (Geneva, 1922-1923).

Isaev, A., "Bezrabotitsa i bor'ba nei v 1927/28 (k kontrol'nym tsifram po trudu," *Voprosy truda,* 11 (1927), 17-28.

———, "Blizhaishie zadachi po regulirovaniiu rynok truda: zadachi po regulirovaniiu gorodskogo rynok truda," *Vestnik truda,* 5 (1927), 10-15.

———, "Bor'ba s bezrabotinets v 1922 godu," *Voprosy truda,* 2 (1923), 26-33.

———, "Bor'ba s bezrabotitsei v 1924 godu," *Voprosy truda,* 1 (1925), 36-43.

———, "Kollektivy iz bezrabotnykh v Moskve," *Voprosy truda,* 2 (1926), 134-137.

Istoriia Moskovskogo avtozavoda imeni I. A. Likhacheva. Moscow, 1966.

Istoriia Moskvy. 6 vols. Moscow, 1957.

Istoriia Moskvy: kratkii ocherk. Moscow, 1974.

Iunost' nasha Komsomol'skaia: dokumental'nye materialy, ocherki i vospominaniia iz istorii Komsomola Kalinskogo raion goroda Moskvy, 1917-1970. Moscow, 1970.

Iz istorii bor'by trudiashchikhsia Moskvy i Moskovskoi oblasti za ustanovlenie Sovetskoi vlasti i sotsialisticheskoe stroitel'stvo: sbornik trudy. Moscow, 1977.

Izmeneniia sotsial'noi struktury sovetskogo obshchestva: oktiabr' 1917-1920. Moscow, 1976.

Johnson, Robert E., "Labor Unrest in Moscow, 1880-1900," Paper presented at the 2nd New England Slavic Association Conference, Cambridge, Mass., April 15-16, 1977.

——, *Peasant and Proletarian: The Working Class of Moscow at the End of the Nineteenth Century.* New Brunswick, 1979.

——, "Peasant Migration and the Russian Working Class: Moscow at the End of the Nineteenth Century," *Slavic Review,* 35, 4 (December, 1976), 652-664.

——, "The Nature of the Russian Working Class: Social Characteristics of the Moscow Industrial Region, 1880-1900," Ph.D. dissertation, Cornell University, 1975.

Juviler, Peter, "The Family in the Soviet System," *The Carl Beck Papers in Russian and East European Studies,* 306 (1984).

K. and Sh., "Zhilishchnoe polozhenie tekstil'shchikov," *Statisticheskoe obozrenie,* 6 (1929), 60-65.

Kabo, Elena Osipovna, *Ocherki rabochego byta.* Moscow, 1928.

——, *Pitanie russkogo rabochego do i posle voiny: po statisticheskim materialam, 1908-24gg.* Moscow, 1926.

Kaplan, Frederick I., *Bolshevik Ideology and the Ethics of Soviet Labor, 1917-1920: The Formative Years.* London, 1969.

——, "The Origin and Function of the Subbotniks and Voskresniks," *Jahrbücher für Geschichte Osteuropas,* 13, 1 (April 1965), 30-39.

Kaplun, S., "Rezhim ekonomii i okhrana truda," *Voprosy truda,* 5-6 (1926), 16-22.

Karchevskii, N., "Opyt aktivnogo posrednichestva Posredsezon-Biuro pri Komitete Moskovskoi Birzh truda," *Voprosy truda,* 11 (1925), 149-157.

Katomin, "Biudzhet bezrabotnogo," *Voprosy truda,* 1 (1924), 61-63.

Katel, M., "Rabochee vremia promyshlennykh rabochikh SSSR," *Vestnik truda,* 5 (1925), 102-115.

Kats, A., "Povyshenie proizvoditel'nost' i okhrana truda," *Vestnik truda,* 11-12 (1924), 89-95.

Katzenellenbaum, S. S., *Russian Currency and Banking, 1914-1924.* London, 1925.

Kholodny, T., *Moscow: Old and New.* Moscow, 1933.

Khotsianov, L. K., *Opyt izucheniia demograf1cheskikh sdvigov v sel'skom naselenii Moskovskoi i Riazanskoi oblasti, 1851-1960.* Moscow, 1963.

Khoziaistvennoe i sotsial'no-kul'turnoe stroitel'stvo v Moskve i Moskovskoi gubernii. Moscow, 1928.

Khrestin, N., *Vysokoe napriazhenie (Moskovskii kabel'nyi zavod).* Moscow, 1962.

Kingsbury, Susan M. and Fairchild, Mildred, *Employment and Unemployment in Pre-War and Soviet Russia.* Report submitted to the World Social Economic Congress, Amsterdam, August 23-29, 1931.

———, *Factory, Family and Woman in the Soviet Union.* New York, 1935.

Kleinbort, L. M., *Ocherki rabochego intelligentsii.* Petrograd, 1923.

Koblents, I. G., *Zhilishchnoe pravo.* Moscow, 1924.

Koenker, Diane, *Moscow Workers and the 1917 Revolution.* Princeton, 1981.

Koenker, Diane G. P., "Moscow Workers in 1917." 2 vols. Ph.D. dissertation, University of Michigan, 1976.

Kolantay (sic), Alexandria, *The Workers Opposition In Russia.* London, 1923.

Kopp, Anatole, *Town and Revolution: Soviet Architecture and City Planning, 1917-1935.* Trans. by Thomas Burton. New York, 1970.

Kosinski, Leszek A., ed., *Demographic Developments in Eastern Europe.* New York, 1977.

Kostomarov, G. D., "Moskovskii sovet i oborona strany (1918-1920)," *Istoriia proletariata SSSR*, 3/19 (1934), 131-155.

Kozhanyi, P., "Zhilishchnyi vopros," *Voprosy truda*, 10 (1924), 54-57.

Kozelov, B., "Osnovaia direktiva VII s"ezda," *Vestnik truda*, 1 (1927), 5-6.

Krasil'nikov, M., "Perenaselenie v 1925 i 1926 godakh," *Statisticheskoe obozrenie*, 2 (1928), 90-95.

———, "Sviaz' naseleniia goroda Moskvy s nadel'noi zemlei," *Statisticheskoe obozrenie*, 6 (1928), 103-107.

Krasnaia Moskva, 1917-1920gg.. Moscow, 1920.

Kritsman, L., *Geroicheskii period velikoi russkoi revoliutsii.* Moscow, 1926.

Kuczynski, Robert R., *The Balance of Births and Deaths.* 2 vols., Washington, 1931.

Kukushkin, Iu., Shelestov, D., *Pervyi kommunisticheskie subbotniki.* Moscow, 1959.

Kulyshev, Iu., Rogachevskaia, L., *Pervye udarnye.* Moscow, 1961.

Kurakhtanov, V. M., *Pervaia sittsenabivnaia.* Moscow, 1960.

Kuromiya, Hiroaki, "Edinonachalie and the Soviet Industrial Manager, 1928-1937," *Soviet Studies*, 36, 2 (April 1984), 31-43.

Kurlat, F. L., "Nekotorye voprosy istorii oktiabr'skoi revoliutsii v Moskve," *Vestnik Moskovskogo gosudarstvennogo universiteta*, 6 (1963), 31-43.

Ladurie, Emmanuel Le Roy, "Famine Amenorrhea (Seventeenth- Twentieth Centuries)," is *Biology of Man in History: Selections from "Annales: Economies, Societies, Civilizations."* Eds. Robert Forster and Orest Ranum. Baltimore, 1974.

Lampert, Nicholas, *The Technical Intelligentsia and the Soviet State.* New York, 1979.

Langsam, David E., "Pressure Group Politics in NEP Russia: The Case of the Trade Unions". Ph.D. dissertation, Princeton University, 1973.

Lapitskaia, S., *Byt rabochikh Trekhgornoi manufaktury*. Moscow, 1935.

———, "Byt rabochikh staroi i novoi fabriki," *Bor'ba klassov*, 6 (1933), 31-43.

———, "Zhilishchnoe stroitel'stvo novoi Moskvy posle oktaibr'skoi revoliutsii," *Bor'ba klassov*, 7-8 (1934), 216-224.

Larin, Iu., *Chastnyi kapital v SSSR*. Moscow-Leningrad, 1927.

———, *Sovetskaia derevnia*. Moscow, 1925.

———, *Voprosy krest'ianskogo khoziaistva*. Moscow, 1923.

Larin, Iu. and Kritsman, L., *Ocherk khoziaistvennoi zhizni i organizatsiia narodnogo khoziaistva Sovetskoi Rossii, 1 noiabria 1917-1 iiulia 1920g.* Moscow, 1920.

Lavrov, V., *Tsentral'no-promyshlennyi raion*. Moscow, 1929.

Le Mouvement Natural de la Population dans le Monde de 1906 a 1936. Paris, 1954.

Leasure, J. William and Lewis, Robert A., "Internal Migration in the USSR: 1897-1926," *Demography*, 4, 2 (1967), 479-496.

Lebit, P., "Rabota Moskovskoi Birzhi truda za 1925-26g.," *Voprosytruda*, 12 (1926), 97-103.

———, "Itogi pereregistratisii bezrabotnykh v Moskve," *Voprosy truda*, 4 (1927).

———, "Promyshlennyi travmatizm v Moskovskoi gubernii," *Voprosy truda*, 1 (1929), 107-108.

Lediaev, D., "Bezrabotitsa v SSSR i bor'ba s nei (1917-1927)," *Voprosy truda*, 10 (1927), 105-113.

Leites, K., *Recent Economic Developments in Russia*. Oxford, 1922.

Lenin, V. I., *Polnoe sobranie sochinenii*. 5th ed. 55 vols., Moscow, 1958-1965.

Leninskii sbornik. 39 vols. Moscow, 1924-1980.

Leridon, Henri, *Natalité, Saisons et Conjoncture Économique*. Paris, 1973.

Les assurances sociales sovetiques au gouvernment de Moscou: sommaire pour l'annee 1926-1927. Moscow, 1927.

Lewin, Moshe, *Russian Peasants and Soviet Power: A Study of Collectivization*. Evanston, Illinois, 1968.

———, "Society, State and Ideology during the First Five-Year Plan," in *Cultural Revolution in Russia, 1928-1931*.

Lewis, Robert A. and Rowland, Richard H., "Urbanization in Russia and the USSR, 1897-1970," in *The City in Russian History*.

Liashchenko, P. I., *Istoriia narodnogo khoziaistva SSSR*. Moscow, 1956.

Lieberstein, Samuel, "Technology, Work and Sociology in the USSR: The NOT Movement," *Technology and Culture*, (January 1975), 48-66.

Lorimer, Frank, *The Population of the Soviet Union: History and Prospects*. Geneva, 1946.

McAuley, Mary, *Labour Disputes in Soviet Russia, 1957-1965*. Oxford, 1965.

Mace, David and Vera, *The Soviet Family*. New York, 1964.

McNeal, Robert, gen. ed., *Resolutions and Decisions of the Communist Party of the Soviet Union*. 4 vols. Toronto, 1974.

Maizel, I., "Massovaia ekonrabota soiuzov (k itogam VII s"ezda profsoiuzov)," *Vestnik truda*, 3 (1927), 69-75.

Makarenko, A. S., *The Road to Life (An Epic of Education)*. 3 vols. Trans. by Ivy and Tatiana Litvinov. Moscow, 1951.

Male, D. J., *Russian Peasant Organization before Collectivization: A Study of Commune and Gathering, 1925-1930*. London, 1971.

Mandel, David, *The Petrograd Workers and the Fall of the Old Regime: From February to the July Days, 1917*. New York, 1983.

————, *The Petrograd Workers and the Soviet Seizure of Power*. New York, 1984.

Markus, B., "K voprosu o semichasovom rabochem dne," *Voprosy truda*, 12 (1927), 3-15.

————, "Nekotorye predvaritel'nyi itogi osushchestvleniia semichasogo rabochego dnia," *Voprosy truda*, 6 (1928), 6-11.

————, "Voprosy okhrany truda v tekstil'noi promyshlennosti (k nachalu 1927/28 goda)," *Voprosy truda*, 2 (1928),23-40.

Markuzon, F. D., "Biudzhet Moskovskogo rabochego v dekabre 1922 goda," *Voprosy truda*, 5-6 (1923), 40-47.

————, "Polozhenie truda v g. Moskve v 1921 godu," *Voprosy truda*, 2 (1922), 136-181.

Marmershtein, N. ed., *Slavnye traditsii: k 100-letiiu zavoda"Krasnyi proletarii" imeni A. I. Efremova*. Moscow, 1957.

Massovaia rabota Moskovskogo i raionnykh sovetov. Moscow, 1927.

Matiugin, A. A., "Iz istorii razvitiia rabochego klassa v period postroeniia sotsializma 1917-1936," *Istoricheskie zapiski*, 48 (1954), 3-42.

————, *Moskva v period vosstanovleniia narodnogo khoziaistva (1921-1925gg.)*. Moscow, 1947.

————, *Rabochii klass SSSR v gody vosstanovleniia narodnogo khoziaistva, 1921-1925*. Moscow, 1962.

———— and Baevskii, D. A., eds., *Izmeneniia v chislennosti i sostave sovetskogo rabochego klassa*. Moscow, 1961.

Mazlov, Petr, *Agrarnyi vopros v Rossii*. Moscow, 1926.

Meijer, Jan M., "Town and Country in the Civil War," in *Revolutionary Russia*. Ed. Richard Pipes, Cambridge, Mass., 1968.

Meyer, Alfred, "The War Scare of 1927," *Soviet Union/Union Sovetique*, 5, 1 (1978), 1-25.

Miliutin, B., "Voprosy sotsial'nogo strakhovaniia v resheniiakh VII s"ezda soiuzov," *Vestnik truda*, 2 (1927), 26-28.

Mints, L. E., *Agrarnoe perenaselenie i rynok trud SSSR*. Moscow, 1929.

————, "Bezrabotitsa v dorevolutiutsionnoi Rossii i SSSR," *Bolshaia sovetskaia entsiklopediia*. 65 vols. Moscow, 1926-1931. Tom. 5, 214-215.

————, "Biudzhety bezrabotnykh," *Statisticheskoe obozrenie*, 10 (1928), 48-55.

————, "K probleme agrarnogo perenaseleniia (k voprosu o kharaktere gorodskoi bezrabotitsy)," *Voprosy truda*, 2 (1928), 15-19.

————, *Rynok truda v Rossii (za 1922g i I polovina 1923g)*. Moscow, 1923.

————, "Rynok truda v sviazi reorganizatsei Birzh truda," *Voprosy truda*, 12 (1924), 23-27.

————, "Sovremennoe sostoianie bezrabotitsy v SSSR," *Statisticheskoe obozrenie*, 3 (1927), 31-39.

Molochko, V. K., "Kommunisticheskaia partiia i massy v period stroitel'stva sotsializma," in *Partiia i massy*. Ed. K. I. Suvorov. Moscow, 1966.

Monkhouse, Allan, *Moscow, 1911-1933: Being the Memoirs of Allan Monkhouse*. London, 1933.

Morozov, Ia., "Trudovaia distsipline v Moskovskikh uchrezhdeniiakh," *Voprosy truda*, 7 (1927), 117-120.

Morozov, L. F., *Rezhaiushchii etap bor'by s NEPmanskoi burzhuaziei (1926-1929gg.)*. Moscow, 1960.

Morrell, Edwin B., "Communist Unionism: Organized Labor and the Soviet State." Ph.D. dissertation, Harvard University, 1965.

Moskovskaia gorodskaia i Moskovskaia oblastnaia organizatsiia KPSS v tsifrakh. Moscow, 1972.

Moskovskaia oblast' za 50 let: statisticheskii sbornik. Moscow, 1967.

Moskva v tsifrakh za gody sovetskoi vlasti: 1917-1967gg. Moscow, 1967.

Moskovskie bol'sheviki v bor'be s pravym i levym opportunizmom 1921-1929gg. Moscow, 1969.

Moskovskii sovet rabochikh, krest'ianskikh i krasnoarmeiskikh deputatov, 1917-1927. Moscow, 1927.

Moskovskii sovet za desiat' let raboty. Moscow, 1927.

Moskva za 50 let Sovetskoi vlasti. Moscow, 1968.

NKVD, *Goroda soiuza SSR. Moscow, 1927*.

Narodnoe khoziaistvo Rossii za 1921g. Berlin, 1922.

"Nash otchet chitateliam," *Voprosy truda*, 1 (1926), 4-7; 1 (1927), 3-9.

Nefedov, M., "Trudovaia i material'naia pomoshch' bezrabotnym v Moskve," *Voprosy truda*, 2 (1926), 134-137.

————, "Okhrana truda moskovskikh rabochikh v 1924-1925g," *Voprosy truda*, 2 (1926), 137-143.

Noskresenkaia, V., Novoselov, L., *Proizvodstvennye soveshchanii—shkola upravleniia (1921-1965gg.)*. Moscow, 1965.

Nove, Alec, *An Economic History of the USSR*. Middlesex, 1972.

Novikov, V., "O trudovoi distsipline," *Voprosy truda*, 10 (1926), 3-6.

O zemle. Moscow, 1921.

Ocherki istorii Moskovskoi organizatsii KPSS: 1883-1965. Moscow, 1966.

Ocherki istorii Moskovskogo organizatsii VLKSM. Moscow, 1976.

Ognyov, N., *The Diary of a Communist Schoolboy*. Trans. Alexander Werth. New York, 1928.

Osipov, G. V., ed., *Town, Country and People*. London, 1969.

Ostapenko, I. P., *Uchastie rabochego klassa SSSR v upravlenii proizvodstvoi (proizvodstvennye soveshchaniia v promyshlennosti v 1921-1932gg.)*. Moscow, 1964.

P., A., "Zarabotnaia plata rabochikh i sluzhashchikh Moskovskoi gubernii v 1927/28," *Voprosy truda*, 12 (1928), 111-116.

Panfilova, A. M., *Formirovanie rabochego klassa SSSR v gody pervoi piatiletki*. Moscow, 1964.

————, *Istoriia zavoda Krasnyi bogatyr', 1887-1925*. Moscow, 1958.

Parkins, Maurice Frank, *City Planning in Soviet Russia*. Chicago, 1953.

Pavlova, A. E., *Bor'ba Moskovskoi partiinoi organizatsii za ukreplenie soiuza rabochego klassa i krest'ianstva v pervye gody nepa, 1921-1923gg*. Moscow, 1959.

Pavlovsky, George H., *Agricultural Russia on the Eve of the Revolution*. London, 1930.

Peremyslovskii, I., "Bezrabotitsa sredi podrostkov," *Voprosy truda*, 8-9 (1926), 39-43.

Pethybridge, Roger, *The Social Prelude to Stalinism*. London, 1974.

Petrochenko, P. and Kuznetsova, K., *Organizatsiia i normirovanie truda v promyshlennosti SSSR*. Moscow, 1971.

Pipes, Richard, ed., *Revolutionary Russia*. Cambridge, Mass., 1968.

Pisarev, I. Iu., *Narodonaselenie SSSR: sotsialno-ekonomicheskii ocherk*. Moscow, 1962.

————, *Naselenie i trud v SSSR*. Moscow, 1966.

Poliakov, Iu. A., *Moskovskie trudiashchiesia v oborone sovetskoi stolitsy v 1919 godu*. Moscow, 1958.

————, *Perekhod k NEPu i sovetskoe krest'ianstvo*. Moscow, 1967.

Poliakova, N. I., "Bor'ba rabochikh-tekstil'shchikov za povyshenie proizvoditel'nosti truda v 1921-1925 (po materialam Moskvy i Moskovskoi gubernii)," *Voprosy istorii*, 6 (1959), 20-37.

Polliak, G. S., "Biudzhet rabochego k nachalu 1923g.," in *Voprosy zarabotnoi platy*. Moscow, 1923.

————, "Dinamika rabochego biudzheta (noiabr' 1926-noiabr' 1927g.)," *Statisticheskoe obozrenie*, 5 (1928), 44-56.

————, "Nevykhody na rabotu po dniam nedeli," *Statisticheskoe obozrenie*, 4 (1927), 48-57.

————, "Zarabotnaia plata i potreblenie," *Statisticheskoe obozrenie*, 3 (1929), 47-68.

Poniatovskaia, N. P., "Vosstanovlenie promyshlennosti i rost rabochego klassa v pervye gody NEPa," in *Leninskoe uchenie o NEPe i ego mezhdunarodnoe znachenie*. Moscow, 1973.

Popov, A., "Ot pervogo kommunisticheskogo subbotnika - k stakhanovskomu dvizheniiu," *Bor'ba klassov*, 12 (1935), 21-31.

Poselianina, A., "Leninskii prizyv (Moskovskii zavod 'Serp i molot')," *Bor'ba klassov*, 1 (1934), 142-149.

————, "Vosstanovlenie zavoda 'Serp i molot'," *Bor'ba klassov*, 7-8 (1934), 189-195.

Rabinowitch, Alexander, *The Bolsheviks Come to Power*. New York, 1976.

Radkey, Oliver H., *The Unknown Civil War in Soviet Russia: A Study of the Green Movement in the Tambov Region, 1920-1921*. Stanford, 1976.

Ransome, Arthur, *Russia in 1919*. New York, 1919.

————, *The Crisis in Russia*. New York, 1921.

Rashin, A. G., *Fabrichno-zavodskie sluzhashchie v SSSR (chislennost', sostav, zarabotnaia plata)*. Moscow, 1929.

————, *Formirovanie rabochego klass Rossii*. Moscow, 1958.

————, *Sostav fabrichno-zavodskogo proletariata SSSR. Predvaritel'nye itogi perepisi metalistov, gornorabochikh i tekstil'shchikov v 1929g.* Moscow, 1930.

————, *Zhenskii trud v SSSR.* Moscow, 1928.

Ratner, B., *Istoriia Moskovskogo instrumental'nogo zavoda.* Moscow, 1934.

Resnikov, I., "Voprosy zhilishchnogo stroitel'stvo," *Vestnik truda,* 3 (1925), 27-30.

Reswick, William, *I Dreamt Revolution.* Chicago, 1952.

Rezvushkin, Ia., "Proletariat na pervom etape sotsialisticheskogo stroitel'stva (ot oktiabr'ia do 'voennogo kommunizma')," *Istoriia proletariata SSSR,* 11 (1932), 59-90.

Rigby, T. H., *Communist Party Membership in the U.S.S.R., 1917-1967.* Princeton, 1968.

Roberts, Paul Craig, "War Communism: A Re-examination," *Slavic Review,* 29, 2 (June, 1970), 238-261.

Rodionova, N., *Gody napriazhennogo truda: iz istorii Moskovskoi partiinoi organizatsii 1921-1925gg.* Moscow, 1963.

Rogachevskaia, L. S., *Lividatsiia bezrabotitsy v SSSR, 1917-1930gg.* Moscow, 1973.

————, "Rabota proizvodstvennykh soveshchanii v pervye gody industriali-zatsii (1926-1927)," *Istoricheskie zapiski,* 57 (1956), 255-275.

Rosenberg, William, "Workers' Control on the Railroads and Some Sugges-tions Concerning Social Aspects of Labor Politics in the Russian Revolu-tion," *Journal of Modern History,* 49, 2 (1977), D1181-D1219.

Rosmer, Alfred, *Moscow Under Lenin.* Trans. by Ian H. Birchall, New York, 1972.

Rowland, Richard H., "Urban In-migration in Late Nineteenth Century Rus-sia," in Michael F. Hamm, ed., *The City in Russian History.* Lexington, Kentucky, 1976.

Rowney, Don Karl, "Proletarianization, Political Control and the Soviet State Administration in the 1920s: Their Impact on Upward Mobility," Paper Presented at the Third Annual Conference of the Seminar on Russian Social History. Philadelphia, January 29-30, 1983.

Russia After Ten Years: Report of the American Trade Union Delegation to the Soviet Union. New York, 1927.

Rysko, Iakov, "Zhilishchnyi vopros v metallopromyshlennosti," *Vestnik truda,* 11 (1925), 34-49.

Safronov, E. D., Tikhomirov, V. A., "Iz istorii resheniia toplivnoi problemy v vosstanovitel'nyi period (1921-1925gg.)," *Istoriia SSSR,* 4 (1973), 112-121.

Safronov, V., "Chto pokazlo obsledovanie proizvodstvennykh soveshchanii i komissii v Moskvy," *Vestnik truda,* 1 (1927), 94-96.

————, "Kak proshli proizvodstvennye konferentsii v Moskve," *Vestnik truda,* 2 (1927), 151-153.

————, "Proizvodstvennye konferentsii po Moskve i Moskovskoi gubernii," *Vestnik truda,* 11 (1925), 176-179.

Schapiro, Leonard, *The Communist Party of the Soviet Union.* New York, 1971.

Schlesinger, Rudolf, ed., *The Family in the U.S.S.R.* London, 1949.

Schwarz, Solomon M., *Labor in the Soviet Union.* New York, 1951.

Seigrist, Henry E. and Older, Julia, *Medicine and Health in the Soviet Union.* New York, 1947.

Semashko, N. A., *Health Protection in the U.S.S.R.* London, 1934.

Serebrennikov, G. N., *Zhenskii trud v SSSR.* Moscow/Leningrad, 1934.

Shastin, L., "Sezonnyi rynok truda v 1926/27 godu," *Voprosy truda,* 2 (1928), 46-50.

Shanin, Theodore, *The Awkward Class: Political Sociology of Peasantry in a Developing Society, Russia 1910-1925.* Oxford, 1972.

Sheer, D. "Travmatizm na Moskovskikh postroikakh," *Voprosy truda,* 9 (1928), 117-118.

Shelestov, D., *Pervyi kommunisticheskie subbotniki.* Moscow, 1959.

Shelley, Louise, "Female Criminality in the 1920s: A Consequence of Inadvertant and Deliberate Change," *Russian History/Histoire Russe,* 9, 2-3 (1982), 265-284.

Shikheev, N., "Iz istoriia zavoda AMO," *Bor'ba klassov,* 3-4 (1931), 57-73.

Shishkov, Vyacheslav, *The Children of the Street: Life in a Commune of Russia's Besprizorniki.* Translated by Thomas Whitney. Royal Oak, Mich., 1979.

Shkaratan, O. I., *Problemy sotsial'noi struktury rabochego klassa SSSR.* Moscow, 1970.

Shmidt, V. V., "Nashi dostizhenniia i nedostatki v oblasti regulirovaniia truda i ocherednye zadachi nashei trudovoi politiki," *Voprosy truda,* 1 (1927) 102-103.

———, "Perspektivy blizhnaisnei raboty NKT," *Vestnik truda,* 5-6 (1924), 40-48.

———, "Regulirovanie truda stroitel'nykh rabochikh," *Voprosy truda,* 2 (1926), 3-11.

———, "Voprosy bezrabotitsy, gosnormirovaniia i okhrany truda sovtorgslu-zhashchikh," *Voprosy truda,* 6 (1927), 5-12.

Sholokhov, Mikhail, *And Quiet Flows the Don.* Translated by Stephen Garry. New York, 1966.

Sirianni, Carmen, *Workers Control and Socialist Democracy: The Soviet Experience.* London, 1982.

Smith, Jessica, *Woman in Soviet Russia.* New York, 1928.

Smith, S. A., *Red Petrograd: Revolution in the Factories, 1917-1918.* Cambridge, England, 1983.

Sochor, Zenovia, "Soviet Taylorism Revisited," *Soviet Studies,* 33, 2 (1981), 246-264.

Sorenson, Jay B., *The Life and Death of Soviet Trade Unionism, 1917-1928.* New York, 1969.

Sorin, V. G., *Rabochaia gruppa ("Miasnikovshchina").* Moscow, 1924.

Sorkin, A., Bondarchuk, S., "Zavod 'Krasnyi Bogatyr' (Moskva)," *Voprosy truda,* 9 (1929), 90-92.

Sorlin, Pierre, *The Soviet People and Their Society from 1917 to the Present.* Translated by Daniel Weissbort. New York, 1969.

Sosnovy, Timothy, *The Housing Problem in the Soviet Union.* New York, 1954.

Sovetskii rabochii klass: kratkii istoricheskii ocherk (1917-1973). Moscow, 1975.

Spirin, L. M., *Klassy i partii v grazhdanskoi voine v Rossii, 1917-1920.* Moscow, 1968.

Starovskii, V. N., "The Analysis of Population Growth," in *Town, Country and People.*

Stepanov, I. P., *25 biudzhetov krest'ianskikh khoziastv Moskovskoi gubernii.* Moscow, 1925.

Stevens, Jennie A., "Children of the Revolution: Soviet Russia's Homeless Children (Besprizorniki) in the 1920s," *Russian History/Histoire Russe,* 9, 2-3 (1982), 242-264.

Stopani, A., "Biudzhet Moskovskogo rabochego," *Statistika truda,* 1-4 (1919).

————, "Eshche ob osebennostiakh nashikh zabastovok," *Voprosy truda,* 7-8 (1924), 38-42.

————, "Nashi zadachi v bor'be s biurokratizm," *Voprosy truda,* 2 (1927), 3-7.

————, "Promyshlennye konflikty na mestakh," *Voprosy truda,* 1 (1923), 29-31.

Strumilin, S. G., "Dinamika produktivnosti truda v Rossii," *Vestnik truda,* 5-6 (1924), 144-146.

————, *Izbrannye proizvedeniia.* 5 Vols. Moscow, 1963-1968.

————, *Na planovom fronte.* Moscow, 1958.

————, *Zarabotnaia plata i proizvoditelnost' truda v Russkoi promyshlennosti v 1913-1923gg.* Moscow, 1923.

Sulianov, A. S., "Shefskaia pomoshch' rabochego klassa derevne v podgotovoke sotsialisticheskogo preobrazovaniia sel'skogo khoziaistva (1925-1929)," in *Rol' rabochego klassa v sotsialisticheskom preobrazovanii derevnii v SSSR.* Moscow, 1968.

Suvorov, Iu. I., *Bor'ba kommunisticheskoi partii za povyshenie effektivnosti proizvodstva v oblasti promyshlennosti (iz opyta khoziaistvennoi deiatel'nosti Moskovskoi partiinoi organizatsii v 1925-1928gg.)* Iaroslavl', 1972.

Suvorov, K. I., *Istoricheskii opyt KPSS po likvidatsii bezrabotitsy (1917-1930).* Moscow, 1968.

Taniuchi, Yuzuru, *The Village Gathering in Russia in the Mid-1920s.* Birmingham, 1968.

Tarasov, S., "Sostoianie rynok truda i mery ego regulirovaniia v 1926/27 khoziaistvennom godu," *Voprosy truda,* 5 (1927), 25-29.

Teodorovich, M., "Zhilishchnye usloviia i prestupnost' v Moskve," *Statisticheskoe obozrenie,* 10 (1928), 89-94.

Thiede, Roger L., "Industry and Urbanization in New Russia," in Hamm, ed., *The City in Russian History.*

Thurston, Robert W., "Developing Education in Late Imperial Russia: Concerns of State, 'Society,' and People in Moscow, 1906-1914" *Russian History/Histoire Russe,* 11, 1 (1984), 59-82.

Tian-Shansky, Benjamin Semenov, "Russia: Territory and Population: A Perspective on the 1926 Census," *The Geographic Review*, 18, 4 (October, 1928), 616-640.

Timofeev, P., "What the Factory Worker Lives by," in Bonnell, ed., *The Russian Worker*, 72-112.

Tolstopiatov, I., "Truddistsipline i proguly," *Voprosy truda*, 1 (1929), 21-25.

———, "Bol'she vnimaniia okhrane truda," *Voprosy truda*, 5 (1929), 18-24.

Traub, Rainer, "Lenin and Taylor: The Fate of 'Scientific Management' in the (Early) Soviet Union," *Telos*, 37 (1978), 82-92.

Trotsky, Leon, *The Challenge of the Left Opposition, 1923-1925*. Ed. Naomi Allen. New York, 1975.

———, *Problems of Everyday Life*. New York, 1973.

———, *The Real Situation in Russia*. Trans. by Max Eastman. New York, 1928.

Trifonov, I. Ia., *Klassy i klassovaia bor'ba v SSSR v nachale NEPa (1921-1925gg.)*. Leningrad, 1969.

———, *Likvidatsiia ekspluatatorskikh klassov v SSSR*. Moscow, 1975.

———, *Ocherki istorii klassovoi bor'by v SSSR v gody NEPa, 1921-1937*. Moscow, 1960.

Tsypkin, G., Goldberg, A., "Predvaritel'nye itogi perekhod na semichasovoi den'," *Statisticheskoe obozrenie*, 11 (1928), 30-35.

Turin, S., "Workers' Family Budget Enquiries in Soviet Russia," *International Labor Review*, 20, 4 (1929).

United Nations, *Methods of Population Projection by Sex and Age*. New York, 1956.

U. S. Public Health Service, National Office of Vital Statistics. *Summary of International Vital Statistics*. Washington, 1947.

Urlanis, Boris, "Some Demographic Trends," in Osipov, ed., *Town, Country and People*.

"VI Vsesoiuznyi s"ezd professional'nykh soiuzov: rezoliutsii," *Vestnik truda*, 11-12 (1924), 235-255.

Vaganov, F. M., *KPSS v bor'be za uskorenie tempov sotsialisticheskogo stroitel'stva (1927-29gg.)*. Moscow, 1967.

Vasil'ev, N., "Ratsionalizatsiia proizvodstva i voprosy truda," *Voprosy truda*, 1 (1929), 26-31.

Vas'kina, L. I., "Rabochii klass SSSR po materialam vsesoiuznoi perepisi naseleniia 1926g," *Istoricheskie zapiski*, 92 (1973), 7-56.

Veinberg, G., "Promyshlennost', zaplata i proizvoditel'nost' truda v leningradtsev," *Vestnik truda*, 2 (1925), 87-88.

Vinnikov, A., "Nekotorye itogi perekhoda predpriatii na semichasovoi rabochii den'," *Voprosy truda*, 9 (1929), 90-92.

———, "Pervyi itogi i perspektivy provedniia semichasovogo rabochego dnia," *Voprosy truda*, 2 (1929), 46-55.

Viola, Lynn, "Notes on the Background of Soviet Collectivization: Metal Workers Brigades in the Countryside, Autumn 1929," *Soviet Studies*, 36, 2 (April 1984), 205-222.

———, "The '25,000ers': A Study of a Soviet Recruitment Campaign during the First Five-Year Plan," *Russian History/Histoire Russe,* 10, 1 (1983), 1-30.

Vol'f, M., Mebus, G. A., *Tsentral'no-promyshlennaia oblast'.* Moscow, 1926.

Volin, Lazar, *A Century of Russian Agriculture: From Alexander II to Khrushchev.* Cambridge, Mass., 1970.

Volkov, E. Z., *Dinamika naseleniia SSSR za vosem'desiat let.* Moscow, 1930.

Von Laue, Theodore, "Russian Labor between Field and Factory, 1892-1903," *California Slavic Studies,* 3 (1964), 33-65.

———, "Russian Peasants in the Factory," *Journal of Economic History,* 21 (March, 1961), 61-80.

"Voprosy zarabotnoi platy i NKT," *Voprosy truda,* 2 (1924), 12-17.

Vsia Moskva, adresnaia i spravochania kniga na 1929g. Moscow, 1929.

Vydro, M. Ia., *Naselenie Moskvy.* Moscow, 1976.

Wells, H. G., *Russia in the Shadows.* London, 1931.

Wrigley, E. A., *Population and History.* New York, 1969.

Zagorsky, S., *Wages and Regulation of Conditions of Labour in the U.S.S.R.* Geneva, 1930.

Zakgeim, E., "Pitanie bezrabotnykh," *Statisticheskoe obozrenie,* 1 (1929), 56-60.

———, "Stroiteli-otkhodniki," *Statisticheskoe obozrenie,* 10 (1929), 66-72.

Zavodovskii, P., "Itogi obshchestvennykh rabot v 1924 godu," *Voprosy truda,* 4 (1925), 3-15.

Zawodny, Jay (Janucz) K., *Twenty-six Interviews with Former Soviet Factory Workers.* Unpublished Collection, Hoover Library, Stanford University.

Zelnik, Reginald E., "Russian Bebels: An Introduction to the Memoirs of Semen Kanatchikov and Matvei Fisher," (Part I) *Russian Review,* 35, 3 (July, 1976), 249-289; (Part II) 35, 4 (October 1976), 417-448.

Zenzinov, Vladimir, *Deserted: The Story of the Children Abandoned in Soviet Russia.* Trans. Agnes Platt. Westport, Conn., 1975.

Zorev, L. K., *Pervaia obraztsovaia.* Moscow, 1962.

Zubov, A., "Sostoianie broni podrostkov v soiuznoi promyshlennosti," *Voprosy truda,* 12 (1929), 98-102.

Index

Workers' antipathy (*cont.*)
109; generational tensions among,
238; juvenile, 34, 109; in Red Army,
32; resentment of other social groups,
128–29; rising expectations of, 297–
98; shortage of skilled, 34, 111–12,
220–21; sources of discontent among,
48–51, 173–74, 228, 231–32, 238,
243, 270, 275–76, 278–282, 283, 286,
296; support for intensification of
labor among young, 236–38; tensions
between other social groups and, 173–
74; unity among, 280, 283, 286. *See
also* Juveniles, Labor conflicts, New
workers, Proletariat, Semiproletariat,
Strikes, Urban workers, Women,
Worker unrest, Working class
Workers' and Peasants' Inspectorate
(Rabkrin): investigations by, 242, 276–
77; on overnight barracks, 193
Workforce: changing size of, 107–8;
characteristics of, 104–5; occupational
structure of, 311
Working class: breach between party
and, 50–51, 261–62; breach between
unions and, 50, 51, 258–59;
centripetal and centrifugal forces
within, 103, 120–21, 246–47, 293,
295–96; composition of, 312;
concentration of, 106; dilution of,
221; disintegration of, 33–35;
heterogenity of, 112; relationship to
party, 293–97, 299; size of, 105;
typology of, 112–21. *See also*
Proletariat, Workers
Working conditions. *See* Labor
conditions
Working population, definition of,
129n.1

Zemliaki, 83, 127, 128
Zinoviev, G., 233

A Note on the Author

WILLIAM J. CHASE was educated at Lafayette College and Boston College. He has received grants from the ACLS, the NEH, and the National Council for Soviet and East European Research. A former Senior Fellow at the Harriman Institute, Columbia University, he has published articles on Soviet labor, demography, and the Communist Party elite. Mr. Chase is an associate professor of history at the University of Pittsburgh.

This book forms part of the STUDIES OF THE HARRIMAN INSTITUTE, successor to:

STUDIES OF THE RUSSIAN INSTITUTE

Abram Bergson, *Soviet National Income in 1937* (1953)

Ernest J. Simmons, Jr., ed., *Through the Glass of Soviet Literature: Views of Russian Society* (1953)

Thad Paul Alton, *Polish Postwar Economy* (1954)

David Granick, *Management of the Industrial Firm in the USSR: A Study in Soviet Economic Planning* (1954)

Allen S. Whiting, *Soviet Policies in China, 1917-1924* (1954)

George S. N. Luckyj, *Literary Politics in the Soviet Ukraine, 1917-1934* (1956)

Michael Boro Petrovich, *The Emergence of Russian Panslavism, 1856-1870* (1956)

Thomas Taylor Hammond, *Lenin on Trade Unions and Revolution, 1893-1917* (1956)

David Marshall Lang, *The Last Years of the Georgian Monarchy, 1658-1832* (1957)

James William Morley, *The Japanese Thrust into Siberia, 1918* (1957)

Alexander G. Park, *Bolshevism in Turkestan, 1917-1927* (1957)

Herbert Marcuse, *Soviet Marxism: A Critical Analysis* (1958)

Charles B. McLane, *Soviet Policy and the Chinese Communists, 1931-1946* (1958)

Oliver H. Radkey, *The Agrarian Foes of Bolshevism: Promise and Defeat of the Russian Socialist Revolutionaries, February to October, 1917* (1958)

Ralph Talcott Fisher, Jr., *Pattern for Soviet Youth: A Study of the Congresses of the Komsomol, 1918-1954* (1959)

Alfred Erich Senn, *The Emergence of Modern Lithuania* (1959)

Elliot R. Goodman, *The Soviet Design for a World State* (1960)

John N. Hazard, *Settling Disputes in Soviet Society: The Formative Years of Legal Institutions* (1960)

David Joravsky, *Soviet Marxism and Natural Science, 1917-1932* (1961)

Maurice Friedberg, *Russian Classics in Soviet Jackets* (1962)

Alfred J. Rieber, *Stalin and the French Communist Party, 1941-1947* (1962)

Theodore K. Von Laue, *Sergei Witte and the Industrialization of Russia* (1962)

John A. Armstrong, *Ukrainian Nationalism* (1963)

Oliver H. Radkey, *The Sickle under the Hammer: The Russian Socialist Revolutionaries in the Early Months of Soviet Rule* (1963)

Kermit E. McKenzie, *Comintern and World Revolution, 1928-1943: The Shaping of Doctrine* (1964)

Harvey L. Dyck, *Weimar Germany and Soviet Russia, 1926-1933: A Study in Diplomatic Instability* (1966)

(Above titles published by Columbia University Press.)

Harold J. Noah, *Financing Soviet Schools* (Teachers College, 1966)

John M. Thompson, *Russia, Bolshevism, and the Versailles Peace* (Princeton, 1966)

Paul Avrich, *The Russian Anarchists* (Princeton, 1967)

Loren R. Graham, *The Soviet Academy of Sciences and the Communist Party, 1927-1932* (Princeton, 1967)

Robert A. Maguire, *Red Virgin Soil: Soviet Literature in the 1920's* (Princeton, 1968)

T. H. Rigby, *Communist Party Membership in the U.S.S.R., 1917-1967* (Princeton, 1968)

Richard T. De George, *Soviet Ethics and Morality* (University of Michigan, 1969)

Jonathan Frankel, *Vladimir Akimov on the Dilemmas of Russian Marxism, 1895-1903* (Cambridge, 1969)

William Zimmerman, *Soviet Perspective on International Relations, 1956-1967* (Princeton, 1969)

Paul Avrich, *Kronstadt, 1921* (Princeton, 1970).

Ezra Mendelsohn, *Class Struggle in the Pale: The Formative Years of the Jewish Workers' Movement in Tsarist Russia* (Cambridge, 1970)

Edward J. Brown, *The Proletarian Episode in Russian Literature* (Columbia, 1971)

Reginald E. Zelnik, *Labor and Society in Tsarist Russia: The Factory Workers of St. Petersburg, 1855-1870* (Stanford, 1971)

Patricia K. Grimsted, *Archives and Manuscript Repositories in the USSR: Moscow and Leningrad* (Princeton, 1972)

Ronald G. Suny, *The Baku Commune, 1917-1918* (Princeton, 1972)

Edward J. Brown, *Mayakovsky: A Poet in the Revolution* (Princeton, 1973)

Milton Ehre, *Oblomov and His Creator: The Life and Art of Ivan Goncharov* (Princeton, 1973)

Henry Krisch, *German Politics under Soviet Occupation* (Columbia, 1974)

Henry W. Morton and Rudolph L. Tökés, eds., *Soviet Politcs and Society in the 1970's* (Free Press, 1974)

William G. Rosenberg, *Liberals in the Russian Revolution* (Princeton, 1974)

Richard G. Robbins, Jr., *Famine in Russia, 1891-1892* (Columbia, 1975)

Vera Dunham, *In Stalin's Time: Middleclass Values in Soviet Fiction* (Cambridge, 1976)

Walter Sablinsky, *The Road to Bloody Sunday* (Princeton, 1976)

William Mills Todd III, *The Familiar Letter as Literary Genre in the Age of Pushkin* (Princeton, 1976)

Elizabeth Valkenier, *Russian Realist Art. The State and Society: The Peredvizhniki and Their Tradition* (Ardis, 1977)

Susan Solomon, *The Soviet Agrarian Debate* (Westview, 1978)

Sheila Fitzpatrick, ed., *Cultural Revolution in Russia, 1928-1931* (Indiana, 1978)

Peter Solomon, *Soviet Criminologists and Criminal Policy: Specialists in Policy-Making* (Columbia, 1978)

Kendall E. Bailes, *Technology and Society under Lenin and Stalin: Origins of the Soviet Technical Intelligentsia, 1917-1941* (Princeton, 1978)

Leopold H. Haimson, ed., *The Politics of Rural Russia, 1905-1914* (Indiana, 1979)

Theodore H. Friedgut, *Political Participation in the USSR* (Princeton, 1979)

Sheila Fitzpatrick, *Education and Social Mobility in the Soviet Union, 1921-1934* (Cambridge, 1979)

Wesley Andrew Fisher, *The Soviet Marriage Market: Mate-Selection in Russia and the USSR* (Praeger, 1980)

Jonathan Frankel, *Prophecy and Politics: Socialism, Nationalism, and the Russian Jews, 1862-1917* (Cambridge, 1981)

Robin Feuer Miller, *Dostoevsky and the Idiot: Author, Narrator, and Reader* (Harvard, 1981)

Diane Koenker, *Moscow Workers and the 1917 Revolution* (Princeton, 1981)

Patricia K. Grimsted, *Archives and Manuscript Repositories in the USSR: Estonia, Latvia, Lithuania, and Belorussia* (Princeton, 1981)

Ezra Mendelsohn, *Zionism in Poland; The Fomative Years, 1915-1926* (Yale, 1982)

Hannes Adomeit, *Soviet Risk-Taking and Crisis Behavior* (George Allen & Unwin, 1982)

Seweryn Bialer and Thane Gustafson, eds., *Russia at the Crossroads: The 26th Congress of the CPSU* (George Allen & Unwin, 1982)

Roberta Thompson Manning, *The Crisis of the Old Order in Russia: Gentry and Government* (Princeton, 1983)

Andrew A. Durkin, *Sergei Aksakov and Russian Pastoral* (Rutgers, 1983)

Bruce Parrott, *Politics and Technology in the Soviet Union* (MIT Press, 1983)

Sarah Pratt, *Russian Metaphysical Romanticism: The Poetry of Tiutchev and Boratynskii* (Stanford, 1984)

STUDIES OF THE HARRIMAN INSTITUTE

Elizabeth Kridl Valkenier, *The Soviet Union and the Third World: An Economic Bind* (Praeger, 1983)

John LeDonne, *Ruling Russia: Politics and Administration in the Age of Absolutism 1762-1796* (Praeger, 1984)

William J. Chase, *Workers, Society, and the Soviet State: Labor and Life in Moscow, 1918-1928* (University of Illinois, 1987)